THE SURVIVAL OF THE PAGAN GODS

The Mythological Tradition and Its Place in Renaissance Humanism and Art

By

JEAN SEZNEC

Fellow of All Souls College, Oxford

TRANSLATED FROM THE FRENCH BY
BARBARA F. SESSIONS

BOLLINGEN SERIES XXXVIII

PRINCETON UNIVERSITY PRESS

TO

THE MEMORY

OF

MY MOTHER

CC

THE SURVIVAL OF THE PAGAN GODS

Published by Princeton University Press, Princeton, N.J.

First Princeton / Bollingen paperback printing, 1972
Second hardcover printing, 1972

THIS IS THE THIRTY-EIGHTH IN A SERIES OF WORKS
SPONSORED BY BOLLINGEN FOUNDATION

This book was originally published in French as
La Survivance des dieux antiques,
STUDIES OF THE WARBURG INSTITUTE, Vol. XI, London, 1940.
It was first published in English in 1953
by Pantheon Books, Inc., New York, for Bollingen Foundation.

Published in Harper Torchbooks paperback edition in 1961

Library of Congress catalog card number: 52-10520

ISBN 0-691-01783-2 (paperback edn.)

ISBN 0-691-09829-8 (hardcover edn.)

Printed in the United States of America
by Princeton University Press, Princeton, N.J.

THE SURVIVAL OF THE PAGAN GODS

Contents

PAGE

THIS TRANSLATION *varies from the original text only where factual errors had to be corrected; the illustrations are the same, and better photographs for them have been provided by the Warburg Institute, London; the bibliography has been brought up to date, and rearranged for the greater convenience of the reader.*

In preparing this new edition, I have again received valuable assistance from the staff of the Warburg Institute. I wish to express my special gratitude to Gertrud Bing, Assistant Director of the Institute, for her unfailing and friendly support.

Jean Seznec

Illustrations

THE SURVIVAL
OF
THE PAGAN GODS

Introduction

THE TITLE of the present work requires a certain amount of explanation. As the Middle Ages and the Renaissance come to be better known, the traditional antithesis between them grows less marked. The medieval period appears "less dark and static," and the Renaissance "less bright and less sudden." [1] Above all, it is now recognized that pagan antiquity, far from experiencing a "rebirth" in fifteenth-century Italy, had remained alive within the culture and art of the Middle Ages. Even the gods were not *restored* to life, for they had never disappeared from the memory or imagination of man.

Many works published in recent years have studied the underlying causes and the means of this survival.[2] We aim to resume this investigation here, developing it along new lines and taking it still further, not merely to the dawn of the Renaissance but to its very decline. We have not focused our attention upon those centers of medieval humanism where the reading of classical texts and the study of traces of pagan art kept the memory of the ancient gods alive in the minds of scholars and the imagination of artists; Jean Adhémar has made a contribution of the greatest interest on this aspect of the question, limited to France.[3] We view the problem from a different angle, and

[1] Haskins, *The Renaissance of the Twelfth Century* (Cambridge, Mass., 1927), Pref., p. vii.

[2] We name here only the most important: F. von Bezold, *Das Fortleben der antiken Götter im mittelalterlichen Humanismus* (Bonn-Leipzig, 1922); H. Liebeschütz, *Fulgentius metaforalis, ein Beitrag zur Geschichte der antiken Mythologie im Mittelalter,* Studien der Bibliothek Warburg, IV (Leipzig, 1926); A. Frey-Sallmann, *Aus dem Nachleben antiker Göttergestalten* (Leipzig, 1931); also the article by E. Panofsky and F. Saxl, which is of fundamental importance: "Classical Mythology in Mediaeval Art," *Metropolitan Museum Studies,* IV (1932–1933), pp. 228–280; and E. Panofsky's article, "Renaissance and Renascences," *The Kenyon Review,* VI (1944), pp. 201–236.

[3] *Influences antiques dans l'art du Moyen-Age français,* Studies of the Warburg Institute, VII (London, 1939).

attempt to show that the gods lived on in the Middle Ages in concepts which had already taken shape at the end of the pagan epoch—interpretations proposed by the ancients themselves to explain the origin and nature of their divinities.

"It is by no means easy," observes Fontenelle in *L'Histoire des oracles*, "to know how the pagan peoples looked upon their own religion." In fact, they found themselves in a dilemma from the moment they first began to reason about their beliefs; for "the myth really possesses its full significance only in those epochs when man still believes himself to be living in a divine world, with no distinct notion of natural laws; but long before the end of paganism, this first naïveté had disappeared." [4] Indeed, the effort of modern mythographers, since early in the nineteenth century, has been to recover the primitive mentality by way of philology and anthropology, and to recapture the intuitions of the earliest periods.

The ancients, however, in their inability to "investigate the origins of their own culture, to learn how their legends were formed and what may have been their earliest meaning," [5] evolved contradictory theories in order to render them intelligible—theories which are brought face to face, for example, in Cicero's *De natura deorum*. In essence, these may be reduced to three: (*1*) the myths are a more or less distorted account of historical facts, in which the characters are mere men who have been raised to the rank of the immortals; or (*2*) they express the union or conflict of the elementary powers which constitute the universe, the gods then being cosmic symbols; or (*3*) they are merely the expression in fable of moral and philosophical ideas, in which case the gods are allegories.

Now it was thanks to these interpretations, which were proposed by the ancients themselves and which integrate mythology in turn with world history, natural science, and morals, that the gods were to survive through the Middle Ages, preserved alike from oblivion and from the attacks of their enemies. But, as we have said, we plan to follow the fortunes of the gods well beyond the Middle Ages, up to the end of the sixteenth century. This will give us an opportunity to show how greatly the art and thought of the Renaissance

[4] E. Renan, *Etudes d'histoire religieuse*, chap. i, "Les Religions de l'antiquité," pp. 25–26.

[5] G. Boissier, *La Fin du paganisme*, II, p. 372.

were indebted to that particular tradition whose astonishing persistence and unsuspected prolongations we hope to reveal.

This *traditional* aspect of fifteenth- and sixteenth-century mythology is, in fact, less striking and less well known than any other. If one attempts to recall, for example, the profane themes most often treated in Italy at this time,[6] what come first to mind are the scenes of seduction or rape, of love or drunken revelry—and admittedly no parallel to these had been seen since the end of the ancient world. The kingdom of Aphrodite and Bacchus, peopled by nymphs and satyrs, with the Antiope of Correggio and the Ariadne of Titian as its reigning princesses, is in truth a new universe, rediscovered after the lapse of centuries; while the predilection of artists and men of letters for voluptuous themes bears witness to the spiritual revolution which has taken place. Once again poets dare to sing of

. . . l'amour vainqueur et la vie opportune

and to glorify Desire as master of gods and of men.

But alongside or above this mythical realm within which nature and the flesh have come into their own again, there exists another realm, less familiar if no less seductive, where reign the great planetary deities, the heroes, and the allegories. It is above all in monumental art that figures of this type are met with—in palace vaulting, in chapel cupolas—and their role should not be mistaken for a purely decorative one. Actually their true meaning and character may be understood only by establishing their connection with their immediate forerunners, the gods of the Middle Ages, who had survived as the incarnation of ideas. In some cases the relationship is obvious: we easily recognize in the combat of Diana and Pallas with Venus and her train, which in Mantegna's painting represents the triumph of Wisdom over Vice, one of the spiritual dramas (*psychomachiae*) dear to the preceding age. At the same time, however, the meaning of other mythological compositions, such as

[6] These themes have been enumerated by S. Reinach, "Essai sur la mythologie figurée et l'histoire profane dans la peinture italienne de la Renaissance" (works prior to 1580, with Index), *Rev. archéol.*, ser. v, vol I (1915), pp. 94–171. The list has been completed by R. C. Witt, "Notes complémentaires sur la mythologie figurée et l'histoire profane dans la peinture italienne de la Renaissance," *ibid.*, ser. v, vol. IX (1919), pp. 173–178. Cf. also L. Roblot-Delondre, "Les sujets antiques dans la tapisserie," *ibid.* (1917), pp. 296 ff.; *ibid.* (1918), pp. 131 ff.; *ibid.* (1919), pp. 48 ff., 294 ff.; the first section of this list deals with "La mythologie, les cycles légendaires, et les Triomphes des dieux," with Index.

those of Francesco Cossa in the Schifanoia Palace at Ferrara or of Baldassare Peruzzi on the ceiling of the Farnesina, becomes clear only if we see them as the outcome of the medieval astrological tradition; even the *Parnassus* of Raphael in the Stanza della Segnatura forms part of a spiritual edifice, the structural elements of which are still largely scholastic.

It is difficult, it must be confessed, to trace the frontiers separating these two great profane cycles (the second of which alone concerns us here), for one melts insensibly into the other. Even the games and dances, the idyls and the Bacchic triumphs, whose sole object is apparently to delight the senses and transport the imagination, often embody some meaning or *arrière-pensée*—are intended, in short, as food for the mind. It is only our indifference to the subject,[7] or our ignorance, which has kept us from examining or identifying it. Patient analysis would in some cases reveal the secret of the work; and at the same time we should recognize, in the classical motif thus "resurrected," the transposition of a medieval theme.

The difference in styles acts as a further hindrance to our awareness of this continuity of tradition, for Italian art of the fifteenth and sixteenth centuries invests the ancient symbols with fresh beauty; but the debt of the Renaissance to the Middle Ages is set forth in the texts. We shall attempt to show how the mythological heritage of antiquity was handed down from century to century, through what vicissitudes it passed, and the extent to which, toward the close of the Cinquecento, the great Italian treatises on the gods which were to nourish the humanism and art of all Europe were still indebted to medieval compilations and steeped in the influence of the Middle Ages.

When conceived of in these terms, our subject, already vast and complex in itself, forces us to cover an immense period of time. We have accepted this challenge, with its inevitable risks. Frequently we have had to limit ourselves to a cursory sketch, but in such cases we have tried to indicate the main outlines without altering the proportions. For the sake of precision, we have at some points restricted our inquiry to some series of special importance, like that of the planetary figures, whose history has served us as an example of certain phenomena of survival and evolution.

[7] See for example a characteristic comment made by Taine on a Veronese painting: "It is an allegory, but the subject hardly concerns us" (*Voyage en Italie* [1866], II, p. 433).

The essential function of the visual image, which plays so important a part in this book, is the summing up of trends or currents of thought. Our examples have been chosen and analyzed—at least for the most part—not from the formal or stylistic point of view, but rather as documents and witnesses. In many cases their mere succession furnishes us with a guiding thread; elsewhere they supplement or complement the texts. They allow us to recognize or to establish the continuity of a tradition and to trace the directions in which it extends. In a word, iconography serves as a constant auxiliary to the study of the history of ideas.

Finally, we have throughout subordinated our ambition to be comprehensive to our regard for clarity. To pioneer in a region which is still scarcely known because it is the meeting place of several disciplines and so belongs specifically to none, to plant signposts there and open up vistas which may help to orient other travelers—this is the end to which our efforts have been directed.

BOOK I

PART ONE: THE CONCEPTS

I

The Historical Tradition

On the appearance, early in the third century B.C., of the romance by Euhemerus which was destined to exert so lasting an influence, the intellectual climate of the Greco-Roman world was in a state exceptionally favorable to its reception.[1] Philosophical speculation and recent history alike had prepared the way for an understanding of the process by which, in times long past, the gods had been recruited from the ranks of mortal men.

Philosophy, from Aristotle onward, had recognized a divine element within the human soul, the nature of which was thus more specifically defined by the Stoics: "Deus est mortali juvare mortalem et haec ad aeternam gloriam via" ("For mortal to aid mortal—this is God, and this is the road to eternal glory").[2] A noble formula this, which Cicero develops in his *Tusculan Disputations:* those men have within them a supernatural element and are destined for eternal life who regard themselves as born into the world to help and guard and preserve their fellow men. Hercules passed away to join the gods: he would never so have passed unless in the course of his mortal life he had built for himself the road he traveled.[3]

At the same time, the superhuman career of Alexander, and above all his expedition to India—where he became the object of adoration similar to that which, according to the myth, had once greeted Dionysus there—had suddenly thrown light upon the origin of the gods. For the generations who subsequently witnessed the official deification of the Seleucids and Ptolemies

[1] See P. Decharme, *La Critique des traditions religieuses chez les grecs* (Paris, 1904), pp. 372–373, and chap. xii: "L'Evhémérisme et l'interprétation historique."

[2] Pliny, *Historia naturalis,* II, 7, 18; in all probability, a translation from Posidonius.

[3] Cicero, *Tusc.,* I, 32; see also *ibid.,* 25–26, and *De natura deorum,* II, 24.

there could be no further doubt: the traditional deities were merely earthly rulers, whom the gratitude or adulation of their subjects had raised to a place in heaven.[4]

The appearance of Euhemerus' work was well timed. Its success was immediate. It was one of the first books to be translated from Greek into Latin; Ennius' version, as is well known, gave it general currency in Rome, where Picus, Janus, and Saturn promptly became princes who had once ruled over Latium. The euhemeristic thesis set at rest for a time the disquiet that the traditional mythology had always inspired in the minds of educated men, who, though unable to accord it their literal belief, had nevertheless hesitated to reject as a mass of outright falsehood the time-honored tales for which Homer himself stood guarantor. A few voices, however, denounced euhemerism as impious and absurd.[5] Above all, its prosaic character made it disappointing to the ever increasing number of persons who had succumbed to the appeal of the supernatural and craved a more emotional type of religious belief.[6]

But euhemerism was to enjoy an extraordinary revival at the beginning of the Christian era. First the apologists, then the Fathers, seized eagerly upon this weapon which paganism itself had offered them, and made use of it against its polytheistic source.

It was only too easy for Clement of Alexandria, who quoted Euhemerus in his *Cohortatio ad gentes* (*PG,* VIII, 152) to declare to the infidel: "Those to whom you bow were once men like yourselves." [7] Lactantius, again, to whom we owe the preservation of a few fragments of Euhemerus and of Ennius' translation, proclaims triumphantly in his *Divinae institutiones* that the gods, one and all, are nothing but mortal beings who have been raised from

[4] Instances of deification of high Egyptian officials at an earlier date are given by Charles Picard in his article, "L'Inhumation 'ad sanctos' dans l'antiquité," *Revue archéologique* I (1947), pp. 82–85.

[5] Cicero, *De natur. deor.*, I, 42. But in a passage in *Tusc.* (I, 12–13), Cicero seems implicitly to admit that all the gods are men who have been raised from earth to heaven: "Totum prope caelum . . . nonne genere humano completum est?" ("Is not almost the whole of heaven . . . filled with gods of mortal origin?")—LCL. Cf. Plutarch, *De Iside et Osiride*, XIII.

[6] G. Boissier, *La Religion romaine, d'Auguste aux Antonins,* II, vii, 2. On the fortunes of euhemerism in antiquity, see Gilbert Murray, *Five Stages of Greek Religion* (ed. 1935), pp. 152–160, and A. B. Drachmann, *Atheism in Pagan Antiquity* (Copenhagen, 1922).

[7] *Οἱ προσχυνοῦμενοι παρ' ὑμῖν ἄνθρωποι γενόμενοί πότε.*

earth to heaven through the idolatry of their contemporaries (*PL*, VI, 190 ff.). Also euhemeristic in inspiration are the *De idolorum vanitate* of St. Cyprian, the *De idololatria* of Tertullian, the *Octavius* of Minucius Felix, the *Adversus nationes* of Arnobius, the *Instructiones adversus gentium deos* of Commodian, and the *De erroribus profanarum religionum* of Firmicus Maternus. St. Augustine, in the *De consensu Evangelistarum* (*PL*, XXXIV, 1056) and the *De civitate Dei* (VII, 18, and VIII, 26), was to subscribe in his turn to this theory, which seemed bound to prove fatal to the adversary.

Thus euhemerism became a favorite weapon of the Christian polemicists, a weapon which they made use of at every turn.[8] In fact, as Cumont has shown,[9] their tactics were not always wholly legitimate, being aimed for the most part at an idolatry long since extinct, and at gods whose existence had been reduced to a mere literary convention. What matters to us, however, is that the Christian apologists bequeathed to the Middle Ages a tradition of euhemerism, with further reinforcement from the commentators of Virgil—especially from Servius, whose errors the Middle Ages accepted as articles of faith.[10]

*

THE EUHEMERISTIC tradition remains a living influence throughout the Middle Ages, although it undergoes a total change of character. The human origin of the gods ceases to be a weapon to be used against them, a source of rejection and contempt. Instead, it gives them a certain protection, even granting them a right to survive. In the end it forms, as it were, their patent of nobility.

First of all, euhemerism at a rather early date loses its polemic venom, to become instead an auxiliary to historical research. Certain men have become gods; at what period, then, were they alive upon earth? Is it possible to assign them a definite place in human history?

[8] And sometimes for contradictory ends. In the towns, Christian preaching encountered a predominantly symbolic or allegorical explanation of the myths, which had to be refuted in a summary and brutal way. In country districts, the chief obstacle to Christianity was offered by the tenacious survival of anthropomorphic cults; here the problem became one of still further humanizing the divinities of springs, trees, and mountains, in order to rob them of their prestige. See P. Alphandéry, "L'Evhémérisme et les débuts de l'histoire des religions au Moyen-Age," *Revue de l'histoire des religions*, CIX (1934), pp. 1–27, esp. p. 13.

[9] *Les Religions orientales dans le paganisme romain* (4th ed., 1929), pp. 186–187.

[10] See Alphandéry, *op. cit.*, p. 18.

This tendency is already apparent in Eusebius. He explains in his *Ecclesiastical History* that the Babylonian god Baal was in reality the first king of the Assyrians, and that he lived *at the time of* the war between the Giants and the Titans (*PG*, XIX, 132–133). The coincidence in time is still only approximate, and it is clear, furthermore, that Eusebius' main concern is to show the religion of the chosen people as antedating pagan mythology. It was he, however, who bequeathed to the Middle Ages, through St. Jerome, the prototype of those crude historical synchronizations which grouped all the events and characters of human history, from the birth of Abraham down to the Christian era (including the gods themselves), into a few essential periods.

After Eusebius, Paulus Orosius does much the same thing. Although he is writing "adversus paganos" and under the inspiration of Augustine, his book is above all an attempt to unravel the past, even the past of fable and legend; this is all the more significant since it remained a manual of the highest authority throughout the Middle Ages and even into the Renaissance, going through twenty editions in the sixteenth century.

But it is in the seventh century, in the *Etymologiae* of Isidore of Seville, that we find the most interesting application of euhemerism to history, in the chapter "De diis gentium" (Bk. VIII, chap. xi; *PL*, LXXXII, 314). "Quos pagani deos asserunt, homines olim fuisse produntur." [11] Not only does Isidore, following Lactantius, accept this principle—he seeks to demonstrate it. He attempts to "place" these gods "secundum ordinem temporum" in world history divided into six great periods: from the Creation to the Flood; from the Flood to Abraham; from Abraham to David; from David to the Babylonian Captivity; from the Captivity to the Birth of Christ; from the Nativity onward. This scheme may appear rudimentary, but Isidore's erudition enabled him to enrich it with a wealth of marvelous detail concerning primitive Egypt, Assyria, Greece, and Rome. Drawing by way of Lactantius on Varro, and even on Ennius, he reconstructed mythological groups and dynasties: Belus, king of Assyria, of whom Eusebius had spoken, was the father of Ninus, etc. Above all, he singled out in these primitive ages the heroic figures who, from Prometheus on, had been leaders and pioneers in civilization—slay-

[11] "Those whom the pagans claim to be gods were once mere men."

ers of monsters, founders of cities, discoverers of arts and skills. The result was to restore dignity and independence to the personages of Fable: as benefactors of humanity they had every right to be held in grateful remembrance. And on the other hand, there was no reason for subordinating them to figures from Holy Writ—to the patriarchs, judges, and prophets; they could be ranked together, even if they were not of the same lineage. By gaining a foothold in history, the gods had acquired new prestige.

This is clearly to be seen, for example, in Ado of Vienne, whose *Chronicle of the Six Ages of the World* stems from the *Etymologiae.* After speaking of Moses and the Exodus, he refers to contemporary events in the pagan world: "In those days, it is said, lived Prometheus, who is believed to have fashioned men out of clay; his brother, Atlas, living at the same time, was regarded as a great astrologer; the grandson of Atlas, Mercury, was a sage skilled in several arts. For this reason, the vain error of his contemporaries placed him after his death among the gods" (*PL,* CXXIII, 35).

Aside from the expression "vain error," this passage has lost all accent of contempt or hostility; instead, we observe a concern for fixing dates, for determining pedigrees and genealogies, with a view to making room for the heroes of Fable in the annals of humanity. Does this not constitute a recognition of the virtues which, in times long past, had earned them their place in heaven? Parallel to the story of Scripture, this account of profane history is no longer subordinate to it; the first neither influences nor overshadows the second. Mercury has his own kind of greatness, as Moses has his. We have come a long way from Eusebius, who derived all pagan divinities from the Moses type, and for whom profane wisdom was merely a reflection of the wisdom of Israel.

*

ADO OF VIENNE is only one among the innumerable continuators of Isidore; in fact, there is hardly a chronicler or compiler of universal history writing after the great encyclopedist who fails to include humanized gods in his enumeration of ancient kings and heroes. We shall not present the endless list of these authors here, especially as it has already been compiled by others.[12] Let us mention only the most important of them all Peter Comestor.

[12] See Alphandéry, *op. cit.,* and J. D. Cooke, "Euhemerism, A Mediaeval Interpretation of Classical Paganism," *Speculum,* II (1927), pp. 396–410.

Around the year 1160, this Peter Comestor, dean of the church of Notre Dame at Troyes and later chancellor of Notre Dame at Paris, wrote under the title of *Historia scholastica* a history of God's people which penetrated to all parts of Europe in the translation by Guyart des Moulins (*Bible historiale* [1294]). In this work, which enjoyed tremendous authority,[13] we recognize in fixed and, as it were, codified form, the euhemeristic orientation that we first saw beginning to take shape in the writings of Isidore.

As an appendix to his sacred history, Peter condenses the mythological material furnished him by Isidore and his predecessors, Orosius and St. Jerome, into a series of short chapters, or *incidentiae*. The parallelism between the two narratives, sacred and profane, is presented with curious precision: clearly, the figures from the world of Fable, though of different lineage, have now achieved a basis of strict equality with the Biblical characters. In both groups, Peter recognizes men of superior stature, geniuses endowed with profound and mysterious wisdom. Zoroaster invented magic and inscribed the Seven Arts on four columns (Gen. XXXIX); Isis taught the Egyptians the letters of the alphabet and showed them how to write (LXX); Minerva taught several arts, in particular that of weaving (LXXVI); Prometheus, renowned for his wisdom, is reputed to have created men, either because he instructed the ignorant or perhaps because he fabricated automata. All these mighty spirits are worthy of veneration, exactly as are the patriarchs, and for the same reasons: they have been the guides and teachers of humanity, and together stand as the common ancestors of civilization.

This tendency of the Middle Ages to establish parallels between pagan wisdom and the wisdom of the Bible has long been recognized. It came clearly to light when study was first undertaken of the representations on cathedral portals[14] associating Sibyls and Prophets, and of the legend of Virgil, whom the medieval imagination had transformed into a kind of sorcerer or mage.[15] The Sibyls and the author of the Fourth Eclogue, it is true, had had intuitive

[13] Yearly editions from 1473 to 1526; another edition, Venice, 1729. Huet quotes the work; Richard Simon refers to its lasting success.

[14] See Emile Mâle, *L'Art religieux du* XIIIe *siècle en France* (6th ed., Paris, 1925), p. 339; *L'Art religieux de la fin du moyen âge,* pp. 268–296.

[15] See Comparetti, *Virgilio nel medioevo* (new ed., Florence, 1937); J. Webster Spargo, *Virgil the Necromancer* (1934), chap. ii: "The Talismanic Arts."

foreknowledge of Christian verity, and had foretold its coming. Applied to the divinities of paganism, this tendency has, as will be seen, surprising results. Not only does it "justify" the false gods by recognizing in them certain real virtues, but it even goes so far as to re-endow them with at least a part of their supernatural character.[16]

If we now look back at the diatribes of Arnobius and Commodian, we shall see that euhemerism was a weapon which cut both ways. What, in the intention of the apologists, it should have demolished, it actually confirmed and exalted. "If deification," Tertullian had argued, "is a reward of merit, why was Socrates not deified for his wisdom, Aristides for his justice, Demosthenes for his eloquence?" Tertullian, in his irony, spoke better than he knew: the Middle Ages were disposed to remedy this injustice. In his superstitious zeal, medieval man was ready to venerate sages whom antiquity itself had not placed among the immortals.

*

As WE have said, the pagan gods were no longer thought to have purloined the magic gifts they were believed to possess from the treasury of Christian wisdom. But might they not have inherited their power from the demons, with whom the first apologists often sought to identify them? [17]

In the tradition with which we are concerned, it might be possible to find traces of this idea—distant recollections, but nothing more. Neither Isidore nor his followers attribute a demonic character to the genius, the supernatural gifts which have brought about the elevation of great men to the rank of gods.[18] True, Apollo and Mercury have taken on the look of magicians, but this is no reason for regarding them with suspicion. They are good magicians, benevolent sorcerers. Humanity has much to thank them for.

That this was indeed the common attitude in the Middle Ages can be clearly seen in the works of popularization. Not only did the *Historia* of Peter

[16] Peter Comestor may have had in his hands the *De incredibilibus* (Περὶ ἀπίστων) of Palaephatus, which he cites (Judges, XX), and which would still further have strengthened his appreciation of the element of prodigy in pagan science.

[17] See, for example, Tertullian, *De spectaculis*, *PL*, I, I, 641 and 643: Venus, Bacchus, Castor, Pollux, etc., are "daemonia." Cf. St. Augustine, *Enarratio in Psalmos*, Psalm 96 (*PL*, XXXVI, 1231–32), verse 5: "Omnes dii gentium daemonia" ("All the gods of the heathen are demons").

[18] We shall study the tradition of the demonic in the next chapter in connection with astrology.

Comestor, which had come into general use as a textbook (a veritable "memento of the history of religions," as Alphandéry calls it), mold generations of readers in orthodox euhemerist views and furnish Vincent of Beauvais with all the essentials of what he wrote of the gods in the *Speculum historiale;* it also directly or indirectly inspired the compilations in vulgar tongues which brought science within reach of the layman.[19] These books go even farther in the same direction. They proclaim the gratitude of humanity toward the men of genius whom antiquity had made into gods. The *Book of the Treasure* of Brunetto Latini places Hercules side by side with Moses, Solon, Lycurgus, Numa Pompilius, and the Greek king Phoroneus as among the first legislators, who by instituting codes of law saved the nations of men from the ruin to which their own original frailty and impurity would have condemned them.[20]

Our medieval compilers feel themselves indebted to all these great men; they also feel themselves their heirs. For civilization is a treasure which has been handed down through the centuries; and as no further distinction is made between the sacred and profane precursors of Christianity who first forged that treasure, it is at last possible for medieval man unreservedly and even with pride to claim the heritage of antiquity. In the twelfth century, cultivated men were already aware of the Greco-Roman origins of their culture,[21] and Chrestien de Troyes affirms the idea that France has garnered the patrimony of antique culture and virtue:

Grece ot de chevalerie
Le premier los et de clergie

[19] See P. Meyer, "Les Premières Compilations françaises d'histoire ancienne," *Romania,* XIV (1885), pp. 38–81. Cf., at a much later date, early in the fourteenth century, the "historical" interpretations found in a poem of essentially "edifying" character, the *Ovide moralisé* (I, vv. 859 ff. and vv. 1101 f.)

Jupiter fut, selon l'estoire
Rois de Crete, et fesoit accroire
Par l'art de son enchantement
Qu'il ert Deus . . .

("Jupiter, according to history, was King of Crete, and by his magic art caused it to be believed that he was God.")

Or vous dirai coment la fable
Peut estre à l'estoire acordable". . .

("Now I will tell you how fable can be made to agree *with history.*")

[20] See C. V. Langlois, *La Connaissance de la nature et du monde au moyen âge,* in *idem, La Vie en France au moyen âge,* III (Paris, 1927), pp. 341–342.

[21] See E. Faral, *Recherches sur les sources latines des contes et romans courtois* (Paris, 1913), pp. 398 ff. The idea of the continuity between the ancient and contemporary worlds is thus seen not to have been peculiar to the Renaissance humanists. Cf., on this point, the controversy between Bremond and Hauser, in Bremond, *Histoire littéraire du sentiment religieux en France,* vol. I: *L'Humanisme dévot,* chap. i, section ii, esp. pp. 4–6.

Puis vint chevalerie a Rome
Et de la clergie la some
Qui ore est en France venue . . .[22]

This idea reappears insistently in the popular encyclopedias of the thirteenth century.[23] And among the "chevaliers" and "clercs," whose glorious tradition the French are so proud of continuing, appear valiant captains at times called Alexander or Caesar, but at others Hercules or Jason, and great inventors, now known as Ptolemy or Aristotle, and again as Mercury or Prometheus.

*

As we have just seen, the French of the thirteenth century believed that the heritage of antiquity was theirs by special right; other peoples had long advanced the same claim. In the fifth century, the Spaniard, Paulus Orosius, boasts of being a genuine Roman; later, a Gregory of Tours, an Isidore of Seville, were to see themselves as belonging to peoples especially privileged in comparison with "barbarian" stock. But this pride of descent, which is hardly ever absent from the learned writings of the Middle Ages, brings with it one curious consequence: in order to justify his pretentions, the scholar turns to the fabled past of antiquity for supporting witnesses, for ancestors and begetters. Thus originate those "ethnogenic" fables (as Gaston Paris called them) which name a hero or demigod as ancestor of a whole people.

One such fable, which proved to be a particularly hardy one, is famed above all—that according to which the Franks were descendants of the Trojan Francus, as the Romans were of the Trojan Aeneas. This legend was an invention of Merovingian scholars,[24] but it should not be dismissed as a mere fantasy of learned minds. It was taken seriously as genealogy, and became a "veritable form of ethnic consciousness."[25] Its plausibility was enhanced by the apocryphal journals of the siege of Troy by the "Cretan" Dictys and the "Phrygian" Dares, which had been popular ever since the Greek decadence:

[22] *Cligès* (ed. W. Foerster), vv. 32 ff. ("Greece had once the leadership in chivalry and learning; then chivalry passed to Rome together with the sum of learning, which now has come to France.")

[23] For example, in *L'Image du monde*. See Langlois, *op. cit.*, p. 73.

[24] The earliest evidence of this legend is met with in the *Chronique de Frédégaire*; the *Liber historiae Francorum* adds new elements.

[25] Alphandéry, *op. cit.*, p. 8.

with their appearance of exact documentation they, as it were, secularized the marvels of antiquity and gave them the color of true history. "These *procès-verbaux* of gods and heroes presented them in such a light that they seemed more convincingly historical than Charlemagne, Roland, or Oliver. . . ." But even when thus humanized, and brought near enough to look like probable ancestors, these figures lost none of their mythical prestige; mortals who claimed relationship with them on historical grounds could boast of their supernatural origin. Did not the Trojan Aeneas, "de' Romani il gentil seme," [26] leave a quasi-divine imprint upon the whole race of his descendants?

The exceptional popularity enjoyed by the legend of Troy in the Middle Ages was therefore not due exclusively to the interest of the romantic narrative in itself; the *Roman de Troie* of Benoît de Sainte-Maure contained a "sort of mythical substratum" where the medieval listener or reader could more or less consciously detect "something of his moral genealogy."

This, then, is one of the effects of euhemerism in the Middle Ages: mythological figures are no longer presented as common benefactors of humanity. They are the patrons of this or that people,[27] the parent stem from which the race has issued and from which it derives its glory.

*

IN THIS regard no break is discernible between the Middle Ages and the Renaissance; the same considerations which have protected the gods continue to

[26] Dante, *Inferno*, XXVI, 60 ("of Romans the noble seed").—In addition to the Romulus story and the legend of Trojan descent, Rome has other and purely mythological origins. In his *Dittamondo*, Fazio degli Uberti relates that Janus was the first king of the Latins; then came Saturn and his sons, "Iddii nomati in terra," who civilized Italy. Cf. *supra*, p. 12. —See A. Graf, *Roma nella memoria e nelle immaginazioni del medioevo* (1882).

[27] Or even of this or that city: medieval scholars did their utmost to prove that their cities had been named for a hero or demigod. According to Flodoard (*PL*, CXXXV, 28), Rheims was founded by Remus; Sigebert de Gembloux (*PL*, CIX, 717) held that Metz was founded by one Metius, "who lived under Julius Caesar," and whose name he had read upon an ancient stone. Other similar examples could be given.

Cf. also the legend of Hercules as protector and symbol of Florence; from the end of the thirteenth century he appears on the seals of the Signoria with the legend: "Herculea clava domat Fiorentia prava" (see Müntz, *Les Précurseurs de la Renaissance* [1882], p. 48). Tradition would have it, on the other hand, that the patron of pagan Florence was Mars, a supposed statue of whom was to be seen in the Middle Ages near the Ponte Vecchio (Dante, *Inferno*, XIII, 143–150). It was believed by some that the fortunes of the city were intimately bound up with this statue (R. Davidsohn, *Storia di Firenze*, II, pp. 1156 ff.)—The Florence statue is actually of the group of Patroclus and Menelaus from which the Roman Pasquino was derived.

assure their survival. They are still given a place in history: not only do the early chronicles, printed and many times reissued, retain their full authority, but the fifteenth-century chroniclers follow their lead, and never fail to devote one or more chapters to the pagan divinities. This is true of the *Rudimentum noviciorum* (1475), the *Fasciculus temporum* (1475), and the *Mer des hystoires* (1488); also of Annius of Viterbo, the pseudo commentator on Berosus,[28] and Jacopo da Bergamo.

The last-named, for example, in his *Supplementum chronicarum*,[29] studies the origin and the pedigrees of the gods (Bk. III, f. 12). Jupiter is a king who has been worshipped under that name because of his resemblance to the planet Jupiter; other kings have borne the same name, notably the king of Candia, a son of Saturn—who is, of course, historical, as are Ops, Caelus, Uranus, Vesta, etc.[30] Then Semiramis is dealt with, and Lot and Isaac; but a little later (f. 15, r and v) the gods reappear—Cybele, Pallas, the Sun, Diana. Next we pass to Jacob, Leah, and Rachel, and to the monarchs of Assyria; then come Ceres and Isis (f. 16, 17 r); and after a paragraph devoted to Joseph, we meet Apollo, Bacchus, Vulcan, Apis, and Osiris. As in Peter Comestor, mythology alternates with sacred history. It is of interest to note also that this compilation by Jacopo da Bergamo includes additional chapters on the Sibyls and on the Trojan war, a geographical section containing a list of all cities famed since the beginning of time, and, last of all, a contemporary history.

The sixteenth century is in this respect a repetition of the fifteenth: the *Promptuaire* of Guillaume Rouille (*Promptuarium iconum insigniorum a saeculo hominum* [1553]), the *World Chronicle* of Antoine du Verdier (*Prosopographie ou Description des personnes, patriarches, prophètes, dieux des gentils, roys, consuls, princes, grands capitaines, ducs, philosophes, orateurs, poètes, juriconsultes et inventeurs de plusieurs arts, avec les effigies d'aucuns d'iceux . . .* [1573]), and the compilation by Eilhardus Lubinus (*Fax poetica sive genealogia et res gestae deorum gentilium, virorum, regum,*

[28] *Commentaria fratris Joannis Annii . . . super opera diversorum auctorum de antiquitatibus loquentium confecta . . .* (Rome, 1498).

[29] Venice (1483); our references are to the edition of 1485.

[30] Similarly, Jacopo da Bergamo distinguishes several different Minervas, etc. In order to make clear these mythological genealogies, he has recourse to Boccaccio's *Genealogia deorum*, of which we shall have much to say later.

et Caesarum Romanorum [1598]), show us gods and heroes, in an apparently secure historical framework, among patriarchs, philosophers, and Caesars.

*

THUS THE EXISTENCE of the gods continues to be sanctioned on historical grounds; furthermore, as in the Middle Ages, there is a disposition to regard them as the forerunners of civilization. This tendency is already very evident in Jacopo da Bergamo. Minerva, he says, was the first woman to understand the art of working in wool (f. 15); Chiron was the inventor of medicine (f. 18, r), Hermes Trismegistus the first astronomer (f. 21, r), Mercury the first musician (f. 20, v). Prometheus taught men to make fire and to wear rings (f. 19, r); Atlas taught the Greeks astrology (*ibid.*). Apollo, Aesculapius, etc., are placed in a section entitled "Viri disciplinis excellentes"; other gods, like Faunus, Mars, etc., appear under the heading: "Viri doctrinis excellentes."

Even more typical, from the same point of view, is the *De inventoribus* of Polydore Virgil.[31] In the preface, already present in the first (1499) edition, we find first a declaration of euhemeristic belief: "And whatsoever things may have been attributed by us to Saturn, Jove, Neptune, Dionysus, Apollo, Aesculapius, Ceres, Vulcan, and to such others as have the name of gods, we have thus attributed to them as to mortal men, and not as to gods, even though we still call them by that name." After this declaration, which he obviously thinks should protect him from any quibbling on the part of the ecclesiastical authorities, Polydore does not hesitate to salute each god as an innovator: Hermes Trismegistus established time divisions (II, 5); from Bacchus, man learned how to make wine (III, 3); Venus taught the courtesans their art (III, 17); Mercury, according to Diodorus and Cicero, taught the alphabet to the Egyptians (I, 6). Pliny attributes man's knowledge of the heavenly bodies to Jupiter Belus; Diodorus, to Mercury (I, 17).

[31] Polidoro Virgilio da Urbino, *De rerum inventoribus.* The first edition (Venice, 1499) consisted of only three books, later increased to eight in the Basel edition of 1521. In spite of all his precautions, Polydore's work was put upon the Index.

On a copy of the *De rer. invent.* with annotations by Rabelais, see Perrat, "Le Polydore Virgile de Rabelais," *Humanisme et Renaissance,* XI (1949), pp. 167–204.

Thus the Renaissance only confirmed the right of the ancient gods—those geniuses responsible for our civilization—to the gratitude of the human

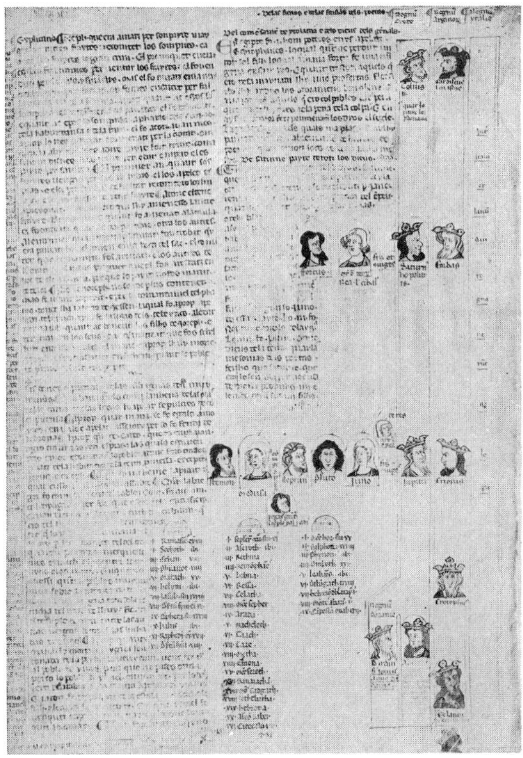

1. Caelus and his descendants

race. It is no exaggeration to say that the Renaissance even restored them to their place in heaven: "Shouldst thou follow in the footsteps of David," wrote Zwingli to Francis I in 1531,[32] "thou wilt one day see God Himself; and near to Him thou mayest hope to see Adam, Abel, Enoch, Paul, Hercules, Theseus, Socrates, the Catos, the Scipios. . . ."

*

[32] *Christianae fidei brevis et clara expositio.*

FINALLY, we have noted during the Middle Ages a strange phenomenon—a whole people claiming a mythological hero as ancestor, choosing him, as it were, for their progenitor and patron. This phenomenon persists into the Renaissance, even taking on new and striking forms.

The legend of the Trojan origin of the Franks was, as is well known, exploited by Jean Le Maire de Belges, in his *Illustrations de Gaule et singularités de Troie,* which attained immense popularity. One reason for this success was that "nearly every nation could find there, as if in an archival setting, its most ancient titles of nobility. Only the Germans and French could boast undisputed descent from Hector himself, but others—Bretons, Flemings, Scandinavians, Normans, Italians, and Spaniards—also found ways of asserting their own relationship with him, to justify either their pride or their ambition." [33] Now Le Maire distributed the names of the various Trojan heroes, like spoils of war, among these claimants: the Bretons were said to be descendants of Brutus, first king of Brittany; the Spaniards of Hesperus, the Italians of Italus, the men of Brabant of Brabo, the Tuscans of Tuscus, and the Burgundians of Hercules the Great of Libya.[34]

Let us further note that Jean Le Maire greatly strengthens the divine element in the legend of Troy. The gods are given a preponderant role in his historico-mythological romance—something which we do not find in Dictys, Dares, or Benoît de Sainte-Maure.[35]

Ronsard's *Franciade* was less successful than the *Illustrations;* the failure and neglect which were to be the lot of this enthusiastically anticipated epic are well known. But the *Franciade* reveals a new tendency which is particularly appropriate to the Renaissance: it is inspired not by "ethnic consciousness" but by dynastic pride. Charles IX personally supervised the composition of the poem,[36] in his concern to have it establish a direct connection

[33] Thibaut, *Marguerite d'Autriche et Jean Le Maire de Belges,* pp. 171–172.

[34] See G. Doutrepont, *Jean Lemaire de Belges et la Renaissance,* pp. 273–274. Goropius Becanus (Jean Becan van Gorp), in his *Origines Antwerpianae* (1569), invents a still more extravagant ancestry for the Flemings. They are Cimmerians, sons of Japheth; their wisdom comes to them from the Thracian Orpheus (Bk. VII).—Etienne Pasquier, in his *Recherches de la France,* and Claude Fauchet, in his *Antiquités gauloises et françaises,* were at last to dispose of the Trojan legend.

[35] See Doutrepont, *op. cit.,* p. 387.

[36] See Ronsard's "Avis au lecteur."

between the sixty-three sovereigns of his own line and the most fabulous antiquity.

Princely pretensions of this sort, indeed, are seldom glimpsed before the end of the Middle Ages. In 1390, however, Jacques de Guise wrote a universal chronicle which bore this revealing title: *Annales de l'histoire des illustres princes de Hainaut, depuis le commencement du monde.*[37] Later, the dukes of Burgundy were to pride themselves on their descent from a demigod; the Trojan legends were in great favor at their court—and that as early as the fourteenth century.[38] Late in the fifteenth, a *Recueil des histoires de Troyes* (1464) was being read there, in which Hercules is given unwonted prominence. The author, Raoul Lefèvre, proposes to deal with his subject in three books, the second of which is to treat of the Labors of Hercules, and to show that he twice destroyed the city of Troy. Furthermore, Hercules appeared in the tapestries decorating the hall where the Banquet of the Pheasant Oath was held (Lille, 1454), and in a pantomime performed at the wedding festivities of Charles the Bold and Margaret of York. Why this special emphasis upon Hercules? It is due to his reputed place as founder of the dynasty. Olivier de la Marche relates in his *Mémoires* that Hercules, journeying long ago into Spain, passed through the land of Burgundy and there met a lady of great beauty and noble lineage, Alise by name. They were wed, and from their union issued the line of Burgundian princes.

Another mythological hero, Jason, was well known at the Burgundian court: Philip the Good put himself under his aegis when, in 1430, he founded the Order of the Golden Fleece. To be sure, a Biblical hero, Gideon, seconded Jason in his functions as patron of the order. But this very partnership, bringing out as it does the parallelism between sacred and profane,

[37] *Annales historiae illustrium principum Hanoniae ab initio rerum usque ad annum Christi 1390;* partially translated into French by Jean Wauquelin around 1445, and published by E. Sackur, *MGH, Scriptores,* XXX, pt. I (1896). (Cf. cod. 9242 of the Bibliothèque Royale, Brussels; see *fig. 6.*)

[38] The library of Philip the Good contained seventeen volumes destined to disseminate the legend. See Doutrepont, "La littérature française à la cour des ducs de Bourgogne," Société d'Emulation de Bruges, *Mélanges,* I (1908). It should be recalled that the *Illustrations* of Jean Le Maire were published from 1509 to 1513—that is to say, long after the last duke of Burgundy had disappeared (1477).

serves admirably to illustrate the persistence of the medieval point of view.[39]

Princely pride found ample satisfaction in these claims of mythological sponsorship and heredity. In addition to the dukes of Burgundy and the kings of France, should we perhaps also cite the example of Pope Alexander VI, who used the Borgia coat of arms as warrant for having the ceiling of his Vatican apartments decorated with frescoes representing the story of Isis, Osiris, and the monster Apis—unexpected antecedents, indeed, for a Christian pontiff? [39a]

Other comparable instances might be found in the seventeenth century. In 1600, the Jesuits of Avignon, charged with organizing the ceremonial reception given by the city to Marie de Médicis, bestowed on her royal consort the title of Gallic Hercules ("Hercule Gaulois"), justifying the extravagant flattery on the following grounds: "L'illustre maison de Navarre a prins sa source de l'ancien Hercule, fils d'Osiris, lequel ayant battu et combattu les Lominiens, qui étaient les trois enfants de Geryon, tyran des Espagnes, et ayant affranchi ce peuple de leur servitude, établit en cette monarchie son fils Hispalus, les neveux duquel succédèrent depuis à la couronne du royaume de Navarre." [40]

*

ICONOGRAPHY, in turn, attests the continuity of the "euhemeristic" tradition, and gives striking illustration to its varied aspects. We shall limit ourselves to a few examples.

In the first place, for visual demonstration of the insertion of the gods into history, let us glance at a Provençal chronicle (British Museum, Egerton ms. 1500) of the early fourteenth century (after 1313). This chronicle, in

[39] See Doutrepont, *op. cit.*, p. 147.—On Jason and Gideon, see Olivier de la Marche, *Epistre à Philippe le Beau pour tenir et célébrer la noble feste de Toison d'Or.* The Jason legend was spread by Raoul Lefèvre (*Jason*), Michaut Taillevent (*Le songe de la Toison d'Or*), and Guillaume Fillastre (*La Toison d'Or*).

[39a] See forthcoming volume of lectures by F. Saxl, to be published by the Warburg Institute, London.

[40] *Labyrinthe royal de l'Hercule Gaulois Triomphant . . . représenté à l'entrée triomphante de la Royne en la cité d'Avignon le 19 nov. de l'an MDC . . .* ("The illustrious house of Navarre issued from the ancient Hercules, son of Osiris, who, having fought and overcome the Lominians, the three children of Geryon, tyrant of Spain, and having freed the people of that country from their servitude, established as head of that monarchy his son, Hispalus, whose descendants later succeeded to the crown of the kingdom of Navarre").

the form of a *rotulus*, is illustrated by tables which are both genealogical and synoptic, and which show us the head of each person named. The first two

2. Biblical and pagan heroes

heads naturally represent Adam and Eve (f. 3, r); then follow their descendants, Noah, Shem, etc. (f. 3, v); next appear the profane dynasties. Here we see, arranged in parallel, vertical rows (f. 6, r), the rulers of the various kingdoms of antiquity. In the Cretan dynasty we find Saturn, beneath Caelus and above Jupiter; on the same horizontal line with Jupiter are his wife Juno, his brothers Plato, Neptune, etc. The gods are included as a matter of course in the historical narrative (*fig. 1*).

3. *Apollo Medicus*

The most typical example of the tradition of the heroes and sages that places profane and sacred history on the same plane, is afforded by the famous series of drawings attributed to Maso Finiguerra, preserved in the British Museum under the title of *Florentine Picture Chronicle.*[41] Sir Sidney Colvin, who had studied the drawings extensively and dated them between 1455 and 1465, related them to a *Sommario,* or *Breve historia universale,* in the Biblioteca Nazionale in Florence (Cat. xxv. iv, 565, ii. iv, 348). These drawings, in fact, present another illustrated world chronicle; they show us, after Adam and Eve, the patriarchs, Noah, Abraham, and their successors, along with "contemporary" pagan figures—Inachus, Cecrops, Codrus, Saturn, Jupiter, etc. What is particularly notable is the parallelism established between all these great figures of the past, historical or legendary, Jew or Gentile—Prophets and Sibyls, judges, warriors, poets, and lawgivers. Especially significant is the prominence given to heroes (Jason,

[41] *A Florentine Picture Chronicle, Being a Series of Ninety-Nine Drawings Representing Scenes and Personages of Ancient History, Sacred and Profane . . . reproduced from the originals with a critical and descriptive text* (London, 1898). To the same family belongs the fine manuscript (*fig. 2*) owned by Sir Sidney C. Cockerell.

Theseus) and to sages; the image of Apollo (*fig. 4;* cf. also *fig. 3,* an Apollo of the tenth century belonging to the same tradition) is of particular interest in this connection. It represents Apollo the Healer:

> . . . *dieu sauveur, dieu des savants mystères,*
> *dieu de la vie et dieu des plantes salutaires.*[42]

Standing at a patient's bedside, with his conjuring books and imps, he seems engaged in some terrifying act of exorcism. He looks like an Oriental magician, and in adjacent drawings we do in fact encounter, similarly accoutered, Hostanes conjuring up demons, and Oromasdes resuscitating a dead person. In the same group appear Zoroaster, Hermes Trismegistus, Orpheus, Linus, and Musaeus—all the esoteric wisdom of Persia, Egypt, and Greece.[43]

4. Apollo as a physician

[42] ". . . savior God, God of learned mysteries, God of life and of health-giving plants . . ."

[43] On the knowledge of Oriental magic and the influence of the Cabala in fifteenth-century Florence, see Colvin, *op. cit.*, Introduction, paragraphs VI–VII.—Cf. F. Cumont and J. Bidez, *Les Mages hellénisés* (Paris, 1939).

On the representation of the sages of antiquity in Renaissance art, see E. Müntz, *Histoire de l'art pendant la Renaissance,* II, p. 125.

Mention should also be made, among the illustrators of this tradition, of Giusto da Padova, whose frescoes in the church of the Eremitani, Padua, have disappeared, but who has left us his drawings for them, executed in the last years of the fourteenth century. See A. Venturi, "Il libro di Giusto per la Cappella degli Eremitani in Padova," in *Le Gallerie nazionali italiane,* IV (1899), pp. 345–376; and, by the same author, "Il libro di disegni di Giusto" (reproduced in its entirety), *ibid.,* V (1902), pp. 391 ff. Cf. also J. von Schlosser, "Giusto's Fresken in Padua . . . ," *Jahrb d. kunsthist. Samml. d. Allerh. Kaiserh.,* XVII (1896), pp. 11–100. The miniatures of Leonardo da Besozzo (1435–1442) derive from Giusto's drawings.

See also *La canzone delle virtù e delle scienze di Bartolomeo di Bartoli* (text and illustrations), published by L. Dorez (1904).

5. *Hercules slaying Cacus*

The parallelism between sacred and profane history is further set forth in one of the most exquisite works of the Renaissance, the façade of the Colleoni Chapel in Bergamo, where alternating bas-reliefs represent events from the Old Testament and from mythology, the punishment of Adam and the Labors of Hercules.[44] At approximately the same date, Lombard sculptors ornamented the zone at the base of the façade of the Certosa of Pavia with medallions which show Prophets side by side with emperors [45] and gods—a strange series of apocryphal portraits in which the infant Hercules strangles serpents and Judas Maccabeus wears a Mercury cap, and which recalls the numismatic fantasies of the "prosopographies." [46]

Of the personages of Fable viewed expressly as inventors of arts and skills we possess some celebrated images in the lowest zone of bas-reliefs on the Campanile in Florence. Not far from the first horseman and the first navigator, we recognize Daedalus, first conqueror of the air; near the mathemati-

[44] The motifs treated are the Creation of Adam, the Creation of Eve, their Fall and Punishment; the Sacrifice of Abraham; the Combats of Hercules with Antaeus, with the Cretan Bull, the Nemean Lion, and the Lernaean Hydra (*fig. 11*).

[45] Chosen by reason of their connection with Christianity. See J. von Schlosser, "Die ältesten Medaillen und die Antike," *Jahrb. d. kunsthist. Samml. d. Allerh. Kaiserh.*, XVIII (1897), pp. 60–108.

[46] See *supra*, p. 21. Several of the Certosa reliefs, furthermore, are inspired by forged medals: see von Schlosser, *op. cit.*, and our article, "Youth, Innocence, and Death. Some Notes on a Medallion on the Certosa of Pavia," *Journal of the Warburg Institute*, I (1937–38), pp. 298–303.

Cf. also forthcoming volume by C. Mitchell on the role of the classical coins in the Italian Renaissance, to be published by the Warburg Institute, London.

6. Diana and her worshippers

cians Euclid and Pythagoras appears Orpheus, father of poetry; still another of civilization's early heroes and benefactors is Hercules, portrayed here as victor over the monster Cacus (*fig. 5*). Here we have the euhemeristic tradition at its purest and noblest; the best commentary on these sculptures is the passage in which Cicero exalts the *animus divinus* of the precursors of civilization: "Omnes magni: etiam superiores, qui vestitum, qui tecta, qui cultum vitae, qui praesidia contra feras invenerunt; a quibus mansuefacti et exculti, a necessariis artificiis ad elegantiora defluximus. . . ." [47]

[47] *Tusc.*, I, 25. ("All these were great men; earlier still the men who discovered the fruits of the earth, raiment, dwellings, an ordered way of life, protection against wild creatures —men under whose civilizing influence we have gradually passed on from the indispensable handicrafts to the finer arts."—LCL.)

Here, again, the illustrated chronicles would furnish many supplementary examples. Among the French manuscripts of the Bibliothèque Nationale we cite cod. 301, *Les livres des histoires du commencement du monde,*

We have further seen that the Legend of Troy, as enlarged upon by pseudo historians, had played a part in the "laicizing" of certain mythological heroes; visual imagery makes this doubly clear. In the Finiguerra drawings Jason and Theseus are shown, and near them Paris and Troilus. Even earlier, however, in the frescoes representing the Trojan war, painted about 1380 in the Steri at Palermo,[48] the ship Argo was to be seen, with Jason, Hercules, Castor, and Pollux. The painter of these scenes, as Ezio Levi has shown, was merely following the text of Guido delle Colonne (*Historia destructionis Trojae* [1273–1287]), which, in turn, is an adaptation of the *Roman de Troie* of Benoît de Sainte-Maure. In the fourteenth and fifteenth centuries, a swarm of illustrated manuscripts of this romance or its derivatives present us with images of the demigods.[49]

Finally, the mythological ancestry on which the Renaissance princes so prided themselves was of course celebrated in works of art.[50] We need mention here only the tapestries of the cathedral of Beauvais, where we see, among other figures, Francus greeting the daughter of the king of the Gauls whom he is to marry, and Jupiter, accompanied by Hercules, bringing the alphabet of civilization to Gaul. These tapestries have their source, as Emile Mâle has proved,[51] in the *Illustrations* of Jean Le Maire. Le Maire sets himself up as the final arbiter of Trojan iconography: "L'histoire véritable de la maison troyenne," he writes, "ne sera plus désormais peinte, figurée, ne patrociniée, pour l'aornement des salles et chambres royales, sinon après la nar-

---

and cod. 6362, *Histoire universelle* (*figs. 7, 8*).

In the 1486 and subsequent Venetian editions of the *Supplementum* of Jacopo da Bergamo, a somewhat crude engraving shows a group of gods whom the text cites as "inventors"; the woodcuts of Wohlgemut and Pleydenwurf (1493) in the *Great Chronicle of Nuremberg* are of interest in the same connection.

48 See E. Levi and E. Gabrici, *Lo Steri di Palermo e le sue pitture* (1932); E. Levi, *L'Epopea medioevale nelle pitture dello Steri di Palermo* (1933).

49 Examples are: Bibliothèque Nationale, cods. fr. 782 and 22.552 (*fig. 9*); Venice, Marciana, cod. fr. 17; Rome, Vatican, cod. Reg. 1505; Milan, Ambrosiana, cod. H 86 sup.; Geneva, Bibl. Munic., cods. fr. 64 and 72; Leningrad, cod. F.v.XIV n. 3 (fr. 2), etc.

50 In 1393, Philip the Bold had acquired from a Parisian *tapissier* two pieces depicting Jason's winning of the Golden Fleece (J. Guiffrey, *Histoire générale de la tapisserie*, Vol. I: *Les tapisseries françaises*, p. 19. These tapestries may have suggested to the Duke the idea of placing himself under the aegis of the hero of Colchis (cf. Doutrepont, *op. cit.*, p. 147). Philip the Good, in 1449, ordered in Tournai eight immense tapestries illustrating the history of the Golden Fleece (Soil, *Tapisseries de Tournai*, pp. 24, 233–235, 374, f.).

See H. Göbel, *Wandteppiche* (1928), II: *Die romanischen Länder*, vol. I, pp. 16, 107, 411, 414, and 552, n. 101.

51 *L'Art religieux de la fin du moyen âge*, pp. 342–346.

ration présente, antique et véritable." [52] In this domain, the artist will from now on be little more than an instrument made use of by some erudite courtier for flattering the pride of his masters.

7. *Rape of Deianira*

8. *Rape of Proserpina*

Later, under Henri II, the French court was to go to even further lengths, acting out literally and in all seriousness the comedy of Olympus.[53] Art and poetry joined forces to attest the divinity of the sovereign, his consort, his favorite, and their entourage.

In the château of Tanlay, the sixteenth-century residence of the Coligny-Châtillon family, a fresco [54] by a pupil of Primaticcio groups a number of contemporary persons in the guise of gods and goddesses (*fig. 10*). There is no doubt as to the interpretation, which has been furnished us by Ronsard

[52] Bk. I, prol. 3–4; cf. II, p. 144. ("The veritable history of the House of Troy shall henceforth be neither painted, imaged, or advocated for the adornment of royal halls and chambers save in accordance with the present narrative, which is from antiquity and truthful.")

[53] See E. Bourciez, *Les Moeurs polies et la littérature de Cour sous Henri II* (1886), II, chap. ii: "L'Olympe nouveau."

[54] See C. Oulmont, "La fresque de la tour de la Ligue au Château de Tanlay," *Revue de l'art*, II (1933), pp. 183–184; and F. E. Schneegans, "À propos d'une fresque mythologique du XVIme siècle," *Humanisme et Renaissance*, II (1935), pp. 441–444.

himself in a *hymne* celebrating the virtues of the Coligny house.[55] The artist must have taken his inspiration from this poem. Jupiter is the king, Henri II;

9. Jupiter vanquishing Saturn

Mars, the Connétable de Montmorency; Themis, the Duchess of Ferrara. As for Mercury,

> *C'est ce grand demi-dieu Cardinal de Lorraine . . .*

In the same year that Ronsard composed these verses, Léonard Limousin

[55] *Hymnes,* I, IV (1555). Cf. *Le Temple de Messeigneurs le Connétable et des Chastillons,* where Anne reigns as Mars, Gaspard as Neptune, etc.; and *Hymnes,* II, II, where Odet de Châtillon appears as Hercules.

reproduced Raphael's *Feast of the Gods* on an enameled plate.[56] Here, again, the place of Jupiter was taken by the king, while Catherine de Médicis appeared as Juno, and Diane de Poitiers as Diana.[57]

Fetes, ballets, dramatic "eclogues," and the co-operation of all the arts continued to support this royal apotheosis, which was to achieve dazzling consummation in the next century at Versailles.

10. The Royal Olympus: Henri II and his court

Thus, at the end of this evolution which has brought us down to the Renaissance, we find the euhemeristic spirit as much alive as ever, still taking the

[56] See Bourciez, *loc. cit.*, pp. 176–177. The plate is described and reproduced in the *Rev. archéol.* (1855), pp. 311 ff. The persons represented, instead of being completely costumed *à l'antique*, are shown wearing plumed toques.

[57] The reader will recall the celebrated Diana at Anet, now in the Louvre; in the same château was formerly a marble medallion (now in the Musée de Cluny) representing Catherine de Médicis as Juno. See also the curious examples assembled by E. Wind, "Studies in Allegorical Portraiture," *Journal of the Warburg Institute*, I (1937–38), pp. 138 ff.

two main forms which we detected at the outset. At times we have to do with a tribute of gratitude and veneration offered to great men; at others, with extravagant adulation of worldly power. In both cases, the recipients are raised to the rank of gods.

11. Hercules and the Lernaean Hydra

II

The Physical Tradition

THE HEAVENLY bodies are gods. "We must assign the same divinity to the stars."[1] This opinion, at the time of its formulation by Cicero, was on the way to becoming general. For a Roman or Alexandrian of that age, the stars were not as they are for us, "bodies infinitely remote in space, which move according to the inflexible laws of mechanics, and whose composition is chemically determinable." They were "divinities."[2]

Every mind which perceives a governing intelligence behind the movement of the spheres instinctively places this divine power in heaven.[3] From this it is but a step to considering the sun, moon, and stars as in themselves divine. Among other determining factors, it was the mythological names given to the stars—in obedience to the same instinct—which above all else encouraged the Greeks, and after them the Romans, to take this step. *Nomen, numen*—the name alone was enough to lend divine personality to each luminous body moving in the heavens, but complete identification was achieved when that name was Hercules or Mars, that is, the name of a god whose appearance and history were already well known. And the mythological imagination of the Greeks, which had created gods on earth, could readily picture them in the skies as well.

However, this identification of the gods with astral bodies, which had been fully accomplished by the end of the pagan era, was the end product of

1 "Tribuenda est sideribus . . . divinitas" (*De natur. deor.*, II, 15).

2 F. Cumont, "L'astrologie et la magie dans le paganisme romain," in *Les Religions orientales dans le paganisme romain*, p. 160.

3 As in Plato, *Laws*, X, 899 b, and *Timaeus*, 36 d ff.

a complex evolution. For the constellations, as for the planets, the process of "mythologization" was steady, if not continuous.[4]

For the constellations, the process had begun in Homeric times: Homer himself speaks of "mighty Orion."[5] But in general the stars and groups of stars were still known merely by the names of objects or animals—the Scales, the Ram, etc. Toward the fifth century B.C., many of the constellations had become associated with myths; in the fourth, the catalogue of Eudoxus of Cnidus—which, though scientific in spirit, adopted the vocabulary of myth—and, a century later, Aratus' poem on the stellar configurations, still further encouraged the same tendency. The famous Farnese Globe in the Naples Museum, copied from a Greek original probably contemporary with Aratus, shows us a sky in part invaded by the gods.[6]

Eratosthenes (284–204 B.C.), in his *Catasterismi*, completes this evolution and standardizes its results: each of the constellations is given mythological significance, and the signs of the zodiac themselves are connected with heroes of Fable. The Lion, for example, is the Nemean lion who was overcome by Hercules; the Bull is the bull of the Europa story. At this stage, the fusion between astronomy and mythology is so complete that no further distinction is made between them: the Augustan poet, Hyginus, is at one and the same time astronomer and mythographer.

But a phenomenon is already beginning to be apparent which is destined to involve this celestial mythology in fearful chaos: the traditional Greek constellations are being supplemented or replaced by exotic constellations. First, thirty-six genii alleged to be of Egyptian origin, the decans,[7] insinuate themselves into the zodiacal band, each one having its own name and face (πρόσωπον) which gives it concrete and independent personality; the decans, too, are both stars and divinities.[8] But these were not the only foreign elements

[4] See E. Panofsky and F. Saxl, "Classical Mythology in Mediaeval Art," *Metropolitan Museum Studies*, IV (1932–1933), pp. 228–280; Cumont, "Les noms des planètes et l'astrolâtrie chez les grecs," *L'antiquité classique*, IV (1935), pp. 5 ff.

[5] Σθένος Ὠρίωνος, *Iliad*, XVIII, 486.

[6] See Thiele, *Antike Himmelsbilder*, Plates II–VI.

[7] The term "decans" derives from the division of the signs into three parts of ten degrees each, where the genii live.—See Bouché-Leclercq, *L'Astrologie grecque*, chap. vii, 2, esp. pp. 221–222; and W. Gundel, *Dekane und Dekansternbilder*, Studien der Bibliothek Warburg, XIX (1936).

[8] See W. Scott, ed., *Hermetica* (Hermes Trismegistus), I, chap. xix, pp. 324 ff., *Asclepius*, and W. Gundel, *op. cit.*, p. 344.—Firmicus Maternus, who on this point follows the Egyptian tradition, still calls them gods. Similarly Celsus alludes to δαίμονες ἢ θεοί τινες αἰθέριοι.

to invade Greek astronomy. Scholars had drawn up lists of the paranatellons, i.e., the stars rising to the north and to the south of each of the zodiacal signs, and we note that the register of these stars, established in the first century of our era by Teucer the Babylonian, contains a great many glyphs or sigils which are likewise of Egyptian origin,[9] or perhaps even Chaldean or Anatolian. Finally, from now on the Greek celestial globe (*sphaera graecanica*) has as a kind of parasite a barbaric globe (*sphaera barbarica*),[10] the mythological elements of which live on, and in the course of the centuries become mingled with those of classical origin.

With the planets the process is even more complicated. Originally the Greeks singled out only one, Venus, Ἑωσφόρος or Ἕσπερος in Homer. They learned from the Babylonians to distinguish the five wandering stars from the fixed stars forming the constellations, and—still following the same example—consecrated each of the five to a different deity. For every Babylonian god a Greek god who bore some resemblance to him in character was substituted as master of the same planet.[11] This identification was probably the work of the Pythagoreans; it came about in the fifth century B.C. Nevertheless, as Cumont emphasizes, the planets in Plato's time have *no true names*, the names of the gods serving merely to indicate possession—ὁ (ἀστὴρ) τοῦ Κρόνου ("star of Kronos"), etc.

During the Alexandrian period the planetary lexicon becomes extraordinarily confused. The planets change masters and their labels are correspondingly multiplied: the patroness of our planet Venus is no longer Aphrodite but Hera, while Mars is placed under the dominion of Hercules rather than Ares. The diversity of cults in the Seleucid Empire which, as we have seen, has already resulted in peopling the Greek celestial globe with barbaric constellations, still further complicates the terminology. To the Egyptians, Mars-Hercules is known as Horus the Red, and Jupiter as Osiris; in Phrygia the planet Venus is sacred to Cybele, mother of the gods. To make matters

[9] Egyptian constellations can be seen beneath the zodiacal signs on the sphere of Dendera in the Louvre. There is a laborer with bull's head, Isis holding the infant Horus, etc.

[10] Ptolemy is very much opposed to these importations. See Bouché-Leclercq, *op. cit.*, pp. 125, 215.—On the origin and use of the latter term, see Cumont, art. *Zodiacus*, in Saglio-Pottier, *Dict. des antiquités grecques et romaines;* F. Boll, *Sphaera* (Leipzig, 1903); and the *Astronomica* of Manilius, ed. Housman (London, 1930), v, pp. xl–xliii.

[11] Diodorus Siculus, II, 30, 3.

worse, the Egyptian decans combine with the planets as they have already combined with the signs of the zodiac.[12]

The Greek astronomers then felt that a fixed nomenclature had become a necessity, and—preceded here too by their Chaldean colleagues—invented for each planet a name derived simply from its physical aspect: for Mercury, Στίλβων, the Brilliant One; for Saturn, Φαίνων, the Shining One, etc. This purely scientific and "lay" nomenclature was in use in the third century in Alexandria; Cicero mentions it still in the *De natura deorum,* and it was naturally in favor with the erudite. But the old designations lingered on, and entered more and more widely into everyday speech. Soon, in fact—from the end of the Republic—the abbreviations *Saturnus* and *Jupiter* begin to be used in prose instead of *sidus* (or *stella*) *Saturni, Jovis,* etc. In the same way, in the Hellenic countries the circumlocution ὁ (ἀστὴρ) τοῦ Κρόνου gives way to the simple substantive Κρόνος. Now this "is not merely a linguistic change; it implies a modification in the religious conception of the planets. They are no longer regarded as being subject to certain divinities who supposedly control their movements or who exert patronage over them. . . . The seven bodies which move periodically within the zodiacal band are henceforth figures within which divinity is incorporated—completely identified with it from this time forward." [13]

*

If we now seek to identify the leading influences which have favored this definitive fusion between gods and astral bodies, we shall find Zeno and his school at the head of the list. Constantly concerned as they were for reconciling philosophy with respect for the ancient beliefs, the Stoics had finally come, through repeated concessions, to acknowledge that a physical meaning lay at the root of each myth: "Physica ratio non inelegans inclusa est in impias fabulas." [14] This system, introduced to Rome, like that of Euhemerus, by

[12] See Bouché-Leclercq, *op. cit.,* pp. 224–228. Cf. the Bianchini Planisphere, in the Louvre Museum.

[13] Cumont, art. cit., *L'Antiquité classique,* IV (1935), p. 35.

[14] Cicero, *De natur. deor.,* II, 24: "These impious fables enshrined a decidedly clever scientific theory." See Boissier, *La Religion romaine,* II, vii.

Ennius, met with the same success there. It brought welcome relief to many moderate minds who asked nothing better than some pretext for adhering to their old religion: if the gods are symbols for the cosmic powers, mythology ceases to appear absurd and immoral.[15] In fact,[16] this rationalist interpretation legitimized for most people the deification of the heavenly bodies, which, as we have already seen, was irresistibly suggested to them by the astronomical nomenclature.

But the decisive influence, beyond any doubt, was that of the Oriental religions. From the day the cults of the East—especially the Persian cult of the sun and the Babylonian cult of the planets—began to spread into the Greco-Roman world, the belief in sidereal divinities was not only confirmed;[17] it took on an extraordinary religious fervor. For the Chaldeans, in fact, the heavenly bodies were the gods par excellence, presiding over the destiny of men and empires. The diffusion of astrology during the decline of the ancient world has formed the subject of a number of works so well known that it needs no extended treatment here.[18] Its most striking symptom was the adoption of the planetary week, which began to spread in the time of Augustus, and has survived to the present day.

Let us note merely that during the last centuries of paganism belief in the divinity of the heavenly bodies grew even stronger. The stars are alive: they have a recognized appearance, a sex, a character, which their names alone suffice to evoke. They are powerful and redoubtable beings, anxiously prayed to and interrogated, since it is they who inspire all human action. They reign over human life and hold in their keeping the secrets of man's fortune and of his end. Benevolent or deadly, they determine the fate of peoples and individuals by the mere accident of their movements, their conjunctions and oppositions. To conciliate these dangerous masters everyone, from the Emperor down to the circus groom, had recourse to the arts of the Chaldean soothsayers, a fraternity as indispensable as it was ill-famed. These charla-

[15] Cf. the opinion of Varro in St. Augustine, *De civ. Dei*, VII, 6.

[16] As Gilbert Murray observes in *Five Stages of Greek Religion*, p. 129.

[17] Cumont (in art. *Zodiacus*) remarks that the materialistic pantheism of the Stoa is intimately related to that of the Chaldeans.

[18] See especially: Cumont, *Les Religions orientales dans le paganisme romain*, chap. vii; Boll-Bezold, *Sternglaube und Sterndeutung*, chap. ii (ed. 1931).

tans boasted that they could bring the spirit of a star down from heaven and render it propitious both for this life and the next. Amulets and talismans were everywhere in circulation. Increasingly—as, for example, among the Neoplatonists of the third century—obsession with the divine and the demoniacal began to mingle with concepts of natural law and mechanics. Science lost ground to superstition and magic, or at the very least became inextricably involved with them.

Let us note, furthermore, that this process of "absorption" of the gods by the stars which we have sketched finally resulted in assuring the gods of survival. One might indeed call it a piece of unhoped-for good luck on their side, for the old mythology had long been bankrupt and the Olympians had become mere phantoms. Now, however, a providential shelter is offered them: "the great gods find honorable refuge in the planets," while the demigods and heroes ascend to people the sky with "catasterisms." [19] Thus, though dethroned or about to be dethroned on earth, they are still masters of the celestial spheres, and men will not cease to invoke them and fear them.[20]

*

SUCH WAS the situation with which Christianity found itself confronted. In its intolerance of all the pagan cults, it is only natural that special hostility should have been shown to their most recent and lively embodiment—belief in powerful stellar divinities, with Helios as their king.

This hostility is in fact apparent from the very beginnings of Christianity: St. Paul reproaches the Galatians for continuing to observe "days and months and times and years" in the name of the "weak and beggarly elements" to which they desire again to be in bondage.[21] Later, the apologists (here, incidentally, echoing the views of Philo of Alexandria) [22] explain that

[19] Bouché-Leclercq, *op. cit.* chap. xvi, p. 604. Perhaps there is an analogy here with the process by which the totem animals of the primitive religions "took refuge" long ago in the zodiac (Cumont).

[20] Astrology, furthermore, created and made her own a mass of new gods, some of whom are singularly abstract—Heaven and Time, the Years, Months, Seasons, etc. The Stoics had already "deified" the elements.

[21] Galatians 4:9–10.

[22] See, for example, Lactantius, *De div. inst.* (*PL*, vi, 277, 281 ff.).

it is a crime to deify the physical world—to worship the thing created instead of the creator. What seems to them particularly impious in the worship of the heavenly bodies, as well as a danger to morals, is that such worship implies a denial of all human liberty and can end only in a discouraging fatalism.[23] At first sight, it would therefore seem that Christianity had nothing but cause to abhor pagan astrology and to oppose it.

In actual fact, however, something quite different took place. To begin with, Christianity itself contained astrological elements;[24] too many traces of the Hellenistic and Oriental religions, too much philosophy and science, were intertwined at its very roots for it to be able to rid itself of them completely. Accordingly, not only did the mythological names for the days of the week survive in spite of a certain amount of protest and some timid attempts to substitute a Christian terminology,[25] but we even see the Church of Rome herself, in the middle of the fourth century, officially fixing the twenty-fifth of December as the date of Christ's nativity—the same day which had marked the birth of the Sun in the pagan religions, since the yearly course of each new sun has its beginning then.[26] Aurelian, in his day, had made the sun a god of the Empire. Later, the first Christian Emperor was to have himself represented in the likeness of the Sun God on a porphyry column in Constantinople.[27]

Thus we see that astrology still had its partisans and believers among the Christians, while even its adversaries made important concessions. Tertullian, not without embarrassment, admits that astrology was valid up to the birth of Christ; now, however, one can no longer look to Saturn, Mars, and

[23] St. Augustine, *De civ. Dei,* v, 1–7.

[24] The Star which guided the Wise Men; the darkening of the sun at the death of Christ; the Morning Star promised in the Apocalypse to the faithful, etc. On these survivals, see Boll-Bezold, *Sternglaube und Sterndeutung,* pp. 29–31.

[25] In the Latin liturgy, the Church adopted new designations: *feria prima, feria secunda,* etc., which are already found in Tertullian; however, these were not welcomed, either by men of learning or by the populace. An unknown Byzantine (*Catal. cod. astron.,* IV, p. 99) proposed for Friday ἡ ἡμ. τῆς Θεοτόχου, Day of the Mother of God; for Thursday, ἡ ἡμ. τῶν Αποςτόλων, Day of the Apostles. Isidore (*Etym.* [*PL,* LXXXII, 181]), and Bede (*De temporibus* [*PL,* XC, 281]), will again protest the mythological names.

[26] The formula Φῶς αὔξει, used on December 25 in the pagan liturgy, as a Greek calendar shows, passed—as is well known—into the Christmas Office of the Church (*Lux crescit*). See Boll-Bezold, *op. cit.,* p. 107, and F. J. Dölger, *Sol Salutis* (Münster, 1925).

[27] It is true that he effaced this image from his coins; however, he commanded an astrologer to draw the horoscope of his capital.

the other "dead" gods for knowledge of the future.[28] Most devout Christians share the view of Origen: supported by texts from the Bible, they still believe in the power of the stars—although that power has certain limitations. The stars, they hold, cannot act in a manner contrary to the will of God; they may not force man to sin. However, they do continue to function as *signs* through which the Deity announces His benevolent or threatening intent.[29] Neither Lactantius nor St. Augustine,[30] again, casts doubt upon the fact of stellar influence, but both believe that it can be overcome by man's free will and by the grace of God. In short, "since, according to the doctrine of predestination, man's eternal salvation or doom depends solely upon the will of God, many see in the compulsion exercised by the stars—an inevitable compulsion, which determines the moral life as well—merely another expression of this doctrine; at all events, God's omnipotence makes manifest its immutable decrees to man through the stars as intermediary." [31]

Furthermore, even when the apologists and Fathers interpret astrology in this way—and even when they condemn it—they leave untouched the underlying belief in demons in which it is rooted. The existence of evil angels is an article of faith with them all, as it is for the Church; but the gods of pagan fable are now combined with the demons mentioned in the Bible in one confused rabble of malevolent spirits.[32] "The things which they sacrifice, they sacrifice to devils and not to God," says Paul, speaking of the Gentiles.[33] For

[28] "Stellas Christi, non Saturni et Martis, et cuiusque ex eodem ordine mortuorum observat et praedicat. At enim scientia ista usque ad Evangelium fuit concessa, ut Christo edito nemo exinde nativitatem alicuius de caelo interpretetur": *De idololatria*, cap. ix. ("Astrology now . . . is the science of the stars of Christ; not of Saturn and Mars and whomsoever else out of the same class of the dead it pays observance to and preaches. But that science was allowed just to the advent of the Gospel, in order that after Christ's birth no one should thenceforward interpret anyone's nativity by the heavens."—Ante-Nicene Library, Vol. XI: Tertullian, I, p. 152 [eds. Roberts and Donaldson].)

[29] Origen denies to man an exact knowledge of these celestial signs; according to him, only the angels and the spirits of the blessed can decipher them.

[30] Lactantius, *De div. inst.*, *PL*, VI, 336 ff.; St. Augustine, *De civ. Dei*, V, 7.

[31] Boll-Bezold, *op. cit.*, p. 32. See a general study on St. Augustine and astrology in L. Thorndike, *A History of Magic and Experimental Science* (1923), I, chap. xxii: "Augustine on Magic and Astrology."

[32] We also find in the Old Testament (Psalms 96:5): "Omnes dii gentium daemonia." On this question, the Doctors of the early centuries were not at all points in agreement. Cf. the *Dictionnaire de théologie catholique*, article *Démons*. See esp. Tertullian, *Apologeticum*, 22, 24.

[33] I Corinthians 10:20: Δαιμονίοις καὶ οὐ θεῷ θύουσιν. Here, again, confusion was helped along by vocabulary, since the Greeks were familiar with δαίμονες.

centuries to come, preachers will still go about the countryside expelling "the demons Jupiter, Mercury," etc., from haunts where they have lingered.[34] It is through the stars and through astrology that these demons often act. In former times, for man's temptation and perdition, they taught him to read the stars.[35] Now, scattered through the air (*aeria animalia,* as St. Augustine says),[36] they make use of the heavenly bodies to aid them in their evil dominion. After this, Augustine's anathema against "mathematicorum fallaces divinationes et impia deliramenta"[37] seems somewhat vain, especially since he elsewhere affirms the corporeal reality of the evil powers of heaven. On this point, the great Bishop is in agreement with the "magician" Apuleius[38]—with the difference that Apuleius admits the existence of friendly demons. And his arguments, aimed at destroying astrology as a religion, sometimes have the effect of reinstating and confirming it.

Last of all, there is one fundamentally important reason why astrology was by no means easily to be extirpated: it stood as an integral and essential element of culture. As we have seen, it had intimately invaded the science of the late pagan world—to such a degree, in fact, that it dominated all the natural sciences. Not only had astronomy fallen under its sway, but mineralogy, botany, zoology, physiology, and medicine as well.[39] A glance at the tabulation reproduced below (p. 47), in illustration of the system advanced by an astrologer of the second century of our era, Antiochus of Athens, will show that all physical beings were thought of as related to the zodiac. It was therefore a simple matter to connect them with the planets as well, by making use of the "fundamental qualities" of the planets as intermediaries. Mars, in fact, was "hot-dry," Jupiter and Venus were "hot-moist,"

[34] As was done, for example, by St. Martin. See Sulpicius Severus, *Dialogi,* II, 13. One resource of the hunted gods is to transform themselves into popular saints. See Boissier, *La Fin du paganisme,* II, p. 67; P. Saintyves, "Les Saints successeurs des dieux," *Essais de mythologie chrétienne* (Paris, 1907).

[35] According to the mythological tradition studied in the preceding chapter, the inventors of astrology were in reality gods.

[36] *De genesi,* III, 10, 4–5.

[37] *Confessions,* VII, cap. vi, par. 8 (". . . the lying divinations and impious nonsense of the astrologers").

[38] Whose teaching he expounds at length, *De civ. Dei,* I, 9.

[39] On the universal solidarity, see Bouché-Leclercq, *L'astrologie grecque,* pp. 73–77, and the whole of chap. X: *Propriétés et patronages terrestres des astres.* The table of Antiochus is taken from Boll-Bezold, *op. cit.,* p. 54. See *Catal. cod. astron.,* IV, 83, 16 ff.

etc. Similarly, correspondence was established between the planets and the elements—between Mars and Fire, between Jupiter and Air, between Mercury and the Moon on the one hand and Water on the other.

Insofar as the Christian community was receptive to pagan culture, therefore, it could not neglect astrology. Now the Church Fathers were urged by two considerations to admit all these studies into the Christian curriculum —their concern that the Christian be in no way inferior to the non-Christian, and their sense of the need for a proper understanding of their own religion. For, as St. Augustine recognizes, knowledge of natural history and astronomy is essential to a right reading of Scripture and a true understanding of divine things.[40]

This theory might prove disturbing to overscrupulous believers. In order to reassure them and to justify profane studies the Fathers invoked a most appropriate Biblical episode: when the Hebrew people emerged from Egypt, they carried away with them vessels of gold and silver belonging to their enemies. Why should Christianity not do the same? [41] It was on the strength of this argument, many times repeated, that ancient science was to pass over into the Middle Ages.[42] But along with it, all sorts of religious elements, classical or barbaric, passed over as well, and were in many cases to outlive the vicissitudes, the periods of eclipse and shipwreck, experienced by science itself.

*

THUS THE CHRISTIAN polemics of the first centuries concerning astrology did not, as might have been expected, result in simply relegating it. Instead, the Church to a certain extent came to terms with it, and even turned to it for support.

The situation remained the same during the Middle Ages,[43] for reasons

[40] *De doctrina Christiana*, II, 29 (*PL*, XXXIV, 57). See H. I. Marrou, *St. Augustin et la fin de la culture antique*, Paris (1938).

[41] *Ibid.*, II, 40. By means of other allegories, also drawn from the Bible, the need of "purifying" these studies was shown. See St. Jerome, *Epistulae*, 70 (*PL*, XXII, 666).

[42] See Roger, *L'Enseignement des lettres classiques d'Ausone à Alcuin* (Paris, 1905), chap. iv, 1.

[43] See Th. O. Wedel, *The Mediaeval Attitude toward Astrology, Particularly in England*, Yale Studies in English, LX (1920); also Thorndike, *op. cit.*, I, bk. 3, and vol. II, bks. 4 and 5.

Signs of the Zodiac	*Seasons*	*Ages of Life*	*Elements*	*Winds*	*Qualities*	*Conditions*	*Humors*	*Tempera-ments*	*Colors*
ARIES TAURUS GEMINI	Spring	Childhood	Air	South	hot-moist	liquid	blood	sanguine	red
CANCER LEO VIRGO	Summer	Youth	Fire	East	hot-dry	gaseous	yellow bile	choleric	yellow
LIBRA SCORPIO SAGITTARIUS	Autumn	Maturity	Earth	North	cold-dry	dense	black bile	melancholic	black
CAPRICORNUS AQUARIUS PISCES	Winter	Old Age	Water	West	cold-moist	solid	phlegm	phlegmatic	white

which are not hard to explain. In the first place, the active principle basic to astrology, the fear of demons, had survived. The Church, it should be recalled, had not completely expelled the antique divinities; they had merely been degraded to the rank of evil spirits. In this form, they still inspired superstitious fears. To be sure, such fears were now to some extent dispelled and held in check by the belief in the omnipotence of a supreme God capable of subduing adverse forces in obedience to His will: God could save man from demons—but they were none the less there, still living and fearsome. We are told in the *Golden Legend* that when St. Benedict was preaching against idolatry to the people of Monte Cassino, he converted a temple of Apollo into an oratory of St. John. But the enraged god returned to torment him in the form of a black monster with flaming eyes.[44]

While the fear of demons continues to haunt the popular imagination, the astrological theory of causation remains in force as an intellectual concept; even the greatest minds do not repudiate it entirely. They do of course see that omnipotence of the stars could constitute a threat to human liberty, but like the apologists and the Fathers, they are satisfied with defining the limits of this power; they do not deny its existence.[45] St. Thomas Aquinas admits that the stars determine individual character, at least in a physical sense, and since most men follow their passions—that is to say, their physical appetites—it is really by the stars that they are led into sin: "Plures hominum sequuntur passiones, quae sunt motus sensitivi appetitus, ad quos cooperari possunt corpora coelestia. . . .[46] And Dante, on this point, faithfully follows in his master's footsteps: while affirming freedom of the will,[47] he at the same time recognizes the influence of cosmic forces on the human soul:

Lo cielo i vostri movimenti inizia. . . .[48]

[44] Jacopo da Voragine, *Leggenda aurea* (ed. Levasti [Florence, 1924–26]), vol. I, p. 407.

[45] Pierre Abélard and Hugues de Saint Victor repudiate astrological predictions as suggestions of the devil; they do, however, recognize a "natural" astrology—that is to say, the influence of the planets on the temperature and on the human body. See Thorndike, *op. cit.*, II, pp. 5–7, 11–13.

[46] *Summa*, I, 115, 4. ("The majority of men follow their passions, which are movements of the sensitive appetite, in which movements heavenly bodies can co-operate. . . ."—Trans. by the Fathers of the English Dominican Province [London, 1912], p. 517.)

[47] *Lume v'è dato a bene ed a malizia*
E libero voler . . . (*Purgatorio*, XVI, 75–76) ("Light is given unto you, for good and for evil, and freedom of will. . . .")

[48] *Ibid.*, 73. ("The stars initiate your movements. . . .")

"Astra inclinant; non necessitant." With this reservation, astrology continues as the foundation of profane culture and the underlying principle of all science, "la fin de toute clergie."

Everything leads back to the stars, and their influence is everywhere exerted. Declining antiquity, as we have seen, had set up a system of concordances in which the planets and zodiacal signs served as the basis of classification for the elements, seasons, and humors. The encyclopedic spirit of the Middle Ages was not satisfied with merely reviving this tradition, with working out more or less ingenious schemes of its own for demonstrating numerical relationships between the component elements—*Mundus, Annus,* and *Homo.*[49] In its preponderant concern for unification, for building a *scientia universalis,* scholasticism still further developed the concordance tables, leaning upon more and more specious analogies as it did so. For example, Alexander Neckam, in his *De natura rerum,*[50] presents in codified form the relationship between the planets and virtues which had first been established in the ninth century; while in the *Convivio,*[51] Dante draws a parallel between the same planets and the seven liberal arts: "Alli sette primi (cieli) rispondono le sette scienze del Trivio e del Quadrivio." Grammar corresponds to the sphere of the moon, dialectic to the sphere of Mercury, etc. Dante thus outlines a complete system of knowledge, corresponding point for point with the astrological system.

But such relationships imply that influences are present: man, who represents the world in summarized form, is dependent on the cosmic forces, which are combined in his make-up in the same proportions as in the universe at large. The theory of macrocosm and microcosm—inherited from Neoplatonism, transmitted to medieval thought by way of Boethius, and developed by Bernard of Tours (called Silvestris) in a famous treatise[52]—finds one of its most curious applications in medicine: in order to learn the fate of a patient, if not actually to cure him, use is still made of strange cal-

[49] (World, Year, Man.) See Wickersheimer, "Figures médico-astrologiques des IXme, Xme, et XIme siècles," *Janus* (1914).

[50] *De nat. rer.,* I, ch. 7 (ed. Wright): *Jupiter intellectus, Sol fortitudinis, Mars consilii,* etc.

[51] II, 14. Similarly, in earlier times, the Pythagoreans had lodged the Muses in the planetary spheres. See Bouché-Leclerq, *op. cit.,* p. 324. These correspondences will be found again in Martianus Capella, I, 28.

[52] *De mundi universitate libri duo sive megacosmus et microcosmus.*

culating machines based upon astronomical data. One such machine was the "sphere of Petosiris," said by F. J. Boll to have been invented in the first century A.D.[53] In treating the patient, it was necessary to remember that, in accordance with the Greek principle of *melothesia*,[54] his anatomy and physiology were governed by the stars. Each zodiacal sign ruled over some part of the body, and each planet over certain organs and limbs. A surgeon must not operate when the moon was in the sign on which the affected member was thought to be dependent; otherwise the planet's moisture would immediately bring about the gravest complications.[55]

It is thus clear to what point astrology had penetrated science, both in theory and in practice. Nor were all these notions confined to learned circles alone. They gained general currency in popular encyclopedias as early as the thirteenth century, pending their further popularization in the fourteenth in the books of hours and calendars.[56]

It goes without saying that mythological terminology survived as a concomitant of astrological doctrine. Timid attempts were nevertheless made to abolish at least the pagan names of the zodiacal signs; we have already mentioned the effort to Christianize the names of the days of the week (cf. *supra*, p. 43). Similarly, during the early Christian centuries, the "astrotheosophers" had wished to transform Cepheus into Adam, Cassiopeia into Eve, and Perseus into Logos,[57] while the Priscillians had replaced the signs of the zodiac by the twelve patriarchs.[58] In the Carolingian period, a certain "Hirenicus" tries, in turn, in a poem on the zodiac, to adjust the signs to Christian symbolism, turning Aries into the Lamb, etc.[59] In the ninth century, in a manuscript now in the ecclesiastical archives of St. Gallen,[60] Cancer has become

53 Wickersheimer, art. cit.

54 Melothesia is the localization of astral influences in the body. There is both a zodiacal and a planetary melothesia. See Bouché-Leclerq, *op. cit.*, pp. 318–325.

55 See K. Sudhoff, "Beiträge zur Geschichte der Chirurgie im Mittelalter," *Studien zur Geschichte der Medizin*, x (1914). Text from Codex Sloane 2320, fol. 20: "Prohibitum est ne aliquis faciet [*sic*] incisionem . . . in nullo membro, dum luna est in signo illud regente."

56 See V. Langlois, *La Connaissance de la nature et du monde au moyen âge*, (Paris, 1911), pp. 225 and 300.

57 See Hippolytos, *Refutatio*, vi, 46–50.

58 See W. Gundel, *Sterne und Sternbilder* (Bonn, 1922), p. 77.

59 *MGH.*, *Poet. Lat.*, iv, pp. 693–695. See R. Salomon, *Opicinus de Canistris*, Studies of the Warburg Institute, i (London, 1936), p. 120.

60 Salomon, *loc. cit.*; see also *Li cumpoz Philippe de Thaun* (ed. Mall [Strasbourg 1875]),

Abraham; Aries, Job; and Leo, Daniel. But these attempts were of no avail; on the contrary, the astronomer William of Conches proclaims the legitimacy of the stellar mythology, and the necessity of knowing it well. He tells us that certain authors have spoken of the astral bodies in terms of myth (*mythice*), mentioning Nimrod, Hyginus, and Aratus, and their accounts of the origin of the zodiacal signs—one example being Taurus, the bull (Jupiter) which abducted Europa. "This way of treating of celestial things is legitimate; without it we would not know in what part of the sky a given sign is located, how many stars it contains, nor how they are arranged." [61]

*

IN THE EVOLUTION of astrology during the Middle Ages, two main periods must be distinguished. Up to the twelfth century, the only learned sources available to Western scholars were Macrobius' commentary on the *Somnium Scipionis*, Firmicus Maternus, the Latin commentators on Plato's *Timaeus*, and the short expositions in Isidore and Bede.[62] During this period, the focus of astrology was in Byzantium, where it reappeared hand in hand with astronomy after the seventh-century decline. In spite of isolated cases of protest on the part of churchmen, it flourished there more and more brightly till the fall of the Eastern Empire, and it is to the interest which it inspired that we owe a large proportion of the manuscripts copied by Byzantine scholars which have preserved for us the treasures of classical science.[63]

But this treasure had been garnered by the Arabs as well. They had inherited physics and the natural sciences from Aristotle, and the *Almagest*

---

in which a Christian interpretation of the zodiac is found:

Li multuns signifie
Le fil Sainte Marie
E li tors signifie
Le fil Sainte Marie.

("Both Aries, the ram, and Taurus, the bull, signify the son of St. Mary.")

In the fifteenth century, Lorenzo Bonincontri (*Dierum solemnium Christianae religionis*, I, 10, 11–12) recognized in the Hydra:

ille malus serpens, qui compulit Evam
in laqueos vitae perfragilesque vices.

In the seventeenth century, attempts were made to "Christianize" the sky. See the atlas of Julius Schiller: *Coelum stellatum Christianum* (1627).

[61] As the *De philosophia mundi* of William of Conches has been falsely attributed to Bede, Honorius of Autun, and William of Hirschau, the Latin text must be sought in the *Patrologia Latina*, either in XC, 1127–1178 (*Bedae opera*, I, bk. ii) or in CLXXII, 39–102 (*Hon. Aug. opera*, II, V, *quot modis auctoritas loquatur de superioribus*).

[62] See Boll-Bezold, *op. cit.*, p. 110 and Appendix, pp. 183–187: "Die lateinische Astrologie des Mittelalters." Thorndike (*op. cit.*, I, pp. 690–691) is of a different opinion.

[63] For the history of astrology in Byzantium, see Boll-Bezold, *op. cit.*, pp. 32–33.

and *Tetrabiblos* from Ptolemy. In due time they were to transmit this heritage to the Occident, enriched by having passed through the hands of their own scholars, like Albumazar and Al-Kabīsī. Thanks to the Crusades, and to the penetration of Arab philosophy and science into Sicily and Spain, Europe came to know the Greek texts with their Arab commentaries, in Latin translations for the most part made by Jews.[64] The result was an extraordinary increase in the prestige of astrology, which between the twelfth and fourteenth centuries enjoyed greater favor than ever before.

It was during this period that the greatest princes took astrologers into their service as intimate counselors—Frederick II of Hohenstaufen and Alfonso the Wise in the thirteenth century, and in the fourteenth Charles V of France. In Italy, astrologers directed the life of cities, *condottieri*, and prelates.[65]

The astrologers were anxiously interrogated, just as the "Chaldeans" had been by Romans of the Empire; strong in its new prestige, astrology inspired new fears. Furthermore, the Arabs had developed one of its most threatening aspects in the theory of planetary conjunction. The appearance together in the same constellation of the three major planets—Saturn, Mars, and Jupiter—could precipitate illness, war, famine, and religious upheavals. The birth of Mohammed, long ago, had actually coincided with such a conjunction, and the Black Death of 1348 again confirmed the same terrible portent.[66] There was a growing sense of inexorable doom threatening from the skies.

Timor fecit deos: the fear of demons revived at the same time. In all these threats which hung over them, men felt evil presences at work, and looked to the magicians for means of escape or propitiation. We are fortu-

[64] There were also direct translations from the Greek. See Haskins, *The Renaissance of the Twelfth Century*, chap. ix: "The Translators from Greek and Arabic." Cf. also G. Sarton, *Introduction to the History of Science* (1927), I, esp. chaps. xviii–xxiv (with detailed bibliography).

[65] The astrologer of Frederick II was the famous Michael Scot whom Dante placed in the abyss reserved for diviners and sorcerers (*Inf.*, XX, 116–117). Thomas, father of Christine de Pisan, was official astrologer to Charles V. Cf. C. Jourdain, "Nicolas Oresme et les astrologues de la cour de Charles V," *Rev. des questions hist.*, XVIII (1875), pp. 136–159.

Cf. an excellent portrait of the Renaissance astrologer in Soldati, *La poesia astrologica nel quattrocento*, Florence (1906), pp. 107–118. Soldati distinguishes between the philosopher-mathematician and the ordinary magician or diviner. In actual fact, they were often one and the same person.

[66] See Boll-Bezold, *op. cit.*, p. 34.

nate in possessing a document of cardinal importance which throws into sharp relief this recrudescence of the demonic in astrology and the state of mind which resulted. This is a manual of magic, composed in Arabic in the tenth century from Oriental and Hellenistic elements, translated into Spanish at the court of Alfonso X, and widely circulated in the late Middle Ages. Some twenty Latin manuscripts are known.[67]

This manual, the Arabic title of which is *Ghâya* and the Latin title *Picatrix* (probably a corruption of Hippocrates), is openly and professedly a treatise on the practice of magic, based on astral science. Indeed, its aim is to conciliate the "spirits" and to utilize their power, though for Picatrix spirits and planets are intimately associated, if not actually interchangeable. "Many instructions are given how to *pray* to each of the planets and to work magic by their aid, just as if they were demons." [68]

For all this there is an established ritual. Picatrix prescribes propitious times and places and the attitude and gestures of the suppliant; he also indicates what terms must be used in petitioning the stars. Here, for example, is his formula for a prayer to Saturn: "O Master of sublime name and great power, supreme Master; O Master Saturn: Thou, the Cold, the Sterile, the Mournful, the Pernicious; Thou, whose life is sincere and whose word sure; Thou, the Sage and Solitary, the Impenetrable; Thou, whose promises are kept; Thou who art weak and weary; Thou who hast cares greater than any other, who knowest neither pleasure nor joy; Thou, the old and cunning, master of all artifice, deceitful, wise, and judicious; Thou who bringest prosperity or ruin, and makest men to be happy or unhappy! I conjure Thee, O Supreme Father, by Thy great benevolence and Thy generous bounty, to do for me what I ask. . . ."

In this pagan prayer one finds, as F. Saxl has pointed out,[69] the accent

[67] The Arabic text of the *Picatrix* was published for the first time by the Warburg Library in 1927. A critical edition of the medieval Latin translation, based on the manuscripts, is in preparation. I am indebted to Dr. E. Jaffé, the editor, for several important items of information. Two further volumes, prepared by Dr. M. Plessner, will contain a modern translation and a full historical discussion of the *Picatrix*.—See, on the same subject, Thorndike, *op. cit.*, II, chap. lxvi; and Hellmut Ritter, "*Picatrix*, ein arabisches Handbuch hellenistischer Magie," *Vorträge d. Bibl. Warburg* (1923), pp. 94–124, esp. p. 113: "Nachleben antiker Götter als Sterndämonen."

[68] Thorndike, *op. cit.*, II, p. 820.

[69] See "Rinascimento dell' Antichità," *Repertorium für Kunstwissenschaft* (1922), pp. 220–272.

and even the very terms of a Greek astrological prayer to Kronos. This is one indication that the sources of *Picatrix* are in large part Hellenistic.[70] But how amazing to think that such prayers were now being raised to the skies in Christian Europe!

Let us now ask by what material means, what tools, the magician hoped to force the astral divinities to lend him their aid. One essential factor was the actual likeness of the god. Engraved, preferably on precious stones, according to the aspect of the heavens at some particularly favorable moment, such images were supposed to receive the greatest possible amount of celestial influence and to store it away, so to speak, for future use. To this end, Picatrix describes some fifty images of fixed stars, planets, and zodiacal signs, the efficacy of which he guarantees.

12. The Olympian Jupiter

Surprises are in store for us as we read these descriptions. To assure the favor of Jupiter, for instance, a white stone should be engraved with the figure of a crowned personage seated on a throne, his hand upraised (see *fig. 12,* taken from the lapidary of Alfonso X); each of the four feet of the throne should rest on the neck of a winged man. Who is this personage? None other than the Olympian Zeus as described by Pausanias: "The god sits on a throne, and he is made of gold and ivory. On his head lies a garland. . . . In the left hand is a scepter. . . . There are four Victories . . . one at each foot of the throne. . . ."[71] To win the benevolence of Mars, one needs a gem engraved with the image of "a young man, naked—at his right a young girl with hair knotted at the back of her head; his left hand rests on her breast, his

[70] It derives also from Babylonian sources. Cf. the article of Dozy and de Goeje on the *Ghâya, Actes du* VIe *Congrès International des Orientalistes* (Leyden, 1885), II, pp. 285 ff.

[71] Pausanias, v, 11, 1–10.

right on her neck, and he gazes into her eyes." The reader will recognize the classical motif of Mars and Venus.[72] Other images are even more perplexing. Here we have a barbaric Saturn: "The form of Saturn, in the opinion of the learned Picatrix, is that of a man seated on a throne, having a crow's head and the feet of a camel." Elsewhere appears a Jupiter with lion's head and cock's spurs. We shall have occasion later to study these puzzling figures more closely; here let us recall merely that ever since the end of the pagan era monsters out of the East had been making their way into the firmament, mingling with the Greek gods who had won a place there.

As a matter of fact, gems bearing effigies of the gods had been in uninterrupted use throughout the Middle Ages. Great monasteries had their collections of antique cameos and intaglios as early as the seventh century. The seal of Charlemagne is a head of Jupiter Serapis; sometimes we even make the surprising discovery of a Venus Anadyomene or a Leda on an ecclesiastical seal. Gems with mythological subjects are often found mounted in crosses, on book covers and reliquaries.[73]

Scholars have been much intrigued by this phenomenon, asking themselves why and in what spirit pagan gems were put to such unexpected uses. The explanation in some cases lies doubtless in mere ignorance, or misunderstanding of the figure represented: thus Poseidon and Athena, under a tree, could be taken for Adam and Eve.[74] But for the most part these stones were used because they were thought to possess special virtues. The Alexandrian lapidaries, both Hermetic and Gnostic—themselves derived from Egyptian and Chaldean sources—recorded the magic effects of stones bearing representations of divinities. Ptolemy himself was thought to have composed a *Liber de impressionibus imaginum in gemmis*. These varied traditions were trans-

[72] Joan Evans, in her *Magical Jewels of the Middle Ages and the Renaissance, Particularly in England* (Oxford, 1922), p. 102, cites the text of a French lapidary derived from the same source as *Picatrix:* ". . . un bachelier nu estant et une pucele que estoit adestre de li nue que eit ses chevus liez entor et le bachelier eit sur le col de la pucele sa main . . ." (B. M. Add. 18.210).

[73] See Demay, *Des Pierres antiques dans les sceaux du Moyen-Age* (Paris, 1877); F. de Mély, "Du rôle des pierres gravées au Moyen-Age," *Revue de l'art chrétien* (1893). E. Babelon, "Les Camées antiques de la Bibliothèque Nationale," Part IV: "A quoi servaient les camées," *Gazette des Beaux-Arts,* XXI (1899), pp. 101–116; W. S. Heckscher, "Relics of Pagan Antiquity in Mediaeval Settings," *Journal of the Warburg Institute,* I (1937–38), pp. 204 ff.

[74] See de Mély, art. cit.

mitted, directly or indirectly, to the Middle Ages: Picatrix combines several of them. But long before his day, belief in the power of engraved stones was very general. Since the art of glyptics had been lost at an early date—between the second and third centuries A.D.—such images were no longer made; [75] but ancient gems corresponding in color and subject to the prescriptions of the lapidaries continued to be used as talismans. It is not till the end of the thirteenth century, however, that the treatises make the action of the stars responsible for the properties which they attribute to gems.[76] To be sure, as Marbod of Rennes says,

> . . . *Nul sage homme doter ne doit*
> *Ken pirres grant vertus ne soit.*[77]

But for the most part these virtues are regarded as being of a medical nature only; so, in his day, old Isidore, speaking "de lapidibus insignoribus," [78] had been at special pains to share none of the "pagan superstitions" on the subject.

On the other hand, and especially during the renaissance of the twelfth century, men who were true humanists made discerning selection—for reasons of taste, or perhaps because of some special personal appropriateness—of gems bearing images of the gods.[79] But in the thirteenth and fourteenth centuries, it is unmistakably as amulets that they are used, and in a distinctly religious spirit. The ferment of diabolism has regained all its old virulence, and the "astrolatry" expressly recommended by Picatrix takes us back to the time of Apuleius—to the days of incantation and sacrifice offered to the astral divinities.

*

IT MAY well be asked how the Church could have allowed astrology to develop to this point, where it constituted a direct threat to the faith. Not only

[75] The formula "Carve in stone . . ." ("Sculpe in lapide . . .") is replaced at an early date by "Should you find in a stone . . ." ("Si inveneris in lapide . . ."). Similarly, in the lapidaries in vulgar idiom the formula begins, "If you find . . ."

[76] See Evans, *op. cit.*, chap. v: "Mediaeval Astrology: Lapidaries of Engraved Gems."

[77] Cited by Evans (ms. 2200, Bibl. Ste-Geneviève, fol. 120, v.)—("No man of sense should doubt that in stones reside great virtues.")

[78] *Etym.*, XVI, 4, ". . . quibus gentiles in superstitionibus quibusdam utuntur." On the other hand, a list of astrological seals will be found in Vincent of Beauvais, *Speculum naturale*, VIII, 35.

[79] See Demay, *op. cit.*, and Adhémar, *Influences antiques dans l'art du Moyen-Age français*, Studies of the Warburg Institute, VII (London, 1939), pp. 106–107.

was it leading Europe back to one of the most demoralizing forms of idolatry, but by representing the various religions and the earthly appearance of their founders as dependent upon the stars, it ranked Christianity on a level with the other faiths and seemed to foreshadow its decline.

And, in fact, the Church did react. Even though, as we have seen, she had conceded the principle of astrology, and had not rooted it out, she understood the extent of the danger. This reaction, which can be detected as early as the twelfth century,[80] was later to be carried at times to the point of utmost rigor. We need only recall Cecco d'Ascoli's expiating at the stake the crime of having calculated the date of the birth of Christ by means of the stars.

Such examples might instill terror; they did not arrest the evil. The dangerous impetus that astrology had gained in the thirteenth century was accentuated in the fifteenth and sixteenth. Here, again, the Renaissance was to prove a continuation of the Middle Ages.

We shall not repeat in this connection all that Burckhardt has shown us in a classic work: [81] never since antiquity had the science of the stars been rated more highly or played a greater role in the lives of states or individuals. The great Cinquecento popes alone may serve as examples—Julius II basing the date of his coronation on the calculations of the astrologers, as Paul III did the hour of each consistory, or Leo X founding a chair of astrology at the Sapienza which was to rival similar foundations at the universities of Bologna, Padua, and Paris.[82] Here we see to what extent the Church, or at least the Vatican, yielded to the prevailing superstition.

It is of course true that at the same time profound intellectual forces were at work which were one day, with Copernicus and Galileo, to lead far beyond the astrological concept of the universe, and to liberate science from magic. But it would be a mistake to view this development as the logical result of a more profound and enlightened culture.

On the contrary, the first effect of humanism was to encourage astrology. The precursors of humanism, men like Petrarch and Salutati, still maintained

[80] According to Thorndike (*op. cit.*, II, pp. 5 ff.), the reaction began somewhat earlier, at the end of the eleventh century.

[81] *The Civilization of the Renaissance in Italy*, pt. VI, chap. iv.

[82] Boll-Bezold, *op. cit.*, p. 36.

the orthodox and reserved attitude of Dante and Thomas Aquinas.[83] As time went on, however, and profane learning gained ground, the barriers within which the Middle Ages had attempted to confine it were steadily weakened. Drawn in large part from the literature and philosophy of late antiquity, the new studies confirmed the astrological concept of causality in a thousand new ways.[84] This concept ended by penetrating all natural philosophy, just as it had formerly sustained the great intellectual structures of the encyclopedists and theologians. It continued to dominate physics and the other natural sciences. The notion of the intimate bond between microcosm and macrocosm, for instance, remained basic to the art of medicine. Paracelsus, following Marsilio Ficino, proclaims that "the physician must have knowledge of man's *other half*, that half of his nature which is bound up with astronomical philosophy; otherwise he will be in no true sense man's physician, since Heaven retains within its sphere half of all bodies and of all maladies." [85] In fact, in order to account for the origin of syphilis and the ravages of the disease, physicians invoked the baleful conjunction of Saturn and Mars.[86]

Attempts were doubtless still made, as in Ronsard's *Hymne des astres*, to differentiate in this connection between *body* and *soul*, the former alone being subject to astral influence:

> *Les Estoilles adonc seules se firent dames*
> *De tous les corps humains, et non pas de nos âmes.*

83 Petrarch, who jests at the astrologers without being himself entirely immune, refers to St. Augustine, *Epist. rer. famil.*, III, 8.—In the *De fato et fortuna*, Salutati regards the heavenly bodies as instruments in the hands of God.

84 In fact, it is *because* he is a humanist and Neoplatonist that Marsilio Ficino believes in astrology: classical antiquity is his guarantor. See, for example, his letter to Rinaldo Ursino, archbishop of Florence (*Epistolae* [Venice, 1495], III, p. lxvi, v.).

85 He adds: "What is a physician who knows nothing of cosmography? He ought, on the contrary, to have a special understanding of it, since it is there that all knowledge finds its confirmation." Ficino, in his *De vita triplici*, had attempted to construct all medicine on astrological bases. Cf. Bonincontri, who in a didactic poem, *De rebus caelestibus*, offers a complete system of astrological physiology in verse, including, for example, an explanation of how all the planets in turn contribute to the formation of the foetus (cod. Laur. XXXIV, 52 c, 23 a, b).

86 See the *Remède contre la grosse vérolle* (Lyons, 1501): "I affirm that the conjunction of two adverse aspects of Saturn and Mars . . . and the conjunction and evil look of the said planets were at its origin. . . . For Saturn causes ill to be suffered in the legs and other members. And Mars is the cause of begetting. . . . Hence the effect of the said conjunction is cause of this malady." Cited by K. Sudhoff, *Aus der Frühgeschichte der Syphilis* (Leipzig, 1912), p. 157.

But physiology and psychology are inseparable; "temperament" is the unfailing determinant of character.

Thus the Renaissance saw no contradiction between astrology and science; rather, the dominion of the heavenly bodies over all earthly things was viewed by some as the natural law par excellence, the law which assures the regularity of phenomena. For Pomponazzi, it was the very form and pattern of universal determinism.[87] And though speculation gradually freed itself from the bonds of this natural philosophy—even more tyrannous for the mind than the bonds of theology—this outcome should not be interpreted merely as a victory of experience and exact calculation over superstition. In fact, as Cassirer has shown,[88] it was essentially for moral reasons that the humanists finally rebelled against the tyranny of the stars.

In a world system all parts of which are interconnected, with no single creature possessing an existence independent of the cosmos, man's position is impossibly humiliating. To be sure, the bonds which attach man to the universe are undeniable; but they now cease to be thought of as a form of imprisonment. Marsilio Ficino still adheres to the notion of "superior" powers with dominion over "inferior" beings (the stars sending their influences down toward the earth). Nicholas of Cusa no longer accepts this subordination of earth to sky; he sees only harmony and correlation, not dependence.[89] Paracelsus goes even further; he suggests that the influence may operate in the other direction—from man to the stars, from *soul* to *thing*, from the inner world to the outer. "It might be said that Mars has more resemblance to man than man to Mars, for *man is more* than Mars and the other planets." [90]

The decisive word has been spoken: mind is superior to matter. "Even where the astrological world picture remains unchanged, a tendency is clearly manifested to create a new place for the individual within the system." [91] This tendency is still more proudly affirmed by Pico della Mirandola. For him, too, acceptance of astrology signifies a reversal of the true order of things—that is, seeing things not so much according to their essence as ac-

[87] *De naturalium effectuum admirandorum causis sive de incantationibus* (Basel, 1556).

[88] *Individuum und Cosmos in der Philosophie der Renaissance* (Leipzig-Berlin, 1927), chap. iii: "Freiheit und Notwendigkeit."

[89] Cassirer, *op. cit.*, pp. 116–117.

[90] *Ibid.*, p. 117.

[91] *Ibid.*, p. 118.

cording to their worth—and is tantamount to admitting the sovereignty of matter over spirit. Against this, the author of the *De dignitate hominis* raises his solemn protest. He refuses, so he says, to honor in great men—in thinkers, statesmen, artists—anything other than their humanity. It is not a better star which creates the genius, it is a loftier mind: "Non astrum melius, sed ingenium melius." And the miracles of the spirit are greater than those of the sky: "Miracula quidem animi . . . coelo majora sunt." [92] To attribute the first to the second is to deny and lower rather than rightly to understand them.

Thus "the true impulse toward liberation came not from a new concept of nature but from a new concept of man's own worth." Humanist pride arose in opposition to astrology even before new methods of observation and reckoning had advanced far enough to condemn it.

However, one grave misunderstanding still persists: *fear* of the stars does not disappear with these proud declarations. The humanists have refused to fetter man to any system of physical causality, to a material principle. But are the heavenly bodies purely material? From the earliest times, as we have seen, they have, on the contrary, been viewed as animated by intelligences (spirits, gods, or demons) who determine their movements, and by more or less malevolent forces. Have the Renaissance philosophers and savants wholly renounced this conception?

To be sure, it is rejected in unmistakable terms by a Pomponazzi, who denies that either demoniacal or divine forces can directly usurp power in violation of the natural laws which govern the production of phenomena. World order would be continually compromised if spirits or angels were able, under cover of the heavenly bodies, to exert a direct influence upon nature and man.

The attitude of Marsilio Ficino is more typical. He maintains that the stars, if they do influence the body, have no compulsive power over the soul; but at the same time his own inner life is shadowed by fear of Saturn, the sinister ancient who presided over his birth. He knows that he cannot escape

92 *In astrologiam*, III, cap. 27, fol. 517 ff. On the controversies aroused by this work of Pico, cf. Soldati, *La Poesia astrologica*, chap. iv.

that baleful influence, which condemns him to melancholy. At the most, he can try to turn it into other channels, to use it for good: Saturn, demon of inertia and sterility, is also the presiding genius of intellectual concentration. But even so, Saturn's patronage imposes strict limitations on those to whom it extends, and it is only within these limitations that man is free to shape his personality. This conviction literally obsesses Ficino, and his friends try in vain to distract him from his somber thoughts.[93]

Thus at the very moment when great thinkers are striving to throw off the humiliating yoke of the cosmic bodies as such, they tremble before the mysterious divinities which inhabit them. Man proclaims the freedom of the will; but there are other wills stronger than his own, and it is Destiny that prevails. The premature death of Pico della Mirandola, which confirmed the predictions of the astrologers to the day and hour, appeared to his contemporaries like a terrifying denial of his proud assertions.[94] And Luther himself, who scoffed at astrology as irresponsible fantasy, or as an unhealthy and pitiable art, admitted that the awe-inspiring conjunction of several planets in the constellation Pisces which occurred in 1524 was a warning from heaven.[95]

Outmoded fears of this kind were stubbornly reborn even in the minds of those who thought themselves most completely emancipated. With how much more reason did they persist among those who lacked the support of philosophical meditation, while no longer wholly accepting the assurances of the faith. Men like these turned to magicians, just as their ancestors had done, to conjure away the evil powers. They searched the treatises on magic

[93] *Epistolae* (Florence, 1495), III, p. lxix, v.: Ficino complains to Cavalcanti of the malign influence of Saturn; Cavalcanti attempts to reassure him, saying that it is impossible for the stars to injure man ("Nullum hercle malum facere nobis possunt astra"). But Ficino continues his lament (p. lxx, r.). Saturn may have good effects, but "I am too timorous about the evil ones"; and he comes back to his horoscope: "This melancholy temperament seems to have been imposed on me from the beginning by Saturn, set almost in the center of my ascendant sign, Aquarius [the Water Bearer] and being met by Mars in the same sign, and by the Moon in Capricorn—while looking toward the Sun and Mercury in the Scorpion, occupying the ninth zone of Heaven."

[94] Boll-Bezold, *op. cit.*, p. 41.

[95] See A. Warburg, *Heidnisch-antike Weissagung in Wort und Bild zu Luthers Zeiten*, *Gesammelte Schriften* (Leipzig, 1932), II, pp. 487–558.

In this regard, the Reformation brought no more essential a break than humanism had done. Melanchthon was an astrologer; even Tycho Brahe, a devout Protestant, believed in the harmful influence of the stars.

for images and formulas with which to placate the astral demons, the very recipes once recommended by astrologers of the thirteenth century. It is from the "Révérend Père en diable Picatrix, recteur de la faculté diabologique," as Rabelais calls him,[96] that Cornelius Agrippa, for example, derives the chapters he devotes to the images of decans and planets suitable to be engraved on talismans;[97] the lapidaries of Camillo Leonardi and Hugues Ragot belong to the same tradition.[98] Henri Estienne reports that Queen Catherine de Médicis, whose passion for astrology is of course well known, always carried a gem on which were engraved names of celestial spirits—one side showed Jupiter, to whom Anubis was offering a mirror, and the other Venus, with her planetary symbol. This talisman had been designed and executed by the Sieur Régnier, a famous mathematician and reputed magician in whom she had great confidence.[99] At about the same time, Benvenuto Cellini had his horrifying nocturnal vision of the Colosseum swarming with a troop of demons which a necromancer had summoned at his request "in Hebrew, Greek, and Latin."[100]

We need not multiply examples of this kind. Still in full force in the sixteenth century, astrology continued to keep alive the veneration for the gods for which it had served as shelter since classical times. Attempts might be made to Christianize or laicize this veneration, to bring it into line with theology or reduce it to a rational theory of universal law; it still bore the imprint of those mythological powers whose names had been preserved by the stars.

*

[96] *Pantagruel,* III, 23; Pantagruel studied under Picatrix in Toledo.

[97] Cornelius Agrippa von Nettesheim (French tran.): *La philosophie occulte* (Paris, 1919), Bk. II, chaps. 36–44. Picatrix also inspired Marsilio Ficino, who believed in the powers possessed by stones engraved with images of the gods.

[98] C. Léonard, *Speculum lapidum* (Venice, 1502): *De figuris sive imaginibus quae similitudinem habent constellationum Caeli et ad quid valent.*—H. Ragot, *Force et vertu des pierres qui sont entaillées.*

[99] H. Estienne, *Discours merveilleux de la vie, actions et déportements de Catherine de Médicis* (1575).

[100] Cellini, *Vita* (ed. Bacci [Florence, 1901]), p. 127. Such demons, responsive to magic arts ("saepius ad magicos solitos conscendere cantus"), are, according to the astrologer Bonincontri, angels who have remained uncertain in their allegiance, belonging neither to God nor to Lucifer. (*Rerum naturalium,* I, cod. Laur. XXXIV, 52 c, 69 b.) The view held by the Church Fathers may be recognized here, especially that of St. Augustine. For the rest, Bonincontri affirms the astral nature of all demons: "astraeumque genus cunctis." Cf. Ronsard's *Hymne des daimons* (ed. A. M. Schmidt [1939], with commentary).

To ILLUSTRATE different aspects of this mythology of the heavens and to convince us that the gods survived as sidereal demons, we have at our disposal an extremely rich and curious iconography. We shall investigate later

13. The sun and the zodiac

in our study (pp. 149 ff.) the process by which this iconography took shape in the course of the centuries, and shall try to trace its singular vicissitudes step by step. Here all that we plan to do is to point out a few of the pictorial themes in which medieval and Renaissance ideas of the nature of the gods found expression.

How are the gods represented in the cosmology of the Middle Ages?

Before the twelfth century, we find little by way of illustration of the world systems of which the gods form part beyond an occasional diagram of more or less summary sort. These diagrams are usually circles containing inscribed rosettes, the interlacings of which form symmetrical compartments: each such compartment bears the name of one of the fundamental qualities, of an element, humor, season, etc. At the center we read the name of Man, who is thus shown as surrounded and hemmed in on all sides by the physical universe. It is easy to recognize in this decorative scheme the table of equivalents (*supra*, p. 47) which, in late antiquity, expressed the correlation and interdependence of all parts of the cosmos.[101] The theme of *melothesia* reappears also, accompanied first by the names and later by the images of the astral deities. As early as the eleventh century a miniature depicts the Sun, a halo of rays about his head, standing at the center of a circular zone made up of the zodiacal signs. Each sign is marked with its own name and the names of the parts of the body which it controls (*fig. 13*).[102]

As the astrological doctrines spread, there is an increase in the number of figures showing the zodiacal symbols distributed over parts of the human body—the Ram on the head, the Fishes under the feet, the Twins grasping the shoulders. In the fourteenth century, this figure is common in calendars; from these it passes to prayer books, where in the fifteenth and sixteenth centuries it serves as a sort of frontispiece. It appears, for example, on a page of the *Très Riches Heures* of the Duc de Berry.[103]

But of greater interest for us are the microcosm pictures in which the planets are represented. One of the earliest examples is a miniature in a manuscript in Munich (cod. lat. Monac. 13002) showing man among the

[101] Cf., for example, a miniature in a seventh- or eighth-century manuscript of Isidore of Seville (ms. 423, Bibl. de Laon), reproduced by E. Fleury, *Les Manuscrits à miniatures de la Bibliothèque de Laon* (1863). The same ms. contains a miniature "De positione septem stellarum errantium." Ms. 422, a ninth-century copy of 423, includes miniatures representing the constellations. Cf. Wickersheimer, art. cit., and J. Baltrušaitis, "L'Image du monde céleste du IXme au XIIme siècle," *Gazette des Beaux-Arts* (Oct., 1938), pp. 134–148.

[102] Bibl. Nat., ms. 7028, fol. 154. Wickersheimer has mistakenly seen here an image of Christ. The original ms. of the *Liber Floridus* composed in 1120 (see Léopold Delisle, *Notices et extraits*, vol. XXXVIII [Paris, 1906]), and preserved in the University Library of Ghent, no. 92, contains a curious microcosm representing the "six ages of the world" (fol. 20, v) and an image of the sun surrounded by the planets (fol. 38, v).

[103] See H. Bober, "The Zodiacal Miniature of the *Très Riches Heures* of the Duke of Berry:

elements, which make up his being as they do the world itself. From the eyes, nostrils, ears, and mouth issue scrolls bearing the names of the planetary deities. A sort of nimbus surrounds the head, inscribed with the legend, "Instar celestis spere" (*sic*). Thus man's head is, as it were, a small-scale image of the sky. Its roundness expresses the curve of the firmament and its seven orifices correspond to the seven great planetary lights (*fig. 14*).

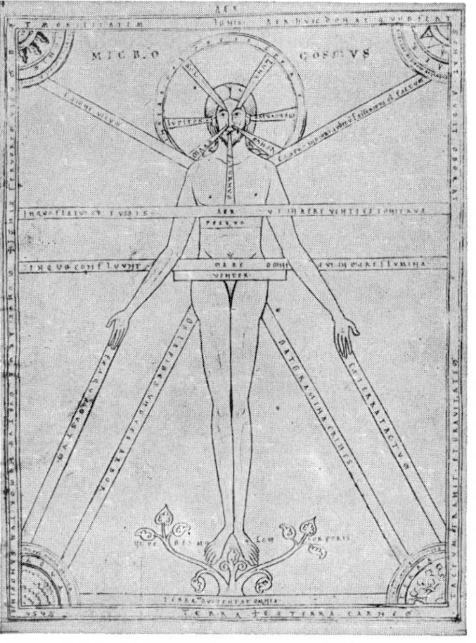

14. Microcosm

Aside from this image, which faithfully reflects the concepts of an Honorius of Autun or a Hildegard of Bingen as to man's relation to the universe,[104] there are others, of later date, in which a new sentiment finds expression. In some of these the figure of a man is enclosed in a series of concentric circles, to which he may be attached by rays; in

Its Sources and Meaning," in *Journal of the Warburg and Courtauld Institutes*, XI (1948), pp. 1–34.—See further, Pierre Gringoire, *Les Heures de Nostre Dame translatées en françoys* (Petit: Paris, 1525). The calendars, almanacs, lot books, and collections of *prognostica* of the fifteenth and sixteenth centuries contain a great many mythological-astrological illustrations; conjunctions of the planets, for instance, are frequently represented. Cf. the rich documentation in Warburg, *op. cit.*, pp. 489–565.

[104] Honorius of Autun, *Elucidarium*, *PL*, CLXXII, 1116: "Man is a little world composed of four elements. . . . His head is round, like the celestial sphere, within which his eyes shine like two of its luminaries."

Hildegard of Bingen, *Causae et curae* (ed. P. Kaiser), pp. 10, 33, 36. "The firmament is like man's head: the Sun, Moon, Stars like his eyes," etc.

On representations of the microcosm, see Saxl, *Sitzungsberichte d. Heidelb. Akad. d. Wissen., Philos.-hist. Klasse* (1925–26), pp. 40–49. It is interesting to note that these drawings combine, from the first, the "scientific" theory of the microcosm with aesthetic theory as to the proportions of the human body. In other words, microcosms inscribed in rectangles or circles are at the same time canons. Cf. P. J. Herwegen, "Ein mittelalt. Kanon des menschl. Körpers," *Rep. für Kunstw.*, XXXII (1909), pp. 455 ff.

others, the figure appears alone, tattooed with inscriptions of the names of the planets.[105] Elsewhere, as in a most curious miniature in a Copenhagen manuscript,[106] the body is covered with disks, each bearing the image of a planet (*fig. 17*). These small images have much to tell us on attentive examination. They betray the conviction which had begun to assert itself in the fourteenth century that man is the prisoner of the heavenly bodies, entirely

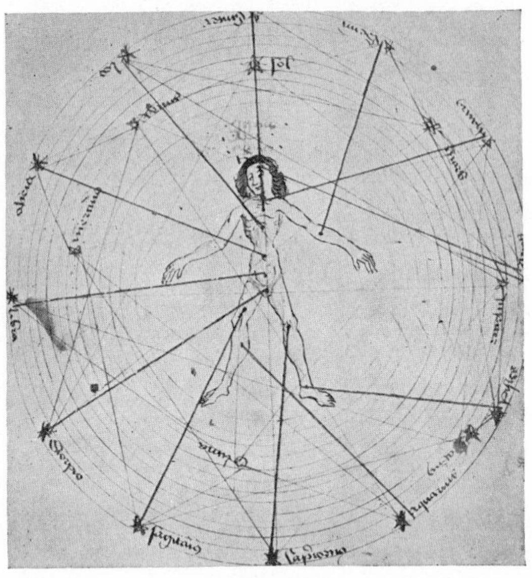

15. Microcosm

at their mercy. This is the impression given by other representations (*fig. 15*) in which he appears as a victim or martyr, fettered, helpless, pierced as if with arrows by the rays of the twelve constellations, his body divided into segments each of which belongs to a given planet or star.[107] But resistance to this tyranny is sometimes expressed as well. In one case (*fig. 16*) we have the figure of a happy child, unconcernedly plucking flowers and paying no

105 E.g., cod. Vindob. 3162, fol. 196, r.

106 Gl. Kgl. S. 78.

107 E.g., cod. Vindob. 5327, fol. 160, r. This fifteenth-century manuscript, of German origin, contains several treatises on the practice of astrology. The illustrations of the other mss., on the other hand, are no more than visual expressions of cosmological theory.

attention to the nine spheres which gravitate around him charged with their dread symbols.[108] In their own way, these naïve images raise the whole problem of necessity versus freedom of the will, the heart-rending conflict which Renaissance thinkers were to make so great an effort to resolve.

Microcosm pictures of this type survive throughout the sixteenth cen-

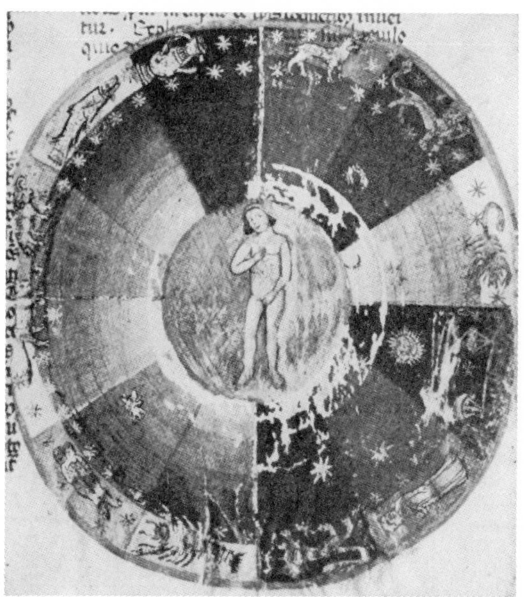

16. Microcosm

tury. We have an example as late as 1572 in the *Livre des portraits et figures du corps humain,* published by Jacques Kerver. In place of a frail puppet and a set of summary inscriptions, we are here shown finely developed athletes, surrounded by circling deities who gracefully launch their hostile bolts from the clouds (*figs. 18 a, b*). But these new pictorial qualities merely clothe the old astro-medical theme. More than a century later, on the ceiling of the astronomical theater of the Archiginnasio at Bologna, Silvestro Giannotti was to carve an array of stellar demigods around the central figure of Apollo

[108] Cod. Vindob. 2359, fol. 52, v. This miniature belongs to the Italian pre-Renaissance.

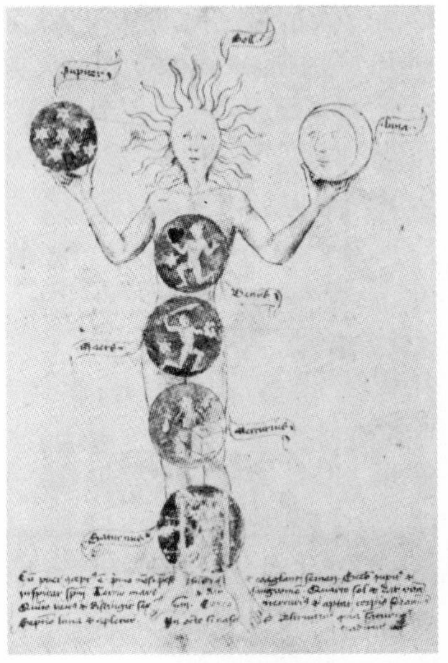

17. *The planets and the human body*

18 a. *The planets and the human body*

18 b. *The planets and the human body*

19. Apollo and the constellations

(*fig. 19*)—homage to the inventor of medicine, but also, without doubt, a distant echo of the principles proclaimed by such men as Paracelsus and Marsilio Ficino: without knowledge of the stars, no one can pretend to know the human body or to cure its ills.[109]

Images of the microcosm are essentially illustrations of the influence of celestial forces on man's physical being. Another iconographical series shows us the same influence as it bears upon his moral existence and his destiny. These representations show us the planets with their "children."[110]

[109] At Milan a medical calendar was still being published in 1754: *Il corso de'Pianeti detto Effemeridi osi il Diario de' moti celesti planetari*, etc.—"a work needed by physicians and surgeons for administering bleedings and medication under the proper aspects of the moon." This corresponds exactly to the medieval theory. See *supra*, p. 50, n. 55.

[110] See Hauber, *Planetenkinderbilder und Sternbilder* (Strassburg, 1916); Saxl, "Probleme der Planetenkinderbilder," *Kunstchronik*, LIV (1919), pp. 1013 ff.

Illustrations of this type first appear in the fourteenth century, a phenomenon which would of itself suffice to attest the revival of astrology at that period, and its popularity. In all astrological calculations the planets are of course the predominant factor. Yet up to this date they have held only a relatively modest place in medieval iconography. In the miniatures decorating astronomical manuscripts they are sometimes met with in the form of busts disposed along the circumference of the sphere, or inscribed in small medallions.[111] From the fourteenth century on, the planets are not only found more frequently in manuscript paintings, but they are revived in Italy in monumental cycles as well. In Venice, they appear on the Gothic capitals of the Doge's Palace (*fig. 21*); in Padua, among the grisailles frescoed by Guariento in the choir of the Eremitani; in Florence, on the Campanile of Santa Maria del Fiore (*fig. 63*), where they occupy the second zone of bas-reliefs, just above the legendary heroes, inventors of the arts, whom we studied in the preceding chapter. Also, in Santa Maria Novella we see them ornamenting the backs of the thrones occupied by the allegorical figures of the arts in the Cappella degli Spagnuoli (*fig. 22*). And in the first years of the fifteenth century, Taddeo di Bartolo represents, in the vault leading to the Chapel of the Palazzo Pubblico in Siena, four mythological divinities, among them Apollo, Mars, and Jupiter (*fig. 42*).

It must be admitted that in these great cycles, as well as in the contemporary miniatures, the gods often take on unwonted aspects—aspects so strange, indeed, that there has sometimes been hesitation in identifying them. They are unmistakably themselves, however, even in the most unexpected disguises,[112] and they are once more beginning to exercise their powerful patronage over humanity. It is they who determine the humors, the aptitudes, the activities of those born under their influence—and this idea, also, receives visual expression. Each planetary divinity presides, so to speak, over an assemblage of persons disposed beneath it in series or groups. These are its "children," whose vocations it has determined. Thus, Mercury presides

111 For the first case, see cod. 448 of the Bibliothèque Municipale of Dijon, fol. 63, v. (*fig. 20*). For the second, cod. Vatic. Reg. 123; and cod. lat. 8663 in the Bibliothèque Nationale, fol. 24.

112 The reason for these profound alterations in the classical type representations of the gods will be explained later (*infra*, pp. 158 ff.).

over an assemblage of painters, writers, and merchants. Schematic representations of this sort, which first took shape in the late Middle Ages,[113] bore fruit in the fifteenth century in a whole family of images, often as beautiful as they are curious. We may cite the illustrations of the *Epître d'Othée* of Christine de Pisan,[114] where the "children" resemble the Apostles receiving the gifts of the Holy Spirit; the frescoes in the Borgia apartments of the Vatican (*figs. 23, 24*); and a whole series of engravings and drawings in which the planets are usually shown riding in chariots, as in the *trionfi* of Petrarch. Among these, in Florence, are the prints of Baldini, of which two versions exist, and which inspired the frescoes in the Cambio in Perugia; and, in Germany, the Berlin *Blockbuch*, also the *Hausbuch* belonging to Prince Waldburg-Wolfegg-Waldsee at Wolfegg, and a Cassel manuscript of 1445.[115] In the sixteenth century, Giolito de'Ferrari and Hans Sebald Beham took up the same theme again, with variants; and toward the end of the century it was treated, with varying success, by a whole group of Dutch and Flemish engravers—Martin de Vos, Crispin de Passe, Goltzius, Sanredam, Thomas de Leu, Gérard de Jode.[116]

20. The planets and the spheres

The appearance of this theme in so many parts of Europe is symptomatic of the wide diffusion of astrological beliefs during the Renaissance.

[113] E.g., Bodl., cod. Or. 133.

[114] Bibl. Nat., cod. fr. 606; Brit. Mus., Harley 4431; Bodl. 421.

[115] See Lippmann, *Les Planètes et leurs enfants*, reproductions published by the Société Internationale de Chalcographie (1895); J. Mesnil, *L'Art au nord et au sud des Alpes à l'époque de la Renaissance*, Brussels-Paris (1911), chap. iv: "Sur quelques gravures du xve siècle."

[116] The Cabinet des Estampes of the Bibliothèque Nationale owns a rich collection of these series: *Imagines septem planetarum, De effectu septem planetarum*, etc. (vol. Td 28).

But not in all cases are we dealing merely with the spreading of a common superstition by means of the visual image; sometimes an original work is born of the encounter between artist and scholar—an encounter which may be especially significant when one is of the South and another of the North. This was the case with Albrecht Dürer's Melencolia. This famous figure is, in

21. The planets and their children

fact, an isolated example of the type of subject which we are discussing; she symbolizes the contemplative life of the "children of Saturn," who, obedient to the laws of their star, meditate gloomily and at length on the secrets of wisdom. Dürer, as penetrating studies have shown,[117] took his inspiration for this work from a distinguished humanist—none other than Marsilio Ficino himself.

[117] See E. Panofsky and F. Saxl, *Dürer's Melencolia I,* Studien der Bibliothek Warburg, II (1923).

Further study has led to the tracing of Cornelius Agrippa's influence in the Dürer design. See K. A. Novotny, "The Construction of Certain Seals and Characters in the Work of Agrippa of Nettesheim," in *Journal of the Warburg and Courtauld Institutes,* XII (1949), pp. 46–57. Cf. *supra,* p. 62, n. 97.

Lastly, we find the "children of the planets" in two vast Italian fresco cycles which constitute a different category, since they incorporate our theme in a complete cosmological ensemble. The first of these series decorates the Palazzo della Ragione in Padua, more commonly known as "il Salone." The

22. The planets and the liberal arts

upper part of the immense fresco which covers the walls of this hall is divided into horizontal zones. These show us, from the lowest to the highest, first the planets and their "children"; then the signs of the zodiac, with the twelve Apostles [118] and the Labors of the Months. Although later restorations make it difficult to judge, the orientation of the hall is apparently such that each month the beams of the rising sun would strike the zodiacal sign which

[118] On the association of the twelve Apostles with the twelve zodiacal signs, see Piper, *Mythologie und Symbolik der christlichen Kunst* (Weimar, 1847–51), I, 2, pp. 292 ff.

the sun was actually traversing in the sky. The uppermost zone holds a row of mysterious figures which have only recently been identified: they are the decans and paranatellons of the "barbaric sphere."[119] A complete world system is thus presented in the Salone: the zones correspond to the concentric spheres enveloping the earth, within which reign the ordering forces of the cosmos.

23. *Mercury and his children*

In the frescoes of the Palazzo Schifanoia, in Ferrara, we find an analogous disposition. Here we have three horizontal bands: the topmost shows not the planetary gods, but the twelve great gods of Olympus ("masters of the months," as Manilius calls them), each mounted on a chariot and surrounded by his "children"; in the central band appear the signs of the zodiac, and the decans (each controlling ten days of the month); finally, in the lowest band, we see the pastimes and

[119] On the Salone, see W. Burges, "La Ragione de Padoue," *Annales archéologiques*, XVIII, pp. 331–343; XIX, pp. 241–251; XXVI, pp. 250–271. Also A. Barzon, *I Cieli e la loro influenza negli affreschi del Salone in Padova* (Padua, 1924). Interpretation of the frescoes as a whole was first given by Dr. Saxl (*Sitzungsberichte der Heidelberger Akademie der Wissenschaften* [1925–1926], pp. 49–68), who found the key to them (1) in the miniatures illustrating the *Anima astrologiae* of Guido Bonatti (cod. Vindob. 2359, fourteenth century), and (2) in an intensive analysis of the *Astrolabium planum* of Pietro d'Abano, published in Augsburg by Johann Engel in 1488, the illustrations of which are in turn derived from a manuscript of Albumazar (cod. Vat. Reg. 1283). Pietro d'Abano is believed to have provided the original program for the Salone (as is usually said, for Giotto), but the frescoes in their present state are not earlier than 1420.

24. *Mercury and his children*

occupations of Duke Borso at different seasons of the year—in other words, a sort of illustrated chronicle or calendar of the life of palace, court, and city.[120] Here, again, the three superposed zones are merely the projection of a spherical system (*fig. 25*), of which the lowest zone, the earth, forms the nucleus or core.[121]

These two great fresco cycles—one ornamenting a public palace and the other a princely dwelling, but both bringing together, in an astonishing synthesis with familiar scenes and episodes of daily life, figures of the sidereal demons drawn from antique and often from barbaric sources[122]—are essential documents for any true estimate of the place of astrology in the fifteenth century. They are the exact and full translation in visual terms of a concept of the universe in which the pagan gods have regained the place of *cosmocrats* (κοσμοκράτορες), of sovereign masters.

But even in ecclesiastical buildings, there appeared in Italy at about the same time astrological representations of an entirely new significance. In the Old Sacristy of San Lorenzo in Florence, and again in the Pazzi Chapel at Santa Croce, it may surprise the visitor to find, just above each altar, a cupola containing mythical figures of constellations (*fig. 27*). We have to do here, as has been proved,[123] with a type of antique decoration already revived by the Arabs.[123a] But what is remarkable about the Florentine cupolas is that they represent no merely random arrangement of the stars: the artist

120 On this score the *Très Riches Heures* of the Duc de Berry may be compared with the frescoes of the Schifanoia Palace; the duke is shown, for instance, feasting and fighting in the months of January and February, beneath the corresponding planet and signs of the zodiac: Saturn, Capricorn, Aquarius.

121 See A. Warburg, "Italienische Kunst und internationale Astrologie im Palazzo Schifanoja zu Ferrara," in *Gesammelte Schriften*, II, pp. 476 ff.

122 These same "demoniacal" figures are found also in the lapidaries and the treatises on magic of which we have already spoken (see *supra*, pp. 54 ff.). Outside the astrological cycle, we sometimes meet with one of the gods conceived of and represented as a diabolical being. A noted example is the Cupid painted by Giotto in the cupola of the Lower Church at Assisi, above the tomb of St. Francis: he has the talons of a bird of prey. The same type appears in a fresco in the Palazzo Castelbarco at Avio, in Tirol, and in a miniature illustrating a poem of Francesco da Barberino (see F. Egidi, in the *Giornale storico della letteratura italiana*, XCVII, pp. 49–70; Zonta, *Storia della letteratura italiana*, I, pl. 14), cited by Boccaccio in the *Genealogia deorum*, IX, 4: "Pedes illi gryphis apponuntur." Here we have Love transformed into a monster, like the Apollo who tormented St. Benedict—a cruel downfall for the fairest gods of Olympus! As if to restore the balance, Christ will be given the features of Love or of Apollo by artists of the Italian Renaissance.

123 See F. Saxl, *La Fede astrologica di Agostino Chigi*, published by the Reale Accademia d'Italia (Rome, 1934), pp. 12–20.

123a See Excursus by F. Saxl on the zodiac of Qusayr' Amra, in K. A. C. Creswell, *Early Muslim Architecture* (Oxford, 1932–1940), I, pp. 289–294.

has preserved the aspect of the sky exactly as it appeared at a given day and hour. Why was this done? Without the slightest doubt, because some event of decisive importance for the Church had taken place at that very moment—an event over which the celestial powers then above the horizon had presided. Aby Warburg was able, in fact, to prove that the arrangement of the stars shown in the Old Sacristy of San Lorenzo corresponds exactly to their posi-

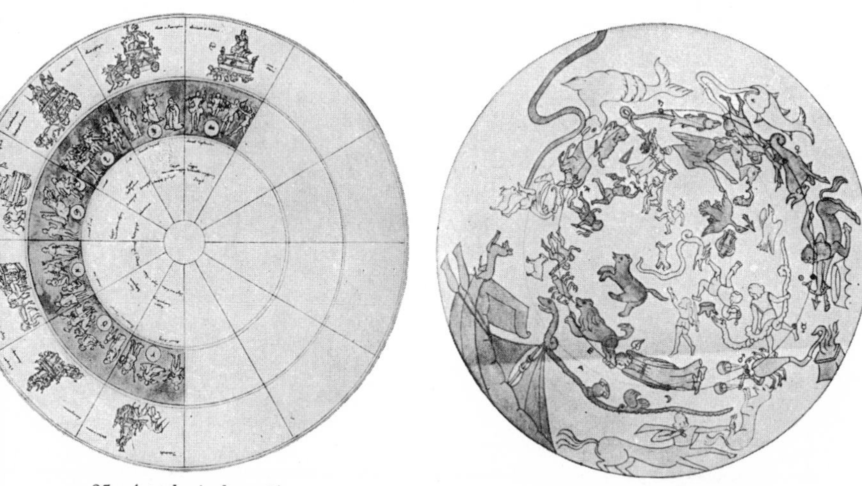

25. *Astrological motif*

26. *Astrological ceiling*

tions in the sky above Florence on July 9, 1422, the date of the consecration of the main altar.[124]

These astral bodies which the Church welcomed into her sanctuaries were later, as we need hardly remind ourselves, to invade the palaces of her popes. The zodiac, the constellations, the planets, play a curiously prominent part in the decoration of the Vatican. To cite only one example, the vault of the Sala dei Pontefici, in the Borgia apartments, decorated by order of Leo X, shows the names of Peter's successors surrounded by celestial symbols; above Boniface IX, Cygnus is seen in flight between Pisces and Scorpio, while in medallions at each side Mars and Jupiter ride past in chariots.

[124] See A. Warburg, "Eine astronomische Himmelsdarstellung in der alten Sakristei von S. Lorenzo in Florenz," in *Gesammelte Schriften*, I, pp. 169–172.

27. *Night sky of Florence, July 8–9, 1422*

And finally, the most radiant period of the Italian Renaissance crystallized in two celebrated works the visual and spiritual elements of this great astro-mythological scheme. Both works were executed at the dawn of the Cinquecento for an outstanding epicurean and humanist, Agostino Chigi. One is profane in character and the other religious, for one is the vault of his palace and the other the cupola of his tomb.

The hall in the Farnesina Palace where Raphael painted his *Galatea*[125] shows us a vault peopled with mythological figures (*fig. 29*), among whom we recognize at first glance Perseus slaying Medusa, Venus with her doves, Leda and the Gemini. In our instant admiration for Baldassare Peruzzi's decorative fantasy and for the skillful distribution of his vivid images in groups and tableaux, we may not at first grasp the connection between this ensemble and the astrological cycles with which we have been dealing. What, in fact, do these noble deities, moving through the serene heights of the ether with an elegance that reminds us of Ovid, have in common with the earth-bound demons of the realistic Paduan and Ferrarese frescoes, or with the schematized sky plan of the Florentine cupolas?

However, the two central scenes of the Peruzzi vault are set against a background of starry sky. What does this indicate if not that here, again, astrology alone can provide the key? And, in fact, careful analysis has shown that precise scientific data underlie the choice and arrangement of the figures[126]—so precise indeed that they have made possible a reconstruction of the corresponding sky map (*fig. 26*), which astronomical calculations have shown to be identical with the aspect of the sky of Rome on December 1, 1466—the very day of Agostino Chigi's birth.[127]

Thus the same fateful powers hold vigil here, disguised in the iridescent garments of Fable. But now they herald the destiny of an individual, who owes his fortune and glory to their favor: Fame, as she sounds her trumpet among the stars of the vault, publishes the fact triumphantly. Whenever he

[125] See F. Hermanin, *La Farnesina* (Bergamo, 1927), and F. Saxl, *La fede astrologica . . .* , p. 11. The Galatea evidently had her own significance in the ensemble so learnedly conceived: she doubtless represented one of the elements, Water. On the other walls, myths relating to the other elements were probably to figure.

[126] We owe this analysis to Saxl, *op. cit.*, pp. 22–23: "Interpretazione astronomica dei singoli quadri della volta."

[127] Arthur Beer, in Saxl, *op. cit.*, pp. 61–67.

glances up at this ceiling, the master of the house may read anew the promises of his horoscope, his heart full of confidence and pride.

Nothing in the Farnesina recalls the Christian world of the spirit; the gods of Olympus reign there alone. But let us not on that account jump to

28. God and the planets

conclusions as to Agostino Chigi's "paganism." Rather let us turn to Santa Maria del Popolo—to the chapel where he rests for all eternity. There another aspect of his thought is revealed. In the cupola, against the blue and gold mosaic background, the divine forms of the planets come again into view, ranged in a circle according to the order of the spheres (*fig. 28*). But this time they are not alone; an angel hovers over each, while surmounting the whole, in the round central aperture, the Creator appears in imperious pose, his arm raised in a gesture at once of benediction and command.

The meaning of the composition is clear: the planetary gods, to whom this earth and the lives of men are subject, are themselves subject in turn.

29. *Horoscope of Agostino Chigi*

They are dependent upon a supreme will, of which they are merely the instruments.

If we wish to confirm this interpretation, we need only turn once more to contemporary texts. In his "sacred hymns" the poet-astrologer Lorenzo Bonincontri addresses the Eternal Father in terms which make His pre-eminence clear:

Te duce, effulgent Jovis astra coelo,
Reddis et clarum Veneri nitorem,
Atque Fortunam variare cogis
Infima summis.[128]

Even more explicitly, Bonincontri elsewhere explains God's intent, in creating the stars, to make them His auxiliaries and agents ("ministras executricesque") in the government of the sublunary world:

Principio Pater omnipotens, ut legibus orbem
Flecteret. . . .
Sublimes caelo statuit stellasque globosque
Errantum: quibus et numeros et nomina finxit,
Naturamque illis praefecit, ut omnia certis
Temporibus mundo starent . . .
His hominum finxit mores, et corpora, et omnem
Fortunam, et casus varios, vitamque, diemque
Extremum, fati seriem finemque laborum . . .[129]

Thus, the stars which determined Chigi's death, after having regulated the whole course of his life, did no more than to execute the decrees of Providence.

But it is in the *Urania* of Pontano that the best commentary may be found on the half-pagan, half-Christian composition of the Cappella Chigi. The celebrated episode of the Assembly of the Gods, in fact, furnishes an exact parallel. The Eternal Father, when about to create inferior beings subject to mortality, convokes in the empyrean a gathering of the most noble beings, who are to be His collaborators. The motivating Intelligences of the seven spheres approach Him—the seven planetary *numina*, each bearing attributes (as in the Cappella Chigi) suggestive of the zodiacal signs in which

128 *Dierum solemnium Christianae religionis libri* IV (1491), I, I, 41–44. ("Under your guidance, Jupiter shines in the sky; you restore her brilliance to Venus, and by you is Fortune obliged to diversify earthly destinies through superior influence.")

129 Laur. Bonincontri, *Rer. nat. et divin. sive de reb. coel.*, II, 12 ff.: "In the beginning, the Almighty Father, in order to rule the world by laws, set high in the sky the stars and the globes of the planets: He gave them numbers and names, and assigned to them such a nature that everything would be determined at definite times. Through them he shaped the morals of men and their bodies, and their whole fortune, accidental happenings, man's life and his ultimate day, sequence of his fate, end of his labors."

it has its "houses," that is to say, where its influence is greatest. Ranged about Him, they wait respectfully:

Ergo ubi convenere animisque opibusque parati
Quales jussi aderant, intenti . . .
Exspectant signum atque alacres praecepta capessunt.[130]

God then addresses them solemnly:

Tum genitor solio placidus sic coepit ab alto . . .[131]

Their role, He tells them, will be to co-operate, each according to his powers, in the great work of creation. To them is entrusted the completion of the work: they are to give shape to the terrestrial sphere and to its mortal inhabitants, as He himself has formed heaven:

Quare agite, et celeres quam primum ascendite currus
Agressi mortale opus et genus omne animantum . . .[132]

He ceases to speak, and with a nod sets Olympus in motion. Each god leaps into his chariot and speeds toward the allotted task.

The poem accords so perfectly with the Chigi cupola that it might almost be a direct description of it. And without doubt Pontano himself was inspired by a recollection of Plato, who in the *Timaeus* assembles a council of δαίμονες around the Demiurge.[133] But his primary concern was to integrate the principles of astrology with Christian dogma. This reconciliation of science with theology, of Providence with necessity—this balancing of two universes, so anxiously striven for by Renaissance thought—is here on a sudden, for one brief moment, realized. But art alone [134] has achieved the miracle—the art of Pontano and Raphael. By some special magic the pagan and the sacred, sensual grace and metaphysical grandeur, are blended here in an exquisite and tranquil light.

130 *Urania*, I, 921–923. ("When they are gathered, with ready minds and resources, as they had been ordered to appear, they await the signal, eager to execute the commands.")—On Pontano's astrological ideas and their evolution, see the interesting analysis by Soldati, *op. cit.*, chap. iv, pp. 232–253.

131 *Urania*, I, 924.

132 *Ibid.*, 946–947.

133 *Timaeus*, 40 D, 41 D.

134 It is true that Pontano, whose early thinking had been so strictly scientific and pagan as to exclude all possibility of a theological concept of the universe, attempted toward the end of his life to introduce a religious corrective into his doctrine. It was then that he adopted the theory of the heavenly bodies as instruments. He even admits the freedom of the will (though with strong reservation), a factor which he had previously neglected. But with these tardy corrections, his philosophic system lacks harmony and unity.

III

The Moral Tradition

THE METHOD of interpretation which consists in endowing mythology with edifying meaning goes back at least as far as the Stoics.[1] Their great desire to reconcile philosophy with popular religion led not only to their attempt, which we have already noted, to regard the gods as symbols of the physical world; they also undertook at times to discover spiritual significance in the figures and even in the names of the gods, and moral lessons in their adventures.

At first glance, this undertaking would seem to have had small chance of success; the Olympians, by and large, were anything but models of virtue. The story of their orgies and cruelties, their incests and fornications, is thoroughly unedifying. It was for this very reason that the exegesis of the Stoics was both legitimate and necessary. It went without saying that Homer, who recounted all these disgraceful acts of the gods, was a great and noble poet. Could he conceivably have told such impious tales without some hidden intent? No, the thing is manifestly impossible; [2] we must therefore make every effort to understand his real meaning when he speaks of the gods—to distinguish between the literal and the deeper meaning. The first may be frivolous but the second has weight, and it is the second meaning which is the true one.

[1] See Decharme, *Critique des traditions religieuses . . .* , pp. 274–275, 288; Gilbert Murray, *Five Stages of Greek Religion*, chap. iv, pp. 165–169; G. Boissier, *La Religion romaine*, II, chap. vii.

[2] "If Homer was not speaking in allegorical terms," says Heraclides, "he was guilty of the greatest impieties." It therefore follows that Homer must have used allegory. See R. Hinks, *Myth and Allegory in Ancient Art* (London, 1939), Introduction: pp. 3–4.

Thus the allegorical method came into being.[3] We find it systematically applied, at the end of the pagan era, in two small treatises—the *Homeric Allegories* of Heraclitus, and Phornutus' *Commentary on the Nature of the Gods.*[4] From them we learn that the manly attributes of Mercurius Quadratus signify the fullness and fecundity of reason,[5] and that the Harpies who rob Phineus of his food are courtesans devouring the patrimony of young men.[6]

The Neoplatonists revive the same method, but they use it on a broader scale and in a different spirit. They apply it not only to Homer but to all religious traditions, including foreign cults; the entire universe is for them nothing but a great myth, endowed with spiritual meaning. Their attitude is no longer one of rationalization, aimed at explaining away shocking absurdities; it is the attitude of believers and mystics, reverently seeking the depths of meaning within a sacred text. One example is Sallust, friend of the Emperor Julian, who in his treatise *On the Gods and the World*[7] fervently defends mythology, the true meaning of which, he declares, is apparent only to the initiate. As proof he deliberately selects fables of the grossest surface immorality—the tale of Saturn devouring his children, or of Attis and Cybele. In the latter, for example, he proves by analysis of the myth and the ritual that we are to see "the trials of the soul in its search for God."[8] Without losing anything of their value as a source of religious emotion, these legends which Cicero and Seneca scorned as "absurdities" and "old wives' tales"[9] are thus given pious and philosophical explanation, ὁσίως καὶ φιλοσόφως.[10]

The weakness of this system of interpretation is obvious: to look for ideas in old images which are no longer understood is to falsify the character

[3] The physical interpretations are also allegories, but for the sake of clarity we have reserved the term for interpretations of a moral character.

[4] *Opuscula mythologica physica et ethica, Graece et Latine* . . . (Cambridge, 1671), for Palaephatus, Heraclitus, Phornutus, Sallustius, etc.—On the interpretation of myths by the Stoics, in general, see Decharme, *op. cit.*, pp. 347–353.

[5] Phornutus, *De natura deorum* (Venice, 1505), p. 32.

[6] Heraclitus, *De incredibilibus* (Rome, 1641), chap. viii. The editor, Allatius, suspects that this Heraclitus was the Heraclides who wrote on the allegories in Homer; it is uncertain which is the correct form of the name.

[7] Sallustius, *De diis et mundo*, chaps. iii and iv.

[8] This explanation, furthermore, is borrowed from Julian's fifth *oratio*, in honor of the Magna Mater.

[9] Cicero, *De natur. deor.*, II, 28: "superstitiones paene seniles"; Seneca, *Fragmenta*, 26: "ineptiae poetarum."

[10] Plutarch, *De Iside et Osiride*, 355.

of the primitive myths.[11] Still, there is much that the Hellenistic philosophers could have brought forward by way of excuse, for they did not, after all, invent allegory out of whole cloth. To say nothing of recent myths, invented or at least elaborated consciously, like the Psyche story, the old legends had long been charged with spiritual elements. Already purified by Homer, they were further ennobled, from Aeschylus to Plato, by serving as themes for poets and philosophers. The gods were no longer elementary beings, "barely detached from the world themselves, covered with soot and with smoke"; nor were they the light and quarrelsome troop of Olympus. Like the statues in the temples, they had come to represent, for the loftiest spirits, magnificent metaphors—signs or steps along man's way to an understanding of the nature of divinity.[12]

There were still other reasons for this leaning toward allegorical interpretation—the taste of antiquity for apologues hiding a moral within a tale, and above all the tendency, shared by Greeks and Romans alike, to personify abstractions. For those who gave divine form and dignity to Health, Victory, Fortune, Concord, and Modesty, it was not difficult to recognize the same qualities in the goddesses of Fable:

Minerve est la Prudence, et Vénus la Beauté.[13]

Virgil's mythology is interesting in this connection, in a dual sense. In the host of malevolent deities who throng the vestibule of Hades,[14] we recognize Discord, Care, and avenging Remorse side by side with monsters of earlier ages, the Gorgons and Titans. In the *Aeneid,* furthermore, the Olympians have taken on a dignified and grave look; Virgil refuses to repeat the frivolous tales about them which Ovid so enjoys collecting. Their attitude inspires respect: Jupiter presides over his council with sovereign majesty,

[11] Cf., for example, E. Renan, *Études d'histoire religieuse,* pp. 26–27: "It is wrong to suppose that humanity, at some remote period, created symbols as a clothing for dogma, or had any distinct view of dogma and symbol." Cf. also Renan, *Vie de Jésus,* 10th ed. (1863), p. 3.

[12] See Murray, *op. cit.,* chap. ii, p. 75: "Hermes, Athena, Apollo, all have their long spiritual history."

[13] On the gods as incarnations of passions, and the "psychological" explanation of mythology, see Decharme, *op. cit.,* pp. 289–291.

[14] *Aeneid,* VI, 273–281. Cf. the description of Fama, *ibid.,* IV, 173–188. See Boissier, *op. cit.,* I, p. 322.

and Venus herself is only a mother who fears for her son.[15] Just as he deifies moral concepts, Virgil "moralizes" the gods.

Mistaken though it was in principle, and often made ridiculous by abuse, the allegorical method thus had its own justification; in their inability to recognize clearly defined periods in the history of the gods, the philosophers were rediscovering elements introduced into mythology by earlier philosophers; they perceived reflections of a wisdom like their own. Furthermore, as we have said, the allegorical method had a very definite *raison d'être:* for many who wished to keep the religion of their fathers it offered a means of giving that religion new life and of bringing it into line with the modern conscience.

*

ON THIS last account, it might be supposed that Christianity could not have shown itself anything but hostile to allegory. In pagan hands, was it not a defensive weapon of the greatest value? By endowing mythology with lofty spiritual significance, Julian, for example, was shielding it from attack by the Christians, who could no longer claim moral superiority for their own religion.

And some voices were indeed raised from among the Church Fathers to contest these interpretations, "which disguise some shameful and miserable error under color of imparting a profound truth." "We are told," St. Augustine exclaims, "that through the myths the small number of initiates were taught to be virtuous; show me the places—or at least remind me of them—where the people received such lessons!" [16] But how could the Fathers condemn without qualification a method which they themselves made use of at every turn? To say nothing of the parables, which are an essential part of the

[15] See Boissier, *op. cit.*, I, p. 286; also De la Ville de Mirmont, *La Mythologie et les dieux dans les Argonautiques d'Apollonios de Rhodes et dans l'Énéide* (1894).

[16] *De civ. Dei,* II, 6: "Nec nobis nescio quos susurros paucissimorum auribus anhelatos et arcana velut religione traditos jacent, quibus vitae probitas castitasque discatur; sed demonstrentur vel commemorentur loca. . . ." Cf. *Epist.*, 91: "Illa omnia, quae antiquitus de vita deorum moribusque conscripta sunt, longe aliter sunt intelligenda atque interpretanda sapientibus," etc. ("All those things which were written long ago concerning the life and manners of the gods are to be far otherwise than literally understood and interpreted by the wise."—*Select Letters*, LCL.)

St. Basil (*Homiliae,* III, 31) also protests against this sort of interpretation.

tradition of Christian teaching, the patristic tendency always to look for profound meanings hidden behind the words of the Scriptural narrative is a matter of common knowledge.[17] This tendency is seen first in the Greek Fathers, who owe it to their Alexandrian antecedents. Thus, according to Origen (and to many other commentators in his wake) the Bride and Groom in the *Song of Songs* represent the Church and Christ.[18] But from Alexandria the allegorical spirit invaded the Western Church as well. The same type of exegesis is found in St. Ambrose, and in Prudentius, famed as the author of the *Psychomachia*, in which the vices and virtues are personified.[19]

But this was not all: for didactic purposes the Fathers often used moralizing interpretations (even in the case of mythology) in no way different from those employed by their opponents. They had, in fact, reluctantly admitted profane poetry into the curriculum, since they recognized it as one of the elements of culture.[20] Was it thinkable that an educated man should know nothing of Homer or Virgil? But in giving his pupils an understanding of the poets, would not the teacher inevitably have to tell them "the scandalous history of Olympus, explain the attributes of the gods, and reveal their genealogy in all its aspects"? [21] In this delicate task, allegory was a great resource. It is easy to believe that Christian teachers of the fourth century gladly welcomed the pagan allegorizing commentaries, like those of Servius on Virgil and Lactantius Placidus on Statius' *Thebaid*.

By these means, it was felt, the gods were being reduced to the level of mere ornaments. Indeed, simply to read of their adventures in school did not seem enough; mythological subjects were taken as themes for compositions. Two centuries after Christianity had become the state religion, topics proposed to young men for literary exercises still included speeches by

[17] See *Dictionnaire de théologie catholique*, art. *Allégories bibliques*.

[18] Some pagan writers, furthermore, criticize this application of allegorical method to the Bible—as, for example, Celsus. Cf. Origen, *Contra Celsum*, IV, 48.

[19] Tertullian, Cyprian, Hilary of Poitiers, and St. Augustine all make use of the same method. On Prudentius, see M. Lavarenne, *La Psychomachie de Prudence* (Paris, 1933); the introduction discusses the history of allegorical literature.

[20] Tertullian, *De idololatria*, 10, sees literature as a necessary instrument: "Cum instrumentum sit ad omnem vitam." St. Jerome, *Epist.*, 21, calls it necessary for the instruction of youth: "In pueris necessitatis est."

[21] See G. Boissier, *La Fin du paganisme*, I, pp. 234–5. Also, H. I. Marrou, *St-Augustin*, p. 117: "*Historia* [understood as the explanation of historical facts indispensable to the understanding of a text] necessarily includes mythology, to which it accords a place of honor."

Thetis or Juno, or the denunciation of a blasphemer guilty of taking a statue of Diana, the virgin goddess, into a house of ill fame.[22] By the same token, mythology is still present as a harmless but indispensable ingredient in the panegyrics of Claudian [23] and the elegies of Ausonius.[24]

Two allegorical monuments mark the beginning of the sixth century—one dealing with the Bible, the *Moralia* of Gregory the Great,[25] the other with the pagan gods, the *Mythologiae* of Fulgentius.[26] In the latter work, "the reader is awe-struck by the acumen of a mind which refers the whole series of fables, philosophically explained, either to the natural order or to man's moral life." [27] Side by side with physical interpretations, Fulgentius does in fact advance explanations of an edifying sort: thus the three goddesses among whom Paris must choose become symbols of the active, the contemplative, and the amorous life (II, 1); the union of Leda and the Swan typifies the coupling of Power and Injustice—the fruits of such a union being, like Helen, inevitable objects of scandal and discord (II, 16).

Gregory of Tours was clearly aware of the dangers inherent in this method, which, under pretext of deriving moral teaching from the pagan fables, actually perpetuated their memory: "Let us have no more of the gods," he said, "and turn rather to the Gospel." [28] But these wise counsels remained without effect. In the Carolingian period, at the same time as the

[22] On these subjects for *dictiones*, see Boissier, *op. cit.*, p. 253.

[23] *Ibid.*, II, pp. 281–282.

[24] *Ibid.*, II, 80–81. Mythology was later to play an analogous role in the educational scheme of the Jesuits.

[25] *Expositio in librum Job sive moralium libri* XXXV.

[26] Fulgentius Planciades: *Mythologiarum ad Catum presbyterum libri* III, in *Auctores mythographi latini*, ed. Van Staveren (Leyden, 1742), pp. 593–734. We should recall here the *Marriage of Mercury and Philology*, of Martianus Capella, which is essentially an allegory of the liberal arts.

[27] This is the verdict of a twelfth-century writer, Sigebert of Gembloux (*Liber de scriptoribus ecclesiasticis*, *PL*, CLX, chap. 28, 554): "Hic certe omnis lector expavescere potest acumen ingenii eius, qui totam fabularum seriem, secundum philosophiam expositarum, transtulerit vel ad rerum ordinem vel ad humanae vitae moralitatem."

[28] "Non enim oportet fallaces commemorare fabulas neque philosophorum inimicam Deo sapientiam sequi, ne in judicium aeternae mortis, Domino discernente cadamus. . . . Non ego Saturni fugam, non Junonis iram, non Jovis stupra . . . commemoro. Sed ista omnia tanquam super harenam locata et cito ruitura conspiciens ad divina et evangelica potius miracula revertamur," *Liber de gloriam martyrum*, *MGH*, *Script, rer. Merov.*, I, 487–488. ("We should neither commemorate the false fables nor follow a philosophy hostile to God, lest we fall into eternal damnation by His judgment. . . . I am not the one to record the flight of Saturn, the anger of Juno, or the adulteries of Jupiter. . . . Instead, looking at all these things as built upon sand and destined to early ruin, let us rather turn our eyes toward the divine wonders recounted in the Gospels.")

Allegoriae in universam sacram scripturam of Rabanus Maurus, appeared a poem by Theodulph, bishop of Orléans, on how to interpret the fables of the poets "philosophically":

> *Falsa poetarum stilus affert, vera sophorum*
> *Falsa horum in verum vertere saepe solent . . .*[29]

He continues by interpreting Proteus as Truth, Hercules as Virtue, Cacus as the bad thief, and comments on the attributes of Cupid in these terms:

> *Mens prava in pharetra, insidiae signantur in arcu,*
> *Tela, puer, virus, fax tuus ardor, Amor . . .*[30]

Thus mythology tends to become a *philosophia moralis* (so titled in an eleventh-century work attributed to Hildebert of Lavardin, bishop of Tours, who draws many examples from the pagan poets, as well as from the Bible).[31] It even tends to become reconciled with theology: the medieval genius for allegory which, renewing the tradition of the Fathers,[32] finds anticipations of the New Covenant in Old Testament characters and episodes, and sees certain characters and episodes of Fable as prefigurations of Christian truth.

In fact, beginning with the twelfth century, when allegory became the universal vehicle of all pious expression, mythological exegesis in this sense grew to astonishing proportions. It was in this period that Alexander Neckam [33] related the gods to those virtues which, according to St. Augustine, had

[29] *Theodulfi Carmina, PL,* CV, 331–332: *De libris quos legere solebam, et qualiter fabulae poetarum a philosophis mystice pertractentur.* —("Poets provide false stories; philosophers often turn these falsehoods into truth.")

[30] "Your depraved mind is depicted in the quiver, your treachery in your bow. Your arrows, child, are your poison; your torch is your ardor, O Love."

[31] *Moralis philosophia de honesto et utili, PL,* CLXXI, 1007 ff.—B. Hauréau (*Notices et extraits des manuscrits,* XXXIII, pp. 100 ff.) attributes this work to William of Conches.

[32] See *Dictionnaire de théologie catholique,* article *Allégories bibliques.* This type of allegory, which foretells the future, is found, for instance, in St. Augustine, *Enarratio in Psalmos,* VII, n. 13: *PL,* XXXVI, 115–116.

[33] *De naturis rerum,* 1, 7; cf. St. Augustine, *De doct. Christ.,* II, 7. Neckam makes the gifts of the Holy Spirit correspond to the planetary gods (see preceding chapter): Saturn = *donum sapientiae,* Mars = *consilii,* Mercury = *pietatis,* the Moon = *timoris dei,* etc.—See E. Rathbone, "Master Alberic of London, *Mythographus tertius Vaticanus,*" *Mediaeval and Renaissance Studies,* I (1941), pp. 35–38; and R. W. Hunt, "Alberic of Montecassino and Reginald of Canterbury," *ibid.,* pp. 39–40. According to Rathbone, the *Mythographus tertius* is not Alexander Neckam, but another Alberic, canon of St. Paul's (1181–1202).

prepared man by degrees for Christian wisdom; that William of Conches,[34] in his commentary on Boethius' *Consolation of Philosophy,* interpreted Eurydice as the innate concupiscence of the human heart and the giants as our bodies, formed of primeval slime, which are in constant rebellion against the soul, Jupiter; that Bernard of Chartres and his pupil, John of Salisbury,[35] meditated upon pagan religion—"not out of any respect for false deities, but because under cover of words truths are hidden which may not be revealed to the vulgar." Above all, it was at this period that the *Metamorphoses* of Ovid were exploited as a mine of sacred truth.

The earliest Christian centuries had shown themselves hostile to Ovid, for the very reason that his work seemed much more difficult to reconcile with philosophy and theology than did that of the graver Virgil.[36] The first indication of a change of attitude is given us by Theodulph, the bishop of Orléans whom we have already quoted. In Ovid's works, he says, although there is much that is frivolous, even more truth lies hidden under a false covering:

> . . . *Quanquam sint frivola multa*
> *Plurima sub falso tegmine vera latent* . . .[37]

Not until four centuries later will this *Ovidius ethicus* or *theologus* come clearly into view, but he will then revenge himself to the full. First of all, he will be given a place of honor[38] in the florilegia, anthologies of edifying *sententiae* culled from classical authors, which were just then attaining great

[34] See Ch. Jourdain, "Des commentaires inédits de Guillaume de Conches et de N. Triveth sur la Consolation de la Philosophie de Boèce," *Notices et extraits des manuscrits,* XX, pp. 55–57.

[35] Johannes Saresberiensis, *Entheticus* (ed. Giles), v, p. 244, verses 185 ff.:

> *Non quia numinibus falsis reverentia detur*
> *Sed sub verborum tegmine vera latent*
> *Vera latent rerum variarum tecta figuris*
> *Nam sacra vulgari publica jura vetant.*

[36] See Lester K. Born, "Ovid and Allegory," *Speculum* (1934), pp. 362–379. We are greatly indebted to this interesting article.—As to the date of the introduction of Ovid into the program of the schools, Born points out (p. 363, n. 5) that scholars are not in agreement. Traube, *Vorlesungen und Abhandlungen,* II, *Einleitung in die lateinische Philologie des Mittelalters,* Munich (1911), p. 115, calls the eighth and ninth centuries *aetas Virgiliana;* the tenth and eleventh, *aetas Horatiana;* and the twelfth and thirteenth, *aetas Ovidiana.* On Ovid's standing during the Middle Ages, see G. Pansa, *Ovidio nel medioevo e nella tradizione popolare* (Sulmona, 1924).

[37] *Loc. cit.,* verses 19–20.

[38] The *Florilegium* studied by Huemer (*Zur Geschichte der klassischen Studien im Mittelalter* [1881], pp. 415–422) is made up of fourteen books, nine taken from "pagan" authors and five from Ovid.

popularity. His authority is invoked, for instance, to prove such propositions as this: "De summa dei potentia et voluntatis eius efficacia" ("The supreme power of God and the efficacy of his will").

In another collection of edifying texts [39] we come, surprisingly enough, upon a set of extracts from the *Metamorphoses* interpreted for use by nuns. As a crowning touch, the goddesses are represented as being nuns themselves. The gods are the clergy, and their marriages are the meetings of monks and nuns:

Abbatissarum genus et grex omnis earum
Sunt Pallas plane, tria virginis ora Dianae,
Juno, Venus, Vesta, Thetis; observantia vestra
Est expressa satis cultu tantae deitatis . . .[40]

But other explanations of the whole of the *Metamorphoses* appear, becoming increasingly numerous.[41] Examples are the prose commentary by Arnolphe of Orléans, and the *Integumenta,* in verse, by John of Garland.[42] But the most important example is furnished us by the mammoth poem known as the *Ovide moralisé,* composed in or near the first years of the fourteenth century [43] by an anonymous author who has sometimes been identified with Philippe de Vitry, bishop of Meaux, and sometimes with Chrestien Legouais de Sainte-Maure.

Here the allegorical principle is clearly formulated. In the *Metamorphoses,* the author declares, instruction may be derived from everything:

Tout est pour nostre enseignement.

In fact, he sees the whole of Christian morality in the poem, and even the Bible itself. The Argus eyes that Juno scatters over the tail of the peacock

[39] W. Wattenbach, "Mitteilungen aus zwei Handschriften der K. Hof- und Staatsbibl.," *Sitzungberichte der K. Bayer. Akad. der Wissensch. zu München,* III (1873), pp. 665–747.

[40] *Loc. cit.,* p. 697, verses 62, ff. ("The abbesses and their flock are obviously Pallas, virgin Diana, Juno, Venus, Vesta, Thetis; the reverence due to you is expressed clearly enough by the cult of so great a deity.")

[41] We shall not cite them all here; see Born, art. cit., and E. Faral, *Les Arts poétiques du 12e et 13e siècle,* pp. 43–60.

[42] Both published by F. Ghisalberti: (1) "Un cultore di Ovidio nel secolo XII," *Memorie del R. Istituto Lombardo di Scienze e Lettere* (1932), pp. 157–232; (2) *Integumenta Ovidii, poemetto inedito del secolo* XIII (Milan, 1933).

[43] See Gaston Paris, "Chrétien Legouais et les autres traducteurs ou imitateurs d'Ovide": *Histoire littéraire de la France,* XXIV.—C. de Boer, *Ovide moralisé, poème du commencement du* XIVe *siècle publié d'après tous les manuscrits connus.* Amsterdam: *Verh. d. Kon. Akad. van Vetensch.* (1915–1938).

are the vanities of this world; the peacock is the vainglorious mortal who flaunts them; Diana is the Trinity; Actaeon, Jesus Christ. Phaëthon represents Lucifer and his revolt against God. Ceres looking for Proserpina is the Church seeking to recover the souls of the faithful who have strayed from the fold. Her two torches are the Old and New Testaments; the child who insults her and whom she transforms into a lizard is the Synagogue.[44]

To the same century belong the *Allegorie* on Ovid of Giovanni del Virgilio;[45] the *Moralia super Ovidii Metamorphoses* of the Dominican Robert Holkott; the *Reductorium morale* of the Benedictine Pierre Bersuire, who "moralizes" Ovid in his fifteenth book, and who states that he is interested solely in the edifying teachings of Fable;[46] the *Metamorphosis Ovidiana moraliter explanata* of Thomas Waleys; the *Allegorie ed esposizioni delle metamorphosi* of Giovanni dei Bonsogni, etc.

Two fifteenth-century commentaries of special interest must be added to these. One, known as the "Copenhagen Commentary," follows one of the manuscripts of the great *Ovide moralisé;*[47] the other accompanies the French translation of the *Ovide moralisé* from Bersuire's *Reductorium morale*—a translation printed in Bruges in 1484 by Colart Mansion. The two commentators make clear their intention from the start: they wish to explain the moral meaning of the fables, since "l'omme doit de toutes choses tyrer sapience et mettre a prouffit pour lui et pour les autres en incitant a bonnes moeurs et fuyant vices."[48] They justify their plans by showing that the Bible authorizes moralization, and that Christ himself made use of parables. Thus far we have seen nothing particularly new; but as Jeannette van't Sant has discerningly remarked,[49] it sometimes happens that the author of the *Commentaire* strays from moral interpretation into the realm of social criticism. In fact, the mythological divinities by no means always symbolize for him vice in gen-

[44] I, verses 4099–4150; III, 635–643; I, 4245–4260; V, 3041–3144.

[45] See Wicksteed and Gardner, *Dante and Giovanni del Virgilio* (Edinburgh, 1902), Appendix I, pp. 314–321.

[46] *Reductorium morale,* prologue: "Non intendo nisi rarissime litteralem sensum fabularum tangere, sed solum circa exposicionem moralem et allegoricam laborare."

[47] See Jeannette van't Sant, *Le Commentaire de Copenhague de l'Ovide moralisé* (Amsterdam, 1929).

[48] "Man should draw wisdom from all things, turning them to his own profit and to that of others as incitement to virtuous ways and discouragement to vice."

[49] *Op. cit.,* p. 12.

eral, but suggest the vices of his own time, and above all the vices of the great —of clergy and princes. Pluto, for example, incarnates the evil prelate; Mars and Neptune, earthly tyrants. In contrast, Saturn, Jupiter, and Apollo upon occasion represent the virtuous ecclesiastic. As for Juno, she remains the incarnation of the Church.

We must treat as a special case the Franciscan John Ridewall, who in the middle of the fifteenth century composed a mythological treatise purporting to be a renewal of Fulgentius,[50] but actually drawing upon the most divergent sources—classical and postclassical authors, the Bible and the Fathers, the encyclopedists and theologians. The chapter sequence is determined by the identification of gods with Virtues. Saturn is Prudence, and since Prudence is made up of Memory, Intelligence, and Foresight, Ridewall next treats of Saturn's children: Juno-Memoria, Neptune-Intelligencia, Pluto-Providencia; and finally of Jupiter-Benevolencia, who sums up Prudentia, Sapientia, and Intelligencia. To Pluto are subordinated Cerberus-Cupiditas and Proserpina-Beatitudo. Similarly, Apollo is Truth; Danaë, Modesty; Perseus, Courage, etc. The detailed working out of this allegorical analysis is carried to fantastic extremes. For instance, Juno, as we have seen, is identified with Memory, and therefore has the following attributes: she is veiled, crowned with a rainbow, and perfumed; she holds a scepter, is bound by a golden chain, surrounded by peacocks, etc.[51] (*fig. 30*). All these details are explained by the very fact that the goddess represents memory.

Memory does, of course, keep alive the recollection of sin: hence the veil behind which Juno may hide her shame. The recollection of sin leads to repentance, and thus to reconciliation with God: this explains the rainbow, sign of divine forgiveness. Reconciliation gives birth to spiritual consolation, which fills the soul with rapture: hence the perfumes. And having, by virtue of Memory, attained repentance and reconciliation, the soul in its new state of blessedness regains that mastery of itself which sin had caused it to lose: hence the scepter, etc.[52] The extraordinary ingenuity of the commentary is ap-

[50] Johannes Ridovalensis, *Fulgentius metaforalis*. See the important study by H. Liebeschütz, *Fulgentius metaforalis, ein Beitrag zur Geschichte der antiken Mythologie im Mittelalter*. Studien der Bibl. Warburg (Leipzig, 1926).

[51] In Chapter 1 of part II we shall trace the various elements of this iconography.

[52] Text in Liebeschütz, *op. cit.*, pp. 88–90.

parent, especially when we consider that each interpretation rests upon at least one supporting authority—Cicero, St. Augustine, or Bernard of Chartres. This is without doubt our most curious monument of the application of Christian allegory to mythology.

*

Rabelais' ironic verdict on the allegorizers, in the prologue of *Gargantua*, is well known: "Croiez vous en vostre foy qu'onques Homère, escrivant l'Iliade et Odysée, pensast es allegories lesquelles de luy ont calfreté Plutarche, Heraclides, Ponticq, Eustatie, Pharnute, et ce que d'iceulx Politien a desrobé? Si le croiez, vous n'approchez ne de pieds ne de mains à mon opinion, qui decrète icelles aussi peu avoir esté songées d'Homère, que d'Ovide en ses Métamorphoses les Sacremens de l'Evangile." [53]

30. Juno-Memoria

It is readily assumed that most of Rabelais' contemporaries shared this attitude of his. In fact, one of the essential differences usually said to exist between the Middle Ages and the Renaissance has to do with this very matter. Whereas the medieval cult of ancient literature was not disinterested, but

[53] "Do you honestly believe that Homer, when he wrote the *Iliad* and the *Odyssey*, had in mind the allegories which have been foisted off on him by Plutarch, Heraclides, Ponticus, Eustathius, and Phornutus, and which Politian has purloined from them? If you do believe this, you are far indeed from my opinion, which is that Homer could no more have dreamed of anything of the sort than Ovid in his *Metamorphoses* could have been thinking of the Gospel Sacraments."

looked to the classics for moral sustenance and studied them only in their "Christian" aspects,[54] the Renaissance, free from such scruples, is thought to have looked on classical literature as a source of pleasure, aesthetic as well as sensuous. As a logical consequence, it must have wished to banish allegory, which hid or disguised the real figures of the gods.

In reality, when examined more closely [55] this traditional distinction is seen to rest on exceedingly insecure foundations. Again we have confirming evidence. First of all, the jeers of Rabelais were no more effective than the diatribes of Luther [56] in checking the vogue for "moralizations" of Ovid. Already numerous in France and Italy [57] at the beginning of the century, toward its close they had spread over all of Europe.[58] This should by no means be interpreted as the survival of an exclusively popular tradition. As we are about to see, the humanists themselves had not abandoned the search for hidden meanings in the literature of Fable, and this despite their direct and familiar contact with antiquity—or should we perhaps say because of that very contact? For the ancients whom they interrogated so passionately were in many cases the last representatives of paganism, the most extreme exponents of mythological exegesis, and in particular of the allegorical method.[59] It is from Heraclitus, Phornutus, the pseudo Plutarch (as Rabelais quite rightly observes) that Politian "purloins" his interpretations of Homer.

The mention of Politian, indeed, opens up a fruitful path of inquiry. This eminent "allegorizer" was close to the circle of Quattrocento Platonists grouped about Marsilio Ficino, leading spirit of the famous Academy whose membership included a number of exegetes bent upon extracting profound

[54] See, for example, Imbart de la Tour, *Les origines de la Réforme* (Paris, 1909), II, pp. 315 ff.

[55] See H. Bremond, *Histoire littéraire du sentiment religieux en France,* I: *L'humanisme dévot,* I, 2.

[56] Luther indeed, in his turn, violently attacks the "moralizers" of Ovid, "who turn Apollo into Christ and Daphne into the Virgin Mary"; his motives are religious (he compares allegory to a seductive courtesan, invention of Satan and of corrupt monks), but he is perhaps also influenced by Melanchthon, who was hostile to the symbolic method. *Enarratio in Genesin,* 30, 9; *Werke,* XLIII (Weimar, 1912), 668.

[57] Editions of Thomas Waleys (Lyons, 1510, 1513, 1518, 1519; Milan, 1517); Nicolò Agostini, *Tutti gli libri di Ovidio Metam.,* with allegories in prose (Venice, 1522); *Le grand Olympe des Histoires poétiques du prince de poésie Ovide Naso . . .* (Lyons, 1532).

[58] *Fabularum interpretatio* (Cambridge, 1584); *Metamorph. Ovidii . . . enarrationibus . . . et allegoriis . . . expositae* (Frankfort, 1536); *Las transformaciones di Ovidio en lengua española con las allegorias* (Antwerp, 1595). —See R. Schevill, *Ovid and the Renascence in Spain* (Berkeley, 1913), pp. 234–250.

[59] See H. Pinard de la Boullaye, *Manuel d'histoire des religions,* II, pp. 148–149.

truths from myth and Fable. Cristoforo Landino refuses to think of the creations of the poets as mere flights of the imagination, and discovers the secrets of wisdom in Virgil; Caelius Rhodiginus sees Kronos as the Divine Intelligence, and the struggle between Ares and Pallas as the combat between Passion and Reason. It has even been thought that Ficino himself was author of a treatise which scrutinizes the inner meaning of the Golden Fleece and the legends associated with it.[60] It is certainly in this milieu that the headquarters of allegory in the fifteenth and the early part of the sixteenth century must be sought. Indeed, what could be more natural? The humanists saw Plato through the eyes of Porphyry, Iamblichus, and Proclus, all three of whom, as edited by Ficino, assumed extraordinary prestige in their eyes. With such persuasive examples before them, they believed that in systematically exploring mythology in search of concealed meanings they were applying the master's own method: "universam poesim aenigmatum esse plenam docet Plato."

Let us note in passing that when the humanists had once begun trying to read the riddles hidden beneath the surface of fable, they were tempted to implant ideas of their own there in turn. The pagan myths did, in fact, serve as vehicle for the philosophical thought of the Renaissance. When Lorenzo Valla treats of free will, he symbolizes divine prescience by Apollo, omnipotence by Jupiter.[61] Later, under the influence of the Florentine Academy, Charles de Bouelles breathed new life into the ancient theme of Prometheus—in this case reverting to pure Platonic tradition, the tradition of Protagoras.[62] The lesser scholars and poets proceeded to "Platonize" in the same sense. A Dorat, for example, was not satisfied with showing his disciples that Homer was in reality a moralist:

Seria multa jocis involvens veraque fictis.[63]

[60] See O. Gruppe, *Geschichte der klassischen Mythologie* (Leipzig, 1921), pp. 27 ff.—Cristoforo Landino, *Questiones Camaldulenses* (Florence, c. 1480); Caelius Rhodiginus, *Lectionum antiquarum Libri* XXX (Venice, 1516).

On the Neoplatonic exegesis of myths in Ficino's circle, see Ch. Lemmi, *The Classical Deities in Bacon, A Study in Mythological Symbolism* (Baltimore, 1933), Introduction, pp. 15–20.

[61] *De libero arbitrio*, fol. 1004 ff.

[62] *De sapiente*, VIII (1510). Edited by R. Klibansky, in E. Cassirer, *Individuum und Cosmos* (1927), pp. 299–412.

[63] ("Mingling many serious thoughts with playful ones, much truth with fiction.") *Poemata*, pt. 2. *Epigrammatum libri* III, I, p. 15. This formula recalls that used by Theodulph of Orléans in speaking of Ovid. Cf. *supra*, p. 92.

He further taught them the necessity of concealing truth beneath the mantle of myth, and how to do it:

> *. . . Comment*
> *On doit feindre et cacher les fables proprement,*
> *Et à bien déguiser la vérité des choses*
> *D'un fabuleux manteau dont elles sont encloses.*[64]

But in the light of Neoplatonism, the humanists discovered in mythology something other and much greater than a concealed morality: they discovered religious teaching—the Christian doctrine itself.

Interpretation by means of symbols, in fact, made it possible not only to discern a lofty wisdom beneath fictions of the most diverse character and the most unedifying appearance: it further led to a grasp of the fundamental relationship between this profane wisdom (variable in its outward form, but immutable in its teaching) and the wisdom of the Bible. Just as Plato accords with Moses,[65] and Socrates "confirms" Christ,[66] so Homer's voice is that of a prophet. And the Magi of Persia and Egypt, who in their turn masked sacred maxims under a cloak of Fable, are linked to the sages of Israel.[67] Against this background, it was inevitable that the same idea which declining paganism had evolved [68] should occur to the humanists—namely, that all religions have the same worth, and that under their varied forms, however puerile and monstrous in seeming, is hidden a common truth. Marsilio Ficino leans toward a sort of universal theism, with Platonism as its gospel.[69] According to others,[70] the ancient peoples, even including the barbarians, shared from the beginning in the Christian revelation; either it became altered in their hands, or the sages of each nation deliberately disguised it in order to protect it from vulgar profanation.

This will explain certain strange utterances, among them Erasmus' sug-

[64] Ronsard, *Hymne de l'automne* (ed. P. Laumonier), IV, p. 313.

[65] *Concordia Mosis et Platonis. Marsili Ficini opera* (Basel, 1561), I.

[66] "Confirmatio Christianorum per Socratica," *op. cit.*, p. 868.

[67] Cf. the parallel between Biblical "wise men" and those of the Gentiles, *supra*, pp. 16 ff.

[68] Byzantine writers had taken up the same idea; in the eleventh century Psellos does his best to make Homer into a prophet of Christianity, and to reconcile Plato and Jesus. Furthermore, Gemistos (= Plethon) is known to have influenced Marsilio Ficino.

[69] Ficino's biography of Plato, placed at the head of his translation (*Omnia divini Platonis opera tralatione M. F.* [Lyons, 1584]), has the character of the life of a saint.

[70] See Agostino Steuco, *De perenni philosophia libri* X (1540).

gestion that more profit is perhaps to be derived from reading the literature of Fable with its allegorical content in mind than from the Scriptures taken merely literally: "Immo fortasse plusculo fructu legetur poetica cum allegoria, quam narratio sacrorum librorum, si consistas in cortice." [71] Or, again, this somewhat disturbing admission of Mutianus Rufus to one of his friends: "Est unus deus et una dea. Sed sunt multa uti numina ita et nomina: Jupiter, Sol, Apollo, Moses, Christus, Luna, Ceres, Proserpina, Tellus, Maria. Sed haec cave enunties. Sunt enim occulta silentio tamquam Eleusinarum dearum mysteria. Utendum est fabulis atque enigmatum integumentis in re sacra." [72]

Thus we may see how far certain humanists were willing to go along this path; they did not stop even at heresy. Neoplatonic exegesis, which had presented them with hitherto undreamed-of possibilities of reconciliation between the Bible and mythology, had now so obscured the distinction between the two that Christian dogma no longer seemed acceptable in anything but an allegorical sense. While it was no doubt best for people as a whole to continue to accept the traditional teachings with naïve faith, learned men, with their more enlightened minds, should be able to discern the inevitable part played in Christianity, as in pagan belief, by the weaving of fables.[73]

*

A PARALLEL influence reinforced that of Neoplatonism. In 1419, Cristoforo de'Buondelmonti, a Florentine priest traveling over the island of Andros, bought there a Greek manuscript which he brought back with him to Italy. This was the *Hieroglyphica* of Horapollo Niliacus, an obscure Alexandrian of the second or fourth century A.D., who claimed in this work to set forth the

[71] *Enchiridion militis Christiani* (Basel, 1518), p. 63. Erasmus gives as examples Circe, Tantalus, Sisyphus, and the Labors of Hercules.

[72] ("There is but one god and one goddess, but many are their powers and names: Jupiter, Sol, Apollo," etc. "But have a care in speaking these things. They should be hidden in silence as are the Eleusinian mysteries; sacred things must needs be wrapped in fable and enigma.") *Der Briefwechsel des Mutianus Rufus* (ed. Krause [Cassel, 1885]), 28.—Mutianus adds: "Tu, Jove, hoc est Optimo Maximo Deo propitio, contemne tacitus deos minutos. Quum Jovem nomino, Christum intellige et verum Deum . . ." ("You, since Jupiter, the best and greatest god, is propitious to you, may despise lesser gods in silence. When I say Jupiter, understand me to mean Christ and the true God.")

[73] See the biography of M. Rufus in F. Halbauer, *Mutianus Rufus* (Leipzig, 1929).

hidden meaning of the sacred symbols used in ancient Egypt.[74] Everyone believed that a real discovery had been made. In reality, all that Horapollo did was to sanction the mistaken view of hieroglyphics which had arisen by way of Apuleius, Plutarch, and Plotinus—namely, that they formed an ensemble of rebuses designed to make religious precepts incomprehensible to the profane. Later, Marsilio Ficino and his circle showed the greatest enthusiasm for this little treatise, which so admirably confirmed their theories. Naturally, they supposed that the great minds of Greece had been initiated into these Egyptian "mysteries"—which, in their turn, were of course one more prefiguration of the teachings of Christ.[75]

The *Hieroglyphica* played a considerable role both in humanistic thinking and in art.[76] The work was printed for the first time by Aldus in 1505, but well before that date it had inspired a chapter of Leon Battista Alberti's *De re aedificatoria,*[77] and had manifestly influenced the illustrations of a famous book, the *Hypnerotomachia Poliphili,* or *Dream of Poliphilo,* by Francesco Colonna.[78] But Horapollo's example inspired the humanists, above all, to look for some contemporary equivalent of the ancient cryptograms. This equivalent was offered by the *emblemata,* the prototype of which was provided by Alciati in his first collection, published in 1531.[79] The "emblem" is a picture which hides a moral lesson; an accompanying explanation makes

[74] *Ori Apollonis Niliaci de sacris notis et sculpturis libri* II (title of the Kerver edition [Paris, 1551]). Furthermore, Horapollo knows the hieroglyphics of the Roman period much better than his contemporaries do. See the critical edition by Fr. Sbordone, *Hori Apollonis Hieroglyphica* (Naples, 1940), and *The Hieroglyphics of Horapollo,* translated by George Boas (Bollingen Series XXIII, New York, 1950).

[75] Cf. the address to the reader in the *Hieroglyphica* of Pierio Valeriano (ed. of 1575): ". . . ut sane non temere Pythagoram, Platonem, aliosque summos viros ad Aegyptios doctrinae gratia profectos intelligas: quippe cum hieroglyphice loqui nihil aliud sit, quam divinarum humanarumque rerum naturam aperire." (". . . you will understand that it is not by mere chance that Pythagoras, Plato, and other great men went to the Egyptians to acquire learning, as speaking through hieroglyphs means nothing less than revealing the nature of things, divine and human.")

[76] We shall naturally treat of the *Hieroglyphica* only in relation to mythology. General studies will be found in K. Giehlow, "Die Hieroglyphenkunde des Humanismus in der Allegorie der Renaissance," *Jahrb. d. Kunstsamml. d. Allerhöch. Kaiserhauses,* XXXII (1915), and in L. Volkmann, *Bilderschriften der Renaissance, Hieroglyphik und Emblematik in ihren Beziehungen und Fortwirkungen* (Leipzig, 1923).

[77] Bk. VIII, ch. iv.

[78] Published in 1499, but written as early as 1467.

[79] See the invaluable work of Mario Praz, *Studies in Seventeenth Century Imagery,* I, Studies of the Warburg Institute, III (1939), a study of the origin and later history of the emblems and devices, seen by the author as products of the same spirit which produced the epigrams and *concetti.*

it possible to recognize the meaning behind the image. Alciati, of course, borrowed from Horapollo, his model, but he used many other sources as well. He took his texts from the Latin fabulists and historians, especially from Martial and the poets of the *Anthology;* the epigram, in its sententious brevity, lent itself ideally to his purpose. As for the pictures, aside from a few bizarre figures these represent animals or plants, sometimes human beings, and sometimes, lastly, gods.

Mythological characters play a prominent part.[80] Leafing through Alciati's *Emblematum liber*, we find Pan, Bacchus, Juno, Thetis, Minerva, Hercules, the Graces and Harpies, Scylla and Niobe, Tantalus and Prometheus, Ganymede, Actaeon, Icarus, Narcissus, Proteus, etc. The eye dwells on these figures with delight; many of them are charming. But we must not forget that they have a further function—either to symbolize some vice or virtue or to embody a moral truth. Faunus represents *luxuria;* Tantalus, avarice; Bellerophon, intelligence and courage overcoming obstacles; Ganymede, the unsullied soul finding its joy in God. Pallas, with the dragon at her side, signifies the virgin's need for strict guardianship and for protection against the snares of Love (*Emblema* XXII):

Vera haec effigies innuptae est Palladis: ejus
Hic draco, qui dominae constitit ante pedes.
Cur divae comes hoc animal? Custodia rerum
Huic data: sic lucos, sacraque templa colit.
Innuptas opus est cura asservare puellas
Pervigili: laqueos undique tendit Amor.[81]

Venus placing her foot on a tortoise (*fig. 39*), an image borrowed from Pausanias, teaches that women should remain at home and be chary of speech (*Emblema* CXCV):

. . . *Manere domi, et tacitas decet esse puellas.*[81a]

[80] Dinet, in his *Cinq Livres des Hiéroglyphes* (Paris, 1614), devotes an entire book—the fifth (pp. 548 ff.)—to the hieroglyphs which can be drawn from the ancient gods.

[81] "This is the true portrait of Virgin Pallas: this is her dragon, at the feet of his mistress. Why is that animal a companion to the goddess? Because it has the custody of things: thus it protects the sacred woods and the temples. Unmarried girls should be guarded with ever-watchful care: Love lays his nets [snares] everywhere."

[81a] Venus with foot on tortoise occurs in ancient examples (Berlin Museum, 5th century B.C.) and in Hellenistic statues, especially at Dura-Europos, Cyrene, etc. (The symbol seems to have been preserved chiefly in the East.) Thus the source may have been not solely literary.

For Alciati's imitators, this figure took on new significance, and was enriched with new details:

La tortue dit que femme n'aille loing,
Le doigt levé, qu'à parler ne s'avance,
La clef en main dénote qu'avoir soing
Doibt sur les biens du mary par prudence.[82]

Each attribute of Bacchus exhibits one of the harmful effects of intemperance,[83] and each of the various aspects of Mercury conceals some sage maxim.[84] But it is the likenesses of Cupid which offer the emblem-maker the richest material, if not the most varied. One image shows him riding in a chariot drawn by lions which he has tamed, proof that the power of Love is irresistible (CV); again, he holds a fish in one hand and flowers in the other, showing that both land and sea are subject to the laws of Love (CVI). Elsewhere (CVII) we see lightning expending itself in vain against his weapons and his wings—he is but made the stronger. Finally, Alciati enumerates and comments critically on the attributes usually assigned to the god by the poets, and tells us how he himself interprets them; he then offers his own description of Love, conforming to the god's true nature.[85] This theme and its variations, derived from the *Anthology* (two of the emblems also portray wounded Love), were certainly thoroughly familiar to the Renaissance academies, where Cupid's arrows, his wings, and his bound eyes were favorite topics of discussion.

At this juncture, one may pause in some surprise at the banal character of the emblems. "What!" one may well exclaim, "is there anything mysterious here? Are these subjects profound, these teachings sacred?" The disappointed reader, finding nothing but commonplaces clothed in transparent dress, begins with good reason to wonder at the presumption which placed such futilities under the patronage of the Sphinx. The truth is that the science of emblems had two contradictory ends in view.[86] On the one hand, it did in-

[82] La Perrière, *Emblèmes* (ed. 1599). ("The tortoise means that a wife should not go far; the lifted finger, that she should refrain from talking; the key, that she should take good care of her husband's possessions.")

[83] XXV: *In statuam Bacchi.*

[84] VIII, XCVIII, CXVIII. Junius, another celebrated emblematist, analyzed Mercury's attributes one by one: *Insignia Mercurii quid?*

[85] CXIII: *In statuam Amoris.*

[86] This has been clearly seen by M. Praz, *op. cit.*

deed aim at establishing an esoteric means of expression; on the other, however, it wished to be didactic, offering lessons which, through their visual presentation, would be within reach of everyone. Its ambition was to be at one and the same time an occult and a popular language. The humanists do not appear to have been disturbed by this contradiction, and unfailingly regarded the emblems as a sublime creation of the human spirit.[87] It should thus not surprise us that this pseudo science led them, as their pseudo Platonism did, to carry their reconciliation of pagan mythology and Christian teaching to the point where the two were actually merged.

In the science of emblems, furthermore, we see the first outlines of a movement which culminated in "the embrace of profane and sacred philosophy." [88] We have already seen Ganymede incarnating the joys of the innocent soul enraptured by God; one of Alciati's glossators even recalls at this point the words of Christ, "Suffer little children to come unto me." [89] But this is not all. Alciati offers us, in addition to a lascivious Cupid, a modest and virtuous Cupid (Emblems CIX, CX) who symbolizes love of virtue—divine love. Alexandrian eroticism had been spiritualized and moralized in the same way by opposing Ἀντέρως to Ἔρως (*figs. 100, 101*). But a further step is soon taken: Cupid yields his bow and arrows to the Infant Jesus, who in his turn uses them to pierce human hearts.[90]

*

THUS THE GREAT allegorical current of the Middle Ages, far from shrinking, flows on in an ever widening channel. And the gods of the Renaissance are still in many cases didactic figures—instruments for the edification of the soul.

Certain later contributions may have rejuvenated mythological allegory in its outward look; they brought to it nothing essentially new. Neither Neoplatonism nor the study of hieroglyphics, in spite of the high expectations

[87] As serious a scholar as Scaliger laid great stress upon them; they are such, he says, as to vie with any mind: "ut cumquovis ingenio certare possint." (*J. C. Scaligeri Judicium*, at the head of the published editions of Alciati.)

[88] Pansa Mutio, *De osculo ethnicae et Christianae philosophiae* (1601).

[89] This commentator is Claude Mignault (= "Minos"), who issued numerous editions of Alciati, beginning in 1571.

[90] E.g., in O. Vaenius, *Amoris divini emblemata*. We shall study the Christian emblems of the late sixteenth century in Bk. II, chap. ii.

that they raised and the bold ventures they provoked, brought about any decisive deviation from the medieval tradition—and that for a very simple reason. As a whole, they merely led the humanists back to the ultimate sources of that tradition. Hence the curious resemblance—sometimes almost amounting to identity—between the mythological "moralities" of the fifteenth and sixteenth centuries and those of the twelfth century, or even of the ninth or sixth. The scholar who believed that he had recovered the secret of the lost wisdom of antiquity was in reality merely returning to the hybrid doctrine that the Fathers had inherited from the last defenders of paganism.[91] He prided himself on walking in the footsteps of Plato, but the paths he followed had been well worn since the time of Fulgentius.[92]

When Alciati comments on the attributes of Cupid, he echoes the voice of Carolingian scholars. Turning back to Theodulph we find:

Tela, puer, virus, fax tuus ardor, Amor . . .[93]

And if the Renaissance transforms Alexandrian eroticism into Christian teaching, such boldness is not new: as we have seen, the Middle Ages read Scriptural meaning into the *Metamorphoses*, and nuns of the thirteenth century were devout readers of the *Ars amatoria*.

Moral or theological truths discovered beneath the mask of Fable and in the figures of the gods, the fleeting reflection of divine wisdom in profane knowledge—nothing of this had actually been invented by the Renaissance. It was, in the words of Pierre de Nolhac, the "rêverie médiévale"[94] to which the Renaissance had succumbed—the haunting chimera, born on the ruins of paganism, of an impossible reconciliation.

The survival of the gods in these different systems of moral allegory is here again confirmed by a wealth of iconographical material from which only a few examples can be chosen.

The first century of the Christian era—to go no farther back in time[95]—furnishes us with two convincing illustrations. The delicate stucco reliefs of

[91] It is significant that for his commentary on Alciati, Mignault invokes now Plato, now the Fathers of the Church.

[92] O. Gruppe, who emphasizes this fact (*op. cit.*, pp. 27–28), is nevertheless surprised that Platonism did not inspire more daring theories.

[93] Cf. *supra*, p. 90.

[94] *Ronsard et l'humanisme*, p. 71.

[95] See R. Hinks, *Myth and Allegory in Ancient Art* (1939).

the subterranean basilica at the Porta Maggiore in Rome offer eloquent proof of the spirituality with which the ancient mythology had come to be suffused. These genii, bacchantes, and demigods are charged with symbolism. Thus the rape of Ganymede by Jupiter's eagle and that of the daughters of Leucippus by the Dioscuri typify the ascent of the soul to immortality; Marsyas, Agave, the Danaids, on the other hand, image the punishments meted out to ignorance and pride.[96] As Carcopino has shown,[97] the decoration as a whole embodies the great esoteric doctrines associated with the Pythagorean sects. Need we recall, moreover, that the Christian art of the catacombs borrowed from mythology the symbolic motif of *amorini* as vintagers which later caused the Basilica of Constantine to be mistaken for a temple of Bacchus! [97a]

Similarly, we see the Middle Ages Christianizing, or "moralizing," pagan figures. In the previous chapter we have remarked upon the singular use made by scholars of gems engraved with likenesses of the gods. They were not always prompted by ignorance or naïveté, but sometimes deliberately transformed the meaning of an image by means of a simple inscription. Cupid became the Angel of the Annunciation, and Minerva the Virgin Mary.[98]

But above all, the allegorical treatises in which the attributes of pagan divinities were systematically interpreted in a moral sense gave rise to curious sets of miniatures. Within their moralizing framework, these treatises contained extremely precise and visually clear descriptions—a source of ready inspiration to the illustrator. It is thus, for example, that a Vatican manuscript (Palatinus 1066) has been provided with lively images of Juno, Neptune, Jupiter, Pluto, and Saturn, which, it is true, bear little resemblance

[96] Lucretius (III, 976–1021), who denies the existence of Hell and Tartarus, saw the torments of the Danaids, and those of Tantalus, Tityos, Sisyphus, etc . . . as the sufferings of souls agitated by vain terrors or guilty passions:

Sed Tityos nobis hic est, in amore jacentem
Quem volucres lacerant . . .

("But our Tityos is here, cast down in love, whom the winged things tear": LCL.)

[97] J. Carcopino, *La Basilique pythagoricienne de la Porte Majeure*, 3rd ed. (Paris, 1926), esp. II, 1: "Mythologie et mystères."

[97a] See also the silver vase from Alexandria with similar subjects. Cf. A. Adriani, "Le Gobelet en argent des amours vendageurs du Musée d'Alexandrie," Société Royale d'Archéologie d'Alexandrie, Cahier 1 (1939).

[98] In the thirteenth century, an abbot of St. Étienne in Caen had the following words engraved around a Cupid: "Ecce mitto angelum meum"; in 1296, the chapter of Noyon surrounded a Minerva with the inscription: "Ave Maria gratia plena." See E. Müntz, "La tradition antique au Moyen-Age" (reviewing Springer, *Das Nachleben der Antike im Mittelalter* [Bonn, 1886]), *Journal des Savants* (Oct. 1887—Jan.–March, 1888); and Alma Frey-Sallmann, *Aus dem Nachleben antiker Göttergestalten* (Leipzig, 1931), chap. ii, D.

to the rulers of Olympus, but in which every pictured detail embodies some moral idea. We thus see Juno:

> *quae pingitur:*
> *vertice velata, iride sertata,*
> *unguentis afflata, sceptro decorata*
> *et auro ligata . . .*
> *avibus vallata*
> *humore rigata et luce lustrata.*[99]

The miniaturist has provided a point-for-point reproduction of this portrait (*fig. 30*), the meaning of which receives a learned explanation in the *Fulgentius metaforalis.*[100]

Such descriptions, issuing from the edifying tradition of Fulgentius and Martianus Capella, and collected, as we shall see later, in mythographical compilations, passed from these sources into literature. It has long been realized that the French epics and romances are full of mythological characters. Frequently these figures issue straight from Ovid; often, however, following the ancient use of ἔκφρασις (*descriptio*), they slip into the rhetorical description of a work of art—of a statue, wall painting, tapestry, tent, or war chariot.[101] But if we turn to the *Roman de la Rose,* we shall find there the tradition which interests us. The predilection of Guillaume de Lorris for allegory is well known; furthermore, it was from the Vatican Mythographers I and II [102] that Jean de Meung derived his knowledge of mythology. That great scholar was unquestionably fitted to recognize, beneath the "integumenz" of Fable,

> *une grant partie*
> *des secrez de philosophie . . .*

99 Liebeschütz, *op. cit.*, p. 88. (. . . "who is depicted with a veil on her head, wreathed by a rainbow, fanned with perfumes, decorated with a sceptre, bound by a golden chain, surrounded with birds, moistened by dew, illuminated by light. . . .") Liebeschütz reproduces the miniatures.

100 See *supra*, p. 94. Cf. the illustrations in another ms. of the *Fulgentius metaforalis* (Rome, Vatican, Palat. lat. 1726 [*fig. 31*]).

101 On ἔκφρασις in antiquity, see R. Hinks, *op. cit.*, pp. 11–12; and A. Frey-Sallmann, *op. cit.*, chap. i. In the *Roman de Thèbes* (vv. 4713–4774), Jupiter, fighting against the giants, is *seen on the chariot of Amphiaraos* (holding thunderbolt and spear):

> *Jupiter est de l'autre part,*
> *Un foildre tient et un dart. . . .*

Also, in the *Lai de Guigemar* (vv. 233 ff.), of Marie de France, Venus is said to have been admirably represented in painting:

> *Vénus la déesse d'Amur*
> *Fu très bien mise en la peinture.*

102 See E. Langlois, *Origines et sources du Roman de la Rose* (Paris, 1891), pp. 134–135.

The illustrations of the *Roman de la Rose* themselves reflect the same tendency.[103] The gods, for the most part, are indistinguishable in dress and attitude from the noble lords and ladies—and resemble them, also, in that their sole function is to clothe abstractions in living and graceful form. A figure, mirror in hand, which we might take to be Venus, is actually "Oiseuse," symbol of the leisure which opens the way to amorous dalliance, and own

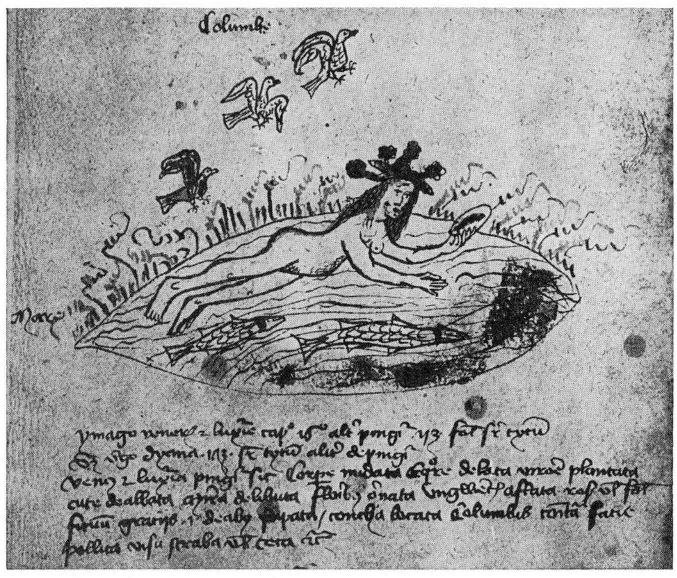

31. Venus-Luxuria

sister of the Luxuria who is contrasted with Chastity in the stained-glass windows of the French cathedrals.[104] In a manuscript of the *Echecs amoureux,*[105] a delightful miniature (*fig. 32*) shows us another Venus with mirror, standing nude in a garden, surrounded by flowers. This is again a symbol—of the Amorous Life, to which are opposed the Active and the Contemplative Life, seen a bit further to the rear in the guise of Pallas and Juno. Three

[103] See A. Kuhn, "Die Illustration des Rosenromans," *Jahrbuch d. Kunsthist. Samml.*, XXXI (1912).

[104] See É. Mâle, *L'art religieux du* XIIIe *siècle*, pp. 120–121 and fig. 59.

[105] Bibl. Nat., ms. fr. 143.

32. Nature with Venus, Juno, and Pallas

goddesses in a beautiful garden? No; three moral ideas, an allegory of Fulgentius.[106] Similarly, some manuscripts of the *Ovide moralisé* (for example, cod. 742 of the Bibliothèque de Lyon) offer us small pictures, ravishing in their delicate irony and freshness, but each containing a lesson or sermon (*figs. 33–36*).

*

HOWEVER they may differ in outward appearance, certain works of art of the Italian Renaissance are in spirit very close to our medieval images.

In the Louvre are two celebrated representations of the *psychomachia* in which pagan divinities incarnate the virtues and vices. Both were painted for the young and cultivated duchess of Mantua, Isabella d'Este. One is Mantegna's *Triumph of Wisdom over Vice* (*fig. 37*),[107] where Wisdom appears in the guise of Minerva. Helmeted, shield on arm and lance in hand, escorted by Diana and by Chastity, she puts to rout Venus, mother of all the Vices, who are shown swarming in a stagnant pool—Dalliance (Otia),[108] Sloth, Hate, Suspicion, Avarice. The other is Perugino's *Combat of Love and Chastity*.[109] Here we have a somewhat timid, though exact, rendering of a theme furnished by the court poet Paride da Cesarea: "Our poetic invention, which I greatly desire you to paint, is a battle between Chastity and Lust, in which *Pallas and Diana* shall be shown manfully struggling against *Venus and Amor*. . . ." Cesarea advised the artist to introduce other episodes into the background of the painting, showing what happens when Chastity succumbs to Love: the Rape of Europa, Daphne pursued by Apollo, Glaucera and Mercury, Proserpina and Pluto. . . . Fable, in other words, is now merely a repertoire of symbolic figures and moral examples.

[106] Cf. *Mythologiae*, II, 1 (see *supra*, p. 89). See another illustration of the *Vita triplex* in Palat. 1066, f. 230 v.

[107] On this painting, see R. Foerster, *Jahrb. der kön. preuss. Kunstsamml.*, XXII (1901–1902), p. 480; and R. Schneider, *Bulletin soc. hist. de l'art fr.* (1920), p. 94; *Revue de l'art ancien et moderne* (1923), p. 14; E. Wind, *Bellini's Feast of the Gods* (Cambridge, Mass., 1948), p. 18.

[108] Along the bank of the pool we read the legend: "Otia si tollis, periere Cupidinis arcus." ("If you banish sloth, you defeat Cupid's bow.") This is the verse from Ovid (*Remedia Amoris*, 139) which inspired G. de Lorris' creation of "Oiseuse"; cf. *Proverbia rusticorum*, 7:

Opera cum mihi do, mihi praebet terga Cupido.
Otia si sequeris, luxuriosus eris.

("When I work, Cupid turns his back upon me; if you give yourself over to idleness, you will become voluptuous.")

[109] On this painting, see C. Yriarte, *Gazette des Beaux-Arts* (1895), II, p. 130.

33. *Jupiter and the gods*

34. *Mercury and Argus*

35. *Diana and Callisto*

36. *Pallas and the Muses*

At the height of the Cinquecento, the *Combat of Ratio and Libido*, by Baccio Bandinelli (*fig. 38*),[110] is grounded in the same tradition. It shows us another psychomachy, in which the gods play similar roles. In a contest waged with bows and arrows, Cupid, Venus, and Vulcan represent the side of Passion, while Apollo and Diana—with Mercury, Saturn, Hercules, and Jupiter in their train—are the champions of Virtue. In the sky above, Reason herself takes part in the battle, sheds light on her fellow combatants, and cov-

[110] Engraved by N. Béatrizet, 1545.

37. Wisdom overcoming the vices

ers her adversaries with dense clouds.[111] The edifying intent of the composition is still further emphasized by the legend:

Discite mortales tam praestant nubibus astra
Quam Ratio ignavis Sancta cupidinibus.[112]

[111] Cf., in Mantegna's painting, the Virtues who contemplate the battle from above, in the clouds; an inscription even refers to the Mother of the Virtues, who, according to Foerster, is the invisible figure of Truth. ("Et mihi virtutum matri succurite divi": "Come to my help, O Gods—to me who am the mother of virtues.")

[112] "O mortals, learn that the stars are as superior to clouds as Holy Reason is to base desires."

Thus, in spite of their classical suggestion and their plastic nudity, these figures, again, are instruments of morality. They take us back, far beyond the Middle Ages, to the very sources of mythological allegory: in the combat of the gods in the twentieth book of the *Iliad*, Anaxagoras early discerned a spiritual conflict, the never-ending conflict between the forces of the soul.[113]

*

ALLEGORICAL EXEGESIS, toward the end of the fifteenth century, was focused chiefly in Florence. As a natural consequence, Florentine art of that period produced great allegorical compositions, rich in inner meaning.

Botticelli's divinities come first to mind—his three Venuses and his Pallas.[114] Their languid grace and dream-filled eyes haunt the imagination but defy analysis. Painstaking and exact research [115] has thrown light on their origin, on the texts, models, and outward circumstances which brought them into being; nevertheless, their ultimate secret has not yet been penetrated—or rather, their secrets, for it is our belief that they hide several layers of allegorical meaning.

First of all, they conceal certain allusions of a personal and private nature, evocations of events prominent in Medici annals [116]—the tournament of 1475 in which Giuliano distinguished himself before the "Queen of Beauty," [117] and the return of Lorenzo, which restored peace to Florence after

[113] See Decharme, *La Critique des traditions religieuses chez les Grecs*, pp. 274–275. The battle of the gods symbolizes the struggle between moral principles (Hermes-Intelligence against Leto-Oblivion; Athena-Wisdom against Ares-Folly) or between physical forces (Apollo-Fire against Poseidon-Water).

[114] *The Birth of Venus* and the *Primavera* in the Uffizi—the Primavera being, as Vasari says (*Opere* [ed. Milanesi], II, 312), another Venus, flower-strewn by the Graces; *Venus and Mars*, in the National Gallery, London; *Pallas and the Centaur*, in the Uffizi. Another Pallas has been lost. See Poggi, "La giostra medicea del 1475 e la Pallade di Botticelli," *L'Arte* (1902), pp. 71–77, and the complementary note on the subject of the marquetry Venus in Urbino; also A. Warburg, "Die verschollene Pallas," in *Gesammelte Schriften*, I, pp. 23–25.

[115] All that need be mentioned here are the penetrating analyses by Warburg, reproduced in the *Gesammelte Schriften*, pp. 1–61, with important appendices, pp. 307–329; and the recent reinterpretation by E. H. Gombrich, "Botticelli's Mythologies, A Study on the Neoplatonic Symbolism of his Circle," *Journal of the Warburg and Courtauld Institutes*, VIII (1945), pp. 6 ff.

[116] See W. von Bode, *Sandro Botticelli*, 2nd edition (1922), IV: "Mythologische und allegorische Darstellungen im Auftrage der Mediceer."

[117] *The Birth of Venus* and *Venus and Mars*. *La giostra di Giuliano*, by Politian, shows the close connection between these paintings and the tournament.

the conspiracy of the Pazzi.[118] They also represent, in disguised form, amorous memorials and tributes dedicated by the two brothers to their "nymphs," Simonetta Vespucci and Lucrezia Donati.[119] Yet there is nothing anecdotal about these figures, with their air of remoteness and the unreality of their set-

38. Combat of Ratio and Libido

ting. They transport us to another world—to the Elysian fields among the Shades,[120] or to a universe of abstractions. The great enigmas of Nature, of Death and Resurrection, seem to hover about these dreamlike forms of Youth, Love, and Beauty, phantoms from an ideal Olympus. In this skein of symbol-

[118] *Pallas and the Centaur* (Wisdom taming brute Force).

[119] Perhaps to others as well; see A. Warburg, *op. cit.*, appendix, p. 325.

[120] The *Primavera.* When the picture was painted, Giuliano and Simonetta were dead, Simonetta's death having occurred in the month of April, as Lorenzo notes (*Commento*

ism, profound speculation and gallant gesture are intertwined, and the chronicle of a small princely court blends with legends from the old cosmogonies.[121]

Modern commentators have undoubtedly at times been guilty of further entangling the skein under pretext of identifying the strands that compose it. But if there is any domain in which ingenuity is called for, and in which even the most daring hypotheses have a chance of arriving at the truth, it is that of the circle of humanists, poets, and philosophers where this singular series of mythological scenes was conceived.[121a]

The painter's whole entourage, his clients and protectors, friends and advisers, formed a coterie of littérateurs and pedants, men who delighted in the spinning of farfetched theory. Politian, the learned interpreter of myths, who paraphrased the Homeric hymn to Aphrodite [122] in his *Giostra di Giuliano*, provided numerous themes for painting and sculpture [123] as well as for amorous rebuses,[124] much in demand at this court where the mania for "em-

---

sopra alcuni de suoi Sonetti, Opere [ed. Simioni], I, 27): "Mori questa eccellentissima donna nel mese d'aprile, nel quale tempo la terra si suole vestire di diversi fiori." ("This excellent lady died in the month of April, in which season the earth is accustomed to clothe herself with a variety of flowers.") —An Elysian Venus appears also in Tibullus, I, 3, 57 ff.—Jacobsen has carried this funereal interpretation to its extremes: "Allegoria della Primavera," *Archivio storico dell'arte* (1897), pp. 321 ff., and "Merkur als Psychopompos," *Jahrb. d. königl. preuss. Kunstsamml.* (1900), pp. 141 ff.

[121] The birth of Venus is a cosmic myth (castration of Saturn), and is so recounted by Politian, *Giostra*, st. 99; it takes place "sotto diverso volger di pianeti"; similarly, it is the appearance of the planet Venus which heralds the return of Spring (*Primavera*), with its dances and its love-making. (Cf. the planetary series by Baccio Bandinelli.)

A. Warburg and his commentators (esp. pp. 325–326) have strikingly brought out how, at this point, Botticelli's two compositions relate directly to the medieval astrological tradition.

[121a] E. Gombrich, *op. cit.*, pp. 7–60.

[122] This (unfinished) work by Politian remains the capital source for explanation of the three Venuses. It contains two sections: (1) a description, according to the principle of ἔκφρασις, of the bas-reliefs which decorate the palace of Venus (six cosmogonic allegories, one of which concerns the birth of the goddess; twelve scenes of amorous seduction, demonstrating Venus' power over the other gods); (2) the appearance of the nymph who is to convert Giuliano to love.

[123] Including the subject of Michelangelo's bas-relief of the Centaurs and Lapiths. It was in the *Giostra* that Raphael found the theme of the *Galatea*. See E. Müntz, *Les Précurseurs de la Renaissance*, p. 206.

[124] Politian composed the *impresa*, or device, of Giuliano: branches of greenwood, in flames, with the motto: "*In viridi teneras exurit flamma medullas.*" See Vasari (ed. G. Milanesi), VIII, 118. In the 1513 edition of the *Giostra*, an engraving represents Giuliano praying before an altar on which these branches burn at the feet of a statue of Pallas (see Warburg, "Die verschollene Pallas," *loc. cit.*) Lorenzo had as his emblem the laurel tree (Lorenzo = Lauro), and for motto "le temps revient" (Luigi Pulci, *La giostra fatta . . . dal Magnifico Lorenzo*, st. 64); he bore this in the tournament of 1469.—We thus see that these paintings by Botticelli are closely allied to the *imprese amorose* commonly painted on *tondi* and *cassoni.*

blems"[125] was so strong. Lorenzo the Magnificent was also Lorenzo the subtle, and one might be tempted to see in the Primavera, pensive among her flowers, nothing more than a veiled echo of his songs.[126] But here the learned voice of Pico della Mirandola is heard; he invites us to look more deeply into the mystery of Venus and the three Graces: "Qui profunde et intellectualiter divisionem unitatis Venereae in trinitatem Gratiarum . . . intellexerit, videbit modum debite procedendi in Orphica Theologia."[127]

Alma Venus quæ nam hæc facies, quid denotat illa
Testudo, molli quam pede diua premis?

39. Venus and the tortoise

And from the whole Florentine circle, gorged as they were with antiquity, there seems to arise a confused murmur of literary recollections—a strophe of Horace here, a verse of Lucretius there, a line of Ovid or Claudian, a page of Seneca or Plato.

We must lend an ear to them all in turn, since Botticelli himself undoubtedly did so. Artistically impressionable as he was, and open to every influence—disciple of Alberti, emulator of Leonardo—he had to harmonize all these voices as best he could, to reconcile these divergent aims, to crystallize the unco-ordinated emotions arising from all this erudition. Hence, perhaps, the feeling of uneasiness and expectancy which these paintings arouse.

[125] And for *mythological* emblems. Mention need be made only of the medals by Niccolò Fiorentino, such as Giovanna Tornabuoni's, with representation of Venus-Virgo and the three Graces—Castitas, Pulchritudo, Amor.

[126] For example, *Selve*, II, 122:

> . . . *Or nel loco alto e silvestre*
> *Ove dolente e trista lei si truova*
> *D'oro a l'età, paradiso terrestre*
> *E quivi il primo secol si rinnuova.*

("In that high and wooded place where languorous and sad she dwells—
In the Age of Gold, the earthly paradise—
There it is that the first century is renewed.")
Cf. the motto: "Le temps revient."

[127] *Conclusiones*, XXXI, 8. ("Whoever understands deeply and with intellect the division of the unity of Venus into a trinity of Graces, will find the proper way of advancing into Orphic theology.") Marsilio Ficino had translated the Orphic Hymns in 1462.

Elsewhere,[128] in his figures of Calumny, Fraud, Ignorance, and Remorse, Botticelli has no difficulty in confining definite concepts and moral ideas within precise contours. But here the same clear-cut and sinuous line is powerless to imprison a subject matter made up of complex ideas and elusive dreams.

40. Prudentia

At the Medici villa of Poggio a Caiano, one of the seats of the Neoplatonic Academy, further enigmas are proposed to the visitor, from the moment of his arrival, by the terra-cotta frieze[129] seen against the blue ground of the pediment. Among these figures, exquisite in their grace and their balance, we recognize Apollo and Diana in their chariot; Eternity in her cavern, with souls emerging from her breast; Janus on the threshold of the temple of War. But other scenes have defied explanation, and the meaning of the composition as a whole has not been deciphered. The artist, unquestionably following a program furnished again by Politian or by some other humanist in Lorenzo's court, was evidently charged with concealing in this work some momentous secret from the wisdom of the ancients. He succeeded only too well in his task.

*

In the first years of the sixteenth century, mythological allegory was to give rise to other supreme masterpieces.

[128] In the *Calumny of Apelles.* On the Renaissance view of this reconstruction, suggested to Botticelli by L. B. Alberti, see R. Foerster, "Die Verleumdung des Apelles in der Renaissance," *Jahrb. d. königl. preuss. Kunstsamml.* (1887), pp. 29 ff.

[129] Attributed to Giuliano da Sangallo. U. Middeldorf, "Giuliano da Sangallo and Andrea Sansovino," *Art Bulletin,* XVI (1934), pp. 112–113, suggests attribution to Sansovino.

Let us visit the famous Camera di San Paolo in Parma, painted by Correggio between 1518 and 1519. Our first impression is a completely captivating one: Diana, mighty huntress, with her bow and dog; the *amorini* playing mischievously among the leaves; above all, the ingratiating forms of deities

41. The punishment of Juno

delicately modeled in *chiaroscuro*—what could be more instantly satisfying to the senses and imagination both? On a more considered view, however, we begin to feel a certain surprise; the choice and arrangement of the supple figures first intrigues, then disturbs us. Many are frankly puzzling, and even if we recognize Adonis or Juno we cannot tell why they are there. And this playful decoration has, in fact, remained an enigma; under its apparent artlessness it conceals a wealth of symbolic intention.

This hall once formed part of a convent—more precisely, of the apartments of the abbess, Giovanna da Piacenza. This circumstance would at first appear to deepen the mystery; as a matter of fact, it provides us with the key. To be sure, a superficial observer might find it "scandalous that subjects from pagan fable should be represented in a monastery of virgins consecrated to Our Lord." [130] But what scandalizes him ought, on the contrary, to reassure him, for these subjects were deliberately suggested to Correggio by the abbess —herself a woman of intellect—or by some humanist belonging to her circle,[131] *for an edifying purpose.* Diana represents Giovanna da Piacenza, guarding her virgin flock. The figures of the Vestals, the scenes of libation and sacrifice, teach the nuns their duty. Tranquillity, Fortune, Abundance—allegories drawn from Roman medals—remind them of the advantages of their state. Finally, other images contain salutary warnings: Tellus, scorpion in hand, serves to recall the sad fate of Orion, the proud hunter who boasted of slaughtering the protégés of Diana; Juno, suspended by her hands, a heavy anvil attached to her delicate feet, as in Homer's account,[132] is a reminder of the punishment inflicted on the goddess by the supreme ruler of Olympus for having persecuted Hercules (*fig. 41*). Possibly these last two themes were meant to impress nuns who might be tempted to forsake their vows, "a coloro che dimentiche delle giurate promesse deviassero mai all'errore." [133] More probably they were intended for the visitor, who is struck by them immediately upon entering.

Thus all these delicate charms which we were but now admiring are spiritual in essence ("intellettuali bellezze," the Padre Affò calls them); each one has its message. Unexpected as the comparison may appear, this hall in a Renaissance convent has more than one trait in common with the first-century basilica that we recently discussed: [134] it is characterized by the same decorative elegance of form, the same underlying gravity of meaning, and the same evocation of sacrifices, rewards, and punishments. This is no arbitrary parallel. The Camera di San Paolo contains an inscription, "Ignem gladio ne fodias," in which we recognize a Pythagorean adage.[135] Although

130 See *Ragionamento del Padre Ireneo Affò sopra una stanza dipinta del celeberrimo Antonio Allegri da Correggio nel monasterio di San Paolo in Parma* (1794), pp. 8–9.

131 Possibly G. Anselmi, who had a daughter in the convent.

132 *Iliad*, xv, 18 ff.

133 Affò, *op. cit.*, p. 47.

134 The Pythagorean basilica at the Porta Maggiore, see *supra*, p. 105.

135 ("Do not poke the fire with a sword.") Diogenes Laërtius, *Vitae philos.*, VIII, 1, 17.

placed above the fireplace, this inscription should not be taken in its literal sense. It is an allusion to the sacred fire guarded by the Christian vestals, and an admonition against irritating the powerful directress of the establishment.[136] It, too, has the force of a warning.

There are, moreover, manifest links between the Camera di San Paolo and the allegorical tradition of the Middle Ages. Three hundred years earlier, as we have seen, nuns found the same precepts of Christian morality and virtue in the fables of Diana and Vesta, piously interpreted:

. . . Observantia vestra
Est expressa satis cultu tantae deitatis . . .[137]

Although perhaps less naïve, the learned abbess who had the words *Di bene vortant* written at the very door of her convent is worthy to be called their sister. She differs from them in being no longer content merely to interpret enigmas; she composes her own. She thus earns a place among those makers of hieroglyphs whose origin, models, and ambitions we have already discussed.[138]

*

THIS PASSION for hieroglyphs with which humanism was so thoroughly impregnated could not fail to leave its traces in the visual arts. The pseudo science of Horapollo and of the "emblematists" who emulated him did, in fact, provide artists not only with new elements of decoration,[139] but also with themes for learned allegories. Pintoricchio, Leonardo, Giovanni Bellini, and Dürer had recourse, each in turn, to this source of inspiration.[140] We shall pause to mention only a "hieroglyph" attributed to Titian, which offers special interest in connection with the tradition which concerns us here.

The work in question is a painting in the Francis Howard Collection,[141]

136 Cf. Alciati, *Syntagmata de symbolis*, Pref., *Emblematum liber* (Paris, 1608), p. 8.

137 See *supra*, p. 92.

138 See *supra*, pp. 100 ff.

139 We have already cited the *De re aedificatoria* of L. B. Alberti, VIII, and the illustrations of the *Hypnerotomachia Poliphili*. In the Latin translation of Horapollo (1517), Filippo Fasanini speaks of these "practical applications" of hieroglyphic art. Alciati alludes to them in a letter to Calvi (1522); he returns to the subject in the dedication of the 1531 edition of the *Emblematum liber*, emphasizes it in the edition of 1551.

140 See K. Giehlow, *op. cit.*, and L. Volkmann, *op. cit.* We have indicated the role of "emblematics" in the allegories of Botticelli.

141 D. von Hadeln, "Some Little-Known Works by Titian," *Burlington Magazine*, XLV (1924), pp. 179–180, reprod. pl. II, b.

representing three male heads—one seen in fullface, the other two in profile —above three animal heads, dog, wolf, and lion (*fig. 40*). The painting had been believed to represent the three ages of life, although astonishment had been expressed at strange features in the composition. Admittedly, Titian's allegories are not always clear,[142] but this six-headed monster is of an unwonted barbarity.

In reality, as recent analysis has shown,[143] we have here a curious combination of two symbols. The human heads represent Prudence, in the terms of scholastic moral theology. If we turn to *Fulgentius metaforalis,* in fact, we find that Prudentia is composed of three faculties—Memoria, Intelligencia, and Praevidentia, whose respective functions are to conserve the past, to know the present, and to foresee the future: "Tripartita perlustrat tempora vitae." [144] Hence the frequent representation of Prudence with a triple head—as, for example, in the pavement of the Siena Cathedral.[145] Thus this first symbol belongs to medieval philosophy and allegory.

It remains for us to interpret the second—the three animal heads. For this we must go much farther back in time. In his *Saturnalia,* Macrobius describes a statue of Serapis whose hand rests on a monstrous creature, at once lion, wolf, and dog. Only the three heads are visible, the bodies, which are fused together, being wrapped in the coils of a serpent. "Easque formas animalium draco conectit volumine suo." What is the meaning of this strange attribute? Macrobius himself gives the explanation. "The lion, violent and sudden, expresses the present; the wolf, which drags away its victims, is the image of the past, robbing us of memories; the dog, fawning on its master, suggests to us the future, which ceaselessly beguiles us with hope." The three symbolic animals are thus the three aspects of Time. It is manifestly this text which inspired Titian.[146] The text was familiar to the Renaissance humanists. With

142 To mention only the *Sacred and Profane Love* of the Borghese Gallery.

143 E. Panofsky and F. Saxl, "A Late Antique Religious Symbol in Works by Holbein and Titian," *Burlington Magazine,* XLIX (1926), pp. 177–181.

144 See *supra,* p. 94.

145 See also the Prudentia in the Baptistry of Bergamo; in the Palazzo Pubblico, Siena, the Prudentia of Lorenzetti holds a torch with triple flame on which is written: *praeteritum —praesens—futurum.* In the Stanza della Segnatura, Raphael has painted a Prudentia with two heads.

146 A direct derivation in the sixteenth century from the statues of Serapis is most improbable.

their taste for pseudo-Egyptian allegories, they must have been attracted by the enigmatic character of the monster and by Macrobius' ingenious explanation. In fact, this *signum triceps* had already come to light in the *Dream of Poliphilo,* and was to be seen later by Pierio Valeriano as a perfect model of the "hieroglyph." [147]

What seems to us particularly interesting in the painting attributed to Titian is the combination of the two symbols. A moment's thought will show the significance of this synthesis. It blends two images which embody two completely distinct ideas. The first, borrowed from medieval morality, represents the three phases of Time as encompassed in Prudence; these are purely intellectual concepts, personified in human form. The second, issuing from the Oriental cults of the late Empire, depicts Time as a mythical force made up of three ravening beasts. But what does this contrast matter? Humanism is a stream into which flow all the waters of the past, mingling the most diverse forms and ideas, fusing Christian allegory with the ancient symbols of the barbarian religions.[148]

[147] A detailed history of the *signum triceps* is given by E. Panofsky, *Herkules am Scheidewege* (Leipzig, 1930), pp. 12 ff.

[148] We have intentionally disregarded the Psyche myth (see *supra,* p. 86), which is of late origin and deliberately charged with spiritualistic implications. In the humanism and art of the Renaissance, it was to achieve exceptional importance. See Gruyer, *Raphaël et l'antiquité,* II, p. 169.

IV

The Encyclopedic Tradition

UP TO this point we have been studying the three great traditions—historical, physical, and moral—within which the gods survived. For the sake of clarity we have distinguished between them, and kept them as separate from one another as possible.

In actual fact, from the very beginnings up to the sixteenth century, they were often intermingled. If in antiquity, as we have seen, the different philosophical schools proposed different interpretations "of the nature of the gods," these interpretations were not mutually exclusive; they were accessible simultaneously to cultivated minds, which did their best to reconcile them. Logic would doubtless have demanded the adoption of one to the exclusion of the rest, but men felt that three keys were better than one. Sometimes one key, sometimes another, seemed more appropriate to the character of a given myth.

Similarly, the scholars of the Middle Ages made no clear-cut choice.[1] We frequently find them applying all three methods to a single personage or episode, or employing one method after the other in connection with different events or people. Thus Pierre d'Ailly, a remote disciple of Isidore,[2] considers the gods, in his *Compendium cosmographiae*, sometimes as heavenly bodies, and sometimes as rulers who gave their names to various parts of the world —thus unhesitatingly advancing contradictory explanations.

On the other hand, intersection of the three systems may be noted at an early date. The points of contact or of overlapping between the historical, physical, and moral spheres are easy to find; at need, intermediate terms

[1] See Alphandéry, *op. cit.*

[2] Petrus de Aliaco, *Ymago mundi* (ed. Buron [Paris, 1930]), chaps. xxiii, xxv, xxviii.

bridge the gaps between them. We have already seen, for example, how the physiological notion of "temperament" facilitates passage from the physical to the moral world, from the planetary gods to the virtues.[3] But morality can also offer a helping hand to history. Boccaccio, for example, in composing his *De casibus virorum et feminarum illustrium*, goes to the heroes of Fable, viewed as historical personages, in search of edifying anecdotes. Finally, and most important of all, these three domains of knowledge in which we have till now attempted to keep the gods confined and partitioned were in the Middle Ages not circumscribed nor distinguished from one another. On the contrary, the whole effort of scholasticism was rather to fuse them into one, and to enclose them in a vaster sphere, which should encompass the whole of human knowledge.

The encyclopedic character of medieval culture, its obsession with a *scientia universalis*, are strikingly shown, from the time of Isidore, in both learned and popular compilations—the *Summae, trésors*, or *miroirs*, where the "natural," the "moral," and the "historical" all have their place. From the twelfth century on, they are apparent in the domain of scholarship. A hierarchy of the sciences does of course exist, with Theology at their summit; but they form an organic whole, a *bloc* which resisted disintegration for centuries. As Soldati has justly observed,[4] "Even when the first fruits of humanism were beginning to ripen in art, the Middle Ages still lived on in doctrinal teaching, which only gradually felt the stirrings of renewal. . . . What was left of encyclopedic science had great vitality, since it antedated 'encyclopedism'—being, that is to say, classical in its sources."

Numbers, as is well known, play a capital role in this reduction of the diversity of the universe to unity. In many cases, the relations established between the themes dear to medieval learning are purely numerical. Like the twelve Prophets and the twelve Apostles, the seven celestial Spheres and the seven gifts of the Holy Spirit, the four Elements, the four or the seven Ages, the nine Worthies and the nine Muses lend themselves to symmetrical treatment, to balanced combinations which seem, after the fact, to bear testimony

[3] See *supra*, pp. 46 ff.

[4] *La Poesia astrologica nel quattrocento*, p. 105.

to profound inner relations, and to manifest a secret harmony between the truths of the faith and those of nature and history. This "sacred mathematics," a renewal of Pythagoras, would of itself account for the integration of mythology in the encyclopedic system of knowledge.

We have already seen, in Chapter II, how, in the concept of the microcosm, the seven planetary divinities brought about the reconciliation of astronomy and anatomy, and how Dante established the concordance between Ages, Spheres, and Arts.[5] This type of equivalence, moreover, has very distant origins; in the same chapter we recalled the synoptic tables drawn up by Antiochus of Athens. It would be easy to go still further back—by way of the Apocalypse, where the seven Seals, the seven Angels, the seven Spirits of God recur constantly—to Assyria, where the seven tables of destiny are oddly related to the seven Seals, the seven Heavens, the seven colors, and the seven days of the week.[6] The hieratic meaning of the number seven would thus be sufficient to assure to the planetary deities an outstanding place in all the world systems elaborated throughout the centuries.

A strange document, recently published,[7] shows the unbelievable complexity which these numerical combinations had attained at the end of the Middle Ages. This is a series of outline drawings in which a fourteenth-century scholar, a native of Pavia in Italy who lived at the court of Avignon, has attempted to translate his conception of the Universe into geometric terms. What we have here are no longer primitive designs like the rosette-shaped forms [8] which gave summary expression to the relationships between Man, the Elements, and the Seasons, but learned diagrams in which notions of every sort—theological, geographical, mineralogical, medical—are combined according to the laws of number and the divisions of physical space. One [9] consists of a map of Europe on which are superposed circles and ovals containing medallions inscribed with the signs of the zodiac, the names of the

[5] *Convito*, II, 14; IV, 24. See *supra*, p. 49.

[6] E. Renan, *L'Antéchrist*, pp. 472–473.

[7] Codex palat. lat. 1993; facsimile reproduction, with commentary, by R. Salomon, *Opicinus de Canistris, Weltbild und Bekenntnisse eines Avignonesischen Klerikers des* XIV. *Jahrhunderts* (The Warburg Institute, London, 1936). Another work of Opicinus was found in the Vatican Library during the second world war, and is to be published by the Warburg Institute.

[8] See *supra*, p. 63, *fig. 13*.

[9] *Op. cit.*, pl. VII.

planets and months, of minerals, parts of the body, the gifts of the Holy Spirit, and the corresponding sins, with the seven Ages of Life dominating all the rest. In another,[10] five points—the five patriarchates, seats of the princes of the Church—determine the surface of the earth. On the site of Jerusalem a crucifix is reared; from the wound in Christ's side issues a straight line, *rivus sanguinis,* which crosses the picture diagonally. Another line, intersecting this one, emerges from the lance of Sagittarius. At the center of the zodiac stands an immense figure of the Virgin; circles symbolize the Church Universal, "spiritualis et sacramentalis," with the Pope in their midst. Along the lines thus created, on the circumferences of the circles, are arranged the Patriarchs and the lesser Prophets, the Planets, the symbols of the stars, the Elements, the parts of the body, and the names of the Months. In still another drawing,[11] two crucifixes symmetrically opposed are surrounded by a rose-like form made up of Winds, medallions containing Virgin and Child, *Sponsus* and *Sponsa,* animals, Evangelists, Dogmas, and Virtues, the Sun and Moon, the Planets and Metals, the Doctors of the Church, and the monastic orders.

Saturn and Jupiter, Mars, Venus, and Minerva are of course no longer shown as masters of this Universe, where the whole normally gravitates and falls into place around some Christian symbol. But they are always present in the general scheme; they go to make up the *Summa.* It is above all the universalism of the Middle Ages which is set forth here in its full range; these compact networks of curved and straight lines express the relations between the cosmic, historical, and moral components of the universe. In a world truly "catholic," a "total" world,

Il ne cesse point continuité, non plus que de l'âme au corps.[12]

*

THIS CULTURAL unity finds its expression in monumental art. Certain plastic themes, assembled according to the laws of a more or less rigorous symmetry, present the medieval harmony and solidarity in concrete form. In the iconography of the French cathedrals, in the sculptures of the porches and

[10] *Ibid.,* pl. XX.

[11] *Ibid.,* pl. XXI.

[12] Paul Claudel.

the motifs of stained-glass windows, Emile Mâle has recognized a magnificent visual encyclopedia, where all human learning is set forth, as in a great illustrated book, from the humblest aspects of nature to the secret of man's own destiny. Even after scholasticism as a whole began to crumble, whole sections of the great edifice remained standing for centuries. Not only did Italian art in the fifteenth and sixteenth centuries still associate the signs of the zodiac and the Labors of the Months, but it continued to develop symmetrical series of the Virtues and the Liberal Arts—the first dating from the ninth century, and the second going back to Martianus Capella. Under the inspiration of the Dominican monk, Filippo de' Barbieri, it even renewed, in the confrontation of Sibyls and Prophets, the old parallels between sacred and profane history.[13]

The gods, then, whose various modes of survival we have distinguished, are, at a very early date, ordinarily integrated with one or another of these series, or with several of them at once. Captured in "the immense net of learning," they figured from the beginning in the miniatures illustrating the encyclopedias;[14] in the late Middle Ages and at the height of the Renaissance, they continued to have their share in vast decorative ensembles which seem like imposing ruins of the temple of universal knowledge.

*

It is difficult to study these ensembles methodically. They are of unequal importance, not only as works of art, but also from the point of view of the thought which they embody. Sometimes current decorative themes are used with no sign of any organic arrangement which might indicate a carefully thought-out program. Sometimes, on the other hand, everything reveals the artist's subservience to the order imposed by the mind.

This reservation made, let us attempt to define the role of the gods in the pictured encyclopedias.

[13] See L. Dorez, *La Canzone delle virtù e delle scienze*, etc. (Bergamo, 1904); P. d'Ancona, "Le rappresentazioni allegoriche delle arti liberali," *L'Arte*, v (1902), pp. 137–155, 211–228, 269–289, 370–381.

[14] We have found them described (*supra*, p. 64, and n. 101) in the illustrated manuscripts of the *Etymologiae* of Isidore; they are met with again, for example, in the illustrated Monte Cassino manuscript of Rabanus Maurus (1023).

The planetary gods, the hardiest of all, are also the most skillful in insinuating themselves, but they win only tardy entrance into monumental art. They have no place in the stone Bible of the French cathedrals, where only the zodiac is admitted.[15] The same holds true of thirteenth-century Italy—heir, also, to the encyclopedic tradition, and at so many points in her iconography dependent upon France. The Planets are missing, for example, on the Fontana Maggiore in Perugia, the bas-reliefs of which sing another version of "the dual poem of science and labor," represented by the Liberal Arts and the Labors of the Months. In the fourteenth century, however, the planetary gods invade the monuments, religious and civil, of Venice, Padua, Florence, and Siena.[16]

In the Cappella degli Spagnuoli and in the Eremitani, for example, they are associated, if somewhat unobtrusively, with traditional elements—the Sciences in the one case, in the other the Ages of Life;[17] but they have at last become an integral part of a vaster and more imposing whole, occupying the

[15] The gods sometimes appear in the stained-glass windows of the cathedrals, but in a different capacity: they are the idols to whom the blessed martyrs refuse to sacrifice. (It is in this role, again, that Fra Angelico will later depict them in the Chapel of Martin V in the Vatican.)—For a special study of the Circe figure at Vézelay, cf. Ch. Picard, "Une scène d'inspiration antique inconnue. Le mythe de Circé au tympan du grand portail de Vézelay," *Bulletin monumental,* CIII (1945), pp. 213–229.

The planets, on the other hand, are included in profane decorations from the twelfth century on. In a Latin poem of around 1107, Abbot Baudry de Bourgueuil (see Phyllis Abrahams, *Les oeuvres poétiques de Baudri de Bourgueuil* [Paris, 1926]) describes in great detail the bedroom of the countess of Blois, daughter of William the Conqueror. The figures of the Liberal Arts decorate the bed; stars and planets are painted on the ceiling; on the wall (doubtless on a tapestry) appear the Golden Age (*Saturnia Regna*) and the metamorphoses of Jupiter. In his paramount desire to show off his erudition, it may be that Baudry has introduced inventions of his own; he is attempting to outrival Claudian's *De raptu Proserpinae,* I, 246. It is also possible that he has seen the famous coronation robe of Bamberg, on which are embroidered the signs of the zodiac and the constellations (but only two planets: Sol and Luna), as well as the Virgin, the Agnus Dei, and St. John. See R. Eisler, *Weltenmantel und Himmelszelt* (Munich, 1910), p. 13. Cf. Maas, "Inschriften und Bilder des Mantels Heinrichs II," *Zeitsch. für christl. Kunst* (1899), p. 321.

[16] We have explained this invasion (*supra,* pp. 52 and 67) as resulting from the vigorous recrudescence of astrology in the fourteenth century.

[17] In the Guariento frescoes, the Ages of Life are also brought into relation with the zodiacal constellations: Youth, for example, is represented with Venus and the sign of the Scales, etc.—A. Venturi (*L'Arte,* XVII [1914], pp. 49–57) has pointed out the correlation between these frescoes and the drawings of a *Liber physiognomie* (cod. Mut. 694, fol. 11); this correlation is probable, although the style of the drawings is very different. See F. Saxl, "Rinascimento," *Rep. für Kunstwiss.,* XLIII (1922), p. 245.

wall of a chapel and the choir of a church. On Giotto's Campanile, their position lends them veritable majesty; under the exalted patronage of the Prophets and Sibyls, they are seated in the same rank as the Virtues, the Sciences, and the Sacraments, and dominate the entire cycle of figures, which recounts the creation of man, his first struggles with matter, the first victories of the spirit, and the great steps in the history of civilization.

But, as we have already noted, the gods appear twice on the Campanile: they are also included among the bas-reliefs of the lowest zone, where they are shown specifically as nothing less than precursors of civilization, as heroes and inventors.

There are other examples of the inclusion of mythical figures in an encyclopedic scheme of decoration; in monumental Italian art, some of these occur at a quite early date. On the Fontana Maggiore in Perugia, allegories of the Months and the Sciences, in combination with scenes from Genesis, make up a history of the world. But local traditions also play their part in this history.[18] In one of the bas-reliefs, Romulus and Remus are a reminder of the fabulous beginnings of Rome, mother of civilization. The statuettes of the upper basin recall the origins of Augusta Perusia herself, and these origins are, in their turn, mythological: the hero Aulestes, legendary king of Etruria, progenitor of the race and founder of the city, stands near the saints Herculanus and Lawrence, who later awakened it to the Christian life.[19]

These heroes and demigods, to some extent merged at times with the Sages of antiquity or the nine Worthies so dear to the Middle Ages, reappear in the fifteenth century in other monumental decorations where, as on the Campanile in Florence, the planetary deities reign at their side.

In the vestibule of the Chapel of the Palazzo Pubblico in Siena, where we have already encountered Jupiter, Minerva, Apollo, and Mars (*fig. 42*), several figures that had become half-legendary, such as Judas Maccabeus,

[18] This has been emphasized by R. Schneider, *Pérouse*, pp. 57–58.

[19] Aulestes is a Trojan hero; we should recall that the Trojan legend, whose affinities with the "historical" tradition of the gods we have already pointed out (see chap. i), is brilliantly illustrated, a century later, in the Steri of Palermo. Aulestes is painted in the Palazzo Braccio Baglione together with other famous men of Perugia; cf. the series of illustrious Florentines painted by Andrea del Castagno in the Villa Pandolfini, and other similar representations.

Aristotle, Curius Dentatus, and Caesar, are also represented. A medallion evokes the origins of Rome, and lastly a procession of Virtues—Prudence,

42. Jupiter and Mars

Force, Magnanimity, Justice—completes the whole composition, in which we know that Taddeo di Bartolo followed the scholarly instructions of Pietro de'Pecci and Cristoforo di Andrea.

A ceiling by Girolamo Mocetto,[20] now in the Musée Jacquemart-André in Paris, brings together similar elements: Roman or Biblical heroes and sages, planetary gods, Sciences and Virtues, together with mythological episodes and two motifs from the *Trionfi* of Petrarch appear in the panels in the order shown in the accompanying plan.

Mars	Rape of Europa	Prudence	Narcissus	Saturn
Lucretia	Classical triumph	David	Classical triumph	Judith
Temperance	Judgment of Solomon	Force	Justice of Trajan	Justice
Philosopher (Aristotle?)	Triumph of Fame	Astronomer (Ptolemy?)	Triumph of Love	Geometer (Euclid?)
Diana	Myrrha and Adonis	Hope	Mucius Scaevola	Mercury

This scheme, in its very strangeness, reveals a didactic intention. On examination, the figures of the ceiling are seen to constitute a summing-up of the great lessons of science and morality and the great examples offered by history; the fables and the pagan gods serve as illustration and setting for the whole edifying scheme.

In the Palazzo Trinci, Foligno,[21] great encyclopedic themes are set forth in a series of frescoes—unfortunately now much damaged—which were painted around 1420. Again, the gods have their part to play, and again the cosmic and historical traditions meet.

20 (See *figs. 43–45*). Attributed also to Girolamo da Santacroce. See Lionello Venturi, "Una risorta casa del Rinascimento italiano," *L'Arte*, XVII, pp. 72 ff. The order of the figures, corrected in 1913, still remains subject to discussion. The Mocetto ceiling may be compared with that painted by Pintoricchio for the Palazzo del Magnifico, Siena, now in the Metropolitan Museum, New York. Almost all the panels of the Pintoricchio ceiling represent mythological scenes. See Bryson Burroughs, "Ceiling Panels by Pinturicchio," *Bulletin of the Metropolitan Museum of Art* (January, 1921), Part II.

21 See M. Salmi, "Gli affreschi del Palazzo Trinci a Foligno," *Boll. d'Arte*, XIII (1919), pp. 139–180.

The frescoes of the Loggia, like the Perugia fountain and the Palazzo Pubblico in Siena, celebrated the fabulous origin of Rome. In the Sala dei Giganti, the tall figures of Scipio, Fabius Maximus, Marius, are still to be seen—a legendary *De viris*. In a corridor are other illustrious names, no longer drawn from Rome alone, but from Greece, Israel, Christianity—Romulus

43. Narcissus

and David, Hector and Caesar, Alexander and King Arthur; [22] facing these, on the opposite wall of the corridor, are the Seven Ages of Man.[23] And again, allegories of the Seven Ages, this time combined with the Hours of the Day,[24] are presented in the magnificent Camera delle Stelle, each associated with a

[22] On the cycle of the Worthies in château decoration, see Salmi, *op. cit.*

[23] Here represented, as the inscriptions reveal, on the basis of an anonymous French poem of the fourteenth century (Bibl. Nat. 1728, fol. 271). See É. Mâle, *L'Art religieux à la fin du Moyen-Age* (1908), pp. 324 ff.

[24] For this relationship between the Ages and the Hours, see the didactic poem by Francesco da Barberino, *Documenti d'amore*. Cf. Fr. Egidi, "Le miniature dei Codici Barberiniani dei *Documenti d'amore*," *L'Arte* (1902), pp. 1–20, 78–95.

planetary divinity—Infancy with Mars and Aurora, Adolescence with Mercury and the Third Hour, Virility with Jupiter and the Sixth. In the same hall, corresponding in position to the gods, are seated the Arts of the Trivium and Quadrivium. In spite of the ravages of time, this cycle of archaic figures is full of poetry and grandeur. The composition reflects a directing intelligence, and traces have in fact been seen in it of the *Quadriregio*, a poem by the Do-

44. Mars

45. Saturn

minican savant, Federico Frezzi, bishop of Foligno. The repetitions appearing in the other frescoes to which we have referred would seem to indicate that there the artists [25] followed no clear general plan. But in the Palazzo Trinci we have unmistakably a *Summa,* in decorative terms, to which the mythical heroes and the stellar powers make an essential contribution.

*

SOME THIRTY years later, another *Summa*—this time in marble—was introduced into the church of San Francesco of Rimini. It was around 1450 that Agostino di Duccio, Matteo de'Pasti, and Francesco Laurana peopled

[25] In Salmi's view, the artists are at least three: one a disciple of Gentile da Fabriano, the second much influenced by French miniature painting, the third a follower of Ottaviano Nelli.

the chapels of this church with sculptures and bas-reliefs representing the Theological and the Cardinal Virtues, Prophets and Sibyls, Liberal Arts, signs of the zodiac, and Planets as well—Mars in his war chariot, Venus

46. *Jupiter*

47. *Apollo*

and her doves, Saturn with his sickle, Apollo and the Graces,[26] Mercury, Diana, and Jupiter (*figs. 46, 47*). From one chapel to the next these figures look out at one another in groups of six, seven, or twelve, surrounded by coats of arms, devices, arabesques, and scrolls where angels and *putti* are seen playing.

There is nothing in this whole decorative ensemble that we have not al-

[26] On the special iconography of these gods, see *infra*, pp. 252 ff. Cf. also Charles Mitchell, "The Imagery of the Tempio Malatestiano," in *Studi romagnoli*, II (1952), pp. 77–90.

ready met with, even in religious monuments. Why is it, then, that the figures of so traditional[27] a cycle should awaken impressions and associations of an entirely different nature? Is it because of the attitudes and movements which animate them? Without doubt, Diana's undulating draperies, like Venus' nudity and her flowing hair, take us far from the grave, hieratic figures of the Campanile of Giotto. But this new rhythm itself betrays new sources of inspiration. No system of didactic thought, no edifying intention, is entrusted to these marble symbols.[28] Instead, they exalt profane sentiments of love and pride. The focus, the ideological center, is no longer to be found in a clerical conception of the Universe, but in the pagan imagination of a humanist. It is the purpose of Sigismondo Malatesta and the genius of Leon Battista Alberti that lend a new accent, almost sacrilegious in its boldness, to this chorus of allegories.

We know that Sigismondo conceived the project of raising a temple to his own glory, to that of his lady, his ancestors, and the men of learning and philosophers of his court. It was to accomplish this that the humble Franciscan church was surrounded with mausolea and triumphal arcades, and the interior chapels were fitted with balustrades and fluted pilasters to give each the look of an ornamental screen surrounding some proud tomb. Everything seems to sing of the vainglory of man: the Prophets and Sibyls serve only as witnesses of the dual triumph of Sigismondo and his house; the planetary gods are his personal protectors, and the *condottiere* himself mounts to the zenith like a new planet.[29] The sacred character of Virtues and Angels serves to heighten the significance of princely emblems, crests, crowns, and heraldic

[27] Its elements are, in fact, purely scholastic. D'Ancona (*op. cit.*: "Le rappresentazioni allegoriche . . .," p. 272) finds it surprising that there should be a return to the elaborating of old motifs at a time when the absolute rule of scholasticism in the schools had come to an end, giving way to the reflowering of ancient philosophy. We have explained (*supra*, p. 123) this surprising vitality of medieval encyclopedism.

[28] G. del Piano, *L'Enigma filosofico del Tempio Malatestiano* (Bologna, 1938), maintains the contrary: he sees in the different chapels illustrations of the great steps in human religion (Egyptian, Greek, and Jewish "theologies"), and their final outcome in Christianity. Certain esoteric meanings cannot be excluded, a priori. But del Piano's thesis is at fault on two essential points: first, he supposes that the Tempio shows an ensemble of complete originality, whereas it is rather with a traditional iconographic cycle that we have to do; second, he affirms, against all the evidence, the predominance of the Christian idea, when it was the *absence* of Christian elements which astonished contemporary observers.

[29] This is the destiny predicted for him in so many words by Basini, who called upon him to choose his own place in the heavens:

elephants. And Love has its part to play in this apotheosis. The beautiful Isotta sleeps in her stately tomb, but her monogram is interlaced with that of Sigismondo at the base of the pilasters and in the frieze of the chapel where Letters, the Arts, and the Sciences pay them eternal homage. Thus the time-honored figures which once composed the Bible of Learning have been, in this sacred place, reduced to the role of courtiers: they escort two princes and two lovers into immortality.

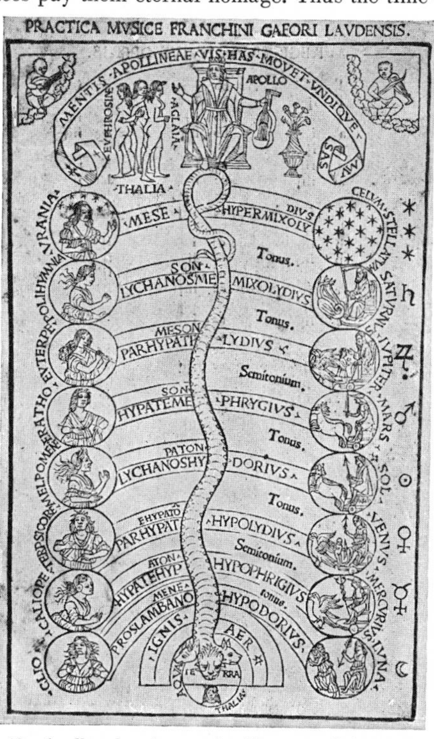

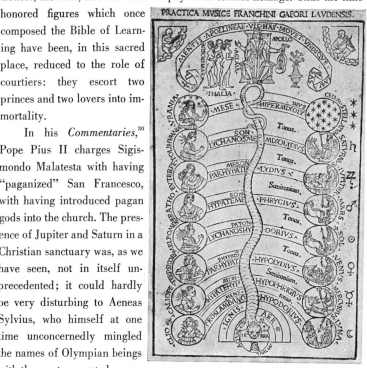

48. *Apollo, the planets, the Muses, and the modes*

In his *Commentaries*,[30] Pope Pius II charges Sigismondo Malatesta with having "paganized" San Francesco, with having introduced pagan gods into the church. The presence of Jupiter and Saturn in a Christian sanctuary was, as we have seen, not in itself unprecedented; it could hardly be very disturbing to Aeneas Sylvius, who himself at one time unconcernedly mingled the names of Olympian beings with the most venerated names

"Interea, tardus quamvis, ad sidera coeli— Accedes quondam serisque vocabere votis;— Cum tamen in numero divorum veneris, opta Qua tibi parte poli, qua sit regione manendum!"—*Astron.*, I, 24–27. ("One day, as late as possible, you will accede to the stars, and will be invoked with earnest wishes. When you arrive *among the gods*, choose that part of the sky where you will take residence.") Similarly, Virgil had marked out a place for Augustus in the zodiac, and Lucan offered Nero one in the sun. Basini was revising his *Astronomicon* at the court of Rimini, at the very moment when work on the Tempio was going forward. See Corrado Ricci's important work, *Il Tempio Malatestiano* (1925), p. 458.

[30] P. 51: "Verum ita gentilibus operibus implevit, ut non tam Christianorum quam infidelium daemones adorantium templum esse videretur."

of the Church. But what makes the association impious in this case is that Christian thinking is subordinated to the classical imagination and to pagan sentiments. The architect who was responsible for the superb reconstruction

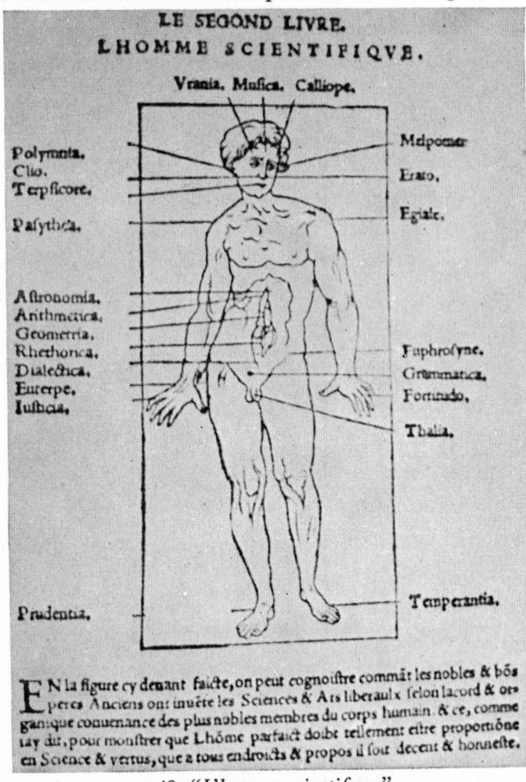

LE SEGOND LIVRE.
LHOMME SCIENTIFIQVE.

EN la figure cy deuant faicte, on peut cognoistre commãt les nobles & bõs peres Anciens ont inuẽte les Sciences & Ars liberaulx selon lacord & organique conuenance des plus nobles membres du corps humain. & ce, comme iay dit, pour monstrer que Lhõme parfaict doibt tellement estre proportiõne en Science & vertus, que a tous endroicts & propos il soit decent & honneste.

49. *"L'homme scientifique"*

of this House of God—still dedicated to His service, if we are to believe the inscription on the façade—could conceive of no higher artistic aim than the building of temples to Diana or Mercury [31] and triumphal arches in honor

[31] Alberti has, in fact, much to say as to how the gods may best be honored by means of temples built in the style most appropriate to each. Temples to Diana, Venus, and the Muses should imitate the female form; robust gods like Hercules and Mars need dwellings which inspire reverence. See *De re aedificatoria*, VII, 3 and 17. In the *De pictura* also, Alberti envisages only mythological compositions, dwelling upon the proper attributes of the gods.

of earthly conquerors. The cult that actually is celebrated in these precincts is not that of Christ. It resembles rather the worship which Rome once offered to her human idols—Augustus, Faustina, or Caesar. The god who is honored here is Sigismondo; the goddess is Isotta—"divae Isottae sacrum."

Similarly, in the Vatican, Pintoricchio was to place the Sciences and the Planets, who had once been vassals of Theology, at the feet of a human being, Alexander Borgia.[32] Sacrilegious flattery, perhaps, but not unnatural, in view of the other frescoes which glorified the mythological ancestors of the Pope,[33] representing him as the heraldic bull among the idols—or, again, of the triumphal procession which passed through the streets of Rome on the day of his coronation, August 16, 1492. Inscriptions composed by Pomponius Laetus celebrated Alexander as greater than Caesar: "The other was only a man; this is a god." [34]

*

THERE IS, however, no final tipping of the scale in favor of paganism. On the contrary, at the very moment the Renaissance, secure in its triumph, was preparing to consummate its unnatural alliance with the papacy, new attempts may be observed to restore the gods to the place which they had rightfully occupied in the medieval encyclopedia—to reduce them once more to the status of mere elements in a Christian universe.

Let us turn from monumental art for a moment to consider a set of engravings which, from this point of view, is of the greatest interest.

We refer to the famous series known as Mantegna's *Tarocchi*.[35] This series is made up of fifty figures, divided into five groups. First come the Conditions of Man—the Beggar, Servingman, Artisan, Merchant, Gentleman, Knight, Doge, King, Emperor, and Pope; then Apollo and the nine Muses; then the ten Sciences—the seven Liberal Arts, Astrology, Philosophy, and Theology. The next group consists of the three Cosmic Principles—Iliaco (Ἡλιακός), genius of Light; Cronico, genius of Time; Cosmico, genius of

[32] Cf. the Liberal Arts carved by Antonio Pollaiuolo on the tomb of Sixtus IV, and those welcoming a member of the Tornabuoni family in the fresco from the Villa Lemmi by Botticelli, now in the Louvre.

[33] See *supra*, p. 26.

[34] See E. Bertaux, *Rome des catacombes à Jules* II (Paris, 1904), pp. 162–163.

[35] See *Die Tarocchi. Zwei italienische Kupferstichfolgen aus dem* XV *Jahrh.* (Berlin, Graphische Gesellschaft, 1910, introduction by P. Kristeller).

Earth—together with the Ethical Principles, i.e., the seven Virtues. Lastly come the ten Firmaments—that is to say, the seven Planets, with the Heaven of the fixed stars, the *Primum Mobile*, and the *Prima Causa*, which dwells in the Empyrean (*figs. 50–53*).

50. *Jupiter*

51. *Philosophy*

There has been disagreement as to the meaning and purpose of these engravings. Apparently they should be thought of as a real game of cards, but an improving and educational game—a type of which we have several examples dating from the fifteenth century, and some even later than that time.[36] Brockhaus believed that he had been able to determine their origin, and hence throw light on their meaning.[37] According to him, the *Tarocchi* were devised and made in Mantua, during a long council which was held

[36] Dating from the same period as the *Tarocchi* are other combinations of images designed to instruct or to convey moral lessons. One example is the game of the Apostles and Our Lord; others are the illustrations of the *Biblia pauperum* and the *Speculum humanae salvationis,* which were also probably used as card games.

[37] H. Brockhaus, "Ein edles Geduldspiel: die Leitung der Welt oder die Himmelsleiter, die sogenannten Taroks Mantegnas vom Jahre 1459–60," in *Miscellanea di storia dell'arte in onore di I. B. Supino* (Florence, 1933), pp. 397–416.

there from June, 1459, to January, 1460; they allegedly served as a pastime for three members of the council, the Cardinals Bessarion and Nicholas of Cusa, and Pope Pius II himself.

And in fact they were not unworthy to occupy the leisure of these princes

52. *Thalia*

53. *Primum Mobile*

of the Church. Their proper order, indicated by the letters A, B, C, D, E for the groups, and the numbers 1 to 50 for the separate figures, reproduces the order assigned by theology to the Universe. Placed edge to edge, they form, as it were, a symbolic ladder leading from Heaven to earth. From the summit of this ladder God, the *Prima Causa,* governs the world—not directly, but stepwise, *ex gradibus,* by means of a succession of intermediaries. The divine power is thus transmitted down to the lowest level of humanity, to the humble beggar. But the ladder can likewise be read from bottom to top; seen in this way it teaches that man may gradually raise himself in the spiritual order, reaching at last the heights of the *Bonum,* the *Verum,* and the *Nobile*—and that science and virtue bring him closer to God.[38]

[38] Cf. Antonio Bettini da Siena, *Monte Santo di Dio* (Florence, 1477), where the ladder of virtues is shown, leading up to God.

Thus, this card game sums up the speculations of St. John Climacus, of Dante, and of St. Thomas Aquinas. It is true that we do not know its rules in detail,[39] but there is no doubt that it was played seriously, with the feeling that each image was, as it were, a piece from the divine chessboard. And we may apply to it the words which Nicholas of Cusa wrote of a similar game, a "geographical globe game," which he uses as an illustration for his philosophical thought: "This game is played, not in a childish way, but as the Holy Wisdom played it for God at the beginning of the world." [40]

In the rigorous hierarchy of the game of *Tarocchi,* mythological figures, as we have seen, appear at two different levels; [41] they occupy inferior ranks in each case, but differ considerably in dignity. The planetary gods appear in the first group, that of the Heavens; Apollo and the Muses are in the next to the highest group—below the Arts, but above Man.

Now these same figures are to be found by themselves, a little later, used to express the Harmony of the Universe. Apollo, in his double role of leader of the Muses and ruler of the Planets, is the soul of this Cosmos, from which every trace of Christianity has disappeared. The primary source of this concept is, indeed, a purely pagan one: we find it in Macrobius' commentary on the *Somnium Scipionis* (II, 3), where the Muses have become the movers of the Spheres.

The same tradition reappears in an engraving illustrating the *Practica musice* by Gafurio, which appeared in Milan in 1496.[42] The image expresses a cosmic theory of the musical tonalities, and at the same time a musical theory of the world; it attempts to demonstrate "quod Musae et Sydera et Modi

[39] The figures carrying *globes* of increasing size (the Emperor; the Muses—minus Thalia; Apollo, Poetry, Astrology, Theology, Iliaco, Cosmico, Octava Sphaera, Primum Mobile, and Prima Causa, which is itself a sphere) undoubtedly were of special importance in the playing of the game.

[40] *Luditur hic ludus; sed non pueriliter, at sic / Lusit ut orbe novo Sancta Sophia Deo.—De ludo globi libri duo* (probably written in 1463), in the third edition of Nicholas of Cusa's complete works (Paris 1514). On this treatise, see E. Vansteenberghe, *Le Cardinal Nicolas de Cues* (Paris, 1920), esp. pp. 275, 335, 337.

[41] And even at three; for, curiously enough, Philosophy is a Minerva, with lance and aegis (*fig. 51*).

[42] See A. Warburg, "I costumi teatrali per gli intermezzi del 1589," in *Gesammelte Schriften,* I, p. 271, and Appendix, pp. 412–415. This engraving may be compared with an illustration for P. Tritonius' *Melopoiae sive Harmoniae tetracenticae super* XXII *genera carminum* . . . (1507). In an oval surrounded by medallions representing the Muses, we see Apollo, with Jupiter above him and Mercury and Pallas at either side.

atque Chordae invicem ordine conveniunt." [43] Apollo is seen enthroned at the summit of the heavens; from under his feet, a long, triple-headed serpent plunges straight downward to the Earth, which is surrounded by Fire, Air, and Water. The names of the musical tones and modes cross the back of the serpent, one above the other, forming as it were the cords of the lyre; at the extremities of each cord are medallions—on one side a Muse, on the other a Planet (*fig. 48*).

How had the correspondence of these different elements been established? There are eight strings, and eight musical modes; there are also eight celestial spheres—the spheres of the seven planets, with the addition of the heaven of the fixed stars, *caelum stellatum.*[44] But the Muses? What shall be done with the ninth, who would make one too many? This difficulty has long since been resolved: Martianus Capella, who also assigned one celestial sphere to each of the Muses,[45] decreed that Thalia should remain on earth. And in fact, at the foot of our engraving, we see her, associated with Terra.[46] In his commentary of 1518, Gafurio justifies this humiliation by referring to Cicero's statement that the earth, being motionless, was therefore silent: "Thaliam enim primo subterraneam veluti silentium ponunt. Constat quidem apud Marcum Tullium (*Somn. Scip.*, v) terram (quod sit immobilis) silentio comparatam, quam tricipiti Cerbero Apollineis pedibus substratum comparant." [47]

It is for this reason that Thalia, instead of taking part in the music of the spheres, rests in the lap of the silent and immobile earth:

Terrae in gremio surda Thalia jacet,

and that she has as companion the triple-headed serpent, the *signum tri-*

[43] ("That the Muses, the Planets, the Modes, and the strings correspond with one another") —Franchini Gafurii *De harmonia musicorum instrumentorum opus* (Milan, 1518), ch. 92. This is a later edition of the *Practica,* but contains a commentary.

[44] As we know, the Middle Ages had added a ninth and a tenth sphere, personified, as in the *Tarocchi,* by *Primum Mobile* and *Prima Causa.* See Dante, *Convito,* II, 3 and 4.

[45] I, 27.

[46] The creator of the *Tarocchi* was doubtless familiar with this tradition, since he has represented Thalia without a globe, seated on the earth (*fig. 52*).

On this "Earthly Muse" cf. also Plutarch, *Sympos.*, LX, 14, 6.

[47] ("They set Thalia underground, as silence, for according to Cicero [*Somn. Scip.* v] the earthly sphere, because motionless, is silent, which is indicated by the triple-headed Cerberus lying at Apollo's feet.")—Cicero's exact words are: "The earthly sphere, the ninth, remains ever motionless and stationary in its position at the center of the Universe."

ceps which we have met before,[48] but which here is the emblem of Silence.

The eminent place given to Apollo, on the other hand, has a dual explanation. Not only does he conduct the choir of the Muses, who set in motion the Planets:

Mentis Apollineae vis has movet undique Musas,

but he himself has his abode in the midst of the Planets "like the Dorian mode amid the strings of the lyre."

In medio residens complectitur omnia Phoebus.

He is thus both the origin and the center of the Universal Harmony.

It would be interesting to follow the subsequent developments of this "Apollonian" tradition. For the moment let us merely call attention to one of its curious derivations. In the second book of the strange work in which he treats of the "science of the proportion of letters," [49] Geoffroy Tory has repre sented the letter O "selon la deue proportion." Tory's O is a divine letter, which represents the sphere of the sun; it is surrounded by all the other letters, each inscribed on one of the sun's rays. "Et entre lesdit [*sic*] rayons du Soleil, j'ay escript aussi," says the author, "et logé les neuf Muses, les Sept arts libéraulx, les quatre vertus cardinales, et les trois Grâces se logeant chacune l'une apart de l'autre et tout au mylieu de le O, je y ay désigné et pourtraict Apollon jouant de sa divine harpe. Pour montrer que la concatenation et ronde perfection des Lettres, Muses, Arts libéraulx, Vertus cardinales et Grâces nous sont inspirées et nories par Apollon." [50]

As is here seen, though the Sun God is retained at the center of the system, the traditional medieval elements have been regrouped around him. Somewhat earlier in the same work, Geoffroy Tory has designed a bizarre figure—a sort of microcosm, a nude man whose limbs and organs are given

48 See *supra*, p. 120.

49 Geoffroy Tory, *Champfleury* (photographic reproduction of the *editio princeps*, 1529), annotated by G. Cohen (Paris, 1931), fol. XXVIII verso, XXIX.

50 ". . . and between the said rays of the Sun, I have likewise inscribed and lodged the nine Muses, the Seven liberal arts, the four cardinal virtues, and the three Graces, placing each apart from the others, and at the exact center of the O, I have designed and portrayed Apollo playing his divine harp. This is to show that the concatenation and full perfection of the Letters, Muses, liberal Arts, cardinal Virtues, and Graces are inspired and nourished in us by Apollo."—Tory undertakes similar demonstrations for the letter I, etc., fols. XIV–XVII.

such unexpected labels as Euphrosyne, Grammatica, Euterpe, Dialectica.[51] According to the author's explanation, the well-formed and well-set-up individual contains in his own person the nine Muses and the seven Liberal Arts; he even contains the Virtues, for his hands and feet are marked Justicia, Fortitudo, Prudentia, and Temperantia—all this serving to show "que l'homme parfaict doibt tellement estre proportionné en science et en vertus que a tous endrois et propos il soit decent et honneste. . . ." Such, it appears, is the lesson of the "nobles et bons pères Anciens." [51a]

*

APOLLO and his college of Muses, Sciences, and Virtues are now to lead us back to monumental art—to that low-ceiled room, small in dimensions but vast in content, which we know as the Stanza della Segnatura.

Concerning this sublime ensemble, "tout est dit, et l'on vient trop tard." We shall attempt no more than a review of the features which make it both the direct outcome of the "encyclopedic" tradition and the august expression of a new and precarious truth.

The didactic character of the work is obvious; at first glance it reveals the profound spiritual kinship which links Renaissance art with the art of the Middle Ages.[52] The use for which the room was intended would have been enough to impose this character: it was a tribunal hall, and originally also contained a library (there is at least good reason for thinking so).[53] As Schlosser has noted,[54] library decoration was traditionally "encyclopedic" in character, following the lines of a program laid down, like the classification

[51] Fol. XXIII, v.: "L'homme scientifique" (*fig. 49*).

[51a] ". . . to show that the perfect man should be so proportioned in science and virtue as to be in all places and circumstances decent and honest."

[52] The Renaissance did not distinguish, any more than the Middle Ages had done, between the search for the beautiful and the search for the good, between doctrinal content and artistic form. Leonardo conceived of painting and sculpture only as truth made perceptible to the senses. Cf. Benedetto Croce, *Estetica* (Milan, 1902), p. 187: "The Renaissance, with reason, did not distinguish didactic poetry from the other types, since in its view all poetry was invariably didactic (*didascalica*)." Similarly, there is no art which exists for its own sake, "gratuitously."

[53] Cf. F. Wickhoff, "Die Bibliothek Julius II.," *Jahrb. d. kgl. preuss. Kunstsamml.*, I (1893); J. Klaczko, *Jules* II (Paris, 1898).

[54] In the important article which we have already referred to several times: "Giusto's Fresken . . . ," part 2: "Der encyklopädische Bilderkreis und die Vorläufer von Raffaels Stanza della Segnatura," pp. 518 ff.

of the books themselves, in the *Biblionomia* of Richard de Fournival.[55] In the Middle Ages, "ingenious paintings" thus honored all the disciplines—jurisprudence, theology, philosophy, medicine, music, etc.—as we see in the library of the Bavarian monastery of Nieder-Altaich, in the monastery of St. Albans, and in the Premonstratensian houses in Brandenburg. And the presence of similar allegories in the Eremitani in Padua is due to the fact that the buildings housed the library of the Augustinians, which was classified according to the same principles. The use of decorations of this type, furthermore, was by no means confined to monasteries, since Melozzo da Forlì depicted the Liberal Arts in the library of the duke of Urbino—where they were seen by Raphael. It is most natural, therefore, that in the Stanza della Segnatura the Sciences and Arts should be represented along with Justice [56] and her sister Virtues, Fortitude, Temperance, and Prudence.

But as we know, the Sciences and Arts do not figure here merely in the form of allegories; they are likewise illustrated in tableaux which give considerable prominence to the pagan world. Even though the Law is glorified by strict ceremonial (in one case entirely ecclesiastical), and Theology by a council gathered about an altar, Poetry and Philosophy have as their representatives the sages and gods of antiquity.

Apollo appears three times. His statue and a statue of Minerva [57] adorn the Portico of Athens, where thoughtful groups, dominated by the lofty figures of Aristotle and Plato, give us one more illustration of the series of Liberal Arts, handmaidens of Philosophy. In the vault, witnessing the torture of Marsyas, Apollo symbolizes the victory of the mind over the dark world of matter. Last of all, in the fresco above the window, he is shown surrounded by Muses, playing his viol on the bank of the Castalian spring—the poets ascending the slope toward him, at the call of his song.

[55] See L. Delisle, *Cabinet des manuscrits,* II, pp. 518 ff.

[56] See the exceedingly interesting observations of E. Wind, "Platonic Justice, designed by Raphael," *Journal of the Warburg Institute,* I, pp. 69–70.

[57] G. P. Bellori, in his *Descrizione delle imagini dipinte da Rafaello d'Urbino nelle Camere del Palazzo Apostolico Vaticano* (Rome, 1695), p. 21, comments in detail on these two statues, which he interprets as representing "moral and natural philosophy." It will be recalled that in the *tarocchi,* philosophy is also a Minerva (*supra,* p. 140, n. 41; see also *fig. 51*).

Two statues of the Diana of Ephesus form the arms of the throne of Philosophy painted on the ceiling. On the Diana of Ephesus in Renaissance art, see H. Thiersch, *Artemis Ephesia* (Berlin, 1935). Cf. our observations (*infra,* Bk. II, chap. i) on the role of the Oriental divinities in art.

Apollo's presence in the Stanza will cause us no great surprise. As we have seen, he long ago made his entrance into the great scholastic cycle, followed by the nine Muses. But how are we to evaluate his appearance here? Is he the center about which these ideal spheres gravitate? Is he the incarnation of pagan art and reason, menacing rivals of the faith?

No; there is no doubt that Apollo is not the principal theme nor the chief organizing force of the whole composition; he is not its soul. For it gives expression to a hierarchy of which he is not the summit. Plato, in the *School of Athens,* points upward at the sky, and the whole movement of the fresco centers in this culminating gesture, through which the Sciences and Arts, and Philosophy herself, give way before the "knowledge of things divine."

How shall this supreme truth be revealed? Not by the ardent discussion which resounds within the Portico, not by the exquisite dreams which hover among the laurels of the sacred mount. It gleams in silence on the altar; in the serene order of their grouping, Doctors, Saints, and Angels contemplate its disclosure, with the Trinity dominating from above.

Thus the balance is not upset, nor the true order of things endangered; the human remains subject to the divine, and ancient philosophy to the Christian revelation. Thus seen, the Stanza della Segnatura marks a return to the great scholastic tradition; it restores, in all its dignity, that mighty edifice which had been weakening ever since the fourteenth century. In the same papal palace, below this very hall in which Theology has regained her true place, are the Borgia Apartments, where earthly pride challenges the majesty of heaven, and where the Seven Wise Virgins have been prostituted to the brutish descendant of Osiris.

But it is no mere restoration which we see in the Stanza. If Raphael has recovered the secret of an ideal architecture, lost since Dante and Giotto, the temple of his rebuilding shelters new thoughts as well.

The disciplined ordering of all the elements in the ensemble must be studied in order to be fully understood, but their intimate accord is instantly and strikingly apparent. In this realm, peopled by images in which two worlds come face to face, there are neither victors or vanquished; it is not the clash of two armies which we hear, but the harmony of a choir. This is not the first great pictured cycle which has given us this impression: some ten years earlier, in the Cambio at Perugia, the two worlds had once before met without clashing. There, facing one another on the two long walls, the ancient Heroes and Sages, the Sibyls and Prophets, formed a harmonious council, over which the Planets and Virtues presided from above. And this council proclaimed the supreme verities of Christian dogma—predicted by some of its members, felt by others with instinctive prescience, and now revealed in the paintings of the end wall, the *Incarnation* and the *Atonement.*[58] Assuredly, this ensemble summarized once again the long-standing tradition of the "Magi" and the "prophets without the Law," with its parallelism between great men in Biblical and profane antiquity[59]—a tradition which looked upon all pagan civilization as an instrument of God's purposes and a preparation for His coming. But beneath this mantle of orthodoxy, more than a hint of Neoplatonic thought could already be detected.

Maturanzio's undistinguished mind and Perugino's timid brush were unable to bring this content into relief—or perhaps did not dare to do so. It remained for the humanism of an Inghirami or a Calcagnini[60] and the genius of a Raphael to reveal its lofty perspectives. "In Rome, in the time of Julius II, the work of enthusiastic electicism begun in the Florence of Lorenzo is brought to completion. . . ."[61] The dream of Marsilio Ficino is realized: the Church welcomes the beauty and wisdom of antiquity into her widened embrace. As though by a miracle, Homer and Dante, Plato and St. Thomas, Apollo and Christ, become brothers. No! it is not the Gothic *Summa* which has been reconstructed before our eyes; it is the pantheon of Alexander Severus—all gods, all truth united in a single cult, and worshipped with the same indiscriminate zeal.

*

THIS RECONCILIATION is only a dream—a dream of scholars and philosophers, for whom the approaching Reformation holds a terrible awakening. The dream will recur later, in frequent revivals, but only to flatter the imagi-

[58] See René Schneider, *Pérouse*, p. 120.

[59] See *supra*, chap. i.

[60] According to Paolo Giovio, the program of the frescoes was offered Raphael by the Pope himself; but there seems to be no doubt that the artist profited from the advice of his friends.

[61] E. Bertaux, *op. cit.*, p. 42.

nation of skeptics, or to torment Christians and humanists with nostalgia for lost Edens. And yet, when we return, even today, to the Stanza della Segnatura, the illusion captivates us anew. The art of Raphael, more supple and persuasive than thought, seems gently to seduce the mind, which feels itself willingly yielding. The forms balance and penetrate one another, the colors respond to one another in perfect amity, the rhythm continues without interruption or jolt. All logical difficulty vanishes—or rather, it would seem, has either never existed or else been resolved with no need of the slightest effort. The ultimate impression is that of "an undulation of harmonies which seems to have had no beginning and can have no end."

PART TWO: THE FORMS

I

The Metamorphoses of the Gods

IN THE PRECEDING chapters we have studied in a general way the factors which determined the survival of the gods in the Middle Ages. The pagan divinities served as vehicle for ideas so profound and so tenacious that it would have been impossible for them to perish.

That being so, why do men so often speak of the "death of the gods" with the decline of the ancient world, and of their "resurrection" in the dawn of the Italian Renaissance? We must remember that it was merely the content of the images of the gods which survived. The garment of classical form had disappeared, having gradually been shed in favor of barbaric disguises which made it impossible to identify the wearers. And, in consequence, until our own day, history has failed to recognize them.

This error and this injustice are all the more easily explained since it was for so long our habit of mind to consider the antique tradition from an exclusively formal point of view. Only those works aroused our interest or held our attention in which the classical style had been preserved or recovered. The gods ceased to exist for us from the moment this style was lost.

In this chapter we hope to show how extraordinary were the adventures in space and time of these gods of the Middle Ages—these hybrid and phantom gods—and how much may be learned of the history of civilization from a study of their metamorphoses and reincarnations.

*

To HELP us in this study we have at our disposal documentation of inestimable value in the drawings and miniatures from astronomical, astrological, and mythological manuscripts, a general inventory of which was undertaken by F. Saxl.[1]

Among these countless figures, dating from the Carolingian epoch to the Renaissance, the singular alterations and ramifications of the antique tradition can be followed, as it were, step by step. The tradition is dual, and we must distinguish between two groups[2] of such figures—those which have visual models as prototypes, and those which are based on the data of descriptive texts alone. In the first case, we have to do with copies; in the second, with reconstructions. In actual practice it is not always easy to differentiate the two, especially since there is an occasional mingling of the visual and literary traditions.

54. Perseus

First let us examine the very important group of illustrations which had as origin a classical image. This group is made up of three great families: the first, of purely Occidental source and character, flourished until about the

[1] *Verzeichnis astrologischer und mythologischer illustrierter Handschriften des lateinischen Mittelalters:* Vol. I, "Handschriften in römischen Bibliotheken," in *Sitzungsberichte der Heidelberger Akademie der Wissenschaften,* Abhandl. 6, 7 (1915); Vol. II, "Die Handschriften der Nationalbibliothek in Wien," in *Sitzungsberichte,* Abhandl. 2 (1927); *Catalogue of Astrological and Mythological Illuminated Manuscripts of the Latin Middle Ages:* Vol. III, "Manuscripts Preserved in the Libraries of London, Oxford, and Cambridge" (to be published by the Warburg Institute).

[2] This idea was brought out by E. Panofsky and F. Saxl, "Classical Mythology in Mediaeval Art," *Metropolitan Museum Studies,* IV (1932–1933). Generally speaking, our treatment of the subject, which we have deliberately reduced to the simplest lines, is based in large part on results due to the penetrating studies of Warburg and Saxl.

twelfth century; the two others, marked in varying degrees by Oriental influence, invade the manuscripts of the late Middle Ages.

The first family is found for the most part in the illustrated manuscripts deriving from Aratus, called *Aratea* in Cicero's translation; their prototypes were in all probability established in the last centuries of the Roman

55. Perseus with the head of Medusa

Empire.[3] Aratus, as we have seen,[4] described the constellations as a mythographer rather than an astronomer, and his poem is as rich in visual themes as in scientific data. In short, it offered ideal subject matter for a picture book, and such is, in fact, the character of the manuscripts traceable to this source.

The Carolingian copies of the *Aratea*—examples are the Leidensis Voss. lat. 79, Harley 647, and Vindobonensis 387, or even Reginenses 309 and

[3] They were imitated, in fact, as we shall see, from the earliest periods of Byzantine and Arabian art. It will be recalled that the Farnese Globe, the figures on which correspond exactly with Aratus' descriptions, is a Roman copy of a Greek original.

[4] See *supra*, p. 38.

123, cod. 188 of the Bibliothèque de Boulogne-sur-Mer (*fig. 56*), and cod. 7 of the Stiftsbibliothek of Göttweig (*fig. 57*), which date from the tenth or eleventh century [5]—have surprises in store for the art historian, and sometimes occasion him real emotion. For, contrary to all expectation, these copies succeed in recapturing the antique model with surprising fidelity. In some of them, the classical style is maintained with such purity that an enlargement of certain small figures irresistibly recalls the frescoes of Pompeii (*fig. 54*). On the other hand, the relative positions and sizes of the stars whose arrangement is supposed to be indicated by the mythological figure, are often incorrect; but in this regard also the copies show respect for the model, even where precision is subordinated to aesthetic considerations. Had not the stars which formed the original basis of the figures already disappeared from certain Roman prototypes? [6]

56. Virgo and the Gemini

We thus have here a surprising—and exceptional—case of the conservation of antique types in form as well as in content.

Nevertheless, as time goes on, changes are introduced into the illustra-

[5] The last manuscript named is the exact copy of a Carolingian model.

[6] See Panofsky and Saxl, *op. cit.* Cf. Bibl. Univ., Leyden, cod. Voss. lat., oct. 15.

tions of the *Aratea,* and since observation of the sky, which might have been used by way of verification, is not even resorted to for correcting the figures, they are gradually altered, becoming more and more fanciful.[7] In the process, they lose their Greco-Roman outlines, taking on instead those of the demigods of Romanesque or Gothic art, an example being the Hercules of cod. Bodleianus 614, who looks like a St. Michael. Isolated examples of antique images do survive, in all purity, up to the fourteenth century;[8] but generally speaking, this whole cycle tends to disappear, from the thirteenth century on. Its degenerate types are supplanted by newcomers.

57. *The Centaur*

These newcomers, who are destined to effect a veritable revolution in the iconography of the gods, issue from the Orient. As we have said, they form two distinct families. The first is comprised in the Arabian astronomical manuscripts and their Western copies.

With regard to the direct inheritance of antique learning, the medieval Orient, as we have seen,[9] had been more favored than the Occident. Whereas

[7] One of the most remarkable examples of such fantasy is offered by a manuscript of the twelfth century (Vindobonensis 12600); the illustrator, completely indifferent to science, has taken the liberty of representing his figures in half- rather than full-length, omitting half the stars. The figures are none the less full of movement and vivacity, but for that reason also are far removed from the ancient types.

[8] Thus, in two Provençal manuscripts of Ermengaut of Béziers' *Bréviaire d'amour* (codices Vindobon. 2563 and 2583x) and another in the British Museum (cod. Royal 19, C. 1), which contain images of the constellations and planets, Venus Anadyomene is depicted nude, in the sea. This extraordinary conservatism may perhaps be explained by the fact that the culture of the last pagan centuries remained alive longer in Provence than elsewhere (*fig. 58*).

[9] See *supra,* p. 51.

the West had inherited only meager extracts of Greek science, and based its clearest ideas of astronomy on the Latin *Aratea*, the Arabian astronomers received from Hellenistic sources the thoroughly scientific catalogue of Ptolemy. Furthermore, while the European Middle Ages allowed the Western heritage to decline, the Arabs developed theirs fruitfully. With regard to the stellar images handed down from antiquity, the two attitudes form a complete contrast. The Occident, careless of observation and reckoning, concentrates chiefly upon the pictorial character of the images, and gives little thought to comparing them with the celestial phenomena. The Arabs, on the other hand, consider them exclusively as symbols of a reality which they attempt to grasp with constantly increasing accuracy.

58. Venus

Hence it arises, as a first result, that the locations, sizes, and groupings of the stars, often neglected by Western illustrators, are scrupulously reproduced, and if need be rectified, by the Arab copyists, whose principal concern is to determine the exact forms of real constellations. But another and no less logical consequence then follows: aside from their scientific value, the Hellenistic sky figures offer no interest to the Arabs. Of what significance to them, indeed, are Hercules, Andromeda, and the host of foreign deities? Indifferent to mythology—and, for that matter, knowing nothing of it—they retain the general outlines of each figure,[10] but make no effort to preserve its Greek type, costume, and attributes. Is it a Hercules that they must reproduce? They carefully locate the stars which make up the constellation, but then wrap

[10] This may even seem surprising; it is explained by the fact that the figures of the Greek globe were traditional and at the same time convenient.

the hero's head in a turban, and give him a scimitar instead of a club. It is in this unexpected disguise that he appears, for example, in a manuscript of Sûfî (Paris, cod. arab. 5036; *fig. 59*).[11] Thus the Greek celestial sphere is

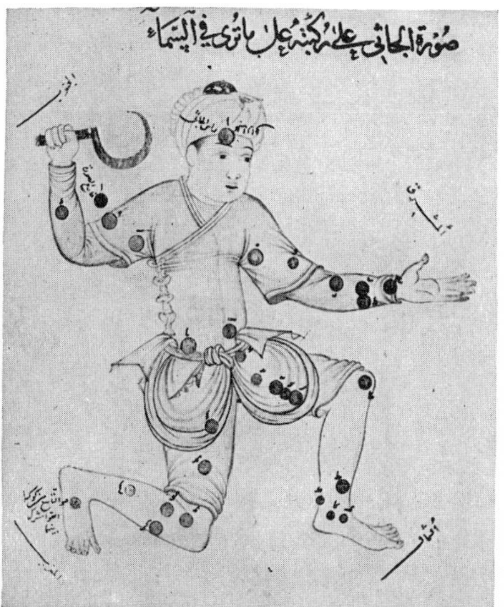

59. Hercules

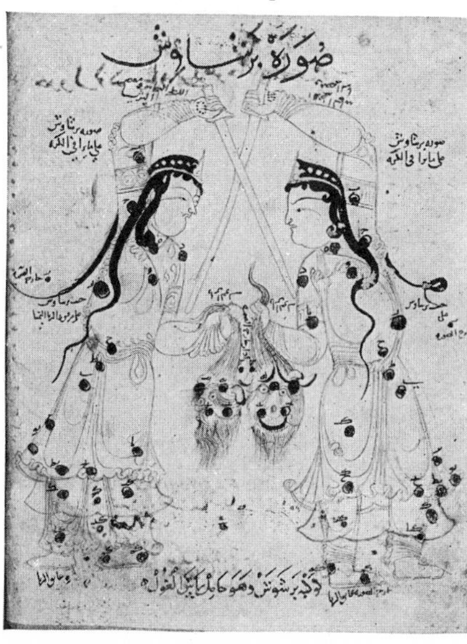

60. Perseus

"Orientalized." At first glance all these masquerading figures seem as farcical to us as do the *turqueries* of Molière, but in reality they hold more scientific information than do the fine Carolingian copies of the Latin *Aratea.* If we look at a sky map drawn by the Arabs, we shall see that the extravagant figures which people it are marked with signs referring to the catalogue of Ptolemy; they fit into a geometric system which makes it possible to locate them exactly.[12]

It is for this reason that the Western Middle Ages, when seized by the reviving passion for astronomy, turned away from the *Aratea* and eagerly collected and copied these Arabian manuscripts. But, strangely enough, the

[11] Sûfî's catalogue became widely known in both East and West. See A. Hauber, "Zur Verbreitung des Astronomen Sûfî," *Islam,* VIII (1918), pp. 48, 49–54.

[12] See, for instance, the copy of an Oriental map in cod. Vindobon. 5415 (fol. 168 r.).

Western copyists appear not to have noted that the manuscripts, while correct astronomically, were mythologically absurd, and so retained Hercules' scimitar, and the bearded demon's head which Perseus was now carrying instead of that of Medusa (*fig. 60;* cf. the "classical" Perseus, *fig. 55*). Was this due to ignorance on their part, or to servile submission to the models? The West no longer recognized its own gods, so greatly had they been disfigured in the East.

As is natural, it was in Sicily and Spain that the Arab manuscripts were first transcribed; these copies, reproduced in their turn, spread the Oriental images of the gods throughout Europe. We know, for example, that cod. Vaticanus lat. 8174 is the copy of a manuscript executed for Alfonso the Wise, and that cod. 1036 of the Bibliothèque de l'Arsenal derives, with several others, from a Sicilian manuscript.

A third family of figures—the most curious of all—remains to be considered. These are the illustrations for the astronomico-astrological treatise of Michael Scot,[13] composed in Sicily between 1243 and 1250 for Emperor Frederick II. We have more than thirty manuscripts of this treatise,[14] which offer us an imagery without precedent—lacking, it would seem, any possible connection with classical antiquity. Thus we discover new constellations: the Viol Player, and the Vexillum, or Standard, appear in Michael Scot side by side with the traditional Cassiopeia, Cygnus, Sagittarius. These innovations, again, are of Islamic origin; most of them are explained, as Boll has shown, by the fact that Scot borrows from the Arabic image of the sky stars which had themselves come from the *sphaera barbarica.*[15] But when we come to the images of the planets, we find novelties still more astonishing; not one of the great planetary divinities has retained his customary appearance. Jupiter is represented as a scholar or jurist or noble personage, seated before a lavishly spread table; Saturn has become a warrior; Mercury is a bishop, carrying a book as his attribute.

This phenomenon is all the more remarkable since up to this time visual representation of the planets has shown almost no deviation from the classical

[13] See *supra,* p. 52, n. 65, and *figs. 61, 62.*

[14] Not of the complete treatise, but of its astronomical section.

[15] See *supra,* p. 39.

iconography. As we have seen,[16] it was only at a comparatively late date that the Greeks learned to distinguish the planets from the fixed stars and, fol-

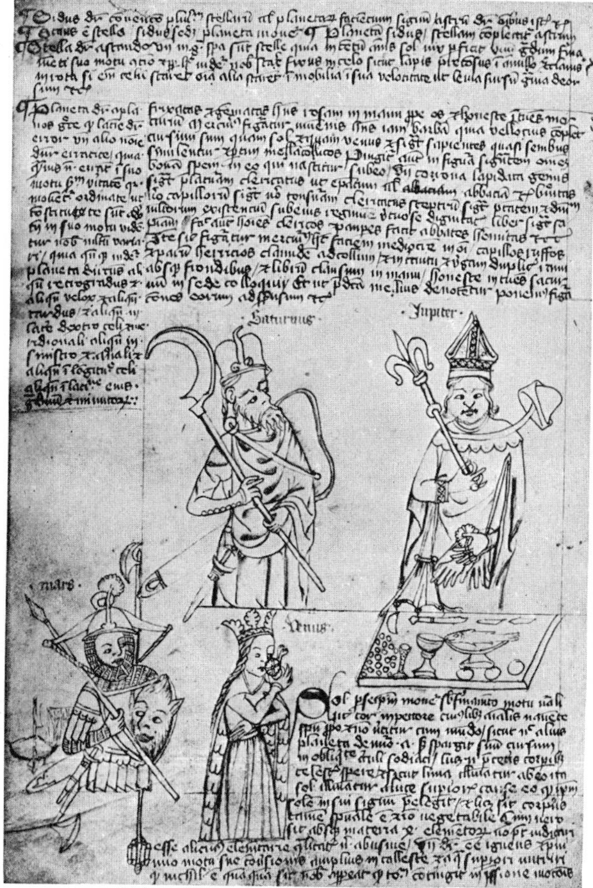

61. *Saturn, Jupiter, Mars, and Venus*

lowing the example of the Babylonians, began to give them the names and likenesses of gods. At that time they invented no special attributes for these

[16] *Supra*, p. 39.

planetary gods, and none were given them by the Romans.[17] They were simply identified with the Olympians, and the Middle Ages continued to reproduce them in the same fashion, with a certain amount of rectification; they can be recognized without too much difficulty, not only in the astronomical manuscripts,[18] but even in the popular series of calendar illustrations [19]—and this remains true until the fifteenth century.

From that time on, however, the gods become unrecognizable. Strictly speaking, a few details—such as Saturn's sickle—could be interpreted as reflections of the Greco-Roman tradition. But taken as a whole, one would look in vain to Olympus for the origin of the gods of Michael Scot. What series of transformations, however fundamental, could conceivably have converted Mercury into an ecclesiastical dignitary?

The origin of these figures must be sought elsewhere. Again, the source is an Oriental one, and again we must thank Saxl for having demonstrated the fact.

In studying the representations of planets in Islamic manuscripts,[20] Saxl found many singular features which on the one hand seemed to relate them to figures illustrating the Michael Scot manuscripts, and, on the other, pointed to an origin much earlier than the thirteenth century. His efforts at localizing this origin in space and time led him in a direct line back to ancient Babylon.

It is, in fact, undeniable that while the Arab figures show almost no relationship with Greco-Roman planetary types, they do offer remarkable resemblances to types found in Babylonian sources. Thus Mercury, as a pious and scholarly figure, corresponds in character to Nebo, the writer-god; Jupiter, as judge, to Marduk, who signs the decrees of destiny. The Sun himself, who in cod. Monac. arab. 464 wears a crown and holds a sword on his knees,

[17] See F. Cumont, *Textes et monuments figurés relatifs aux mystères de Mithra* (Brussels, 1899), I, p. 74.

[18] For example, in the two manuscripts of Ermengaut of Béziers cited above. Nevertheless, a "modern" Jupiter is seen near planets of Greek type in cod. Vindobon. 2563.

[19] See *supra*, pp. 64, 70.

[20] "Beiträge zu einer Geschichte der Planetendarstellungen im Orient und im Okzident," *Der Islam*, III (1912), pp. 151–177.

Among these Islamic manuscripts, let us note cod. Bodl. Or. 133; cod. Monac. arab. 464, an illustrated copy of the *Cosmography* of Qazwînî (d. 1283) executed in Damascus in 1280; the codex Sarre, another copy of Qazwînî, made around 1420; Persian translations of the same work, etc.

is much closer to Shamash than to Phoebus Apollo. In spite of minor divergencies and difficulties of detail, the primary conclusion must therefore be that the Arab figures of planets reflect in reality the Babylonian gods Nebo (Mercury), Marduk (Jupiter), Ishtar (Venus), Ninib (Mars), and Nergal (Saturn).

62. Mercury as a scribe

What remains to be discovered is how the Babylonian types could survive and be transmitted across the centuries to the Arabs. In spite of the almost complete absence of figural documents between the Sassanian period and the twelfth century, it is possible to give a precise answer to this question. We do, in fact, possess an uninterrupted textual tradition dealing with the planetary cults and with ritual images of the planets. These texts, the most important of which is an eleventh-century book on magic, the *Ghâya*,[21] make it clear that in certain isolated districts of Mesopotamia the old autochthonous religion, astrolatry, still had at that date its temples and its devotees. The Haranite Sabeans, for example, continued to invoke the planetary gods and to venerate their images.[22] Thus, in a "dead angle," to use Saxl's apt expression, local paganism survived in its primitive state, sheltered from outside influences[23]

[21] The *Ghâya*, of which we have already spoken (*supra*, p. 53, n. 67), was translated in part by Dozy and de Goeje, *Actes du* VIe *Congrès International des Orientalistes* (1885). Another important text is that of Masudi (tenth century), followed much later by Dimâski (*Manual of Cosmography*, translated by A. F. Mehrens [Copenhagen, 1874]).

[22] Under Roman rule, Haran was called Carrhae.—A Sabean of Haran, Tabit b. Kurra, is the author of a *Liber de lectionibus recitandis ad singulas septem planetarum accomodatis*.

[23] With the exception, that is, of certain borrowings from Hellenistic thought (Stoicism, Hermetism) with which the Haranite "philosophers" colored their teachings; and certain Greco-Roman elements introduced in late antiquity into the iconography by way of strengthening its syncretistic character. On the last point, see M. A. Lanci, *Trattato delle*

—those of the Greco-Roman world as well as those of Islam and Christianity. The effigies which adorned the sanctuaries of Haran preserved unaltered, through the centuries, the types of the astral deities. Now the illustrations of the Arab manuscripts conform perfectly with those effigies, as described in the *Ghâya;* and since there exists, on the other hand, a certain relationship between the Michael Scot pictures and those of the Arab manuscripts, we are justified in connecting them, in their turn, with the Babylonian tradition.

In exactly what way did the Occident fall heir to this tradition? Saxl thought that in certain cases the illustrators actually had Arab models before their eyes, but that often they must also have been inspired by texts. One of the essential intermediaries here was the *Picatrix,* which, as we have already seen, was widely known in the Occident.[24] The *Picatrix,* as has been said, was in fact a translation of the *Ghâya* and reproduces literally the descriptions that are found there.

*

IT IS all the more important to have clarified the origin of this family of figures, since it played an extensive role in the Italian monumental art of the fourteenth century. It provides the explanation of representations contained in the great decorative cycles whose content we have studied above,[25] but which we are only now fully able to understand.

In Florence, the planetary gods sculptured on the Campanile of Giotto appear, as we have noted, in disconcerting guise. The Sun, for example, is a king holding a scepter in his left hand and in his right a sort of wheel. What we have here is distinctly not Apollo, the classical deity, but a descendant of the Asiatic solar gods.[26] Similarly, in the Cappella degli Spagnuoli, Saturn holds a spade in addition to the classical sickle;[27] Mercury appears there as a scribe—indicating that we are looking at the scholarly Nebo. For the same reason, in the choir of the Eremitani at Padua, and on a capital in the Doge's Palace in Venice (*fig. 21*), Mercury has assumed the likeness of a teacher.

---

simboliche rappresentanze arabiche (Paris, 1845–6).

[24] See *supra,* pp. 127 ff.

[25] See Part I, chaps. ii and iv.

[26] We find this figure again in the Eremitani and the Salone in Padua, in the first case wearing the imperial diadem, in the second the papal crown. In the Cappella degli Spagnuoli in Florence, he merely holds a sphere.

[27] He is seen with this spade in the codex Sarre, for one example; elsewhere he appears holding a pick.

There is no doubt that we have definitely penetrated the secret of this strange iconography. Nevertheless, some difficulties remain. In spite of the attributes which reveal their origin, these gods in Florence, Venice, and Padua are represented as if they were contemporary personages—in other words, in Trecento costume. In this respect (an oddity they share with the illustrations in Michael Scot) they differ profoundly from the Arabian figures, in which we find the Babylonian types retaining their exotic character. More remarkably still, not only are they wearing Occidental dress, but in some cases they have even donned ecclesiastical ornaments. We have already called attention to the case of Nebo-Mercury as bishop. A related example is in the choir of the Eremitani—Shamash-Apollo wearing the tiara. But the climax is offered by the Marduk-Jupiter of the Campanile in Florence, muffled in a monk's robe, holding a chalice in one hand, and in the other a cross (*fig. 63*).

63. Jupiter as a monk

These difficulties are not insoluble. First of all, let us not forget that even when these Western figures of the planets represent the same gods as do the Arab manuscripts, they are not copied from those manuscripts. However impregnated with Oriental elements the treatise of Michael Scot may be, the artists who illustrated this work allowed themselves, even while following the indications of the text, to take their models from the life around them. Even with the Arab drawings before their eyes, they did not attempt to imitate them. We must remember, moreover, that Michael Scot himself had been no merely passive recipient of those elements from the East. He had elaborated them, combining them in each description with material from Western sources; and to this description he added, in the manner dear to medieval theology, an allegorical commentary in which he attempted to reconcile these different data and to give them unity [28]—a method, be it noted, completely in accord with the cultural character of southern Italy, the link between Orient and Occident, between Islam and Christianity.

This effort at adaptation and fusion makes Europeans and even Christians out of the astral divinities of Babylon. Mercury, for instance, who in the Eastern representations carries a book and sometimes has a halo, is a scholar, a dervish, a holy man; why should his Western equivalent not be a bishop? In this way pagan cosmogony meets, and is at the same time brought into harmony with the Christian concept of the world.

We should, however, avoid generalizations. The Christianizing of Babylonian figures may have other causes, as in the case of Jupiter. On the Campanile in Florence we found Jupiter represented as a monk; the same thing occurs in the Cappella degli Spagnuoli, and in certain manuscripts.[29] Is this another case of assimilation, a Christian interpretation of Marduk? Nothing could be less certain; it is possible, on the other hand, that this image is directly derived from an Oriental text.

According to the astrological system, each planet holds sway over a certain region of the earth. The Indies, for example, as Qazwînî tells us in his *Cosmography*, are under the dominion of Saturn; that is why Saturn is represented in certain manuscripts in the guise of an aged Indian. Jupiter is the ruler of the Western countries, and for that reason, as the *Ghâya* expressly states, is the patron of the Christians. In consequence, he looks like a Christian himself; and furthermore, according to the principles of sympathetic magic, those who claim his help ought to dress as he does. When praying to Jupiter, the *Ghâya* says explicitly, "Be humble and modest, dressed in

[28] Cf. Ridewall's method in the *Fulgentius metaforalis*, of "converting" pagan images and texts. See *supra*, pp. 94 ff.

[29] In particular in Urbin. lat. 1398, of the fifteenth century (*fig. 64*), where the illustrations are often very close to the Campanile reliefs; also in an engraving of 1492, representing Fortune's wheel. Elsewhere (for example, in Vindobon. 2378, fol. 12 v.) Jupiter wears a miter.

the manner of monks and Christians, for he is their patron; act in every way as the Christians do, and wear their costume: a yellow mantle, a girdle, and a cross."

Thus our Christian Jupiter is not, as might be supposed, the result of a transformation, but is the direct illustration of an astrological magic text; this example may serve to show what care should be used in the study and classification of these figures. We shall see later that innumerable errors and misunderstandings in the transmission and reproduction of the images renders such a classification even more hazardous and delicate. For the moment, one conclusion may be drawn from this summary presentation of the subject: in the domain of planetary and stellar iconography alone, several families of gods outlive the ruin of the ancient world and continue to propagate themselves, but we hesitate to call them by their names—either because they are of barbarian origin, or because the original types from which they arose have become altered by means of successive misalliances or degradations.

*

IF WE wish to pursue our study of the "pictorial" tradition beyond the illustrations in astronomical manuscripts, we shall find abundant material only in Byzantine art.

In the Byzantine Empire, in fact—with its nearness to the sources and its abundance of Hellenistic models—mythology left an imprint in educated minds and even in popular sensibility, the living force of which is attested by the arts.[30] Let us recall briefly the miniatures in profane manuscripts, such as those in the Theocritus of the Bibliothèque Nationale where, in the fourteenth century, the god Pan is still represented with goat's head and cloven hoofs,[31] and even the illustrations of certain religious texts, like the magnificent Paris Psalter, where demigods and nymphs mingle in scenes from the story of David, within landscapes which still seem bathed in the air of classical poetry.[32] We should think also of the charming ivory caskets whose motifs are

[30] See L. Bréhier, *L'Art byzantin* (Paris, 1924), chap. iii: "Le courant profane et mythologique," pp. 44–45.

[31] Cod. grec. 2832, fol. 48 b; the same manuscript contains a representation of Apollo.

[32] Bibl. Nat., cod. grec 139 (tenth century), fol. 16: See H. Buchthal, *The Miniatures of the Paris Psalter*, Studies of the Warburg Institute, Vol. II (1938).—Cf. the Zeus, Artemis and Acteon, Chiron and Achilles, in manu-

inspired by Alexandrian works, even when not literally copied from them; these motifs are for the most part Cupids, Centaurs, Bellerophon, Pegasus, or the Labors of Hercules.[33] "It has generally been supposed that these exquisite works began to be made in Constantinople in the period when the iconoclastic emperors wished to replace religious art by themes belonging to the Alexandrian tradition; but most of the caskets are contemporary with the brilliant literary renaissance of the eleventh and twelfth centuries."[34] Lastly, several bas-reliefs, some of which, for example, still adorn the façades of San Marco in Venice and the Torcello Cathedral, treat again of these same mythological themes. Now these reliefs, as is well known, were brought from Constantinople in 1204, with the famous bronze horses.

In the West, outside the domain of astronomy and astrology, such cases of survival are rare. The manuscripts of the classical poets were not illustrated: of the two Vatican Virgils, for example, no medieval copy has been found, and we have no illustrated manuscript of Ovid. Even though they do not directly form part of our subject, we might perhaps note the Carolingian representations of the Passion in which Sun, Moon, Earth, and Ocean have kept their classical forms;[35] but these are related to the *Aratea* types, and like them degenerate or disappear during the following centuries.

We must direct our search elsewhere. The first encyclopedias, which seem like the debris of classical culture, usually devote one or more chapters, as we have seen,[36] to mythology—"de diis gentium." There we may perhaps find some figure to interest us.

Of the first of the encyclopedias, the *Etymologiae* of Isidore, the library of Laon owns two illustrated manuscripts, of the seventh and eighth (or ninth) centuries; but in these, again, the gods appear only in the guise of

scripts of Gregory of Nazianzus: see C. Diehl, *Manuel d'art byzantin,* 2nd edition (Paris, 1925–26), II, pp. 628–629 and figs. 301–305. In the last two of the figures cited from Diehl (304 and 305), Zeus looks like a *basileus,* and the goddesses like patrician ladies.

[33] For example, Hercules and the Nemean lion, on the casket belonging to the cathedral of Lyons; the same subject on a casket in Cividale, etc.

[34] Bréhier, *op. cit.,* p. 48. Cf. also A. Goldschmidt and K. Weitzmann, *Die byzantinischen Elfenbeinskulpturen des* X–XIII *Jahrhunderts* (Berlin, 1930–34).

[35] Cf., in Byzantine compositions of a religious nature, the type of the bearded river god, who represents the Jordan in the Baptism mosaic of the Ravenna Baptistery; and the "Hades," Hell in chains, in the mosaic at Daphni representing the Descent into Limbo. See J. Ebersolt, *Mélanges d'histoire et d'archéologie byzantines* (Paris, 1917), p. 10.

[36] Book I, Part 1, chaps. i and iv.

64. The planetary gods

constellations.[37] We shall fare better with the *De rerum naturis* of Rabanus Maurus; of the original manuscript of this work, which has disappeared, we possess the famous copy executed in 1023 and preserved at Monte Cassino.[38] Here we have some ten divinities, among whom are Bacchus, Juno, Pan, and Mercury. Their appearance is crude and bizarre (*fig. 65*), yet a classical model can be more or less vaguely discerned behind each one. Relationships have been shown, for instance, between the figure of Pan and a classical statuette in the Louvre.[39]

65. Vulcan, Pluto, Bacchus, Mercury

66. Vulcan, Pluto, Bacchus, Mercury

But now comes the surprising fact: this little group of gods in the Monte Cassino Rabanus manuscript, classical in origin,[40] and therefore a relatively correct set of models for the Middle Ages, remained without posterity for centuries.[41] It immediately fell

[37] Cod. 422 and 423; see *supra*, p. 64, n 101.

[38] See A. M. Amelli, *Miniature sacre e profane dell'anno 1023 illustranti l'Enciclopedia medioevale di Rabano Mauro* (Monte Cassino, 1896), Pl. CXII.

[39] See F. Saxl, *Antike Götter in der Spätrenaissance*, Studien der Bibl. Warburg (Leipzig, 1927), Pl. III; A. Goldschmidt, "Frühmittelalterliche illustrierte Enzyklopädien, *Vorträge der Bibliothek Warburg* (1923–24); see also F. Saxl, "Illustrated Mediaeval Encyclopaedias, I: The Classical Heritage," in volume of lectures to be published by the Warburg Institute.

[40] With the exception of the dog-headed Mercury (Anubis).

[41] As we shall see later, it was copied in the fifteenth century (*fig. 66*).

into oblivion, giving place to absolutely new types which lacked even the slightest connection with classical art.

*

THESE NEW types originate exclusively in literary sources. They are found, from the twelfth century on, in the manuscripts of those allegorical treatises on the gods whose contents we have already had occasion to study.[42] These treatises are made up of two parts: a descriptive section, generally brief, in which the author outlines the figure and attributes of each of the pagan gods; a moral section, much the more important of the two, in which each figure and its attributes are interpreted in an edifying sense.

The elements of these descriptions, and often those of the commentary as well, are drawn for the most part not from the classical authors, but from late mythographers or scholiasts, pagan or Christian, who resemble one another in their inclination to search for the secrets of science or wisdom beneath the surface of Fable—authors, for example, like Macrobius, Servius, Lactantius Placidus, Martianus Capella, and Fulgentius. We know, moreover, that in the fifth century mythology had long ceased to be a religion, and had become instead a theme for didactic disquisitions.[43] It is this mixed erudition, thoroughly impregnated with allegory, which serves as a base for our medieval compilers,[44] who collect and juxtapose material from late sources of this type and then, in turn, pile up their own glosses on the slight descriptive data which serve as groundwork for the whole medley. Thus did Rémi of Auxerre graft his commentary on Martianus; thus, later, did Ridewall remoralize Fulgentius.[45]

Now from around the year 1100, illustrations begin to appear in the margins of these treatises. A manuscript of the commentary of Rémi on Martianus, for example,[46] contains a whole series of gods: Saturn, Cybele and the Corybantes, Jupiter, Apollo, Mars, Mercury. Without the inscriptions we

[42] See Book I, Part 1, chap. iii.

[43] *Supra*, pp. 88 ff.

[44] This has been demonstrated with extreme precision by O. Gruppe, *Geschichte der klassischen Mythologie*, chap. I, A, i: "Die Quellen der mythologischen Kenntnisse des abendländischen Mittelalters"; B, "Mythologische Studien von der Völkerwanderung bis zur karolingischen Zeit"; C, v, "Die Erneuerung der Wissenschaften unter Karl dem Grossen"; C, vi, "Das Wiederaufblühen der symbolischen Mythenauslegung." This chapter is fundamental for the study of medieval mythology.

[45] In his *Fulgentius metaforalis*; see *supra*, p. 94.

[46] Cod. Monac. lat. 14271, fol. 11 v.

would have trouble in identifying them, for at first glance neither the style of the drawings nor the trappings of the figures recall the classical images; these deities look much more like contemporaries of the first German emperors (*fig. 67*).

Yet as we examine them more carefully, we see that the artist has not indulged in pure fancy; on the contrary, he has taken pains to follow as carefully as possible the directions of a certain text. He has, in fact, given to each personage the attributes assigned to it by that text: to Cybele, "mater deorum," her tympana and her sacred tree, the pine of Attis; to Apollo, the bow, arrows, and aureole; to Jupiter, the raven of prophecy [47] and the oak of Dodona. These attributes, however, do not by themselves provide a correct portrayal of the gods, for in the absence of any sort of visual model the artist has not known how they ought to be represented. The text tells him, for instance, that Apollo carries the three Graces in his hand.[47a] Rémi has taken this detail from Macrobius, who had it from Pausanias: "Apollinis simulacra manu dextera Gratias gestant" (*Saturnalia,* I, 17). What is called for here is thus a small replica of the group of the three Graces. Our draftsman, however, who has never *seen* anything of the sort, naïvely pictures a kind of bouquet out of which emerge three female busts. Similarly, Saturn is given a veiled head—"caput velatum," says the text. Representations of Saturn are known which show the god with a fold of his toga thrown over his head, as in the fresco from the House of the Dioscuri, now in the Naples Museum. But the illustrator of Rémi has supposed that the veil to be represented must be ample and majestic like a sort of canopy. Thus those very accessories which should identify the gods serve to disguise them, and even when a classical representation is intended, the text, sedulously translated into visual form, engenders images which are completely nonclassical.

At a distance of several centuries, the illustrations of the *Fulgentius metaforalis* [48] offer us an even more singular pantheon; these *ymagines secundum Fulgentium* are little more than caricatures of antiquity (*figs. 30*

[47] The raven is found in Cicero, *De divinatione,* I, 7: "Jupiterne . . . corvum a dextra canere jussisset"; I, 39: "Cur a dextra corvus."

[47a] Cf. R. Pfeiffer on the Delian Apollo, in *Journal of the Warburg and Courtauld Institutes,* Vol. XV.

[48] Cod. Palat. lat. 1066. These miniatures are reproduced in H. Liebeschütz, *op. cit.*

and *31*). Lacking a model, as did his Romanesque predecessor, the Gothic miniaturist has fallen into the same errors. He also has naturally adapted his mythology to the taste of the day, introducing crenellations, turrets, armor, and long furred mantles; and he, also, has been completely ingenuous in his literal interpretation of the text before him.[49] Jupiter is surrounded by a flight of heraldic eaglets; Iris' rainbow forms an aureole for Juno which

67. Saturn, Cybele, Jupiter, Apollo, and other gods

[49] It must be said, in his behalf, that the text itself often departs from the classical data.

might be the halo of a saint; a postilion drives the quadriga of Apollo, and Pluto's Inferno suggests the setting for a mystery play (*fig. 80*).

The illustrations in these two manuscripts show us, therefore, how the Middle Ages, with no help except that of the texts, attempted in different periods to restore the visual embodiments of the pagan gods, and that the resulting figures are completely foreign to antiquity. At the same time, neither Rémi of Auxerre nor John Ridewall can be said to have created types. They founded no tradition, for the images which they inspired seem not to have enjoyed any great diffusion. The case is quite otherwise with another treatise, which exerted a profound and lasting influence on the iconography of the gods; this is the *Images of the Gods* of the "philosopher Albricus."

*

FROM a very early date and until quite recently, two distinct authors were confused under the name Albricus.

A Latin manuscript in the Vatican Library, Reginensis 1290, seemed to substantiate this error. The manuscript contains two texts:

1) a fairly long treatise, *Albrici philosophi liber ymaginum deorum* (fol. 8v.–29r.);

2) a series of very short chapters, illustrated with pen drawings, and attributed to Albricus, with the title, *De deorum imaginibus libellus* (fol. 1r.–8r.).

The attribution of these two texts to a common author seemed at first perfectly convincing, since to a superficial view they appeared to be two different forms of the same work, the *Libellus* being only an abridgement of the *Liber*. "The mythographer Albricus," says R. Raschke, "as Varro had already done before him, reduced his larger work to the form of an *epitome*." [50] In reality, as we shall prove, the relationship between the two texts is much less immediate, and more complex. But first of all we must clarify the personality of Albricus, the "first" Albricus, author of the *Liber*.

The *Liber ymaginum deorum* is known under other titles; it was identified long ago with the anonymous treatise published in 1831 by Angelo Mai

[50] *De Alberico mythologo* (Breslau, 1913).

and by him attributed to a "Mythographus tertius." [51] Furthermore, in the fourteenth century it was commonly known as the *Poetarius,* or again as the *Scintillarium poetarum.* It is under the latter title, for example, that Raoul de Presles refers to it in his commentary on the *Civitas Dei* (*c.* 1375); in the list which he draws up of the "docteurs et auteurs desquieux a esté prinse l'exposicion de ce livre," he cites "Albericus Londoniensis in sintillario [*sic*] poetarum." [52]

One is struck by the adjective "Londoniensis." [53] Was Albricus, then, an Englishman, or the pseudonym for an Englishman?

In certain manuscripts in Cambridge (cod. Cantab. Trinity College 884), Oxford (cod. Digbeianus 221), and at Worcester Cathedral (cod. 154), the *incipit* or the *explicit* of the *Scintillarium* replaces the name Albricus with "Alexander Nequam." [54] For his part, Robert Holkott, in his *Commentary on the Wisdom of Solomon,* cites "Alexander Nequam in Scintillario poetarum," while another Englishman, Ridewall, author of the *Fulgentius metaforalis,* calls the text which is one of his principal sources *Mithologia Alexandri Nequam.* According to this tradition, then, Albricus would be the pseudonym of the celebrated philosopher Neckam, author of the *De naturis rerum,* who died in 1217. The oldest known manuscript of the *Images of the Gods*—cod. Vat. 3413—is of exactly contemporary origin. The "Mythographus tertius," Albricus, and Neckam would thus be one and the same person. Some caution must still be maintained, however, with regard to this hypothesis.

What, now, are the sources of the *Liber ymaginum deorum,* and what are its true connections with the text and pictures of the *Libellus?*

[51] Cod. Vatic. 3413. See A. Mai, *Classicorum auctorum e Vaticanis codicibus editorum* (Rome, 1828–38), III, preface, pp. X–XV. Jacobs (*Zeitschrift f. d. Altertumswissenschaft* [1834], pp. 1059–1060) was the first to demonstrate the identity between the "Mythographus tertius" and Albricus.

[52] Bibl. Nat. ms. fr. 22912, fol. 1. Albricus is, indeed, the chief authority referred to by Raoul de Presles for mythology. See A. de Laborde, *Les manuscrits à figures de la Cité de Dieu* (Paris, 1909), chap. IV, p. 60: "For the mythology of fable and the representation of pagan divinities, he has recourse chiefly to Albricus, whom he seems to know by heart. He quotes him frequently, and is led to speak of earlier mythographers by what he finds said of them in his work."

[53] The same adjective reappears in the *editio princeps: Allegoriae poeticae seu de veritate ac expositione poeticarum fabularum libri* IV *Alberico Londoniensi authore* (Jehan de Marnef, Paris 1520).

[54] The name Albricus is preserved in the margin of cod. Digb. 221, and at the end of the Worcester manuscript. See the discussion in Liebeschütz, *op. cit.,* pp. 16–18, n. 28.

Like the other treatises of the same general sort, Albricus' work condenses the mythological material collected by the grammarians and compilers of the last centuries of antiquity. He enriches this material with additions from his medieval forerunners. His chief sources, in fact, are the *Mythologiae* of Fulgentius, Servius' *Commentary on the Aeneid,* the *Saturnalia* and the *Commentary on the Dream of Scipio* by Macrobius, the *Marriage of Mercury and Philology* by Martianus Capella, the *Etymologiae* of Isidore, and the *Commentary* of Rémi of Auxerre on Martianus. There are very few direct borrowings from classical literature, if we except the *De natura deorum* (utilized only for the interpretation of the names of the deities), and rare citations from the poets, for whom Albricus seems to have consulted chiefly the scholiasts.[55]

Like the other treatises, that of Albricus still searches the myths for their "hidden" meaning, lending them in turn historical, physical, and, above all, moral significance. The story of Venus and Mars, for example, becomes Lust dishonoring Virtue. When the Sun unveils their guilty love, Venus revenges herself by leading astray the five daughters of the Sun—that is to say, the five senses: Pasiphaë, the sense of sight; Medea, hearing; Circe, touch; Phaedra, smell; Dirce, taste.

Such as it was, with its heavy allegorical apparatus, the work appears to have enjoyed a great vogue and great authority among the educated. We have an example in Raoul de Presles, who knew it by heart;[56] and, in fact, as a mythological manual or dictionary, it constituted a precious auxiliary in reading the poets. Hence its appellations of *Poetarius* and *Scintillarium poetarum.* But it was also to become an aid to artists, furnishing them with themes of inspiration; we shall see this when we examine the links which connect the work with the *Libellus de imaginibus deorum.*

In spite of appearances, the *Libellus* is not a simple abridgement of the *Liber.* It does indeed derive from it, but indirectly, and after an interval of two centuries. Between the two works stands, first of all, an intermediary of prime importance, since it is no other than Petrarch himself.

[55] He has made use of the scholia on Horace, Statius, Persius, Lucan. See the detailed analysis of his sources in R. Raschke, *op. cit.*

[56] See *supra,* p. 171, n. 52.

Pierre de Nolhac noted years ago [57] that Petrarch's library contained a collection which, among other manuscripts, included the *Liber mythologiarum* of Fulgentius, and the *Poetarius Albrici viri illustris, unde idolorum ritus inoleverit, ubi omnis vetustas deorum antiquorum exprimitur.* Petrarch, it thus appears, made use of our Albricus, and drew from it a good part of his mythological knowledge. Better still, he made direct use of it in writing the third canto of his Latin epic, *Africa,* composed to honor the memory of Scipio.

In the poem Lelius, on a mission as ambassador to Syphax, King of Numidia, is received in a splendid hall, the decorations of which he admires at length. Among these decorations appear the gods of Olympus:

Undique fulgentes auro speciesque Deorum
Et formae heroum stabant atque acta priorum.[58]

Petrarch describes them individually, in 123 verses (140–262), following step by step the indications of Albricus. However,—and this should be even more interesting for us—since his aim is simply to describe and not to moralize, of the mythological material from which he thus borrows, he retains only the pictorial elements, the visual details indicative of the pose, costume, and attributes of each god:

Jupiter ante alios, augusta in sede superbus
Sceptra manu fulmenque tenens; Jovis armiger ante
Unguibus Idaum juvenem super astra levabat.
Inde autem incessu gravior tristisque senecta
Velato capite et glauco distinctus amictu,
Rastra manu falcemque gerens Saturnus agresti
Rusticus aspectu natos pater ore vorabat;
Flammivomusque draco caude postrema recurve
Ore tenens magnos sese torquebat in orbes . . .[59]

[57] *Pétrarque et l'humanisme* (Paris, 1892), pp. 169–171, and p. 133. Petrarch also made use of Albricus in drawing up his *De viris.*

[58] *Africa,* III (ed. Festa [Sansoni, Florence, n.d.]), vv. 138–139. ("Everywhere, glittering with gold, stood the figures of the gods and heroes, and the deeds of the forefathers.")

[59] *Op. cit.,* vv. 140–148. ("First Jupiter, superb on his majestic seat, holding in hand his scepter and thunderbolt; Jupiter's armor-bearer, with its claws, lifted above the stars the young Idean; then, with heavy pace and saddened by old age, with veil on head and clothed in a grayish cloak, came Saturn, holding in his hand—like a peasant—a rake and a sickle; he devoured his own children, while a

Thus Petrarch preserves only those details which have the value of images; as a humanist and man of taste, he disregards what was meant to improve or instruct. But stripped thus to essentials, the "images of the gods" which he traces one after the other with his elegant and precise hand, form a little repertoire at once clear, detailed, and likely to be of immediate use to the artist who might turn to it for inspiration. In short, we find in this third Canto of the *Africa* the prototype of a *Libellus de imaginibus deorum;* better still, as we shall soon see, we find in it the true model of our *Libellus.*

But the road which leads from Petrarch to the "second" Albricus is not a direct one. Once again the figures of the gods, to which the classicizing poet had attempted to restore their purity of contour, are to serve as themes of medieval allegory. Between the *Africa* and the *Libellus* comes the *Ovide moralisé* composed in Avignon, around 1340, by Petrarch's friend, Pierre Bersuire,[60] following the counsels of the poet and the lines of his *Africa.* This *Ovide moralisé,* is in fact a sort of appendix to the *Reductorium morale,*[61] the great work in which Bersuire laboriously, in thirteen books, gave moral meaning to the *Liber de proprietatibus* of Bartholomaeus Anglicus. In order to complete this vast work of moralization, he added to it three more books: the fourteenth treats of the marvels of nature, the sixteenth of difficult passages in the Bible. As for the fifteenth, it brings us the *Metamorphoses,* interpreted according to the same principles and with the same intent. As introduction to this fifteenth book come seventeen chapters dealing with the form of each god. In this section, as in all the others, the author is seeking truths, more or less profound, beneath surface appearances; but at the beginning of each chapter he gives us a short introduction which, this time, treats only of the god's image as such. He pens a brief description which is to serve

---

flame-vomiting dragon, holding its curved tail in its mouth, twisted itself in great circles.")

[60] This is the work which was later published in a French translation in 1484 by the Bruges printer Colart Mansion (see Part I, chap. iii, p. 93). It was long attributed to the Dominican, Thomas Waleys—as, for example, in the Latin edition of F. Regnault (Paris, 1515): *Metamorphosis Ovidiana moraliter a magistro Thoma Waleys anglico de professione predicatorum sub sanctissimo patre Dominico explanata.* B. Hauréau ("Mémoire sur un commentaire des Métamorphoses d'Ovide," *Mémoires de l'Academie des Inscriptions . . . ,* XXX, Part II, pp. 45–55) restored the work to its true author.

[61] See *supra,* p. 93.

as profane nucleus for the moralization. From whom has he borrowed these portraits of the gods? He tells us in the clearest of terms:

"Sed antequam ad fabulas descendam, primo de formis et figuris deorum aliqua dicam. Verumtamen, quia deorum ipsorum imagines scriptas vel pictas alicubi non potui reperire, habui consulere venerabilem virum magistrum Franciscum de Petato [*sic*], poetam utique profundum in scientia et facundum in eloquentia et expertum in omni poetica et historica disciplina: qui prefatas imagines in quodam opere suo eleganti metro describit, discurrere etiam libros Fulgentii, Alexandri [62] et Rabani, ut de diversis partibus traham figuram vel imaginem, quam diis istis ficticiis voluerunt antiqui secundum rationes phisicas assignare." [63]

However distorted the name may be (the edition of Colart Mansion was to translate it as "François du Pré"),[64] it is not difficult to recognize "Petato" as Petrarch; as for the "opus quodam," this is evidently *Africa.* To assist his friend in his search for information "de formis et figuris deorum," Petrarch, with his customary generosity, has communicated to him the verses in which he has described the palace of Syphax [65]—and this, incidentally, might have made it unnecessary for Bersuire to turn to the poet's own sources: Fulgentius, Rabanus Maurus, and Albricus.

It is these brief introductions of Bersuire on each of the gods, brought together and once more freed of their commentaries, that finally made up, toward 1400, the *Libellus de imaginibus deorum* which, as a whole, follows very closely the text of the *Ovide moralisé.*[66] The author of the work

[62] Alexander Neckam (?), Albricus.

[63] Second edition Regnault, fol. 11 r. ("But before I come to the fables, I will say something about the shapes and figures of the gods. Since, however, I could nowhere find descriptions or paintings of the gods themselves, I had to consult the venerable master, *Franciscus de Petato,* poet as profound in learning as he is well versed in every poetical and historical discipline: he did describe the said figures *in one of his works,* in elegant verse. I also ran through the books of Fulgentius, Alexander, and Rabanus, in order to extract from these various sources the images or figures which the ancients, in giving them physical interpretation, assigned to these fictitious creatures.")

[64] See M. D. Henkel, *De Houtsneden van Mansion's Ovide moralisé, Bruges, 1484* (Amsterdam, 1922), p. 5.

[65] P. de Nolhac, *op. cit.,* pp. 71 and 424.

[66] There exists in the Ambrosiana (cod. G III in f.) a version of this text in verse: *Carmina composita per me Bertilinum de Vavassoribus super figuras deorum 17.* This poem, like the *Libellus,* adheres very closely to Bersuire's text, which follows it in the manuscript: *Prologus in metamorphosim moralisatam: de formis et figuris et imaginibus deorum.*

has remained anonymous, but we now have no trouble in understanding how he could have been confused with Albricus. We need do no more than compare the image of Saturn, for instance, as found in Alexander Neckam(?), Petrarch, Bersuire, and the *Libellus*, to satisfy ourselves that the tradition has varied but slightly from one author to another (see accompanying table).

NECKAM(?) = MYTHOGR. III = ALBRICUS I	PETRARCH *Africa* Can. III, vv. 143–48	BERSUIRE *Ovide moralisé* Chap. I	ALBRICUS II *Libellus* Chap. I
Bode ed., pp. 153 f.	Festa ed.	1509 ed.	Van Staveren ed. (1742), pp. 896–7.
Primum deorum Saturnum ponunt. Hunc maestum, senem, canum, caput glauco amictu copertum habentem, filiorum suorum voratorem, falcemque ferentem, draconem etiam flammivomum qui caudae suae ultima devorat, in dextra tenentem, inducunt.	Inde autem incessu gravior tristisque senecta, Velato capite et glauco distinctus amictu, Rastra manu falcemque gerens Saturnus agresti Rusticus aspectu natos pater ore vorabat, Flammivomusque draco caude postrema recurve Ore tenens magnos sese torquebat in orbes.	Saturnus pingebatur et supponebatur homo senex curvus tristis et pallidus, qui una manu falcem tenebat et in eadem draconis portabat imaginem que dentibus caudam propriam commordebat, altera vero filium parvulum ad os applicabat et eum dentibus devorabat. Caput galeatum amictu coopertum habebat.	Saturnus primus deorum subponebatur: et pingebatur, ut homo senex, canus, prolixa barba, curvus, tristis et pallidus, tecto capite, colore glauco, qui una manu, scilicet dextra, falcem tenebat et in eadem serpentis portabat imaginem qui caudam propriam dentibus commordebat. Altera vero, scilicet sinistra, filium parvulum ad os adplicabat et eum devorare videbatur.[67]

However, the difference between the "first" and the "second" Albricus is profound, for the spirit has changed. Whereas the *Liber ymaginum* brought together the mythological substance encumbered with the medieval glosses, the *Libellus*, renewing Petrarch, and again separating the images from the allegorical ensemble in which Bersuire had reinserted them, offers us a clear text, determinedly profane and purely iconographical. The same formula recurs in it constantly: "Pingebatur." This formula tends to freeze the god in some one typical and immutable attitude and setting, which can be

[67] Liebeschütz, *op. cit.*, pp. 58–64, gives other synoptic tables, invaluable for the history of the formation of the *Libellus*. He goes back to Fulgentius, Martianus Capella, and Rabanus Maurus.

easily studied and endlessly reproduced. It seems, in fact, to demand illustration, and illustrations of it were not lacking.

Cod. Reginensis 1290, which contains the text of the *Liber* as well as that of the *Libellus,* is decorated, as we have seen, with curious pen drawings, executed around 1420. These drawings lack neither life nor charm, but the

68. Apollo and the Muses

divinities which they present offer almost no kinship with the antique types. In the absence of any sort of visual model—the lack of which we have already noted in the case of Rémi's and Ridewall's illustrations—the most scrupulous artist will inevitably fall into blunders and anachronisms. But in the *Libellus* we have a vivid example of another weakness inherent in reconstructions of this sort, due to the fact that they are based on heterogeneous texts and are therefore made up of unrelated fragments. Let us, for example, analyze the image of Apollo as the *Libellus* has described it and as it has been faithfully represented by the artist (*fig. 68*). The table on the following page makes clear its composite origin.

Thus, strictly speaking, the illustrations of the *Libellus* are grounded not on any one text, but on a mosaic of texts. It is this which gives them their doubly artificial character: they are composite portraits, formed of scattered

Pictured Detail	*Source*
Apollo a beardless young man.[68]	Fulgentius, *Mythol.*, I, 17
Golden tripod on head.	Rémi, *Comm. ad Mart.*, V, fol. 83 a, v, 28 ff.
Bow, arrows, and quiver in right hand; in left, the zither.	Servius, *Comm. Aen.*, III, 138
Three-headed monster beneath the god's feet, frightful in aspect, its body that of a serpent and its heads those of dog, wolf, and lion. (The heads are separate, but the body common to them all.)	Macrobius, *Sat.*, I, 20, 13–14
Crown of twelve precious stones on Apollo's head.	Martianus Capella, I, 75 (p. 22, 3–4)
Laurel tree at his side, with black raven flying above it.	Fulg., *Mythol.*, I, 14
The raven sacred to Apollo.	schol. on *Theb.*, III, 506
Under the laurel tree, the nine Muses, forming a choir.	Fulg., *Mythol.*, I, 15
At a slight distance, the great serpent Python, which Apollo pierces with an arrow.	Fulg., *Mythol.*, I, 17
Apollo seated between the two summits of Parnassus,	Isidore, *Etymol.*, XIV, viii, 11
from which springs the Castalian Fount.[69]	Mart. Cap., VI, 651 (p. 221, 12–16)

features, of *membra disiecta,* welded together after a fashion, but necessarily lacking in unity. Hence the awkward and bizarre look of these gods, burdened with anomalous attributes which they do not know how to carry all at once.

But, all the same, these artificial and "synthetic" gods live and multiply. There can be no doubt, in fact, that the text of the *Libellus,* in its definitive state, or even in its preceding phases, often inspired artists, to whom

[68] The text adds: ". . . nunc in facie puerili, nunc juvenili, semper imberbis nunc autem in cana diversitate apparentis" (". . . sometimes with the face of a child, or that of a young man, always beardless, or again as an old man"). This feature comes from Martianus, I, 76.

[69] See Raschke, *op. cit.*, for analysis of the other descriptions.

it served as a repertory or manual of iconography. Aside from Reginensis 1290, there are many manuscripts in which we find the gods pictured according to the tradition of Albricus. The earliest till now known, Paris 6986 and Vat. Reg. 1480,[70] hardly go back farther than 1370, but the common model which served for both may have been executed in the first half of the fourteenth century.[71] In any case, we possess a very rich series of miniatures [72]—French, Flemish, and Italian—which bear witness alike to the diffusion and the stability of the Albricus types, all of whose features have been once and for all standardized by the *Libellus*.

*

IF WE have dwelt at some length upon Albricus and upon the tradition that he founded, it is because of his exceptional importance. He is, in reality, not merely a precursor, but one of the principal agents of the Renaissance, since it is in part by way of his text and the visual images engendered by his *Images of the Gods* that the Olympians regain their sovereignty.

Indeed, as we shall soon show, the text of Albricus is to continue, directly or by way of Boccaccio,[73] to serve as a base to mythographers and a source to humanists, while its illustrations remain the standard types for artists throughout the Quattrocento and even beyond.

*

THE FOREGOING exposition has brought us down to the first years of the fifteenth century—in other words, to the threshold of the "Renaissance." By this date, the two great iconographical traditions which we have traced from late antiquity have led, each in its own way, to a profound alteration of the classical types of the gods.

We have observed the reasons for these alterations as we went along. If we omit the cases of substitution (such as the replacing of Olympian figures by the Babylonian planetary types), they may be reduced in essence to two:

[70] The *Ovide moralisé* in verse, attributed to Chrétien Legouais by Gaston Paris, who studies its relations with the moralization of Ovid by Bersuire; see *supra*, p. 92.

[71] See F. Saxl, "Rinascimento dell' antichità," *Rep. f. Kunstwiss.* (1922), pp. 220 ff.

[72] Several of these manuscripts will be studied in the next chapter.

[73] That is to say, through the *Genealogia deorum*, see Bk. II, chap. i.

either the artist has a visual model but, being ignorant of the subject—that is to say, lacking an explanatory text—is unable to render it correctly, or he has nothing but a text, and in this case his reconstruction, even when carefully made, is bound to entail a certain risk, because there is no model which would permit him to check its accuracy.

69. Mars and Venus; Mercury

A typical example of the first case is the curious transformation of the Medusa head in the illustrations of astronomical manuscripts: the Arab copyist, knowing nothing of Greek mythology, mistook the blood dripping from the severed head for a beard, and changed the Gorgon into a hirsute demon.[74] His error is even perpetuated in the terminology of modern astronomers, who still give the name Algol, meaning "demon," to the strange star in the constellation Perseus whose brightness varies periodically.

On the other hand, we have seen (*figs. 67* and *12*) what amusing caricatures result from the attempts of the medieval illustrators to reconstruct, on the basis of Pausanias, a statue of Apollo[75] or of the Olympian Zeus.[76]

It might be instructive and diverting to list the manifold forms taken on by one specific deity. As we do so, we shall be unable to decide whether it is

[74] See, for example, cod. Vat. 8174, cod. Vindob. 5415 (sky map), and the Perseus of the lapidary of Alfonso X; a Sûfî ms., Paris, Bib. Nat. cod. arab. 5036; a ms. of Qazwînî, cod. Vindob. 1437; Brit. Mus. cod. Or. 5323 (*fig. 60*).

[75] See *supra*, pp. 167 f. (Monac. lat. 14271).

[76] See *supra*, p. 54 (lapidary of Alphonso X).

through copying or reconstruction that he has suffered most. Let us take Mercury, for example. The illustrator of Rémi of Auxerre has given him virtually the aspect of an angel (Monac. lat. 14271); in Rabanus Maurus[77] his winged feet have been mistaken for a bird flying between his legs;[78] with the Arab copyist, in a manuscript of Qazwînî (Vindob. Fl. 1438, N. F. 155), the wings are attached to the god's belt rather than to his feet, and the little wings on his cap have become a cockscomb (*fig. 69*). In one of the manuscripts of the Albricus tradition, these wings have so increased in size that they entirely cover the legs, and the chin and ears, and meet above the head to form a sort of crest (Bodl. Rawlinson B. 214, f. 198 v.; see *fig. 70*). The caduceus is another source of embarrassment for the artists. In one case, we see the two serpents reduced to a single one, which crawls at the feet of the god instead of twining about his rod

70. Venus and her train; Mercury

[77] This figure is inspired, incidentally, by a type of the Mercury-Anubis.

[78] Cf., in a German ms. of the fifteenth century (Morgan Library, New York, 384), the transformation of the lionskin worn by Hercules into a living animal, looking up over the hero's shoulder.

(Monte Cassino ms. of Rabanus Maurus; *fig. 65*); again, it has become a sort of fork (Monac. lat. 14271; *fig. 67*), and still elsewhere, a candelabra bearing two candles (Monac. lat. 826).

Occasionally errors arise which are only to be explained by corruptions in the text itself, or by misreadings.[79]

Thus Pluto, in the Rabanus Maurus manuscript (although the illustrations are derived from an antique model), carries in his hand a jar; this unaccustomed attribute arises simply from a confusion between *orca,* meaning jar, and *Orcus,* the realm of the dead (*fig. 65*). Comparable misunderstandings have been produced through translation—as is true, for example, in lapidaries.[80] Thus, the mysterious figure who holds sometimes a book, sometimes a hare, in the French lapidaries, is in reality the zodiacal sign of the Scales: *libra* has become *liebra* in Spanish, *livre* or *lièvre* in French.[81] The Latin manuscripts of *Picatrix* contain variants capable of producing wholly different images: thus the figure of Saturn, "according to the learned Mercury," is that of a man having under his feet, as is said in some texts, "similem unius lagori id est racam"; in others, "aliquid simile racemo." In the first case, a lizard must be placed beneath Saturn's feet; in the second, a bunch of grapes.

Still more surprising is what happens to Andromeda. In the *Apothecarius* of the library at Chartres we read: "Si inveneris Andromadam quae habeat crines sparsos atque manus remissas, ille lapis . . . habet potestatem reconciliandi inter se virum et uxorem." Now this is the version found in ms. F. fr. 9136 of the Bibliothèque Nationale: "Si tu trouves un dromadaire qui ait les cheveux épars sur les épaules, icelle pierre rend paix et concorde entre mari et femme." Andromeda has been changed into a dromedary, through the intermediary of *dromedarius.*[82]

In the Arab texts, homonyms have similarly been responsible for unexpected representations. Thus in the manuscript of Qazwînî (cod. Vindob.

[79] We disregard the casual substitutions of one thing for another, which are frequent in the miniatures and the calendar engravings of the late Middle Ages: Mars represented instead of Jupiter, Mercury instead of the Sun, etc.

[80] See F. de Mély, "Du rôle des pierres gravées au Moyen-Age," *Revue de l'art chrétien* (1893); and *supra,* pp. 54 ff.

[81] De Mély, *op. cit.*

[82] The name of the stone *androdamas* (hematite) has added to the confusion; in both cases the ability to reconcile husband and wife is asserted.

Fl. 1438, N. F. 155), Jupiter holds a phallus in his raised hand instead of a scepter; the word used in the text might signify either object.[83] Other representations find similar explanation, such as that of Cassiopeia with a bleeding hand, etc.

And all these misunderstandings, confusions, false interpretations, which sometimes end by completely corrupting the images, are at bottom attributable to something still more general—the fact that the gods have traveled widely.

Let us recall their itineraries: sometimes they go from East to West, from Egypt, Syria, even Mesopotamia, to Sicily and Spain; sometimes from North to South, from England into France and Italy. Now each of these removes, with the translations and adaptations which it involves, adds to the chances of error. On the other hand, all these roads end undoubtedly, sooner or later, by bringing the classical gods back to the lands of their birth—but after how many centuries, how many wanderings and detours, and in what a state! Europe, in short, recovers her gods very much as she received Aristotle—"mutilated, botched, crippled, turned from Greek into Arabic and from Arabic into Latin." [84] Their long absence and their vagabond paths—leading sometimes so far from their native shores—have made them into foreigners.

But now that they have at last returned to their homeland, we shall see them gradually undergoing formal reintegration—regaining, at least in large part, their natural bearing and their familiar look.

[83] See F. Saxl, *Verzeichnis astrol. und mythol. ill. Handschrift. in röm. Bibl.*, Introd., p. XII, n. 1. In the same manuscript, Mercury also holds a phallus, apparently for the same reason (*fig. 69*).

[84] J. Michelet, *Histoire de France au seizième siècle: Renaissance* (Paris, 1857), Introd., p. 94.

II

The Reintegration of the Gods

WE HAVE seen how, in the Middle Ages, the gods lost their classical form, either because it underwent gradual change, or because it was dropped in favor of the most unexpected disguises.

How and why did it come about that, in the second half of the fifteenth century, the original form was reintegrated? This is the problem which remains for us to solve. We shall consider it according to the plan adopted in the preceding chapter—that is to say, by limiting ourselves to certain iconographical series, and by distinguishing between the visual and the literary traditions, from which our examples will successively be drawn.

*

WE HAVE followed, in the illustrations of the astronomical manuscripts, the alteration of the Hellenistic types of the constellations. A few of these types, however—those of the Aratus manuscripts—were retained in relative and sometimes even surprising purity beyond the Carolingian period; but in the end they, too, underwent deterioration before being replaced, toward the dawn of the thirteenth century, by the Orientalized types.[1]

Now, in the fifteenth century, we come upon a family of manuscripts, embracing the whole century in date, but all issuing from a codex of the *Aratea,* discovered in Sicily, which Poggio is known to have had in his hands.[2] Of these copies, one was executed for the Duke of Urbino (Urbinat. 1385), another for the Medici (Laurent. 98 sup. 43), and another for Ferdinand of

[1] See *supra,* pp. 150 ff., and *figs. 54–60.*

[2] See A. Breysig, *Germanici Caesaris Aratea* (Berlin, 1867), and F. Saxl, *Verzeichnis* (Rome), *Einführung,* pp. xv–xvii.

Aragon, king of Naples (Barberin. 76). They mark the return to an authentic tradition, and this is of itself extremely interesting; but much may also be learned from a comparison of them. The earliest of the copies, executed by artists still half immersed in the medieval tradition, have not successfully reproduced the style of the model: attitudes and draperies rather betray the influence of their own time. On the other hand, the last copyist, represented by the Naples manuscript, has freed himself from this influence. Even though he is less skillful than the others, he has a better understanding of the qualities of the prototype, restoring to it its dignity, its equilibrium—even the frame which surrounds it and the delicacy of its color modeling (*fig. 71*). Thus, from now on, the evolution tends to come full circle: instead of moving farther away from the antique model, it approaches it more and more closely.

The same phenomenon is seen even more clearly in the Orientalized series of astral figures. There, as the reader will recall, the Hellenistic demigods had undergone disguise at the hands of the Arabs into characters from the *Thousand and One Nights*. But they likewise now slowly revert to their original aspect.

Let us take the example of Hercules. We have spoken of his strange reincarnations: a short jacket, crossed in front, and a pair of breeches had been given him to mask his muscular nudity; on his head he wore a turban. In the same process, he had lost his lion's skin and had exchanged his club for a scimitar.[3] Let us now see how he appears in a Vienna manuscript which contains a sky map (Vindobon. 5415). This manuscript dates from before 1464 and comes from southern Germany; its illustrator, though German, has followed the designs of a North Italian artist.

The Oriental descent of this Hercules is recognized at first glance by means of the scimitar which he brandishes, but he has already lost much of his exotic look—for one thing, he no longer wears a turban. But he still has a certain distance to travel before his true form is fully regained, and it is Dürer himself who will aid him in the process. Dürer, in fact, was inspired by our Vienna manuscript, or by one of the same family, when he composed

[3] E.g., cod. Paris. arab. 5036 (*fig. 59*).

his famous sky map of 1515, the first chart of the heavens to be printed. But he introduces modifications, or rather, decisive rectifications, into the style of the figures; he frees Hercules from his outworn Eastern trappings, the Nessus shirt which has encumbered him for centuries: the club is placed in his right hand again, and the lion's skin on his left shoulder. The hero, in short, once more emerges as his true self (*fig. 72*).

71. *Jupiter*

Perseus may be taken as a similar example, and perhaps an even more instructive one. We have described his Arabic outfit and the bearded head of the demon Gûl which he carries instead of the bleeding Medusa head. He continues to be represented in this form in Western manuscripts which copy the Arab astronomical figures without recognizing in them the old pagan divinities.[4] Now in the same Vienna manuscript of which we have just spoken, which continues the Arab tradition even while mitigating its exotic character,[5] Perseus is represented nude; however, his victim's head is still that of the demon—"caput Algol."[6] Here again it is Dürer who accomplishes the restoration of the original image. In his version, not only has Perseus regained his winged feet, but it is now

72. *Hercules*

[4] E.g., cod. Vat. 8174 (end of fourteenth century).

[5] It is remarkable, as F. Saxl observes, that in this manuscript we find, along with astronomical tables belonging to the Arab tradition, and works by modern astronomers, others which belong to the old European tradition, Aratus as reworked by Bede, and a poem on the stars (*Epitome phaenomenon*).

[6] A new advance is to be seen on an Italian

the head of Medusa which he grasps by its serpent locks. In order to dispel all doubt, Dürer has added the words "caput Meduse."

In the Michael Scot manuscripts, which form a separate group, the figures again evolve in the same direction. Thus—and as early as the first half of the fifteenth century—the illustrator of cod. Vindobon. 3394 (fol. 222 v.), an Italian, substitutes the classical Perseus for the frightful Oriental gnome who still represents him around 1400 (for example, in cod. Vindobon. 2378, fol. 7 v.).

But Dürer's restorations deserve a moment's attention; let us try to define the spirit which has inspired them. What Dürer has given back to the celestial demigods is not merely their traditional attributes: it is the life and breath of paganism. For his immediate predecessors, and even for the Italian draftsman whose work he is transposing, Hercules and Perseus are hardly more than what they had been for the Arabs—mere outlines, graphic symbols. Dürer now endows these diagrams with flesh, vigor, and relief; muscles stand out, heads take on expressive power. Thus transfigured, his heroes share in the same animal force which he restores to Dog, Bear, and Bull. In his sky, swarming with its unleashed monsters, resounding to the heavy galloping of Sagittarius, the gods in their turn are roused from their torpor; mixed though it may be, the blood which flows in their veins is warm and pulsating, and restores them to their fabled existence.

However, this reawakening of a sense of plastic values and mythological correctness is not accomplished at the expense of scientific accuracy; on the contrary, the map of 1515 represents both effort and progress in that direction. The stars which form the substance of Dürer's drawings have had their positions scrupulously assigned by Conrad Heinfogel, with due attention to the work of the Arab astronomers; none of the celestial globes hitherto made had offered as solid or precise a base for study of the heavens.

This alliance of strength and energy, of calculation and life, is without doubt characteristic of Dürer's personal genius, but it is also a sign of the times. To recover the forms used by the ancients as well as their learning, their poetic imagination, and their knowledge of the universe—to reconcile,

celestial sphere (*c.* 1500) in the Musée de Cluny (*fig. 73*). The hero has regained his winged heels, and holds a buckler on which the Gorgon's head is shown; in spite of this, the inscription is still "caput Algol."

as they did, mythology and geometry—such was to be the dream of the greatest spirits of the Renaissance.

The great gods, like the heroes, were eager to resume their rightful visage. Curiously enough, it is in Germany again that we witness other interesting attempts to aid them in doing so. In the course of the fifteenth century, certain Northern artists appear to have become suddenly aware of the incongruity of representing Jupiter or Mercury under the extravagant aspect which he had taken on, either through Michael Scot or in the illustrated encyclopedias; these artists turned to the pre-Gothic period for models closer to antiquity.

Thus, in the Palatinate, the illuminator of Palatinus lat. 291 copies, around 1430, the illustrations of the celebrated treatise of Rabanus Maurus, *De rerum naturis;* [7] now among these figures, as we have seen, were images of the Olympic gods—images crude and in many respects faulty, but as a whole of indisputably classical descent. For more than four centuries they had fallen into complete oblivion, and were looked at by no one. A local miniaturist now discovers and sets out to copy them. Admittedly, his copy has a contemporary flavor of its own, but it establishes a new link with the great pictorial tradition, and at the same time prepares the way for the reappearance of the gods in their classical form (*fig. 66*).

We have seen how, in the manuscripts of Michael Scot, the figures of the planetary gods had, toward the end of the Middle Ages, assumed the most unexpected forms. We have explained the relevant influences, finding descendants of the Babylonian gods clothed in Giottesque costumes. But now, in the first half of the fifteenth century, we note in certain copies of these manuscripts the disappearance of the barbaric types, and their replacement by figures much closer to the Greco-Roman originals. How is this to be explained? Like the painter of the Rabanus Maurus illustrations, one of the illuminators of Michael Scot [8] has turned back to a relatively pure source: he has taken as model a Carolingian copy of the "Calendar of 354," and in so doing he also, despite his lack of skill, has placed himself in contact with the classical prototypes.

[7] The original manuscript of the ninth century is lost, but we possess a replica of it in the Monte Cassino manuscript, executed in 1023; see *supra*, pp. 166 f., and *fig. 65*.

[8] Cod. Darmstadt 266.

These are, of course, isolated examples. We should nevertheless note the symptomatic character of the German "pre-Renaissance," which makes use

73. Perseus

of the most authentic documents available to it, until such time as the statues and bas-reliefs themselves shall again be ready to hand.

*

LET US now see what has become of the literary tradition. As will be remembered, this term designates the ensemble of figures illustrating the allegorized mythological treatises—the common character of these figures (which begin in the fourteenth century to supplant other types) being that they are based exclusively on texts. They are reconstructions.

We have sketched the history of this tradition, in which the "Mythographus tertius," Albricus, occupied a leading place. A whole family of gods emerged from his *Liber ymaginum deorum* and its successive recastings. Conceived without the benefit of any real model, and without the slightest contact with classical art, these artificial gods might appear to have had but small chance of survival; nevertheless, not only did they beget offspring of their own, but against all expectation they gradually prepared the return of the rightful gods.

77. *Mars*

The slightest familiarity with these types—not a hard thing to acquire, since they are distinct from all others—will show them to us on every hand. It would seem that, outside the astrological tradition, which in general adhered to its own types and laws, they constituted the chief repertory which artists continued to draw upon from the fourteenth to the end of the fifteenth century, and even later. We meet with them in France, England, Flanders, Germany, Italy—in miniatures, tapestries, and enamels, in painting and sculpture.

It would be easy to trace, for example, the type of Mars in fury, mounted in a chariot drawn by two horses, helmeted, whip in hand, and accompanied by a wolf. It is thus that Petrarch describes him, following Albricus, who has constructed his own picture out of fragments of Servius and Statius:

. . . Mavortis imago
Curribus insistens aderat furibunda cruentis:
Hinc lupus, hinc rauce stridentes tristia Dire;
Cassis erat capiti fulgens manibusque flagellum.[9]

[9] *Africa*, III, 186–189. ("The furious image of Mars stood on a bloody chariot: on this side a wolf, on the other the hoarse Furies with their shrill and mournful cries. He had a

74. *Mars*

76. *Mars*

75. *Mars*

78. *Mars*

And thus [10] he appears in French,[11] Flemish,[12] and Italian [13] drawings and miniatures; in Flemish,[14] Italian,[15] and German [16] engravings; in the fresco by Taddeo di Bartolo in the Palazzo Pubblico, Siena (*fig. 42*); in a relief by Agostino di Duccio in the Tempio Malatestiano at Rimini (*fig. 78*); on a chimney piece in the Landshut Residenz [17] toward the middle of the sixteenth century (*fig. 79*); and on a Flemish tapestry in the royal collection in Madrid.[18]

Although these different representations are un-

gleaming helmet on his head and a whip in his hands.")

[10] Chaucer (*The Knightes Tale,* vv. 2041–2, 2046–8, in *Works,* ed. W. W. Skeat) describes him in almost the same terms:

> *The statue of Mars upon a carte stood,*
> *Armed, and loked grim as he were wood;*
> . . . .
> *This god of armes was arrayed thus:*
> *A wolf ther stood biforn him at his feet*
> *With eyen rede. . . .*"

According to Boyd Ashby Wise (*The Influence of Statius upon Chaucer* [Baltimore, 1911]), Chaucer is here following Statius (*Thebais,* VII, 70) by way of Boccaccio (*Teseide,* VII, 37). See *figs. 74–77.*

[11] Bibl. Nat., mss. fr. 6986 and 143 (*figs. 74* and *75*); Vat. lat. 1480; Brit. Mus., Cott. Jul. F. VII; Bibl. de l'Univ. de Genève, ms, fr. 176.

[12] Copenhagen, ms. Thott. 399 (*fig. 76*).

[13] Regin. 1290; Marcian. 4519. The pedigree of this last "Mars" is not certain; it is the beautiful miniature by Francesco Pesellino, executed around 1450, and described by C. Bartoli to Vasari, who copied the description in the second edition of the *Vite,* in the note on Attavante (ed. Milanesi, II, p. 523). See reproduction in *Dedalo* (Feb., 1932).

[14] In the *Ovide moralisé* of Colart Mansion (Bruges, 1484). See *fig. 77.*

[15] The *Tarocchi* of Mantegna.

[16] The illustrations of Herold's *Heydenwelt,* 1554.

[17] See A. Warburg, *Gesammelte Schriften,* II, p. 457 and fig. 105; also Mitterwieser, *Die Residenz von Landshut* (Augsburg, 1927).

[18] One piece in the series of Vices and Virtues; see reprod. in Guiffrey, *La Tapisserie,* p. 124. Mars is on foot, but he carries a flail; other details in the same tapestry (Amor, etc.) recall Albricus.

79. Mars and other gods

mistakably related, curious variations are to be noted between them. At times, these even affect the iconographical details. Thus, the war-god holds in his hand in some cases a whip, in others a sword, halberd, or flail. Several of these variations can be explained as mere errors. Thus, when the illuminator of ms. Thott. 399 and the engraver of the *Ovide moralisé* of the Colart Mansion edition replace the whip by a flail, it is because the French text had translated Albricus' Latin *flagellum* as *flayeu* (*fléau*).[19] Even more curious than this substitution of attributes is the appearance of quite different persons as escort for the god. Thus, the Mars of the Tempio Malatestiano is preceded by an

[19] Cf. another amusing error in the image of Juno: the peacocks appear to be licking her feet. "Pavones autem ante pedes ejus lambebant," (i.e., "peacocks were pecking before her feet"), says the *Libellus*, and the *Ovide moralisé* translates, "ils lui leschoient les pieds." Again, in the Bibl. Nat. ms. fr. 373 (end of fourteenth century), fol. 207, Venus has in her hand not a shell, but a duck, which she holds by the neck. This is probably the result of a faulty reading: *auca marina* for *concha marina.*

advancing female figure, who holds the reins of the horses in one hand, and in the other an object that appears to be a trumpet. On the bas-reliefs at Landshut this figure does not appear; instead, two men are seen engaged in mortal combat beneath the chariot. It is apparent that here the sculptor has followed the version of the *Libellus*: [20] "Et quia Romani fratres geminos urbis primos fondatores, scilicet Romulum et Remum, Martis filios esse finxerunt, quorum Romulus Remum interfecit, ideo sub ejus curru idem Romulus depictus erat, qui et fratrem Remum occidebat." At Rimini, on the other hand, Agostino di Duccio seems to have been following the text of Petrarch which we have quoted above:

. . . . *hinc raucae stridentes tristia Dirae.*

The divergencies between the two representations would thus correspond in this case [21] to different branches of the Albricus tradition.

But the variants in which we are now most interested are those bearing upon the style of the figures; in one case, for example, Mars is seen driving through a rural landscape in a heavy peasant's wagon, much after the fashion of Lancelot, the knight, in his cart; [22] elsewhere he resembles a Roman legionary mounted on a veritable battle chariot.[23] At the same time, in passing from the type *alla francese* to the type *all'antica*, the formal character of the image undergoes marked changes.

It is the stages in this formal evolution of our series of images which we now wish to sketch in their main outlines. This story, it may be said, parallels that of the geographical diffusion of the types; broadly seen, it appears like a struggle or an exchange of influences between Northern and Western Europe, the region from which the images come, and Italy, which they are doing their best to conquer.

[20] ("And since the Romans claimed that the twin brothers Romulus and Remus, who founded the city, were sons of Mars, and since Romulus killed Remus, under the chariot of the god they depicted Romulus in the act of killing Remus.") The *Libellus* is here taking over and developing a brief reference by Albricus: "Romulum et Remum ejus fingi filios constat." ("It appears that Romulus and Remus were supposed to be his sons.")

[21] Cf. also the representations of the wolf, which sometimes carries sheep in its jaws, or even on its back (Regin. 1290). This detail agrees with the text of the *Libellus:* "ante illum vero lupus ovem portans pingebatur" ("before him they painted a wolf bearing a sheep"), but it is not found in Albricus, Petrarch, or Bersuire.

[22] E.g., ms. Copen. Thott. 399.

[23] In the Tempio Malatestiano; cf. the Mars of the *Tarocchi,* A 45.

The treatise of Albricus, it should be remembered, is the work of an Englishman; of the miniatures which derive from it, the earliest are found in French manuscripts of the *Ovide moralisé* (Paris 6986 and Vat. Reg. lat. 1480), both dating from the end of the fourteenth century. The Gothic accent in these miniatures is strongly marked. Apollo wears an elegant doublet and long, pointed shoes; Mars, a helmet and gauntlets; Juno, an ermine cotte. But their anachronism is not the only distinguishing feature of these naïve images; they also tend to become distinctly more sober and restrained. They adhere faithfully to the text in all essential points, but they do not translate its every detail. Generally speaking, they reduce the overrich content of the Albricus descriptions. Thus, the illustrator of the Vatican manuscript shows neither the Muses in his picture of Apollo nor the merchants and thieves with his Mercury. The significance of these simplifications will easily be gathered: they eliminate all that would overload the composition and disturb the layout on the page or the framing. The images, thus disencumbered, are clearly organized; sometimes they are even quite symmetrical. This effort at stylization—not, by the way, equally advanced in all the manuscripts—is particularly striking if we recall the illustrations in the manuscript of Rémi of Auxerre[24] the tradition of which was followed by Albricus. There, the artist spared us no detail, no accessory; in his concern to reproduce the whole content of the text, he scattered its details diffusely over the page.

These qualities of the French miniatures, which they were to retain throughout the fifteenth century (*figs. 75* and *80*), later passed into Flemish engraving; we find them in the woodcuts of the *Ovide moralisé* printed in Bruges in 1484 by Colart Mansion[25] (*fig. 77*).

Are we to see here the traditional qualities of French art, and in particular that mastery of composition which gives such legibility to the little scenes inscribed on the bas-reliefs of the cathedrals? Or shall we rather, with Saxl, look for a reflection of Giottesque style? At about this same time,

[24] Monac. lat. 14271, fol. 11 v. (*fig. 67*).

[25] These woodcuts take over the miniatures of a manuscript of Bersuire (Copen. Thott. 399); cf. M. D. Henkel, *De Houtsneden van Mansion's Ovide moralisé, Bruges, 1484* (Amsterdam, 1922), and E. Schenk zu Schweinsburg, "Bemerkungen zu M. D. Henkel, De Houtsneden . . . ," etc., *Der Cicerone*, XVI (1924), pp. 321 ff.

Their influence may still be felt in the sixteenth century, in certain woodcuts illustrating the *Heydenwelt* of Herold (1554).

Taddeo di Bartolo, in the Palazzo Pubblico of Siena, represented four divinities [26] who are not connected—at least not directly—with the Albricus tradition,[27] but who have also been reduced to the simplest lines, even though preserving a marked medieval flavor in attitude and costume.

80. Pluto and Proserpina

Around 1420, we find the images of the gods entering upon a new phase. The pen drawings illustrating the *Libellus* text in ms. Vaticanus Reginensis 1290 contrast in several points with the sober Gothic effigies: they are gay, imaginative, free, and exuberant (*fig. 68*). Far from suppressing any figures, this artist has invented them as he pleased. Thus, in the group around Venus, he adds a woman as target of one of Cupid's arrows; [28] at Mercury's

[26] See *supra*, pp. 128 f.

[27] The Mars type, however, is that of Albricus. See *supra*, pp. 189 ff., and *fig. 42*.

[28] Possibly, it is true, a confusion with Apollo. The text says: "*Cupido . . . Apollinem sagittaverat.*" In ms. Rawl. B. 214 (fol. 198 v.),

side he places a kneeling figure who, like the god himself, is playing a flute. Another striking novelty is the introduction of several nude figures. For the most part, to be sure, the figures are clothed—and in the fashion of the time: Orpheus might be a troubadour and the Corybantes mace-bearers. But Venus is once more Anadyomene, and the three Graces sport with her among the waves.

We shall find this same freedom in composition, this mingling of naked bodies with contemporary costume, in other representations from the first half of the fifteenth century, such as the miniatures of an English manuscript at Oxford (Rawlinson B. 214; *fig. 70*), or a series of drawings in the Dresden Print Cabinet.[29] Even outside the Albricus circle, indeed, a parallel evolution of mythological types is to be noted. This becomes clear if we compare two series of pictures of the planets of which we have already spoken [30]—the frescoes by Guariento in the choir of the Eremitani in Padua, and the miniatures of a Modena manuscript, the *Liber physiognomiae* (*figs. 85* and *87*). The two series are connected, as has long been recognized; [31] but the fourteenth-century Venus, with her solemn bearing and her drapery, recalls the allegorical type of the French cathedrals—Luxuria, for instance, who also holds a mirror; [32] in contrast, in the *Liber physiognomiae,* which dates from around 1430, Venus is a young woman, naked and smiling, her hair unbound, who has shed her quasi-ecclesiastical dignity along with her garments.

It would seem, therefore, that a new spirit has begun to animate mythology; but the transformation is not yet final. On the contrary, this whole group of representations is characterized by its ambiguity. If certain deities —Minerva, for instance—are obviously striving to recover their classical form, the majority still wear their bourgeois disguises. And the nude forms themselves have not the slightest sculptural quality; they suggest rather the fragile Eves of the French manuscripts. In reality, these images offer us a sort of compromise between Franco-Flemish naturalism and the idealistic

referred to below, it is really Apollo who is wounded by the arrow: in the Dresden drawing, it is a nude woman who holds a lyre.

[29] Reprod. in P. Lavallée, *Le Dessin français du* XIII*e au* XVI*e siècle* (Paris, 1930), fig. 27. Lavallée sees in these drawings the influence of the artists who worked for the duc de Berry, and of the Burgundian masters (pp. 16–17).

[30] See *supra,* p. 127, n. 17.

[31] See A. Venturi, *L'Arte,* XVII (1914), pp. 49–57. But Venturi, counter to all probability, sees in the manuscript the model for the frescoes.

[32] See *supra,* p. 107.

whims of Italy. The phenomenon is particularly apparent in the illustrations of the *Libellus* executed in northern Italy—that is, at the meeting point between Western and Southern influences. Moreover, as we know, the relations between Flanders and the Florence of the Medici were to bring about an even greater penetration of the Western style. We must not be surprised at finding these same contrasts and contradictions in the famous illustrated *Chronicle*[33] attributed to Finiguerra: demigods accoutered as pages or knights, but posed like statues (Paris, Troilus, Jason, Romulus); ladies wearing the hennin headdress (Helen); nude forms already skillfully drawn (the men and women recreated by Deucalion and Pyrrha); a couple *alla francese* under a frieze *al-l'antica* (Rape of Helen). At the same time, these disparate elements do not clash; instead, we find everywhere the same balance between realism of character and idealism of attitude which is to give Florentine Quattrocento art its unique savor.

81. Hellenistic Hermes

In these gropings, this timid showing of the nude among figures heavily draped, this alternating rhythm of serene immobility and gay vivacity, we should perhaps not only see an effort to reconcile two different spirits, two distinct artistic climates, but also distinguish between the two concepts of classical antiquity which alternately attracted the precursors of the Renaissance. The ambiguity that we note in this period in the form and attitude of the gods is doubtless due in part to their allegiance to both North and South,

[33] See *supra*, p. 28.

but also to the fact that the spirit which animates them is sometimes Dionysian in essence and sometimes Apollonian.

*

Let us now see what has become of the gods of Albricus in the second half of the fifteenth century. We re-encounter them, around 1465, in the famous *Tarocchi* of Mantegna, the subject matter of which we have already thoroughly examined,[34] where several of them appear in the character of planetary powers.

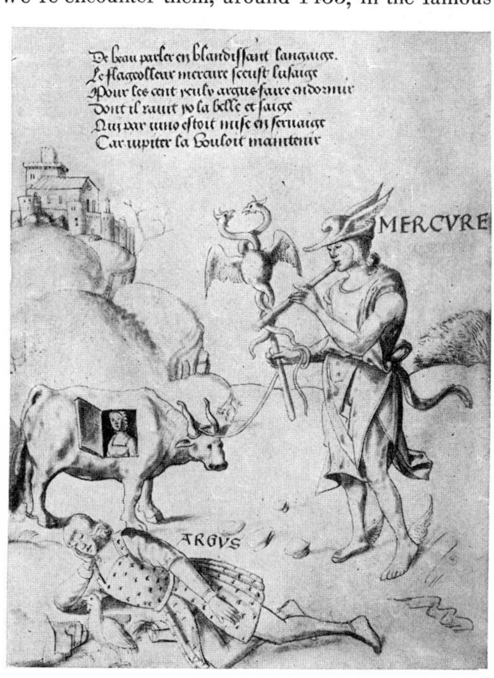

82. *Mercury and Argus*

The pedigree of these figures is not open to doubt. Thus, the image of Venus (A 43; *fig. 86*) corresponds point for point with the description in the *Libellus*. She is bathing ("nuda et in mare natans") and holds a shell in her right hand ("in manu sua dextera concham marinam continens"); beside her are the Graces ("et coram ipsa tres astabant juvencule nude, que tres Gracie dicebantur") and Amor with bow and bandaged eyes ("Huic et Cupido . . . cecus assistebat . . . sagitta et arcu . . ."); above her is a flight of doves ("et columbis circa se volantibus comitabatur"). On the other hand, the influence of the Western miniatures still makes itself felt; thus Jupiter (A 46; *fig. 50*) is shown seated not on a throne, as the text would have it, but

[34] See *supra*, pp. 137 ff.

in a rainbow just as he is in a French fourteenth-century manuscript (Paris. 6986);[35] even more significantly, his position exactly recalls that of the Christ in Majesty on Romanesque tympana and capitals (or, to take a later example, in the Apocalypse tapestry at Angers), for the Christ, also, is surrounded by an almond-shaped frame which cuts across the rainbow.

83. Mercury

However, certain types have been modified. Apollo[36] still has his crown, but instead of treading on the three-headed monster beneath his feet, he is seated on two swans, and his feet rest on a celestial globe. Mercury has kept some of his attributes—the flute, the cock, and the Argus head—but he is dressed in a loose tunic, wears a sort of cap with pointed visor, and is shod in soft boots (*fig. 83*). What is the source of these alterations in the traditional types?

The origin of the new Apollo is still shrouded in mystery. But Saxl succeeded in discovering that of the new Mercury[37]—a discovery, as will be seen, of the highest interest: the model which inspired the artist of the *Tarocchi* (indirectly, it is true) was a Hellenistic relief.

This bas-relief had been found some years earlier, and copied by Cyriacus of Ancona during a voyage to Greece and the Archipelago. A copy of his drawing is in the Bodleian today (ms. Canonicianus lat. misc. 280); we recognize in it a Hermes of archaic or rather of archaistic type, with pointed beard (*σφηνοπώγων*), as he is ordinarily represented on black-figured vases. The same image appears, moreover, in line-for-line identity, in a relief

[35] The same rainbow is seen in the Dresden drawing (see Lavallée, *op. cit.*, fig. 26).

[36] The Apollo shown here is the leader of the choir, in the series of the Muses (D 20); in the planetary series (A 44) only the chariot of the Sun is represented, with Phaeton's fall.

[37] *Rinascimento dell'antichità*, pp. 252 ff., fig. 21.

from Panticapaeum [38] which is an exact replica of the one seen by Cyriacus.

Delighted by his discovery, in which he saw a happy omen for a traveler,[39] Cyriacus let his friends know of it. Carlo Avellino, for instance, writes in this connection to Poggio:

> *Kyriacus nobis misit modo munera, Poggi,*
> *Mercurium, propria pinxerat ille manu;*
> *Ut vidi obstupui . . .*[40]

It is thus clear that the drawing passed from hand to hand; the type soon began to penetrate Italian art: one finds it on the *cassoni,*[41] in the Riccardiana Virgil,[42] in a medal made by Noccolò Fiorentino for Lorenzo Tornabuoni,[43] in a wood engraving illustrating the *Metamorphoses,*[44] etc. It is natural, therefore, that it should have been introduced into the series of the *Tarocchi;* [45] but, curiously enough, it was not substituted for the medieval type—it was combined with it. The general look and pose, and the costume, are derived from the relief, but the accessories are still those enumerated in the *Libellus.* These diverse elements, however, do not clash, perhaps because the archaizing silhouette of the Hermes, ancient but not classical in the strict sense of the word, easily falls into line, in its picturesque oddity, with the other Albricus images. However that may be, we have here a singular instance of assimilation: an antique figure is grafted onto the medieval stem, and draws from it the nourishment of Western naturalism.

[38] See S. Reinach, "Un bas-relief de Panticapée au Musée d'Odessa," *Monuments et mémoires Piot,* II (1895), pl. VII (*fig. 81*). The relief has now been identified as Hellenistic.

[39] See *Bollettino dell' Istituto di Corrispondenza Archeologica per l'anno 1861,* pp. 183 ff.: "Intorno alcune notizie archeologiche conservateci de Ciriaco d'Ancona. Lettera del Prof. O. Jahn al Cav. G. B. de Rossi."

[40] *Ibid.* ("Cyriacus has just sent us a present, Poggio: a Mercury painted with his own hand; when I saw it I was amazed.")

[41] See P. Schubring, *Cassoni* (Leipzig, 1915): *cassone* of Ulysses, Lanckoronski Coll., Vienna, plates LIV and LV. The Neptune representation has also been influenced by this type: *ibid.,* pl. XLVIII.

[42] Cod. 492, fol. 66 v.

[43] See A. Heiss, *Les médailleurs de la Renaissance florentine,* Pt. I (Paris, 1891), pl. VII, 3.

[44] *Ovidio Metamorphoses vulgare* (Venice, 1522), pl. XVI, v.

[45] One of the engravers, who reproduces certain details correctly (the headdress, for example), seems to have followed Cyriacus' drawing closely; the other has reproduced it only indirectly, though without apparently having copied the first. Two series do, in fact, exist: on their differences and similarities, see A. M. Hind, *Early Italian Engraving* (London, 1938), vol. IV (plates 320–369) and *Catalogue,* Part I, pp. 221–250.—See also the Mercury in the Bibliothèque de l'Arsenal, cod. fr. 5066 (*fig. 82*). This manuscript is particularly interesting in that it contains three cyclic series: the Triumphs of Petrarch, *Tarocchi,* Proverbs. See V. d'Essling and E. Müntz, *Pétrarque* (1902), p. 271.

Nevertheless, taken as a whole, the mythological types of the *Tarocchi* mark a certain progress toward classicism. Compared with figures of the first half of the century, they strike one at first by their sobriety and balance of composition. They eliminate a large number of details and secondary personages in the interest of a more concentrated arrangement. From this point of view, they recall the severe, stylized types of the French fourteenth century.[46] But an entirely new elegance and dignity have now appeared, serving as a corrective for the Gothic dryness. The previously slender forms are more ample, and the proportions have gained in breadth; there is generosity in the gestures and rhythm in the movements, and a quiet harmony seems gradually to do away with any sharp or shrunken look left over from the miniatures. A slight grimace or a frown may still distort the faces of the gods, but we feel that they are on the point of recovering their superhuman serenity along with their marble physique.

Before leaving the gods of the *Tarocchi,* we should note that they serve, around 1471, to illustrate the manuscript of a poem by Ludovico Lazzarelli, *De gentilium deorum imaginibus.*[47] Around 1500, Apollo and his train of Muses decorate a cupola in a palace on the Via Belvedere, Cremona.[48] At this period they have already emigrated northward; by 1490 we find them in Nuremberg.[49] Pursuing his strange destiny, the famous Hermes of Cyriacus of Ancona becomes a naturalized German, thanks first to Dürer [50] and later to Hans Burgkmair.[51] He even travels to the Hanseatic provinces: a Lübeck calendar [52] so popularizes him that he becomes a common motif of decoration for the façades of German and Austrian houses.[53]

[46] See *supra,* p. 195.

[47] Vatican, cod. Urb. 716.

[48] This cupola is now in the Victoria and Albert Museum, London (*fig. 84*).

[49] See V. von Loga, "Beiträge zum Holzschnittwerk Michael Wohlgemuts," *Jahrb. d. preuss. Kunstsamml.* (1895), pp. 236–238.

[50] Dürer copied the *Tarocchi* several times, though the copies are only in part by his own hand. See H. Tietze, *Der junge Dürer* (Augsburg, 1928), pp. 306–309, and F. Winkler, *Die Zeichnungen A. Dürers,* Vol. I (Berlin, 1936). The copies of the *Tarocchi* are reproduced in figs. 122–141. Dürer knew the Mercury type from another source as well (see *infra,* p. 203, n. 58). On the relations between Dürer and Cyriacus of Ancona, see O. Jahn, *Aus der Altertumswissenschaft* (Bonn, 1868), pp. 333–352: "Cyriacus von Ancona und Albrecht Dürer." Cf. also: R. Egger, *Österreichischer Jahresbericht,* XXXV (1943), pp. 99 ff., and fig. 68; A. Grenier, *Comptes-rendus de l'Académie des Inscriptions* (1946); J. Martin, *Würzburger Jahresbericht* (1946), pp. 359 ff.

[51] See A. Warburg, *Gesammelte Schriften,* II, p. 486 and fig. 118.

[52] See Warburg, *loc. cit.* ("Über Planetengötterbilder im niederdeutschen Kalender von 1519"), pp. 483–486 and fig. 117. Warburg tells the story of this figure in detail, and determines exactly how it passed from Italy into Germany by way of a citizen of Hamburg resident in Perugia.

[53] *Ibid.,* p. 486 and Appendix, p. 646.

In Nuremberg we also find traces of the Apollo with the two swans. He, too, was copied by Dürer,[54] and Peter Vischer gives him a place of honor among the bronze figures on the base of the shrine of St. Sebald.[55]

The diffusion of these mythological types throws a curious light on the penetration of the Italian Renaissance into Germany. Engravings, as we have

84. Apollo and the Muses

seen, were extremely active as agents in this process, even where, as at Nuremberg, the humanists—men like Celtes, Schedel, and Pirkheimer—were acting as advisers to artists.[56] Thus, Schedel's *Collectanea* contains a drawing of Mercury which corresponds exactly to the bas-relief copied by Cyriacus;[57] it was this drawing which inspired Dürer's *Gallic Hercules*.[58]

With the frescoes of Francesco Cossa in the Palazzo Schifanoia in Ferrara, we reach the concluding stage of this evolution. As will be recalled,

[54] See Tietze, *loc. cit.*

[55] For the other mythological representations on the tomb and their role, see A. Feulner, *Peter Vischers Sebaldusgrab in Nürnberg* (Munich, 1924), pp. 19, 34–37; also L. Réau, *P. Vischer et la sculpture franconienne* (Paris, 1909), and our note in the *Journal of the Warburg Institute*, II, p. 75.

[56] Réau points out (pp. 122–123) that one of the Muses on the tomb is taken from an engraved illustration of Celtes' *Quatuor libri Amorum*, etc.

[57] Cod. Monac. 716.

[58] Dürer thus knew the type via two different channels. See A. Springer, "Vorbilder von zwei Dürerschen Handzeichnungen in der Ambraser Sammlung, *Mittheil. d. k. k. Centralcommission*, VII, 80; and the frontispiece of the *Inscriptiones* of Apianus (Ingolstadt, 1534).

these frescoes, painted around 1470, represent (or rather, represented, for several of them have been ruined) a complete astrological system, which we have already had occasion to analyze.[59]

In the upper zone of the paintings reign the "masters of the months," as named by Manilius—that is to say, the twelve great Olympian deities. These

85. *Venus*

86. *Venus and the Graces*

gods, also, derive from the Albricus tradition. The connection is not at first obvious, because of the difference in presentation. The gods are no longer surrounded by their legendary companions, as in the *Libellus* illustrations; from a chariot, each deity dominates a crowd of figures that are mere mortals, dressed in contemporary costume. Near Minerva, a group of young women busy themselves with weaving and embroidery; and lovers embrace each other tenderly on the banks of the river where glide Venus' swans. Each scene is thus organized according to the traditional scheme of the "children of the planets," and illustrates the thesis we have already seen evolving,[60] namely,

[59] See *supra*, p. 74.
[60] See *supra*, pp. 69 ff.

that human beings share in the properties of the divinity who presides over the month of their birth.

But though the artist has followed the astrological tradition in his compositions, his types conform to the prescriptions of medieval mythography.[61] Thus Venus, though she is not shown swimming in the sea, is still crowned, as

87. Venus

in the *Libellus,* with a wreath of white and red roses ("rosis candidis et rubeis sertum gerebat in capite ornatum").[62] She has not even lost her escort: Amor, her son, no longer at her side, is painted on her girdle, and at a little distance appear her attendants, the three Graces, standing on a rocky plateau (*fig. 89*).

These details betray the continuity of the literary tradition; others, still more striking, attest the persistence of influences from the North. At Venus'

[61] See A. Warburg, "Italienische Kunst und internationale Astrologie im Palazzo Schifanoja zu Ferrara," in *Gesammelte Schriften,* II, p. 471.

[62] In certain manuscripts, in consequence of one of those misunderstandings of which we have already cited so many examples, these roses are scattered around the goddess (e.g., ms. fr. 373, fol. 207 v.) or are arranged in a sort of halo or aureole (e.g., Rawl. B. 214, fol. 198 v.).

feet kneels a warrior, attached to her chariot by a chain. Who would recognize Mars, the terrible, in this gallant knight who, as the code of courtly love prescribes, kneels before his lady, at the mercy of her glance? He might be a Lancelot, even a Lohengrin. This group invites comparison with a Flemish miniature,[63] or with a curious salver in the Louvre, which expresses, in a somewhat crude form, the sovereignty of Venus over the knights of all history.[64]

This conversion of an antique fable into a romance of chivalry [65] gives ample proof of the degree to which the court of Ferrara was impregnated with Occidental culture.

But all this, it will be said, hardly seems like a reversion to classicism. This is true; the Ferrara Mars and Venus, as well as the Minerva, Jupiter, and Cybele, look indeed so much like the ladies and gentlemen of their entourage that if they descended from their chariots they might easily be mistaken for any of these. But it is precisely this familiar association between men and gods that is symptomatic of the new time; its significance will become more clear if we compare the Schifanoia frescoes with the miniatures of a Flemish manuscript of the same period.[66]

In one of these miniatures, which represents Diana, a profane personage has joined the cortege of nymphs—but in how humble a fashion! He is shown as a tiny figure, timidly kneeling in a corner in the pose of a donor,[67] looking as if he felt completely out of his element in this fabulous world. At Ferrara, on the other hand, the contemporary figures seem to consider the presence of the gods as the most natural thing in the world; the gods, for their part, do not appear ill at ease in the midst of this little Italian court—and they ought, by

[63] The Swan Knight, ms. Gall. 19, Bayrische Staatsbibliothek, Munich, reprod. in F. Winkler, *Die flämische Buchmalerei des* XV *und* XVI *Jahrhunderts* (Leipzig, 1925), pl. 60.

[64] Venus is nude, in a mandorla; rays emanating from her womb strike the faces of six kneeling adorers, one of whom is Lancelot. See S. Reinach, *Tableaux inédits ou peu connus des collections françaises*, pl. XXX. Cf. also a French miniature of the early sixteenth century, Bibl. Nat. *fonds fr.* 594; d'Essling and Müntz, *Pétrarque*, p. 226.

[65] On the influence of the knightly spirit on the representation of antique personages, see E. Faral, *Recherches sur les sources latines des contes et romans courtois* (Paris, 1913), pp. 394–395 (for the twelfth century); and J. Adhémar, *Influences antiques . . .* , pp. 292–296: "L'antiquité romanesque."

[66] Ghent Cathedral (*fig. 88*); cf. cod. 9242 of the Bibl. Roy. of Brussels (*fig. 6*).

[67] This figure is undoubtedly the poet Horace; in fact, at the foot of the miniature are several verses of his hymn to Diana (*Carm.*, III, 22), the first of which seems to issue from his mouth.

rights, to feel at home there. Exiles in the Northern countries, they have recovered in the South their true climate, and their compatriots.

And now at last the gods begin to recover their ancient look. In the same

88. Diana, Pan, and nymphs

89. Triumph of Venus

frescoes, where for the most part they are still costumed and posed like Quattrocento princes, one group stands out in contrast. This is the group of the three Graces, in which, perhaps for the first time in centuries,[68] the classical

[68] F. de Mély ("Les Très Riches Heures du duc de Berry et les trois Grâces de Sienne," *Gazette des Beaux Arts* [1912], pp. 195–201) believes that he has found in the figures of the Microcosm (*supra*, p. 64) reminiscences of the antique group in Siena.

qualities reappear. They reappear first of all in the proportions and modeling of the three bodies: these youthful nudes, though still slightly frail and meagre, mark a step on the way to full plasticity. But it is above all the composition that merits our attention.

The antique motif of the three Graces, which goes back to the end of the fourth or the beginning of the third century B.C., had undergone a gradual disintegration during the Middle Ages. In the twelfth century, the "Mythographus tertius" (Albricus) still described it correctly, in the manner of Servius (*Aen.*, I, 720; ed. G. Thilo [1881], pp. 199 f.): two of the figures are seen from the front, the third from the back, and all three hold one another by the arms:

Quarum prima quidem nobis aversa, sed ambe
Ad nos conversos oculos vultusque tenebant
Innexae alternis percandidis brachia nodis

as Petrarch was later to say in his polished hexameters.[69] But in Bersuire the tradition alters: their arms are no longer linked, and two of the figures are seen from the back. This explains why, in a great number of manuscripts of the *Ovide moralisé*, in the *Tarocchi*, and even in the *Practica musice* of Gafurio,[70] they merely stand side by side, two seen from behind or in profile. In the *Libellus*, it is true, two again face the spectator, but they are still shown as separate figures, frolicking each by herself in the sea. Furthermore, the one who turns her back is not the one in the center; this detail is significant. It has not arisen through an error, for the text says only: "Ex quibus duarum facies versus nos adverse erant, tercia vero dorsum in contrarium vertebat." [71] No text, furthermore, expressly indicates the relative positions of the three goddesses. What has happened is rather that the artist has lost his concern for certain aesthetic laws. If the anonymous painter to whom, according to Pausanias, we owe the original motif of the three Graces,[72] placed the girl whose back is turned *between* her two companions, it was for reasons of

[69] *Africa*, III, vv. 216–218. ("The first one had her back turned to us, but the other two had their eyes and faces toward us; their arms were interlaced in ties of exquisite whiteness.")

[70] See *supra*, p. 140, and *fig. 48*.

[71] "Two of them were facing us, the third one turned her back."

[72] Pausanias, IX, 35, 6, 7. The original might have been a painting, the group thus being seen from one side only. See *Roscher's Lexikon*, I, 884 (*s.v.* "Charis").

alternation and balance: it was these qualities which gave the group its significance. In the Middle Ages on the other hand, its meaning was derived mainly from the supposed moral content—from the principle, that is, to which the group seemed to give ingenious illustration: "A benefit conferred is twice repaid." For this, it was enough that any *one* of the Graces should turn her back to the spectator; her place with reference to the other two was a matter of no interest, since it did not affect the meaning.

With Cossa, the three Graces have returned once more to their original positions and posture; their interrupted round has been formed again. The graceful inflection of their bodies, the bending of their heads, and the garland of their intertwined arms once more begin to outline in space their lovely curves, their "enceintes magiques"—to compose "un petit temple rose et rond, qui tourne lentement, comme la nuit." [73] We now see all that is implied in the restoration of this classical group—the renewal of an order, the reawakening of a harmony. By way of this literary tradition, of which his work marks the final outcome, Francesco Cossa has regained contact with the pure plastic tradition of antiquity. His Graces are sisters to those of Raphael.[74]

*

AND SO WE have gradually arrived at the threshold of the Renaissance. By way of a long and laborious evolution, artists have at last begun to restore an ideal youth to the antiquated medieval models; or, more often, they abandon these models in favor of the statues and bas-reliefs which now smile at them with a beauty undimmed by time. The gods who return to people the vaults and walls of the Farnesina, all more or less freely inspired by antiquity,[75] seem to have been reinstated overnight in all their ancient splendor.

[73] Paul Valéry.

[74] Musée Condé, Chantilly; cf. also the reverse of a medal made by Niccolò Fiorentino for Giovanna Tornabuoni, showing "Castitas, Pulchritudo, Amor." On Botticelli's dancing Graces, see A. Warburg, "*Der Frühling,*" in *Gesammelte Schriften,* I, pp. 28–29. On other fifteenth-century representations of the Three Graces, see *ibid.*, p. 29, n. 3; and the article by W. Deonna, "Le groupe des trois Grâces nues et sa descendance," *Revue archéologique,* XXXI (1930), pp. 274–332.

[75] Peruzzi and Giulio Romano, for example, copied sarcophagi; Raphael assimilated classical types without forcing himself to imitate any precise model. See F. Saxl, *La Fede astrologica di A. Chigi,* pp. 41 ff.: "L'antichità negli affreschi della Farnesina."

The importance should be stressed of the part played by the engravers (such as Marc Antonio Raimondi and Bonasone) in giving currency to the antique types which had been thus rediscovered; these types became so popular that they were adopted by decorators of majolica and other artisans.

But this dazzling revenge should not make us forget the centuries which have been needed to bring it about. Sometimes, indeed, at the height of the Renaissance and of the gods' new glory, some sign or detail will intervene to remind us of their long years of exile and adventure. In the church of San

90. Pegasus and Perseus

91. Mercury

Domenico, in Naples, the funeral chapel of the princely Caraffa family is ornamented with bas-reliefs executed around 1512, on which the constellations are represented. For the most part these reliefs reproduce the beautiful classical types of the first *Aratea*, but in the hand of Perseus we see, instead of the Medusa head, the head of a bearded demon (*fig. 90*). This detail recalls the hero's strange past: the head which he holds is a remnant of the disguise imposed on him by the Arabs. It proves the survival, in Italy,[76] of the pictorial tradition with its century-long process of change.

Some vestiges of the literary tradition also survive. Between 1540 and 1545, Jacopo Sansovino made four admirable statues for the Loggetta in

[76] It will be recalled that in Germany at about the same time (1515) Dürer corrected this error (*supra*, pp. 186 f.).

Venice which are still to be seen there: Apollo, Mercury, Pallas, and Peace.[77] There is a singular contrast between the first two figures: Apollo, in his radiant nudity, recalls the Apollo Belvedere; Mercury, in a tunic, wears a triangular hat and soft boots. He has no other attribute, but his right foot rests on the severed head of Argus (*fig. 91*). We recognize this Mercury, whose history we know: he is the Mercury of the *Tarocchi*, in whom the traits of the archaistic Hermes were so oddly combined with those of the medieval type transmitted by Albricus.[78]

*

THE PRECEDING study has rested upon a too restricted and specialized body of material to serve as a basis for general theories and laws. It does, however, authorize us to define more exactly, or to rectify, certain ideas and terms—first of all, the very notion of "Renaissance" itself.

In the light of these analyses, the Renaissance appears as the reintegration of antique subject matter within the antique form: we can speak of a Renaissance from the day Hercules resumed his athletic breadth of shoulder, his club, and his lion's skin. Not for a moment is there any question of "resurrection"; Hercules had never died, any more than Mars or Perseus. As concepts and as names, at least, they had survived tenaciously in the memory of man. It was their appearance alone which had vanished, Perseus living on in his Turkish disguise and Mars as a knight of chivalry.

Nor must we conclude too hastily that the classical form under which the gods had once been known had completely disappeared from view. In spite of long periods of eclipse, it survived during the Middle Ages—as a memory maintained and revived at certain privileged epochs by the sight of ancient ruins and the reading of the poets.[79] Better still, a vivid feeling for

[77] See F. Sapori, *Jacopo Tatti detto il Sansovino* (Rome, 1928), pls. 43–46.

[78] See *supra*, pp. 199 ff. Tiziano Aspetti represented Mercury in the same way, in a bronze formerly in the Figdor Collection, Vienna: see L. Planiscig, *Venezianische Bildhauer der Renaissance* (Vienna, 1921), figs. 647, 648. Aspetti, again, alternately models a Venus of antique inspiration, and a Mars in contemporary costume, with a plumed helmet and a gun (*ibid.*, figs. 619, 618).

[79] This has been shown methodically and at length by J. Adhémar, *Influences antiques* . . . ; cf. also A. Goldschmidt, "Das Nachleben der antiken Formen im Mittelalter," *Vorträge d. Bibliothek Warburg* (1921–22), pp. 40–50.

sculptural beauty in the representation of the gods breathes through some verses written in Rome in the twelfth century by Hildebert de Lavardin:

> . . . *Hic superum formas superi mirantur et ipsi*
> *Et cupiunt fictis vultibus esse pares.*
> *Non potuit natura deos hoc ore creare*
> *Quo miranda deum signa creavit homo*
> *Vultus adest his numinibus potiusque coluntur*
> *Artificium studio quam deitate sua.*[80]

The gods are jealous of their own statues; they it is, and not the gods themselves, that inspire devotion.

This admiration did not remain a matter of words only. Certain aspects of medieval sculpture give evidence of an effort to perpetuate or to rediscover the ancient canon of beauty; and if the understanding of the plastic genius of antiquity is frequently of only a superficial order, at other times—in Rheims, for instance, in the first years of the thirteenth century—it is intimate and profound.

But at Rheims it is no longer the gods who are represented; instead, saints and virgins stand before us, draped in their noble and tranquil majesty. The formal qualities from the past, like the togas and peplums, serve to clothe new ideas; they now belong to Christian subjects. This observation may appear somewhat less obvious if we recall that the manuscripts have presented the opposite phenomenon, that of the pagan gods taking on contemporary costume and even ecclesiastical attributes and gestures. Have we not seen a tonsured Jupiter, a mitered Mercury—whereas one or another of the Rheims Virgins might easily be taken for a priestess of Vesta?

These examples—chosen from among the extreme cases—highlight the process of disintegration or dissociation which in reality had begun in the last centuries of antiquity. Form and subject survived in isolation, so to speak, each distinct from the other. As pagan ideas gradually became severed from expression in art, Christian ideas came forward to inhabit the forms

[80] *De Roma*, in *PL*, CLXXI, 1049. ("Here the gods look at the figures of the gods, and they themselves would like to resemble their own images. Nature could not create gods with faces as on the admirable statues of the gods created by man. They are revered for the work of the artist rather than for their own divinity.") See E. Mâle, "Etudes sur les églises romaines," *Revue des Deux Mondes* (Dec. 1, 1938), p. 592.

thus abandoned, just as the Christian cult took over the empty temples or the imperial baths. And the heroes of Fable, for their part, at length sought shelter within the priest's robe or the knight's armor.

In this strange game of changing places, Christ may become a Roman emperor, an Alexandrian shepherd, or an Orpheus,[81] and Eve a Venus. On the other hand, Jupiter may appear as one of the Evangelists, Perseus as a St. George, Saturn as God the Father. But no god is now represented in his traditional form as a divinity. The mythological heritage, like the classical patrimony as a whole, has so disntegrated that in order to take stock of its remains, we find it necessary to distinguish between a pictorial and a literary tradition which had become completely separate. Neither tradition, by itself, was able to keep intact the memory of the gods. Without a pictorial model as corrective and support, the descriptions of the mythographers were powerless to evoke their true forms; but even where the model had been handed down, it could engender only more and more debased replicas, since understanding of the subject had been obscured or lost.[82] Linked together, and checked one against the other, these two traditions would have made it possible to rebuild the unity of ancient art; this, indeed, is what took place when the figures of the constellations first began to regain their mythological significance, and as the bizarre types issuing from Albricus took on once more the gestures and proportions of statues. More than once during the Middle Ages, a revival of ancient arts and letters appeared to be coming about, and went far enough for us to be able to refer to the Carolingian period and the twelfth century as having been, each in its own way, a "Renaissance." It is quite true that the two traditions moved nearer together at those moments: there were scholars capable of explaining the sarcophagi to the artisans who copied them, while the same scholars, like true humanists, observed the ancient marbles and made collections of works of art.[83]

Thus the Renaissance, rightly seen, is in no sense a sudden crisis; it is the end of a long divorce. It is not a resurrection, but a synthesis.

*

[81] Cf. J. von Schlosser, *Präludien* pp. 9 ff.

[82] See *supra*, pp. 154 ff.

[83] See J. Adhémar, *op. cit.*, esp. pp. 104 ff., 200 ff.

FROM another angle, what we have said of the migrations of the gods throws light at certain points on the part played by Italy. Italy's role was of capital importance, but it differs slightly from the one usually attributed to her.

First of all, Italy received a great many classical themes from outside sources; this is particularly striking in the case of the gods. Not all the ancient divinities were reborn, as has usually been imagined, on the soil where they once reigned; they returned from distant exile, some after strange detours. It is impossible to overestimate the significance of Petrarch's having turned to an Englishman, "Albricus," as his authority in delineating the figure of Jupiter or Neptune—Petrarch, the greatest Italian humanist of the fourteenth century.

Furthermore, it was not merely her own indigenous deities that Italy thus received from abroad; the legends of other nations came to her as well. When, in the Trecento, Guido delle Colonne revived the *Roman de Troie*, he was merely adapting the work of Benoît de Sainte-Maure, a French poet of the twelfth century; similarly, the *Faits des Romains*, which recounted the exploits of their ancestors to the Italians of the late Middle Ages, were composed in Paris in the first years of the thirteenth century.[84]

Thus, contrary to all expectation, it is not always on classical soil that classical memories have remained most alive; more than once it happens that material from antiquity turns up in Italy not as a direct heritage, but as an imported product.

At all events, it will be said, Italy transformed this material and reassimilated it. This is of course true, but not of Italy alone. The countries of the North and West, which played so essential a role in the conservation and transmission of antique themes, contributed also to the restoration of forms. We need but recall the curious experiments of the German artists who, in the fifteenth century, began again to copy the Carolingian manuscripts; or the decisive corrections made by Dürer in the types of the stellar divinities;

[84] See L. F. Flutre, *Li Fait des Romains dans les littératures française et italienne du 13e au 16e siècle* (Paris, 1933); and Sneyders de Vogel, "La date de la composition des Faits des Romains," *Neophilologus*, 17 (1932), pp. 213–214, 271.

However, Flutre points out that the legend of Caesar, the last to appear in France—after the tales of Alexander, Thebes, Troy, etc.—preceded the others in Italy, for the very reason that there Caesar had the character of a "national" hero.

above all, the influence of French and Flemish naturalism on the Trecento and Quattrocento in Lombardy, Siena, and Florence. In this last respect, moreover, the story of the gods is but one episode in the general evolution of art: it has long since been shown [85] that the "Gothic" spirit coming from France, Flanders, and the Rhine valley breathed over Italy as early as the Trecento, and made itself felt down to the sixteenth century. This was one of the influences which "awakened" Italy, and prepared her to understand the teachings of her own past.

Admittedly, the mere mention of a Niccolò Pisano, and later of a Ghiberti, should be enough to prevent us from pushing this view to the point of paradox; these names should also remind us that the evolution of art is not uniform, and that the sculptors were the first to discover truths toward which the painters were still groping. And lastly, as we have seen, it is sometimes difficult to determine the direction in which influences move: if those from the North and West, for instance, left their mark upon the Italian primitives, the French illuminators were in their turn influenced from the South. When Dürer is drawn toward the classical style, he has been preceded by Pollaiuolo and Mantegna, and is following their example.

Nevertheless, the fact remains that the North prepared the way for the reintegration of the gods, furnishing the necessary elements and, in order to bring them to life, lending them something of its own blood and soul.

[85] See L. Courajod, *Leçons professées à l'Ecole du Louvre*, II: *Les origines de la Renaissance* (1901).

BOOK II

I

The Science of Mythology in the Sixteenth Century

THE TRIUMPH of the ancient gods in Renaissance Italy and then in Europe as a whole, and the immense place which they occupy in the art and literature of the sixteenth century, have often been emphasized, but less often accounted for on specific grounds. By what means, through what channels, did the knowledge of mythology become so diffused that it took on the character of a veritable invasion? It has usually been thought enough to give some such reply as this: "The ancient poets were by this time in every hand. . . . The humanists drew their nourishment from Virgil and Ovid, profane Bibles which they knew by heart. The artists, for their part, copied the reliefs and medals which the collectors were so avidly assembling. Thus the knowledge of Fable became more and more widespread, and the images of the gods were multiplied."

Actually, however, in the special case of mythology the men of the Renaissance did not always turn straight to the sources for their inspiration. We shall try to throw light on the obscure but extensive role played by certain intermediaries in making generally known the religious traditions of antiquity. These intermediaries were contemporary works, manuals and dictionaries in which information concerning the names of the gods, their outward aspect, and their adventures was made easily available to all readers. As we shall have occasion to prove later, men of letters and artists as well were often content with secondhand information of this kind. The disadvantages and dangers of the method are obvious, though no great harm would have resulted if the manuals had offered a true image of classical antiquity, based upon a judicious choice of texts and illustrations. But this was by no means the case. What is demonstrated in fact by even a superficial study of these works is that all of them, to a certain extent, derive from the Middle Ages and continue, both in spirit and content, that medieval mythographical tradition of which we have sketched the history.

*

THE CHIEF LINK between the mythology of the Renaissance and that of the Middle Ages is Boccaccio's *Genealogy of the Gods.*[1]

The *Genealogy*, indeed, is essentially a work of transition— "simul ante retroque prospiciens," looking both forward and backward, to use an expression of Petrarch's. In date, in general conception, in sources and method, it still belongs to the Middle Ages, yet here and there symptoms of the new time may be found.

Boccaccio undertook the work at the request of Hugues IV, king of Cyprus, toward the middle of the fourteenth century, and devoted to it the last twenty-five years of his life. Its range greatly exceeds that of the earlier compilations; [2] but in its very breadth the plan of the work recalls the great medieval encyclopedias, the *trésors, miroirs*, or *mers des histoires*, while the attempt "to reduce the whole of classical mythology to a system, and to bring each god, demigod, and hero into connection with the mighty father of the race, marks Boccaccio as a child of the Middle Ages." [3]

Let us see from what materials the work is composed. Boccaccio would have us believe that he always obtained his materials at first hand. In the Dedicatory Epistle he claims that he knows no other study of the subject; furthermore, it would be absurd to look in minor rivulets for what can be drawn from the main spring: "Insipidum est ex rivulis quaerere quod possis ex

[1] The best general study of the *Genealogy of the Gods* since the great work by A. Hortis, *Studii sulle opere latine del Boccaccio* (1789), pp. 155–219, is that of Cornelia C. Coulter, "The Genealogy of the Gods," in *Vassar Mediaeval Studies* (1923), pp. 317–341.

[2] Boccaccio touches upon many other subjects besides mythology, especially in the last books; but mythology remains the essential theme of the work, and the reason for its success.

[3] C. Coulter, *op. cit.* This view is, however, open to question; what of the *Theogony* of Hesiod?

fonte percipere" (xv, 7). Both affirmations are exceedingly ill-advised. The reader soon sees: (*1*) that Boccaccio's knowledge of classical literature is for the most part indirect; (*2*) that he has not scrupled to make extensive use of his predecessors' works.

Certainly, he knows a little Greek; he has heard Leonzio Pilato read from the original text of Homer, and takes legitimate pride in the fact.[4] But his quotations from the Greek generally derive from Latin authors, or even from medieval compilations. With the Roman poets and prose writers, Virgil, Ovid, Cicero, Seneca, he seems to be familiar; but in many instances he has read them or quotes them by way of writers from the period of decadence, even when the originals were immediately accessible to him. He quotes Ovid, for example, from Lactantius and Theodontius. Much of his material comes to him from Apuleius, Servius, Macrobius, and Martianus Capella; much also from the Fathers of the Church, especially Lactantius and St. Augustine. He even draws occasionally upon the encyclopedists, from Isidore to Rabanus Maurus and Vincent of Beauvais. Lastly, he utilizes the treatises devoted to mythology alone, and even those of most recent date—not only Hyginus and Fulgentius, but also his immediate precursors, i.e., Albricus, whom for that matter he holds in high esteem,[5] and another and most mysterious figure whom he calls Theodontius.[6]

This Theodontius, whose work has been lost, was still completely unknown to Hortis;[7] Hauvette supposed[8] that he was some "Latin compiler of the extreme decadence"; but Carlo Landi in his monograph[9] is more pre-

[4] "Meum est decus mea est gloria, scilicet inter Ethruscos Graecis uti carminibus." And he adds, "Etsi non satis plene perceperim, percepi tamen quantum potui." ("It is my privilege and my glory among the Tuscans to make use of Greek poems. . . . If I did not understand everything, at least I perceived as much as I could.")

[5] He cites him frequently: thus, in the Italian edition of G. Betussi (1606), p. 143: "Et Alberico . . . afferma ella (Giunone) aver allevato Nettuno"; p. 144: "poi come dice Alberico"; p. 145: "dice poi Alberico . . . testimonia Alberico . . . Favonia poi, secondo Alberico"; p. 148: "Secondo Alberico," etc. C. Coulter (*op. cit.*, p. 333) wrongly assumes that the *Libellus* is merely an abridgement of Albricus.

[6] In his youth, he copied from the *Collectiones* of Paolo da Perugia "ea quae sub nomine Theodontii apposita sunt" (xv, 6); but he speaks elsewhere (x, 7) as if he had actually had a manuscript of Theodontius in his hands.

[7] *Op. cit.*, p. 464: "Perhaps that much-talked-of Theodontius will one day be discovered, on account of whom Boccaccio was accused of being an impostor."

[8] *Boccace* (1914), p. 425.

[9] *Demogorgone, con saggio di nuova edizione delle Genealogie deorum gentilium del Boccaccio e silloge dei frammenti di Teodonzio* (Palermo, 1930), esp. pp. 18–20.

cise. Theodontius was probably a philosopher of Campanian origin who wrote between the ninth and eleventh centuries. He furnished Boccaccio with the debris of a curious and very mixed tradition; he knew the Olympic pantheon, but there are also signs of a syncretistic mythology, memories of the cosmogonic speculations of the Greek philosophers, and even fragments of a Greek historian of the fourth century B.C.[10] It is to Theodontius that Boccaccio owes his famous "Demogorgon," whom he presents as founder of the whole race of gods,[11] but of whom classical antiquity never heard. Demogorgon is a grammatical error, become god.[12]

This detail alone should serve to put us on our guard as far as Boccaccio's documentation is concerned, and his independence with regard to his sources. As a matter of fact, Boccaccio treats all the authorities and histories which he uses as equally reliable. His own claim is of course quite different—as with regard to Jason, for instance. "Verum ego," he says, "plus fidei antiquae famae exhibeo: qua habemus Jasonem Esonis fuisse filium, quam auctori novo" (XIII, 31).[13] But this declaration of principle does not prevent him from following the Latin poets rather than Homer (IX, 2; XII, 15), or from confidently quoting opinions as late as those of Gervase of Tilbury. Similarly, we find him rejecting this or that fable because of its improbability, and in the next breath accepting some no less absurd fabrication. Basically, all writers of the past, Christian or pagan, inspire him with the same reverence: they are, without exception, recipients of wisdom from on high. It is in this respect that, in spite of stirrings of a more critical spirit, he remains essentially a man of the Middle Ages.

Through his method of interpretation, also, he places himself in the same category. In the first place, he is not concerned with resolving the contradictions that he notes in his authors or in the myths themselves; his busi-

10 This historian is Philochoros. See Lenchantin, "Nuovi frammenti di Filocoro," *Rivista di filologia e d'istruzione classica*, 10 (1932), pp. 41–57.

11 Theodontius himself owed to a Byzantine, the pseudo "Pronapides, Athenian," the idea of presenting all the gods as descendants of Demogorgon.

12 Landi, *op. cit.*, pp. 14–17. Demogorgon was destined for a long career in literature and art. Landi (pp. 46–53) studies his adventures in magic, alchemy, poetry, etc. M. Castelain ("Démogorgon ou le barbarisme déifié," *Association G. Budé, Bulletin:* No. 36 [July, 1932], pp. 22–39) studies what happened to him in English literature.

13 "But I would rather trust the old tradition, according to which Jason was the son of Aeson, than a recent author."

ness, he expressly says, is to record all this, not to unravel it: "If these things and others are erroneous, it is not my intention to disprove them, nor to correct them in any way, should they not lend themselves to some kind of orderly redaction. I shall be content with reporting what I have found, and shall leave philosophical controversies aside." [14] He will not even attempt explanations: "nedum explicare queam" (VII, 24). At the most, following an expedient already practiced by Cicero and the Stoics, and transmitted to him by Theodontius, he makes an effort to reconcile conflicting versions of the same myth by recognizing that the same name has been applied to several different deities—to three Jupiters, four Minervas, five or six Bacchuses. But on the other hand, however passive and timid he may be in analyzing the content of the fables, he shows abundant energy and boldness when it comes to reading meanings into them. Convinced as he is that the chief *raison d'être* of a poem is the sense hidden under its surface (XIV, 10, 12), he develops Rabanus Maurus' idea that there may be several ways of interpreting the same story. Thus the fable of Perseus decapitating the Gorgon and rising into the air with the help of his winged sandals may be taken literally, as the account of an actual happening; morally, as a symbol of the wise man's ascent to virtue after his conquest of sin; or allegorically, as a symbol of Christ triumphant over the Prince of this World and rising toward His Father.

We recognize this method; [15] we have followed its applications from Phornutus to Fulgentius, from Ridewall to the moralizations of Ovid. Here, too, Boccaccio borrows from his predecessors. For example, he takes from Fulgentius his allegorical interpretation of Antaeus, image of earthly lust which the virtuous man can overcome only by chastity (I, 13). But he yields

[14] Dedicatory Epistle: "Quae quidem et alia si quae sunt a debito variantia non est meae intentionis redarguere vel aliquo modo corrigere, nisi ad aliquem ordinem sponte sua se sinant redigi. Satis enim mihi erit comperta rescribere, et disputationes philosophicas linquere."—Cf. Boccaccio's conclusion, after his exposé of conflicting views of Io and Isis: "Sane solertibus hujus varietatis inquisitio relinquatur," IV, 46 ("Surely an inquiry of this kind should be left to the experts"), and, à propos of Apis: "Deus rei hujus videat veritatem: ego quidem has intricationes non intellego," VII, 24 ("Let a god perceive the truth of this: as for me, I don't understand these intricacies").

[15] See *supra*, Bk. I, Pt. 1, chap. iii.—Boccaccio gives an express account of his method of interpretation in his *Vita di Dante* (ed. Moutier [1833]), pp. 56–57.—On the other works by Boccaccio rich in allegorical content, *L'amorosa visione* and the *L'Ameto,* see D. Bassi, "La mitologia nelle prime imitazioni della Divina Commedia," *Aevum,* XI (1937), fasc. 1–2, pp. 203–235.

nothing in ingenuity to the earlier writers when he himself allegorizes on his own account: Pasiphaë, daughter of the Sun, is the soul, child of God; her consort, Minos, is human reason, which governs the soul and leads it along the right path. Venus, her enemy, is lust; the bull represents the pleasures of this world, and from the union of the soul with pleasure is born the Minotaur, the vice of bestiality (IV, 10).

This approach—which consists in a determination to reveal edifying meanings everywhere, come what may—is in line, moreover, with the dictates of prudence. In showing the great lessons of Christian morals beneath the pagan fables, Boccaccio is safeguarding himself against criticism or reproach on the score of impiety. He is careful, furthermore (and there is no question of his sincerity), to give constant assurance of his orthodoxy [16] in order to ward off attack from the theologians.

Thus, in spite of some symptoms of a new spirit, the *Genealogy* is still rooted in the medieval past, which nourishes it and animates it. This in no way detracted from its contemporary success or its wide circulation, which are attested by the large number of manuscripts and, after the invention of printing, the large number of editions brought out in Latin,[17] Italian, and Spanish.[18] It became, and remained for two centuries, the central storehouse from which educated men drew their knowledge of the gods.

*

IT WAS NOT, indeed, until the middle of the sixteenth century that Italy saw a renewal of the authentic mythographical tradition. It is a curious fact that the Renaissance, in its most brilliant phase, produced no work in this field—the reason perhaps being that the very contact with and immediate intuition of antiquity rendered such scholarly aids unnecessary. Perhaps, also, other publications, besides the *Genealogy* of Boccaccio, were a response in at least a provisional manner to the needs of the time.

What were these publications? Were they perhaps, as might be imagined, the most important classical texts, made generally available through the

[16] Each book opens with a prayer to Christ; a profession of faith ends the work.

[17] Eight between 1472 and 1532.

[18] See E. H. Wilkins, "The Genealogy of the Editions of the *Genealogia deorum*," *Modern Philology*, XVII (1919), pp. 423–438.

advent of printing? No; this was not the case. Indeed, the truth of Michelet's verdict must be acknowledged: "Printing at first served for little more than to propagate and assure the survival of barbaric literature. . . . Though some classical works were published, they were far outnumbered by the recurrent editions of medieval writings, especially the textbooks, the *Summae*, the *précis* or abridgements." [19] As a matter of fact, printed editions of ancient mythographers did appear, from the end of the fifteenth century on; but as Gruppe has observed,[20] with the exception of the *De natura deorum,* these were chiefly the works on which the Middle Ages had most thrived. Also, they were printed in an order almost exactly inverse to that of their true value: the *Commentary* of Servius (six editions between 1470 and 1475); Fulgentius; the *Homeric Allegories* of Palaephatus, the treatises of Heraclitus and Phornutus (Aldus, 1505); Macrobius (Macrobius "integer," Paris, 1515 and 1524; Basel, 1535; Lyons, five editions between 1522 and 1544). The *Bibliotheca* of Apollodorus was to appear only much later (1555). On the other hand, the medieval mythographers were constantly reissued. Aside from Boccaccio's *Genealogia,* the success of which we have described, and which continued to be the leading mythological source book through the first half of the sixteenth century, Martianus Capella, for instance, went into no less than eight editions between 1499 and 1599; the *Images of the Gods* of Albricus and the *Libellus de imaginibus deorum* were brought out, the first at the end of the fifteenth century (Rome, *c.* 1480; Florence, *c.* 1492, and 1495–1500; other editions: Vienna, 1510 and 1523; Rome, 1510; Basel, 1549 and 1570; Paris, 1578; Lyons and Geneva, 1608, etc.), the second in 1520 (Paris, Jean de Marnef: *Allegoriae poeticae seu de veritate ac expositione poeticarum fabularum libri quatuor Alberico Londoniensi authore nusquam antea impressi*). The *Libellus,* which, as we have seen, was attributed to Albricus from the fifteenth century on, was presented to the public in glowing terms:

Arma deum, formasque velis si noscere lector
Albrici exiguo codice cuncta leges

[19] *Histoire de France au* XVIe *siècle: Renaissance* (1857), Introd., pp. 105–106.

[20] *Geschichte d. klass. Myth.,* p. 31, par. 17. Dr. E. P. Goldschmidt has kindly communicated valuable information concerning the editions of Albricus.

or in what might be the accents of a dithyramb:

> *Numquid opus Phidiae, vel Mentoris, anne Myronis?*
>
> . . . .
>
> *Falleris. Albrici labor est, dum conderet ista*
> *Archetypos habuit qui (mihi crede) Deos.*[21]

Making due allowance for rhetoric and for the desire to publicize the work, there would still seem to be a certain effrontery—or a strange blindness—in proffering "Albricus" as a rival of Phidias, and in claiming that he copied the gods "d'après nature."

*

THESE VARIOUS treatises, of ancient or more modern date, were several times brought together in collections where mythographical, allegorical, and astronomical texts of very unequal value were juxtaposed. Thus the *Libellus*, supposedly by Albricus, appeared in Basel in 1549 together with the *Fables* and the *Astronomy* of Hyginus, Palaephatus' *On Incredible Things*, the *Mythologies* of Fulgentius, Phornutus' allegorical *On the Nature of the Gods*, the *Sphere* of Proclus, and the *Phenomena* of Aratus.[22] Later,[23] this same collection was to be enriched by the new *History of the Gods* of Giglio (Lilio) Gregorio Giraldi (Lilius Gregorius Gyraldus); later still,[24] through résumés and commentaries by Macrobius, Marsilio Ficino, and a contemporary mythographer, Conti.[25] In the same period, Italy and all of Europe were of course inundated by editions of the *Metamorphoses*, but these were moralized versions.[26] Thus the chief sources for knowledge of the gods during the first

21 Edition of Vienna, 1523: *Albrici philosophi et poetae doctissimi libellus de Deorum imaginibus* (with Fenestella, *De magistratibus . . . Romanorum*). ("If you want to know the arms and the figures of the gods, you will read about them in Albricus' small treatise. . . . Is this the work of Phidias, of Mentor, of Myron? You are mistaken. It is the work of Albricus, who, believe me, had the gods themselves as original models.")

22 An earlier edition of this collection (1535) does not include the *Libellus*.

23 Basel, 1570.

24 Lyons, 1608.

25 On the history of the publication of the mythographers in the sixteenth and seventeenth centuries, see Struve, *Syntagma . . .* (1701), pp. 50 ff.: "Mythographi Latini"; pp. 55–56: "Recentiores scriptores de Diis"; and J. A. Fabricius, *Bibliographia antiquaria*, 3rd ed. (1760), chap. viii: "Scriptores de Diis," etc., esp. par. 8, "Deorum nomina, imagines, genealogiae."

26 We have given (Bk. I, Pt. 1, chap. iii) a list of these editions. The moralization attributed to Thomas Waleys, alone, was published five times in Italy between 1510 and 1519. See E. K. Rand, *Ovid and his Influence* (London, 1926); on the illustrated editions of the *Metamorphoses*, see M. D. Henkel, *Illustrierte Ausgaben von Ovids Metamorphosen im* XV., XVI. *und* XVII. *Jahrhundert, Vorträge der Bibl. Warburg* (1926–27), pp. 58–144.

half of the sixteenth century were either the authors whom the Middle Ages had read, or the medieval authors themselves.

*

NEVERTHELESS, need began to be felt for a more systematic treatment which would collect these scattered notions and bring them into some kind of order, replacing the old *Genealogy*, which in the meantime continued to do fairly good service.

Some works which appeared in the first half of the century prepared the way for this new "codification" of mythology: thus, dictionaries of ancient proper names, like that of Robert Estienne,[27] performed a certain summarizing function with regard to the material of Fable. Similarly, the books of "examples" or "lessons" (*antiquae lectiones,* or *exemplorum libri*)—that is to say, the haphazard compilations of anecdotes, sayings, and curiosities culled at random from ancient authors, to which the sixteenth century was as partial as the Middle Ages had been [28]—usually contained a mass of detail concerning the pagan divinities. The model of the genre, the enormous *Officina* of Ravisius Textor,[29] is a mine of information on the origins and pedigrees of the gods, their attributes, the places, offerings, and festivals sacred to them, etc.; moreover, it has its source in Boccaccio, for it again introduces Demogorgon.[30] Lastly, the books of hieroglyphs and emblems, in which, as we have already seen, the gods played an important part,[31] made a mass of information, citations, and even illustrations readily accessible to the reader; they thus offered, in their own way, the rudiments of a mythological compendium. Nevertheless, none of these works performed the service of a specialized and complete treatise.

[27] *Dictionarium nominum virorum, mulierum, populorum, idolorum, urbium etc. quae passim in libris prophanis leguntur* (Paris, 1512): "Fabulas," says Estienne, "ex Servio Acrone ceterisque nobilibus grammaticis deprompsimus" ("As for the Fables . . . I have borrowed them from Servius, Acron, and other famous philologists"). Analogous works are: Herman Torrentinus, *Elucidarius carminum et historiarum, vel vocabularius poeticus: continens fabulas,* etc. (Strasbourg, 1510 [?]); Montefalco, *De cognominibus deorum* (Perugia, 1525); R. Textor, *Epithetorum opus absolutissimum . . . lexicon vere poeticum, uberem omnium et verborum copiam complectens* (Basel, 1558).

[28] See J. T. Welter, *l'Exemplum dans la littérature religieuse et didactique du Moyen-Age* (Paris, 1927).

[29] Ravisius Textor, *Officina partim historicis partim poeticis referta disciplinis* (Basel, 1503). Cf. the compilations by Caelius Rhodiginus and Petrus Crinitus.

[30] In a chapter entitled, "De deis, filii deorum et heroum," fol. 256v.–259r., etc.

[31] See *supra,* pp. 101 ff.

It is to a German, Georg Pictor, that the credit belongs of having been the first sixteenth-century author to renew Boccaccio's undertaking—though, it is true, on a more modest scale. His *Mythological Theology,* appearing in 1532,[32] and republished in 1558 as the *Magazine of the Gods,*[33] is presented in dialogue form. Theophrastus, a professor, teaches his disciple, Evander, the names, appearance, and "allegory" of each god, beginning with the "Magni Dei" and arriving thereafter at the "Selecti," and the "Indigetes," or tutelary divinities.

Evander is especially curious about the appearance of the gods: "Dic imaginem!" he insists, when the description has not yet been given. It is therefore on this point that Theophrastus dwells at greatest length. He usually offers several descriptions of the same god, based upon different authors and documents. Several of the authorities whom he invokes are old friends of ours: Fulgentius, Martianus Capella, and the *Libellus* (which Pictor paraphrases, when he does not copy it word for word).[34] We find him basing a description of Juno on the statue by Polycletus of which Pausanias speaks, or even on a medal of Faustina (p. 19). But these types are a little too familiar to satisfy Evander, who demands something new and rare: "Habes ab hac aliam minus communem?" (p. 12). To satisfy this taste, Theophrastus sometimes leaves Greece and Rome to hunt for less well-known images in the East (*fig. 94*). Thus, in treating of the great Greco-Roman gods, he does not fail to call attention to their Oriental equivalents: the "Assyrian" Apollo, with basketlike headdress, or the bearded Cypriote Venus. He even devotes several chapters to the Egyptian gods: Isis, Osiris, Harpocrates, etc. Here we merely note the appearance of this exotic tendency, this mythology of other peoples ("exterarum gentium," says the title). We shall meet with it soon again.

32 *Theologia mythologica ex doctiss. virorum promptuario, labore Pictorii Vill. in compendium congesta. Videlicet De nominum deorum gentilium ratione. De imaginibus aut formis, insignibusque; earumd. et omnium imaginum explanationes allegoricae* (Freiburg i.B., 1532); another edition was published in Antwerp in the same year.

33 *Apotheseos tam exterarum gentium quam Romanorum deorum libri tres, nomina imagines et earumdem imaginum complectentes allegorias, auctore D. Giorgio Pictore Villingano . . .* (Basel, 1558). Pictor is also the author of the *Physicarum quaestionum centuria tres . . . quis verus deus, unde gentiles dei* (Basel, 1568).

34 See, for example, p. 26 (ed. 1558): "audi nunc quam totam fere ex Albrico philosopho habemus" ("such as we have almost entirely from the philosopher Albricus"), said of Apollo; p. 38: "Albricus hoc ferme linearum ductu hanc depingit" ("Albricus describes thus clearly"), of Mercury; "Albricus fingit" ("Albricus represents"), of Ceres, etc.

As each description ends, Evander asks to have it explained,[35] taking up one after the other various details of the god's features, clothing, etc. "Why has Jupiter no ears? Why does he hold a scepter in his left hand, thunderbolts in his right?" With untiring compliance the master provides the desired interpretation—sometimes a physical or cosmogonic interpretation, but more often an edifying or moral one. The book ends, as it began, with a completely orthodox expression of faith, a prayer to the true and eternal God of gods, to Him who "verus et sempiternus omnium deorum deus est."

94. Mithra

In short, Pictor's treatise falls thoroughly into line with the medieval tradition. It is related to the *Libellus* by its descriptive method;[36] in its allegorical preoccupations it is a sequel to Boccaccio and his forerunners.

*

BETWEEN 1548 and 1556 there appeared, one after the other, three Italian manuals of much greater importance, both in size and popularity. These are:

The History of the Gods, by Lilio Gregorio Giraldi: *De deis gentium varia et multiplex historia in qua simul de eorum imaginibus et cognominibus agitur*, etc. (Basel, Oporinus, 1548).

The *Mythology* of Natale Conti: *Mythologiae sive explicationis fabularum libri decem* (Venice, Aldus, 1551).

[35] For each one, of course, is "cum sale intelligendus" (p. 20). Cf. p. 9: "Habent fortassis singula plus in recessu quam fronte promittant" ("They have perhaps in the background more than they promise in the front").

[36] The edition of 1558 is illustrated, but the engravings do not correspond to the text; they are taken from another German mythological treatise, the *Heydenwelt* of Herold (see *fig. 94*), published at Basel in 1554. As Herold to a large extent derives from Giraldi, we shall be dealing with him somewhat later.

The Images of the Gods, by Vincenzo Cartari: *Le imagini colla sposizione degli dei degli antichi* (Venice, Marcolini, 1556).

It would be well to recapitulate briefly what is known of these three authors, of their lives, work, and reputation among their contemporaries.

Lilio Gregorio Giraldi is one of the great figures of humanism.[37] Born at Ferrara in 1479, he led a wandering existence, encountering many setbacks of fortune. In Naples, he became the friend of Pontano and Sannazaro; in Milan, he studied Greek under Demetrios Chalcondylas (1507). In Modena, he became the tutor of Ercole Rangone; when Rangone was made a cardinal, Giraldi accompanied him to Rome, where he had lodgings in the Vatican (1514). There his reverses began: his ambitions were frustrated, his health began to fail. Then came the disaster of the sack of Rome in 1527; he lost all his possessions, even his books. As the crowning misfortune, Cardinal Rangone died in the same year. Giraldi then sought refuge with Gianfrancesco Pico della Mirandola, but this patron was assassinated in 1533. Ill, embittered, without resources, he then returned to his native city, where the benevolence of Duchess Renée and the friendship of Manardi and Calcagnini rescued him from want and brightened his latter years. He died in 1550 or 1552.

Author of Latin poems, of the celebrated *Discourse against Letters and the Literati,* which expressed his bitterness and disillusion,[38] and of several learned works (*Treatise on the Muses, On the Enigmas of the Ancients and the Pythagorean Symbols, On the Years and Months, History of the Poets of Antiquity,* etc.), he undertook his great *History of the Gods* only toward the end of his life—"senex et aeger . . . iam grandaevus et paene moribundus." He insists—and his editors will insist after him—on the painful conditions

[37] See G. Tiraboschi, *Storia della letteratura italiana* (Rome, 1782–1797), VII, pp. 190–195; Giannandrea Barotti, *Memorie istoriche di letterati ferraresi* (Ferrara, 1792–93), I, p. 265. Giraldi himself furnishes many autobiographical details, as for instance in the *History of the Gods* (Dedication, Chaps. IV and XIV: his disappointed hopes; his affairs and health ruined) and in the *Poemata* (*Opera,* II, p. 914: sack of Rome; death of Cardinal Rangone).

[38] *Progymnasma adversus literas et literatos,* in *Opera,* II, pp. 422–455 (Basel, 1580). This discourse was probably written under Leo X and revised around 1540. On the condition of the humanists and their decline, see J. Burckhardt, *The Civilization of the Renaissance in Italy,* chap. xi: "Fall of the Humanists in the "Sixteenth Century."

under which he brings the work to an end,[39] ravaged by gout which nails him to his bed, "gravato decumbens, saevissima arthritide correptus."

Giraldi, whom Jensius, in the 1696 edition of his complete works, hails as one of the pioneers of the Renaissance,[40] is, to quote Moreri, "generally regarded as one of the greatest geniuses produced by Italy in the last centuries." And, in fact, he was held in high esteem by the contemporary humanists Scaliger, Casaubon, and Vossius, while Montaigne writes: "I regard it as a disgrace to our century that we have, as I understand, allowed two men of the highest learning to die in extreme want: Lilius Gregorius Gyraldus in Italy, and Sebastianus Castalio in Germany."[41]

We know less of the life of Natale Conti[42]—only that he was born in Milan around 1520, and that after several years of study in Venice he returned to his native city, serving in the household of the jurist Gabrio Panigarola as tutor to his son, the future Fra Francesco Panigarola. Of his other relations, and his milieu, we know very little. He addresses verses to Venetian senators, composes a poem on the Hours for Cosimo de' Medici. He seems to have had correspondents and patrons in France, for he dedicates one of the editions of the *Mythology* to Charles IX.[43] In addition to the last-named work, he is the author of several translations (for example, of a Latin version of the *Deipnosophistae* of Athenaeus), of Latin elegies in the manner of Ovid (*Carmina*), and—still in Latin—of a treatise on hunting (*De venatione*) and works on contemporary history (*Commentarii de Turcorum bello in insulam*

39 At the end of *Syntagma* v he writes: "Hunc . . . laborem omnem exegi XVII calend. Novembris MDXLIII."

40 ". . . primum quasi ver renascentibus ac respirantibus a barbarie litteris."

41 *Essais,* I, 35: "J'entends avec une grande honte de nostre siècle qu'à nostre veüe deux très excellens personnages en savoir sont morts en estat de n'avoir pas leur soul à manger."

42 See G. Tiraboschi (VII, pp. 195–196), who makes use of Foscarini (*Della letteratura veneziana,* p. 284). Johann Fabricius (*Historia bibliothecae,* VII, p. 332) attributes other Latin works to Conti.

43 Edition of 1567; another edition is dedicated to G. B. Campeggi, bishop of Majorca. Conti refers several times to a Parisian magistrate, Arnaud du Ferrier, as one source of encouragement to him in his work; another source was the Venetian inquisitor, Valerio Faenzi.

Conti's *Mythologia* is discussed in the article by D. Bassi, "Un' opera mitologica del sec. XVI," *R. Istituto lombardo di scienze e lettere, Rendiconti,* LXX (1937), pp. 9–20; Bassi points out that Conti was of noble birth, and refers to G. Arditi di Casteltevere, "Memorie delle famiglie Conti ed Arditi," *Revista di araldica e genealogia* (Naples, 1933). The same article contains errors concerning the editions of the *Mythologia.*

Melitam gesto anno 1565; Universae historiae sui temporis libri XXX [1572?]).

It is to his *Mythology*, apparently, that he owed his chief reputation; even so, his fame came late and was not undisputed. Moreri tells us that he passed for one of the most learned men of his time ("l'un des plus sçavans hommes de son temps"); Heinrich Ursinus considers him the first of mythographers. But Scaliger refers to him disdainfully as a negligible compiler not worthy to be quoted.[44]

Vincenzo Cartari, the third of this group of Italian mythographers, is a very mysterious figure. We know almost nothing of his life, except that he was born in Reggio Emilia early in the sixteenth century. Like old Giraldi, he was a protégé of the dukes of Ferrara, and probably lived in their entourage.[45] He dedicated his treatise on the gods to Luigi d'Este, as Giraldi had dedicated his to Ercole II. Furthermore, through his publisher, Marcolini, he must have been in contact in Venice with the circle of humanists surrounding Aretino.

All of Cartari's works are in the vulgar tongue; aside from his *Images of the Gods,* he was author of a translation of and commentary on the *Fasti* of Ovid (*Fasti d'Ovidio tratti alla lingua volgare,* 1551; *Il Flavio intorno ai fasti volgari,* 1553), and of an abridgement of Paolo Giovio (*Il compendio dell'istoria di M. Paolo Giovio,* 1562). The name of Cartari is rarely mentioned by his contemporaries; nevertheless, Armenini cites him as an authority,[46] and Lomazzo recommends his *Images* to artists.[47]

As we see, the three mythographers were by no means equal in celebrity, but the success of their works was not directly related to the more or less brilliant place which they occupied in the history of humanism and the opinion

[44] In a letter (*Epistolae,* XIV, 309, p. 614) to Calvisius (Setho Calvisio) he definitely recommends "ut scriptorum quorumdam minorum gentium mentione, qualis est Natalis Comes, vir futilissimus, abstineas. Dolet enim magnis viris illos pannos tuae purpurae assui." ("Refrain from mentioning minor writers such as Natalis Comes, a very untrustworthy man. It is painful to the great to see you sew these rags to your purple.")

[45] See the allusions at the beginning of the *Flavio.*

[46] Giovanni Battista Armenini, *Precetti della Pittura* (Ravenna, 1587); cf. 1820 edition, p. 318.

[47] Giovanni Paolo Lomazzo, *Trattato dell'arte della pittura* (Milan, 1584); cf. 1844 edition, III, p. 272.

of scholars: Cartari, the most obscure of the three, found more readers than did Giraldi, the most learned and highly regarded.[48]

*

THERE IS no need, we feel, for separate analyses to be made of the *History of the Gods*, the *Mythology*, and the *Images*, since the resemblances between the three works greatly outweigh the differences. Let us note merely:

1) That Giraldi, the earliest in date,[49] undoubtedly influenced the other two; Natale Conti, it is true, affects not to know him, and even feigns amazement that "no one, up to this date, has undertaken a comprehensive explanation of these fables, based on the ancient authors" (I, 1); this attitude, which rightly amazes Tiraboschi (VII, 195), is proof not so much of ignorance on Conti's part as of an excessive vanity, which we shall have occasion to note elsewhere;[50] Cartari, on the other hand, willingly acknowledges his borrowings from Giraldi—borrowings so extensive that Lessing could regard him as a plagiarist.[51]

2) That they bring different aptitudes and aims to bear upon a common subject: Giraldi, the learned philologist, concentrates upon names, epithets, etymologies, to the detriment of the myths themselves; Conti professes himself a philosopher, and takes special interest in a more profound interpretation of the fables; Cartari is essentially an iconographer—his dominant if not exclusive preoccupation being to describe the gods.

With these reservations, we may place the three works on the same level and look at them collectively. For, in spite of appearances, none of them represents a really decisive advance over the earlier treatises; not one contains

[48] This will be shown as we study the dissemination of the three works, Book II, chaps. ii and iii, *infra*.

[49] Ill-informed critics have tried to maintain the contrary. Scipione Casali (cited in the *Dictionnaire universel*, article *Cartari*) affirms that "Cartari was the first writer after Boccaccio to summon mythology from the obscurity into which it had fallen: in fact, the Latin works on the same subject by L. G. Giraldi and N. Conti did not appear till several years later." The dates given above show that this assertion is baseless.

[50] He also omits all mention of Boccaccio, to whom, however, he is much indebted. One of Conti's editors (Frambottus, 1637) was later to name Giraldi among his predecessors.

[51] G. E. Lessing, *Wie die Alten den Tod gebildet*, first edition (Berlin, 1769), p. 79. According to Lessing, Cartari is nothing more than a pocket Giraldi. In our opinion, Cartari also owed much to Pictor; in any case, the two have an astonishing number of common sources.

anything essentially new. On the contrary, what we find—in varying proportions, but in all three—are the materials, methods, and even the images of the past.

*

IT CANNOT be disputed that the information brought forward by these authors is broader, and their erudition more self-assured. But in their choice and classification of sources, they abide by the medieval habits.

Although they have a better and more direct knowledge of classical writers—Conti, for instance, borrows extensively from the Greek tragedians—they continue to draw largely upon the late scholiasts and compilers, Hyginus, Servius, Lactantius Placidus, Macrobius, Martianus, Fulgentius; upon the Church Fathers and the encyclopedists; upon Albricus and Boccaccio;[52] lastly, upon their own contemporaries—sometimes those who are least trustworthy. That Giraldi should evoke the authority of Politian, of Pico della Mirandola, Leon Battista Alberti, and Budé is certainly admissible. But he repeats the tales of a certain Alexander of Naples,[53] whose fables are made use of by Pictor also and later by Cartari in describing the gods.

At the same time, when carefully sorted, this confused mass of evidence is not without its value; for "it is not to the writers of the most brilliant period that the mythographer should turn for evidence; in order to recover the most genuine expression of a myth, one must look much earlier or much later."[54] There is a great deal to be gleaned from the mythographers of the late Empire, who were themselves gleaners. Even the compilers of the Middle Ages are not necessarily negligible: they may have collected the debris of myths which would otherwise have been lost.[55] But did our Italian authors sift this

[52] Giraldi cites both, with reservations to which we shall call attention later. Conti pretends not to know them.

[53] P. 170: "Scribit vero Alexander Neapolitanus suo quoque tempore visum hominem marinum et melle servatum, ex Mauritania in Hispaniam delatum." ("Alexander of Naples writes that in his day a merman was seen, preserved in honey, and brought from Morocco to Spain.") G. Tiraboschi (VII, p. 211) gives a summary biography of this Alessandro degli Alessandri (1461–1523). His *Dies geniales* (1522), an imitation of the *Attic Nights*, contains descriptions of the gods. See ed. 1550, pp. 204–205: "Imagines variorum deorum quomodo pingi solitae" (". . . as they are usually painted"). In reality, his descriptions are by no means the usual ones. See the *Dictionnaire* of Bayle.

[54] P. Decharme, *Mythologie de la Grèce antique* (Paris, 1879), Introduction.

[55] This is true of Boccaccio; see *supra*, p. 222. It is also true of Natale Conti himself. Louis Ménard (*Du Polythéisme hellénique* [Paris, 1863], p. 81) finds in Conti's *Mythologia* (VII, 13) "three verses of the *Little*

heterogeneous matter with an eye to the relative value of their authorities?

On this score, they themselves offer many assurances; if we are to believe their own protestations, the critical sense which their predecessors lacked forms their own chief virtue. Not in their pages will be found, as in Boccaccio, "invented deities, of whom there is no trace in any ancient author." [56] Giraldi prides himself on working from authentic texts, and from the actual manuscripts; [57] Cartari, in his turn, boasts that he uses only the good authors, the writers most deserving of belief.[58] Unfortunately, they fall into the error of attributing too great an antiquity—and hence authority—to writers like Hermes Trismegistus, whom Giraldi places earlier than Plato, and with whom he begins his enumeration of the opinions of the ancients concerning the gods; [59] but above all, as we have seen, these proud declarations do not prevent them from quoting many nonclassical authors.

True enough, they speak of these authors with mistrust and disdain. Hyginus is merely a compiler; [60] Fulgentius is not to be relied upon; [61] Albricus still less,[62] and he contains ridiculous tales. As for the *Genealogy* of Boc-

---

Iliad of Lesches which I have not as yet discovered in any edition of the Epic Cycle." Conti, like Boccaccio, preserved fragments of Philochoros. See Lenchantin, art. cit.

[56] Giraldi on Demogorgon: "Nusquam Demogorgon iste, nusquam inquam apparuit" ("Nowhere, nowhere did this wretched Demogorgon appear). Cf. Cartari: "But I have never yet found or seen mention of him in any ancient writer."

[57] P. 152: "ut in aliis codicibus legitur" ("as is read in other manuscripts"); p. 403: "ne mirere si in citandi Phornuto non edita exemplaria plerumque sequor: nam apud me est manuscriptus codex, illis et castigatior et locupletior" ("do not be surprised if in quoting Phornutus I for the most part do not follow the printed editions, as I have in my possession a manuscript which is both richer and more correct than they are"); p. 463: "quod et agnoscitur ex Cardinalis Maffei codice manuscripto" ("which is also made clear by a manuscript belonging to Cardinal Maffei"); pp. 252, 277, 301, 388: discussion of his lessons; p. 391: "in graeco codice haec nomina corrupte leguntur" ("these names are incorrectly given in a Greek manuscript").

[58] 1571 edition, p. 43: "I do not affirm this, since I have not found it in any trustworthy author"; p. 181: "I have already said several times that I do not wish to assume anything about which the ancients have not written."

[59] P. 26. On the slips and errors made by Giraldi—due less to negligence, his publishers tell us (1696), than to old age and illness, and also to the fact that he did not have at his disposal the aids and instruments of scholarship which were available to later students ("destitutus melioribus rei literariae instrumentis ac praesidiis quae secuta demum subpeditarunt tempora")—see O. Gruppe, *op. cit.*, p. 33.

[60] See Frambottus, editor of Conti (1637): "Julius, quaeso, Hyginus, quid praeter fabularum congeriem adfert?" ("What does Julius Hyginus bring us, I wonder, other than a chaotic mass of fables?")

[61] Giraldi, p. 158: "quamvis hic autor non omnino mihi, vel fide rerum, vel loquendi proprietate satis probatur" ("although this author does not seem to me entirely reliable, either for factual accuracy or for propriety of expression").

[62] Giraldi, p. 153: "qui auctor mihi proletarius est nec fidus satis" ("this author stands low in my estimation, and is not sufficiently trustworthy"); p. 178: "ex Albrico ignobili scriptore. Risum vix continui cum apud

caccio, "one is astounded at finding persons who accord him so much belief, as if his testimony had any value. Certainly, Boccaccio was a cultivated spirit for his time, but he committed gross errors." [63]

After strictures like these, one would expect the untrustworthy authorities to be avoided. But not only are Martianus Capella [64] and Fulgentius [65] cited *in extenso;* they are even on occasion quoted in opposition to the classical authors themselves. For instance, while according to Ovid Apollo's chariot is drawn by four horses, Cartari hastens to add that Martianus mentions only two.[66] As for the most recent authors, Albricus and Boccaccio, Giraldi quotes Albricus apropos of Vesta ("Sunt qui deam supra pinnaculum templi statuant, ut scribit Albricus"), and Boccaccio in several connections. On such subjects as Eternity, the Sirens, Apollo, etc., Cartari often brings forward testimony from Boccaccio.[67]

*

THE FIRST result of this mingling of sources is the surprisingly high proportion of barbarian or pseudo-antique divinities.

From the chapter titles one would judge that our manuals dealt exclusively with Greco-Roman gods: Jupiter, Mercury, Juno, Diana, etc. These Olympians, however, are in fact lost in a crowd—or, to recall an expression

nescio quem legi, Cereris effigiem in bove sedentem cum legione et seminum calatho, assistentibus agricolis, aliisque" ("from Albricus, an obscure writer. . . . I nearly laughed when I read in I don't know what author that Ceres was represented seated on an ox, with a basket full of seeds, among peasants and other people"). This *nescio quis* is the author of the *Libellus.* Frambottus (*loc. cit.*) writes of the *Libellus*: "Quid succincta deorum Iconologia Albricus philosophus proficit?" ("What is the use of Albricus' short iconology of the gods?")

[63] "Saepe miratus . . . nescio quos, qui tantam illius genealogiis auctoritatem impenderint ut non illas modo in testimonium citent, sed etiam (ut audio) interpretati sint": Giraldi, Dedication to Ercole d'Este. In this same dedication, Giraldi congratulates himself on having composed not only a more learned work, but a more complete one as well: "Non genealogias dico, sed et nomina, et cognomina, effigiesque, etc. ("I speak not of the genealogies only, but of the names, figures," etc.); cf. p. 219: "Buccatius insulse tripodem putavit lauri speciem" ("Boccaccio foolishly thought that a tripod was a kind of laurel"). True to his system, Conti pretends not to know the *Genealogia.* Cartari notes, after Giraldi (see *supra*), that Demogorgon is nowhere found in antiquity.

[64] By Giraldi for the figures of Jupiter and Saturn; by Cartari for *all the gods* who are described in the *De nuptiis.*

[65] Giraldi quotes Fulgentius apropos of Neptune, and does so with rather great frequency (pp. 15, 118, 134, 138, 140, 142, 158, 194, 207, 212, 218, 251, etc.).

[66] Cf. p. 282: "The ancients gave him [Pluto] a chariot drawn by four wild black horses . . . although Boccaccio says that there were only three."

[67] P. 176: "But Boccaccio would have it otherwise, and says . . . ," and p. 177: "But Boccaccio has a long tale to tell," etc.

of Nietzsche's, a "cosmopolitan carnival" of divinities. One's first impression on turning the pages of the illustrated edition of Cartari arouses amazement; not one in ten of the gods represented could be named with certainty.

92. Two images of Jupiter

93. Diana and Apollo

Here, for example,[68] we have a strange personage dressed in white, his mantle bespangled with stars. In his left hand he holds a nine-stringed lyre, in his right two globes—one of gold, the other of silver. His footgear, the text tells us, is emerald green in color; he has a trident beneath his feet, and his seat is covered with a sort of drapery woven of peacock's feathers. Who would recognize Jupiter with these accouterments? Yet it is he—point for point like the description of him given by Martianus Capella.[69] It is not on Olympus that

[68] Cartari, *Imagini* (1571 edition), pl. 148. This Jupiter has already been described by Giraldi, *Syntagma* II.

[69] *Martiani Minei Capellae De nuptiis philologiae et Mercurii lib.* VI (Basel, 1532), pp. 12–13. The other engravings inspired by Martianus are as follows: Saturn, p. 42 (*De nuptiis,* 12–13); Apollo, 68 (31); Hecate, 117

he thus appears, but at the nuptials of Mercury and Philology. On the same plate, moreover, Zeus appears with his lightning and his eagle: thus the classical gods are brought together in surprising promiscuity with their hybrid descendants (*fig. 92*).

As for the foreign gods, it should be recalled that our mythographers sum up and continue a syncretistic tradition; they turn for information above all to the last adherents of paganism—that is, to a period when all the cults were being merged and all the gods amalgamated. Medieval mythology preserved many traces of this intermingling: to speak of illustrated manuscripts alone, Monac. lat. 14271 (11 v.) offers us a Cybele (who, admittedly, became a Roman goddess at an early period); the Rabanus Maurus of Monte Cassino, a Mercury-Anubis;[70] Palat. 1066 (224 v.), a Jupiter Ammon. In the *Libellus*, Apollo receives the *signum triceps* belonging to Serapis.

But in our manuals, divinities of the Oriental cults are given extraordinary prominence, especially in Cartari. First of all, the Egyptians: Serapis, Osiris, Isis, Horus, Harpocrates, Anubis, Typhon, the "Moon of Apollinopolis," the "Apollo of Elephantinopolis" (*fig. 93*); the Egyptian Jupiter, beneath the lotus; Canopus, the god formed like a vase. Then come the Syrian gods, Jupiter Ammon, the Assyrian Apollo, Hadad, Atargatis, the Phoenician Venus, Juno Syria of Hierapolis; then the gods of Asia Minor, the Black Stone, Jupiter Labrandeus, also those of Persia (Mithra), and even those of Scythia and Arabia Petraea—Mars in the form of a stone, and Mars as a scimitar mounted on a pyre of wood.

We have already had occasion to note in Pictor[71] the same unusual or even disproportionate place given to the Oriental divinities; it is due, in our opinion, to a contemporary influence—that of the "hieroglyphics," which drew the attention of humanists[72] to Egypt, and to the Orient in general. After Aldus Manutius published the little book by Horapollo, and Pierio

(30); Isis, 120 (30); Juno, 180 (13); Cybele, 207 (14); Neptune, 250 (14); Mercury, 326 (2) and 331 (31).

[70] Cf. Bersuire (1509 edition), chap. vi: "Aliqui etiam, ut dicit ibidem Rabanus, depingebant eum cum capite canino" ("Some, as Rabanus says in the same passage, depicted him with the head of a dog"); and the *Libellus:* "Aliqui vero eum capite canino pingebant" ("Some, however, depicted him with the head of a dog").

[71] See *supra*, pp. 228 f.

[72] See Bk. I, Pt. 1, chap. iii.

Valeriano, the most fertile of its commentators, had drawn from it a veritable bible of symbols, the Eastern religions, with their intriguing qualities of mystery and the picturesque, exerted a steadily increasing attraction.

95. Venus and the Graces

In fact, Giraldi and Cartari not only pillaged the eleventh book of Apuleius, the Περί ἀγαλμάτων of Porphyry, the *Saturnalia* of Macrobius, etc.; they read Horapollo and Valeriano, quoted them as authorities.[73] Some of their most bizarre descriptive details are taken from Alexander of Naples.[74]

To aggravate the confusion, our manuals—whose authors claim, in fact, that they treat of *all* the gods of paganism, "tutti i dei della gentilità"[75] —introduce into their pantheon remnants of Celtic and Germanic mythology,

[73] Giraldi, p. 384: "Sed Horus Apollo, quem in graecam linguam transtulisse creditur Philippus quidam, Annum describens, ita propemodum de Isidis stella haec prodit" ("But Horapollo, who is believed to have been translated into Greek by a certain Philippus, when he describes the Year has something like this to say of the star of Isis"). Pierio Valeriano's descriptions of Mithra, Serapis, Hecate Tergemina, and Isis are identical with those of Cartari; he also cites Alciati.

[74] From Alexander of Naples Cartari takes, for example, the figures of Serapis, Jupiter Labrandeus, Jupiter Ammon, Vulcan as protector of the king of Egypt, the male Venus (the Cypriote Aphroditos), etc.

[75] It will be recalled that this was also the aim of Pictor: "tam exterarum gentium quam Romanorum deorum."

or of what passes as such. Cartari describes a Celtic Jupiter, another borrowing from Alexander of Naples; following Pictor and Giraldi, he makes use of the *Saxon Chronicle.* In this source he finds many singular figures,[76] among others a Venus crowned with flowers, whose breast supports a lighted torch; her left hand holds a globe, and her right three golden apples (*fig. 95*). The history of this "Saxon" Venus is not easy to unravel. The *Saxon Chronicle* itself is a work by Conrad Botho (Bote). Under the title of *Cronecken der Sassen* it was first issued at Mainz in 1492 by Schöffer, with engraved illustrations; [77] but in an earlier French chronicle published in Paris by Pierre Le Rouge in 1488, *La Mer des hystoires,* which contains several chapters (XI to LX) on the gods, the following description is already to be found (p. lx, col. 2): "Selon Theoctetus, le simulacre et l'imaige de Venus estoit telle. Une femme nue de plaisant regard les cheveus pendans sur les espaules aiant une couronne de mirte sur sa teste entrelassée de roses vermeilles riant et aiant en sa bouche une autre rose vermeille. En son coeur une facule ou petite torche ardant et une sayete [78] de trois darts. Tenoit en sa senestre le monde divisé en trois parties cest assavoir ou ciel terre et mer: en sa dextre trois pommes d'or."

Of the mysterious Theoctetus we know nothing. As will be seen, the ancestry of this Venus is exceedingly doubtful. It is therefore all the more puzzling to find her in several sixteenth-century manuals of mythology besides those of Giraldi and Cartari. She appears in two German handbooks—the *Theologia mythologica* of Pictor, and the *Heydenwelt* of Herold—her presence being in these cases somewhat easier to explain.[79]

[76] As, for example, a Saturn standing on a fish, carrying a vase and a wheel as attributes.

[77] See Leibniz, *Scriptores rerum Brunsvicensium . . .* (Hanover, 1707), III, pp. 247–423: "Chronicon Brunsvicensium picturatum, dialecto Saxonico conscriptum autore Conrad Bothone cive Brunsvic."; cf. Schaër, *Conrad Botes niedersächsische Bilderchronik, ihre Quellen und ihr historischer Werth* (Hannover, 1880). All the engravings in the first edition are reproduced by A. Schramm in *Der Bilderschmuck der Frühdrucke,* XIV: *Die Drucker in Mainz* (Leipzig, 1931), pls. CXIV to CCIV. The 1492 engravings reappear in all later editions, at least up to 1596. Several actually represent old Germanic divinities, *Abgötter der alten Sachsen,* such as Armetule, Prono, Eidergast—but these are difficult to identify. In the Magdeburg edition of 1570, the Venus image appears to be derived from a statue which once stood in Magdeburg and was there worshipped as a goddess ("Bildnis der Veneris Myrthiae, wie ehmals zu Magdeburg gestanden und als eine Göttin geehret worden").

[78] Cartari does not repeat these details, but they are in Botho.

[79] Herold, whose text owes much to Giraldi, has derived his illustrations from fifteenth-century engravers. The illustrations of the *Heydenwelt* were taken over (see *supra,*

It should be added that later, early in the seventeenth century, the editors of Cartari were to publish as an appendix to the *Images* a discourse on the gods of Mexico and Japan.[80] With this, Olympus, overrun from all sides, became sheer pandemonium.

*

IN ORDER to find their bearings in this motley array, it would have been necessary for the authors to introduce some kind of order, to organize the material along geographical and historical lines. But our mythographers are even more lacking in historical sense than in critical faculty. They pay no attention to place or time. They mix together all the gods, regardless of their place of origin, the most ancient with those of later times. Giraldi seems to have had some notion [81] of the importance of localizing the divinities, but not to have suspected any need for establishing their chronology. He outlines a geographical classification, but gives no thought to a division into periods. He does not even distinguish between Greek and Roman deities.

Ideas of milieu and evolution are, admittedly, recent achievements, and it would be a manifest injustice to reproach scholars of the sixteenth century for not having possessed them. Furthermore, classical antiquity itself had by its own example encouraged intermingling and disorder. The ancients, who at so early a date had forgotten the meaning of their own myths, possessed no clear idea of their origin or relative age. As Renan says, "Homer, even for his day, was a very poor theologian." [82] The Olympus of Virgil contains gods of all times and peoples,[83] while the fictitious chronology of the *Metamorphoses*

p. 229, n. 36), in one of the later editions of Pictor (Basel, 1558).

[80] Lorenzo Pignoria, *Discorso intorno le deità delle Indie Orientali et Occidentali, con le loro figure,* etc. . . . appended to the *Imagini* (Padua, 1615). We have published a study of this *Discorso* in an article in the *Mélanges d'histoire et d'archéologie* (1931): "Un essai de mythologie comparée au début du XVIIe siècle," pp. 268–281.

[81] *Syntagma* I, par. 3: "Topici dei 'qui locorum, regionum, urbium peculiarem tutelam gerebant'" ("Local gods 'who assumed the special protection of places, regions, towns'").

[82] *Études d'histoire religieuse: Les religions de l'antiquité,* p. 27. Renan further admits that mythology is not referable to history and that it eludes critical examination, by virtue of its mobility and multiplicity: "Contradiction is of its essence" (pp. 36–37). This does not prevent him from reproaching Creuzer for his lack of historical sense: "Time does not appear to exist for M. Creuzer" (p. 14); and from congratulating O. Müller and L. Preller for having "opened the way to a truly scientific mythology," the first by distinguishing different races (p. 43), the second by distinguishing periods (p. 45).

[83] See G. Boissier, *La Religion romaine,* I, pp. 278 ff.

is in reality full of anachronisms (Ovid, for that matter, was already consulting compilations and manuals).[84] Why should our mythographers have seen any necessity for clarifying what the ancients themselves had left in confusion?[85]

96. Jupiter, Juno, Neptune, and Mercury

Even with this reservation, however, we are forced to pass rather severe judgment upon their methods of documentation and presentation. For the most part, what they offer us is a confused mass of erudition, a jumble that neither criticism nor history has done anything to bring into shape.[86] From

[84] See Lafaye, *Les Métamorphoses d'Ovide et leurs modèles grecs* (Paris, 1904), pp. 57 ff., 77 ff., 110–112.

[85] L. Ménard (*op. cit.*, chap. xiv) begs indulgence for the modern mythographer: "In order to find his way through the tortuous labyrinth of mythology . . . he has need of the thread of Ariadne. The road is a difficult one, and error is excusable, since the ancients themselves, who lived in the midst of their mythology, lost their way more than once."

[86] The chief effort of contemporary criticism, on the other hand, has been to localize the myths and to distinguish their different phases. This tendency may be seen, for example, in M. P. Nilsson, *A History of Greek Religion* (Oxford, 1935), and in Gilbert Murray, *Five Stages of Greek Religion*

this point of view, their superiority over their predecessors is a purely relative one.

*

THERE IS another domain, however, in which that superiority ought by rights to be absolute—the study and turning to account of figural monuments. In addition to the literary sources, our mythographers did, in fact, have at their disposal a documentation of infinite value which had been unknown to their medieval forerunners.

When Pierre Bersuire, in the middle of the fourteenth century, apologized for having borrowed elements of his iconographical notes on the gods from his predecessors,[87] he alleged in his own defense that he had no other choice—for, he said, he had been unable anywhere to find real images of the gods themselves: "quia deorum ipsorum figuras alicubi non potui reperire." The defects of Boccaccio's *Genealogy*, as Tiraboschi rightly observes, stem from the same cause: "What could be accomplished at a time when there was so little knowledge of the monuments which would have served as the surest guide?"[88]

Two centuries later, coins, reliefs, and statues had been excavated by thousands; collections were overflowing with marbles and bronzes; all this material was being listed, reproduced, made available. At the same moment as our manuals, in the very year of the first publication of Cartari (1556), the catalogue of Aldrovandi appeared as an appendix to the *Antichità* of Lucio Mauro: *Tutte le statue antiche che in Roma si veggono*. Collections were multiplying of *icones statuarum*, executed in the studios of Lafreri, Cavalieri, Franzini, and Vaccaria.[89]

(Oxford, 1925). Certain writers even refuse to "venture" further, renouncing interpretation on the grounds that all effort to explain the myths presupposes a definitive classification (see, for example, J. Toutain, *Études de mythologie et d'histoire* [Paris, 1909], pp. 81–84; *Nouvelles études de mythologie et d'histoire* [1935]). Our sixteenth-century scholars, who make no attempt to classify, are on the contrary, as we shall see, eager to interpret.

87 See *supra*, pp. 174 f.

88 *Storia della lett. ital.*, VII, 190–191.

89 See Salomon Reinach, *L'Album de Pierre Jacques* (Paris, 1902); Huebner, *Le statue di Roma, Grundlagen für eine Geschichte der antiken Monumente in der Renaissance* (Leipzig, 1912).

Reinach observes (Introduction, p. 15) that the taste for archeology develops above all in the second half of the sixteenth century, at a time when the great creative spirits have disappeared. "The Renaissance, sensing its approaching end, recapitulates its conquests, and draws up its balance sheet."

One would naturally expect to see Giraldi, Cartari, and Conti profit by this treasure which was within their reach. But Giraldi appears to be the only one of the three who thought of making direct use of it; he alone shows some familiarity with archeology. Doubtless his long stay in Rome was to a large extent responsible for this, since there the vestiges of the past were daily before his eyes. We know that he saw two different statues of Neptune (p. 159: "sed et cum buccino et fuscina, qualem marmoreum vidi; . . . nunc nudus etiam cum tridente et concha, quo modo ipse conspexi"); at San Martino ai Monti he read the epitaph of an *archigallus* (p. 140). He visited private collections, those of Cardinals Salviati, Maffei, and Cesi, and others as well (p. 468: "Fortuna conservatrix e cippo utrinque insculpto et inscripto . . . Romae . . . in domo Marcellis Capicasi"; p. 385: "Isis triumphalis in marmore, in domo Cardinalis Caesii Romae," etc.). His friends kept him informed of the latest finds (p. 385: "Sane hujus modi simulachrum repertum Romae fuit, cum ego ibi optimam viae meae partem ingratis contererem . . ."; *ibid:* "Isis Pelagia etiam cognominatur, ut datur intelligi ex marmore quodam vetusto, reperto in vinea Joannis Poggii pontificii quaestoris, extra portam Flaminiam"). While working on his history, he still took an interest in excavated objects, as for example in a statuette of Harpocrates found in Modena (p. 57: "His pro-

97. Mercury and Peace

xime diebus Augustinus Rheginus Magister theologus Franciscanus mihi ostendit aeneam imagunculam hujus Harpocratis Dei, nuper exfossam ex Mutinensibus ruinis").[90]

But it does not take long to see that Giraldi's curiosity is in general limited to inscriptions and medals,[91] which, at the most, help him to trace certain allegorical images: Fortune (pp. 387, 458, 463), Virtue (27), Health (36), Hope (30). It is also apparent that he knows some divinity types only from engravings. "I have seen," he says (p. 297), "in a book of antiquities an image of Mercury: youthful body, beardless face, wings above the ears; entirely nude except for a short mantle; in his right hand a pouch resting on a ram's head, in his left the caduceus; at his feet, a cock and a ram." This book of antiquities was the *Inscrip-*

98. Apollo and Jupiter

90 ". . . with a horn and a three-pronged spear, as I saw him in marble; . . . sometimes naked, with trident and shell, as I saw him recently."

"Fortuna conservatrix from a gravestone carved on both sides with an inscription . . . in Rome . . . in the house of Marcello Capicaso."—"Isis triumphant in marble in the house of Cardinal Cesio in Rome."

"A statue of that kind was found in Rome at the time when I was treading there, thanklessly, the best part of my road . . ."—"She is also called Isis Pelagia, as it appears from an old marble found on the estate of Giovanni Poggi, pontifical quaestor, outside the Porta Flaminia."

"A few days ago a Franciscan theologian, Agostino Reggio, showed me a small bronze image of this god Harpocrates, recently excavated from the ruins in Modena."

91 The 1696 edition of the *History of the Gods* contains a plate of mediocre reproductions of medals: "*nummi quorum auctoritate Gyraldus passim nititur.*" Giraldi alludes to other medals: pp. 118, 383, 387, 393 (Diana Lucifera), etc.

tiones sacrosanctae vetustatis by Petrus Apianus, published in Ingolstadt in 1534 (*figs. 97, 99*). In that work we find (p. 422) exactly the Mercury described by Giraldi, the original of which, indeed, has come down to us.[92] These same *inscriptiones* were to be literally pillaged by Cartari, who appropriated all the engravings,[93] one after the other, even when they represented forgeries.[94]

99. Mercury

In Cartari's documentation, indeed, original works of art play a very small part. At rare intervals he notes that some figure or other is being described "after ancient medals and marbles," and in the preface of his Latin edition,[95] du Verdier goes so far as to praise Cartari for having brought together in a corpus "imagines multiplices ex veterum scriptis, lapidibus et antiquis numismatibus." But in reality even Cartari took from the medals little more than allegories: Virtue, Victory, Fortune, the genius of the Roman people. Furthermore, the suspicion arises that he knew these only through the *Imagini* of Enea Vico,[96] or the *Religion des anciens Romains* of du Choul.[97]

This work by du Choul, "gentilhomme français," merits something more

[92] S. Reinach, *Répertoire de reliefs grecs et romains*, II, pp. 86, 5.

[93] Apianus and his engraver very frequently copy an earlier illustrated collection, containing inscriptions collected by Peutinger and Huttich (Mainz, 1520). On the real or supposed relations of the Apianus engravings with Dürer, see E. Panofsky, *Dürers Stellung zur Antike* (Vienna, 1922), Excursus I: "Die Illustrationen der Apianischen Inscriptiones in ihrem Verhältnis zu Dürer." It should be noted that Apianus cites authorities like Rabanus Maurus and Boccaccio in identifying the statues which he reproduces. Cf. also J. Colin, *Les antiquités romaines de la Rhénanie* (Paris, 1927), chap. viii: "Les images et les résidences des dieux."

[94] For example, the "Three Fates" (Apianus, p. 385), copy of a pseudo-antique plaque found in Styria in 1500 by Conrad Celtes. This plaque is also reproduced in one of the medallions which decorate the base of the Certosa of Pavia. The original is a medal executed in 1458 by G. Boldù.

[95] *Imagines deorum olim a V. C. ex variis auctoribus in unum collectae, . . . nunc vero ad communem omnium utilitatem Latino sermone ab A. V. expressae* (Lyons, 1581).

[96] *Le imagini con tutti i riversi trovati e le vite degl'Imperatori tratte dalle medaglie e dalle historie degli antichi* (1548).

[97] *Discours de la religion des anciens Romains illustré d'un grand nombre de figures retirées des marbres antiques,* etc. (Lyons), 1556.

than passing mention. It is a beautiful book, magnificently illustrated,[98] which in its own time enjoyed a high reputation.[99] Du Choul also undertook the composition of a *Traité sur les images des dieux,* more classical in conception, it would seem,[100] and less exclusively based on literary sources, than our Italian mythologies. Unfortunately, this treatise never saw the light of day.[101]

Archeology thus plays a singularly limited role in Cartari's documentation, just as it does in that of Giraldi himself. With Natale Conti, its role is nonexistent—or virtually so.[102]

On the other hand, we often find in all three authors descriptions taken from other descriptions; this results when, instead of referring to works of art which they have actually seen, they copy what they have read in Philostratus or Pausanias. Thus, even in this domain, texts—and nearly always texts alone—are still their source of information.

*

EVEN THOUGH devoid of new documentation or new mythological content, do the sixteenth-century manuals offer at least some renewal of spirit and interpretation?

Further disappointments await us here, and further surprises. Interpretation, though developed by each in different degrees, appears to all three

98 Perhaps by Bernard Salomon (called le Petit Bernard or Bernardus Gallus), who is probably also responsible for the fine medallions of Strada's *Thesaurus.* Strada and du Choul were friends; in his note to the reader, Strada speaks with admiration of the learning of du Choul and the wealth of his collections (see *fig. 96*).

99 Montaigne owned a copy of the work which bore his signature (now in the collection of M. Henri Bordès in Bordeaux). In the opinion of P. Villey (*Sources et évolution des Essais,* I, p. 121), he made use of it in the *Apologie de Raimond Sebond.*

100 An inference which may legitimately be drawn from the spirit of the *Religion des anciens Romains* and its illustrations; and from a phrase which appears on p. 133 of the same book: "as will be seen from the illustration taken from antique sources in the Latin work which I have written, *De imaginibus deorum.*"

101 In 1572, Abraham Ortelius (*Deorum dearumque capita ex antiquis numismatibus* [Antwerp], p. 4) includes Guglielmus Choulius, *De imaginibus deorum,* in a list of mythographers, but adds "nondum excusus" ("not yet printed"). Cf. Struve, *Syntagma* (ed. 1701), p. 56: "Idem quoque Choulius librum suum de natura Deorum citat, qui tamen cum aliis ab eodem promissis adhuc latet" ("This same du Choul quotes his book on the nature of the gods which, however, like other works promised by the same author, has not yet appeared").

102 In Book VII, chap. 16, in connection with Daedalus Conti draws up a long list of painters and sculptors of antiquity, and enumerates their works.

mythographers as an essential part of their task.[103] But they have no original system to apply. They revert to the three types of explanation offered by antiquity itself—historical, physical, and moral—the fortunes of which during the Middle Ages we have studied at length. They do not choose between these divergent explanations, being content in general merely to place them side by side. Giraldi, for example, is perfectly aware that the ancients were not in agreement as to the nature of Saturn (*Syntagma* IV): for some, Saturn was Heaven, or Time; for others, an early king of Italy; for still others, Fertility. But he does not linger over these contradictions nor choose between them; neither does he attempt to reconcile them. With Conti, this attitude becomes a veritable method. At the end of his book he adds, in condensed form, a summary in which the interpretation of each god is given according to the three traditional points of view—*de Jove historice, physice, ethice,* etc.

At the same time, it is easy to see where Conti's own preferences lie. As a philosopher, he is convinced that mythology holds teachings of the highest wisdom, accessible, it is true, only to those who are not satisfied merely with the outward shell of the fables, their literal meaning: "ad exteriorem corticem fabularum, hoc est, ad simplicem omnibus obviam explicationem." [104]

From the earliest times, says Conti (I, i), the thinkers first of Egypt, then of Greece, deliberately concealed the great truths of science and philosophy under the veil of myth in order to withdraw them from vulgar profanation. With this aim, they invented not only the stories of the gods, but even their very figures: it was they who gave the lightning to Jupiter, the trident to Neptune, bow and arrows to Cupid, the torch to Vulcan. Later, when it was possible for the great sages to teach publicly, without subterfuge, disclosing their precepts in the full light of day, the earlier vehicles of knowledge, the fables, seemed like nothing more than deceitful fiction or old wives' tales; but it is the task of the mythographer to recapture their original content.

Pursuant to this principle, Conti makes his grouping of the myths depend upon the type of teaching to be found in them. Some myths contain se-

[103] Highly developed in Giraldi, with Conti it assumes a disproportionate importance; Cartari, whose interest is in the figures themselves rather than in their meaning, restricts without entirely eliminating it—*Le imagini colla sposizione degli dei. . . .*

[104] Hence his scorn for his predecessors, who have been unable to penetrate the deeper meaning of the myths. It is for this reason that he does not quote them.

crets of Nature: the myths of Venus, the Cyclopes, etc.; others, lessons of morality: man's duty to endure the vicissitudes of fortune (Phoebus herding the flocks of Admetus), to be courageous (Hercules), and neither miserly (Tantalus) nor overbold (Marsyas), etc. Conti reverts to this distinction several times (I, vii: "Partim res naturae occultas habent; partim mores informant"), and the last book of his mythology, the tenth, concludes the demonstration which has been aimed at throughout: "quod omnia philosophorum dogmata sub fabulis contineantur." [105]

In the nineteenth century, Conti was hailed as a precursor by the religious historians of the symbolist school. Louis Ménard, for example,[106] praises "the excellent work of Natalis Comes, much more complete and discerning than most of the treatises on mythology published since his day." In point of fact, Conti was anything but a precursor. On the contrary, in spite of his own denials, he is heir to an agelong tradition, the development of which we have followed down to Boccaccio,[107] and even to Pictor [108]—the allegorical tradition, which persists in seeking the fruit of ancient wisdom beneath the "integuments" of Fable (Conti uses the word often).

Thus Conti's mythological exegesis offers no innovation, and marks no advance. Is this to be wondered at? Bolder minds than his, coming after him, were enmeshed in the same errors. A critical genius like Francis Bacon, theorist of exact research, could still make every effort to discover the "sapientia veterum" hidden beneath the forms and adventures of the gods.[109] The thunderbolts of Zeus, stolen by Typhon and restored by Hermes, symbolize, he says, the authority and the fiscal power that a revolution sweeps away, but that may be recovered by eloquence informed with wisdom. Every youth who rushes forth to meet perils in reckless self-confidence is a son of the

[105] ("All the doctrines of the philosophers are hidden within fables.")—". . . manifestum esse ducimus ex iis quae hactenus explicata fuerunt: omnia priscorum instituta tum ad cognitionem rerum naturalium, tum ad rectorum morum rationem pertinentia, fuisse ab antiquis sub fabulosis integumentis occultata" (". . . we consider it obvious from what has been thus far explained that all the teachings of the ancients relating either to the knowledge of natural things or to moral conduct were hidden by them under the cloak of Fable").

[106] *Op. cit.*, Introd., p. III.

[107] See *supra*, pp. 223 f.

[108] See *supra*, p. 228.

[109] *De sapientia veterum liber* . . . (London, 1609). On Bacon's mythology, see Ch. W. Lemmi, *The Classical Deities in Bacon. A Study in Mythological Symbolism* (Baltimore, 1933). Lemmi proves, in fact, that Bacon made extensive use of Conti's *Mythologia*.

Dawn, a Memnon to be mourned at sunrise—that is to say, at the outset of any great enterprise.[110]

However, in the last years of the sixteenth century an interesting evolution in the interpretation of myth begins to take form; at the root of this movement lies the powerful impetus given by the Reformation to Bible study. The false but fertile hypothesis that Hebrew was the first language [111] led, in fact, not only to the view that other languages were derivatives of Hebrew, but that the myths of other peoples were corruptions of the original revelation.[112] In this way foundations were laid for a kind of comparative mythology, which was to produce its monuments in the following century in the works of Huet, Bochart, and Vossius.

It might be possible to see in Conti the very sketchy outline of an analogous method. In his first book (chap. vii) he hints at a theory that the gods, coming originally from Egypt, were imported into Persia and Greece, then into Rome, spreading from Rome over the entire rest of the world. But he does nothing to develop this idea.

*

IN SHORT, if a collective judgment of the three Italian manuals is to be offered, we must admit that, from the scientific point of view, they are far from marking any decided advance. Their extremely mixed contents are not critically sifted, not brought into order by an historical sense, nor illuminated by new hypotheses.

Let us now examine their value from the aesthetic point of view. We must remember that each is, in fact, addressed to poets and artists, and, not content with supplying simply one more lexicon to aid in the comprehension of ancient works, undertakes to offer models and themes of inspiration.

110 Bacon doubtless was under no great misapprehension as to the value of his interpretations. His allegorical tendency is to be explained in part by his lack of poetic instinct: he can see in mythology only intellectual concepts deliberately transformed into symbols. This was later to be the attitude of Voltaire; cf. the *Dictionnaire philosophique*, art. *Fable:* "The older the fables, the more allegorical they are."

111 See P. D. Huet, *Dissertation de l'origine de la langue hébraïque* (ed. Tillardet [The Hague, 1720], I, 2).

112 This hypothesis had already been anticipated by the Fathers, by Annius of Viterbo, etc., but the progress of linguistic studies was to bring it out into the light.—On the Greek myths compared to those of the Old Testament, in the sixteenth and seventeenth centuries, see A. H. Krappe, *Mythologie universelle*, parag. XVI.

Giraldi, for example, hopes that his work may be of use to painters and sculptors (*Syntagma* VII, p. 251): "Nunc igitur equos solis, quos illi poetae ceterique scriptores ascribunt, tibi assero, ut pictoribus et statuariis nonnullam opem his nostris Syntagmatibus afferamus." [113]

With Cartari's *Images,* this becomes the essential object. The foreword of the publisher, Francesco Marcolini, is explicit enough on this point: "Many have written of the ancient gods . . . but none, until Vincenzo Cartari, has spoken of their statues and representations. This initiative will be agreeable and useful to all who take an interest in antiquity; it is also of a nature to be gladly welcomed by painters and sculptors, providing them with themes for a thousand inventions with which to adorn their statues and painted panels."

Thus the work was meant not only to promote a better understanding of the ancient literatures ("ad intendere bene i poeti antichi e gli altri scrittori"), but also, and to an even greater extent, to furnish subjects for artists. This must be insisted upon, for the author himself reverts to it incessantly. It sometimes happens, for instance, that he pauses over details of a fable which have no direct bearing on the representation of the gods, but he invariably catches himself up with the words: "This has no interest for those wishing to delineate this divinity." [114] Sometimes, on the other hand, he justifies digressions or long parentheses on the ground that they may serve an iconographical end. For instance, the story of the Vestal Claudia and the Magna Mater, if told at full length,[115] could perhaps serve to inspire a painter of allegories: "della quale ho raccontato, perchè questo fatto potrebbe servire à chi volesse dipingere la Pudicitia." [116] Cartari never loses sight of his mission as "provider of pictorial subjects," and herein lies, indeed, the chief originality of the *Images,* which is inferior to the *History of the Gods* and the *Mythology* in erudition and thought.

113 "Now then I am mentioning the horses of the Sun, ascribed to him by poets and other writers, in order that this work of ours may be of some help to painters and sculptors."

114 See 1571 edition, pp. 45, 48, 108, 293, etc.

115 *Idem,* pp. 210–211.

116 Cf., in reference to the Judges of the Nether World and the Fates, p. 273: "Of these I shall first tell what is to be read of them in Plato, since it seems to me most beautiful and delight-provoking, and since it shows us how these three ought to be depicted. Therefore I have recounted all these things after him, in order that anyone wishing to represent one of the figures on his authority, may have the necessary information."

It is therefore relevant to examine the value of the three treatises from the standpoint of art; let us ask what gods they present, and whether these gods might conceivably inspire the imagination of an artist.

*

IN THE MANUALS the place of honor is given, as we know, to divinities from the late periods, and especially those imported into Rome from the Orient. It is not the Olympians alone, but a complete barbaric pantheon which is summoned before our eyes by the illustrations in Cartari: [117] the horrible three-headed Hecate (*fig. 93*); Aphroditos, the bearded Venus, with comb in hand; the Apollo of Elephantinopolis, with blue skin and ram's snout; the unspeakable Typhon, whose scaly body bows his soft, snakelike legs—in a word, creatures of the strangest and most misshapen sort, a nightmare mythology, the vision of St. Anthony in the desert.[118]

In comparing the religious imagination of the Greeks with that of the Orientals, Renan [119] observes the great difference in plastic quality. In the gods of the Orient, "conceived in the absence of all proportion," he decries especially the complex weight of allegory beneath which all form is stifled. "India sees no better way of extolling her gods than to pile up sign upon sign, symbol upon symbol; Greece, better inspired, fashions them in her own image: Helen, in honoring the Minerva of Lindos, offers her a cup of yellow amber made to the exact measure of her own breast."

It is the very essence of the Oriental cults, in fact, to "sacrifice form to meaning." This is seen in late antiquity, when the Roman pantheon came to be filled with enigmatic and monstrous images—the same images which look at us from every page of Cartari's book. As Cumont writes in this connec-

[117] The first illustrated edition of the *Imagini* is that of 1571. In a new dedication to Cardinal d'Este (1569) the author expresses his satisfaction with the "belle e bene accomodate figure" provided by Bolognino Zaltieri for the enrichment of the work. Later Lorenzo Pignoria, editor of the 1615 and 1647 editions, lays great stress on the new illustrations by Filippo Ferroverde, which, he insists, are far ahead of those of Zaltieri. In reality, in spite of several notable additions and a different setting on the page, these illustrations are very close to Zaltieri in their inspiration. See *infra*, p. 256, n. 132.

[118] In *La Tentation de St. Antoine*, a great many of the Oriental gods represented in Cartari are made to pass before the eyes of the saintly hermit. Flaubert has chosen them for their very ugliness or deformity. On monsters in ancient art, in Asia and the Occident, see Focillon, *L'Art des sculpteurs romans* (1931), pp. 168–180.

[119] *Études d'histoire religieuse: les religions de l'antiquité*, pp. 30, 31, 61.

tion,[120] "The Levantines impose on the plastic arts and on painting the complicated symbolism in which their own abstruse and subtle mentality delights. . . . The religious art of declining paganism does not aim at beauty. Increasingly, it obeys a tendency to give expression to learned ideas." Our manuals, in their manifest preference for the Eastern rather than the Olympic divinities—a preference furthered by the contemporary Egyptomania and the taste for enigmas [121]—consequently emphasize symbolism to the detriment of plastic sense. Artists are turned away from the pure nude forms of Greece toward the portrayal of terrifying or baffling allegories.

By way of a parenthesis, a backward glance over the century may here be permitted us. We are already familiar with the dangers inherent in this type of inspiration: an illustrious example has brought them to our attention. When Agostino di Duccio started to represent the planetary deities in the Tempio Malatestiano, it was not always the Greco-Roman types which he adopted. His Jupiter, Apollo, and Mercury are disconcerting in aspect. The Jupiter, brandishing a whip in one hand and holding in the other a sheaf of wheat, is an Assyrian sun symbol, as described by Macrobius (*Sat.* I, 23: "dextra elevata cum flagro, in aurigae modum; laeva tenet fulmen, et spicas"). The Apollo is hardly less strange. He wears a shield on his back; one hand holds the three Graces, the lyre and laurel, and the other, the bow and arrows. He appears to be walking on a globe, with a swan and raven at his feet. This overabundance of attributes alludes in the main to aspects of the solar system, to the deadly or benevolent effects of the planet, etc. Porphyry has commented upon these effects, and explained them, in his study of the Egyptian cult of Osiris as the Sun.[122] As for Mercury, he is a sort of magus capped with a pointed bonnet. Small winged beings, who seem to emerge from a well, grasp the stalk of his enormous caduceus, about which are entwined four serpents; other similar *puttini* seem to slip and fall back. What is this figure, which belongs, as Yriarte remarks, to neither Rome, Greece, Assyria, nor Persia? It is reminiscent at once of Hermes, the guide of souls

120 *Les Religions orientales dans le paganisme romain,* pp. 8, 15, 28, 29.

121 See *supra,* pp. 238 f.

122 See Cartari (1571 ed.), p. 62: "Servius reports all this, taking it from a certain book of Porphyry called that of the Sun." Some elements of the same figure are also to be found in Macrobius, *Saturnalia,* I, 17 (*figs. 46, 47, 98*).

to the underworld or *psychopompos*, and of the Egyptian Thoth, who teaches the soul to raise itself by degrees to a knowledge of divine things.

Art historians have underlined the bizarre nature of these figures (whom, for that matter, they have not always recognized);[123] they have agreed in criticizing their "lack of composition, of solemnity, and of character" (C. Ricci). But if the images betray a certain lack of ease, it is because of the difficulties encountered by the artist in attempting to impose the rhythm and unity, the vibrant harmony of the work of art, upon the complex and predominantly intellectual material of allegory. If he has not succeeded, in spite of a perceptible effort at stylization,[124] it is because the problem was by its very nature insoluble, at least for an artist of the South. Excess of meaningful content is a hindrance to plastic expression. After a certain level of symbolism has been reached, the balance between form and idea can no longer be successfully maintained.

*

THE PLACE accorded by the manuals to the Oriental mythologies would thus of itself justify certain fears as to the aesthetic value of the models which they propose. But another and more general consideration still further restricts that value, i.e., the fact that all the descriptions of monuments they contain are based on texts, and not on the monuments themselves.

We have dwelt at some length on this point:[125] our three mythographers have read many more or less trustworthy authors, but with rare exceptions they seem not to have looked at statues or reliefs. As a general rule, their descriptions reproduce other descriptions; ἐκφράσεις are brought together,

[123] C. Yriarte (*Un condottiere au* XV*e siècle, Rimini* [Paris, 1882]) says nothing of a figure of Jupiter, but reproduces it (p. 26) under the name of Saturn. E. Burmeister (*Der bildnerische Schmuck des Tempio Malatestiano zu Rimini* (Diss. [Breslau, 1891], pp. 27–29) does not arrive at exact identifications.

[124] This effort will be apparent if we compare the Rimini Jupiter and Apollo with those represented in Cartari's *Imagini* (p. 60; see *fig. 98*), which are derived from the same sources. Agostino di Duccio has suppressed several attributes; he has attempted to preserve a certain freedom of attitude in spite of the symbols with which his deities are burdened (*figs. 46, 47*).—One curious detail: in representing the three Graces in Apollo's hand, he resorts to a device analogous to that used by the Carolingian miniaturist of cod. Monac. lat. 14271 (*fig. 67*), showing them as issuing from a tuft of laurel. Let us recall that the colossal Apollo of Delos, by Tectaios and Angelion, held the Charites in his right hand. This statue had been reproduced on coins, and these might have been seen by Agostino di Duccio.

[125] See *supra*, pp. 243 ff.

recopied, juxtaposed—but never, or almost never, brought face to face with a classical model.

This method, which, as we have often said, seems paradoxical in mid-sixteenth-century Italy, develops its disastrous effects to the full in the illustrations of Cartari. Zaltieri, who designed the first engravings for the *Images of the Gods,* in 1571, does not once take his inspiration directly from the antique. His engravings are not copies of works of art, but reconstructions based upon written accounts. Frequently his gods are composite portraits, made up from quotations given him in the text of the work itself. In this, it will be seen, Zaltieri proceeds exactly in the manner of the medieval illuminator. Just as the illustrator of the *Libellus* composed his Apollo out of extracts from Servius, Lactantius Placidus, Fulgentius, Martianus, or Isidore,[126] so Zaltieri assembles the *membra disiecta* of the immortals, and combines them as best he can into awkward and baroque shapes.

Sometimes, however, the text does provide a representation that is complete in itself, as when it cites Pausanias' detailed description of the works of art that he saw during his trip to Greece. At such times the engraver's task is easier, but he does not necessarily achieve a happier result. Among such representations are the statue of Juno at Corinth by Polycletus (p. 180; Paus., II, 17, 4); the celebrated painting of the Cnidian Lesches at Delphi, where Polygnotus had depicted the demon Eurynomus (p. 279; Paus., x, 28, 7; cf. Decharme, *Mythol.,* p. 392); Night, Sleep and Death, Diana, and the other sculptured images on the chest of Cypselos (pp. 336, 105, 265, 468; Paus., v, 18, 1, etc.).[127] But however meekly Zaltieri may have followed the indications of the text, his figures have not retained the faintest Greek character—a deficiency which may be ascribed, without doubt, to the mediocrity of his talent, but even more to his complete ignorance of classical style.[128]

126 See *supra,* pp. 177 f.

127 Another image taken from Pausanias, but appearing only in the 1647 edition, revised by Pignoria, is that of the Zeus of Phidias (p. 87). The god is unrecognizable in this "reconstruction"—as lamentable in its way as that in the lapidary of Alfonso X (*fig. 12*). The *Imagines* of Philostratus also provided Zaltieri with elements of several of the illustrations: Comus (p. 416), the Rivers (265), Neptune (250), Bacchus (413, 420, 424, 433).

128 The greatest artists of the Renaissance, from Botticelli to Mantegna, Raphael, and Titian, attempted more than once to reconstruct or resuscitate masterpieces of ancient art, taking their inspiration more or less literally from Philostratus, Callistratus, or Lucian. See A. Pellizzari, *I Trattati attorno le arti figurative in Italia . . . dall'antichità classica al Rinascimento* (Naples, 1912),

Cartari sometimes boasts, it will be recalled,[129] that he has utilized marbles and medals as part of his documentation, but actually it is in books, and only there, that he has seen them. His illustrator follows the same method. He copies, not the objects themselves, but engravings from contemporary works: for medals, Enea Vico and du Choul; [130] for bas-reliefs and statues, Apianus.[131] Thus, even his purported copies of antique objects are merely reproductions of reproductions. From this it will be seen that the Renaissance mythographers depart as widely from the original models as they do from firsthand documents, even when they claim to adhere to them most faithfully.[132]

On the whole, this mythology—to characterize it briefly—is both bookish and barbaric; seen in this light, it is antiaesthetic in a double sense. And lastly, it marks a striking regression, a return to the Middle Ages; it forces the gods back into the matrix of allegory, decking them out again in the exotic finery which they had shed with such difficulty at the end of the earlier period. It interrupts the contact with classical art through which, from the fifteenth century on, the gods had been gradually regaining their incarnation in human shape.[133]

It is thus essential for us to investigate the extent to which the manuals were read, especially among the poets and artists for whom they were intended. If they were generally used, they must have influenced in curious ways the manner in which the declining Renaissance envisaged the gods and their world.

chap. i; and esp. R. Foerster, "Wiederherstellung antiker Gemälde durch Künstler der Renaissance," *Jahrb. d. preuss. Kunstsamml.*, XLIII (1922), pp. 12–13.

129 See *supra*, pp. 246 f.

130 See *supra*, pp. 246 f.

131 See *supra*, pp. 246 f.

132 The 1615 edition of the *Imagini*, revised and corrected by Pignoria, marks an interesting reaction. Pignoria criticizes Cartari for taking his information entirely from literary sources, and calls attention to the inaccuracies or errors of Zaltieri. However, the new illustrator, Ferroverde, as we have already said (see *supra*, p. 252, n. 117), for the most part reproduces Zaltieri's plates. But he adds a certain number of new engravings, either in the text or in the *Aggiunte*. Several of these are still borrowed from works of contemporary numismatists, Vico, Erizzo, Agostini; but others are directly inspired by intaglios or cameos that Ferroverde has actually seen. He even copies with remarkable accuracy a Mithraic relief seen in 1606 on the Piazza del Campidoglio, and the Diana of Ephesus found under Leo X. And other interesting additions introduce into Cartari's book some of the classical images of the gods which were not previously there: Apollo in his chariot, Apollo and Daphne, Apollo and the Muses, Diana and her companions of the chase, etc. All these attempts, however, do not profoundly alter the essentially bookish character of the work, nor even its bizarre aspect as a whole.

133 See Bk. I, Part 2, chap. ii.

II

Theories Regarding the Use of Mythology

BEFORE TURNING to the art and humanism of the declining sixteenth century for positive proof of the influence of the mythological manuals, we wish to show their appropriateness to the tastes and needs of the time.

The books on the theory of the fine arts published in Italy during this period will provide the main material for such an investigation. These writings are of two kinds, the first group arguing from aesthetics and the second from theology. Both discuss at length the use properly to be made of mythological figures; they thus interpret for us the contemporary attitude toward the problem in which we are interested.

*

THE AUTHORS of dogmatic treatises on painting have much to say of the importance for the artist of consulting books in which he may learn how to treat the subjects which he himself chooses or which are proposed to him by others. These subjects, generally speaking, are drawn either from the Scriptures or from Fable; landscape, genre subjects, and historical scenes are almost never dealt with on their own account.[1] Thus, information about the gods is indispensable to the artist.

In his *Precetti della pittura*,[2] Giovanni Battista Armenini enumerates the authors who, in his opinion, should be in every artist's library. After

[1] The portrait, of course, is in a class by itself. Historical painting is known in Venice and Florence, but is saturated with allegorical and mythological elements. Cf. Ch. Dejob, *De l'influence du Concile de Trente sur la littérature et les beaux-arts* (Paris, 1884), p. 261.

[2] Giovanni Battista Armenini, *De'veri precetti della pittura* (Ravenna, 1587); the reference is to the 1820 ed., Milan, p. 318.

mentioning the standard authorities on sacred history, he recommends for the fables Boccaccio's *Genealogy of the Gods,* Ovid's *Metamorphoses,* and the work of "Alberico, cioè del Cartaro." This confusion between the names Albricus and Cartari is most peculiar. But above all it is striking to see the *Images of the Gods* put on the same level with that "painters' Bible" of the epoch, the *Metamorphoses.*

The famous Lomazzo, in his *Treatise on Painting,*[3] devotes almost a whole book (VII) to the iconography of the gods, and says in conclusion: "Much else . . . can be in large part studied in the authors cited in the *Genealogia* [*sic*] *dei Dei degli antichi* and in the exposition of their images there presented by Vincenzo Cartari—the which I omit for reasons of space, it being too long a task to report them here. . . ."

A few pages earlier,[4] in speaking of the image of Eternity, Lomazzo has already referred to Cartari as the translator of a passage from Claudian. He forgets, however, to tell us that all the poetic passages about the other gods that he quotes are likewise Cartari's translations. Above all, Lomazzo neglects to tell us that his own text, in the major part of that Book VII treating of the gods, is substantially Cartari's. In twenty-one chapters,[5] he has done no more than to plagiarize the *Imagini degli dei* in abridged form.

The fact that our critics feel it necessary to put books of this type in the hands of artists is remarkable in itself, for it exposes the artists' limitations of culture and imagination. Many of them were, in fact, ignorant men, or had received only a superficial education.[6] This, however, is a minor fault (for surely the great Renaissance masters had not in every case been scholars!), but they also lacked creative force. This is why we find the artists of the time so often appealing to a learned adviser for aid,[7] not merely in planning an entire work, but even in the execution of its slightest detail.

One can easily imagine that the manuals of Boccaccio, of Giraldi, Conti,

[3] Giovanni Paolo Lomazzo, *Trattato dell'arte della pittura* (Milan, 1584); the reference is to the 1844 ed., III, p. 272.

[4] *Ibid.*, p. 257.

[5] Of the thirty-three chapters of Book VII, four only are reserved for sacred iconography. All the rest, with the exception of the Introduction, the Conclusion, and chapters 23 and 28, deal with the pagan gods.

[6] See in this connection Dejob (*op. cit.*, pp. 261 ff.) on the Zuccari, Carracci, Albani, Guido, Vasari.

[7] See *infra*, p. 287 and *passim*.

and especially Cartari, to which they were referred by the arbiters of aesthetic taste, appeared to them as providential aids.

It may be asked, of course, if the presence of so many men of letters capable of tracing the broad lines of the artist's canvas, and prodigal of detailed instructions, did not make it somewhat needless for him to consult a manual. When we study the great mythological cycles of the end of the century we shall have occasion to deal with this objection. One thing, at all events, is clear: the manuals became steadily easier to consult. The revisions that they underwent for each new edition shaped them more and more into the form of reference works or catalogues. Thus, the first edition of Conti's *Mythology* was already provided with an extremely clear table of proper names, referring, for each episode, not only to the page, but to the line as well. In the 1581 Venice edition the lines are numbered. In the Latin edition of Cartari of the same date, the translator, du Verdier, emphasizes the convenience of the summary placed at the end of the volume, in which he has condensed "imaginum designationem absque explicatione, ex universo libro collectam."

Indeed, du Verdier himself was one of the very writers who emphasized the usefulness of the work for painters; he even saw in this usefulness one of the reasons for its success. The 1608 Padua edition shows an even greater concern for making the book easy to consult. Cesare Malfatti vaunts its clarity: the illustrations, instead of being confusingly mixed, will now be found "più ordinate ed a luoghi suoi meglio accomodate." In opening the book at a given picture, so he says, one will immediately grasp "its meaning and its allegory, with the allegorical explanation of the animals and hieroglyphs, thus saving the trouble of reading two, three, or four pages in order to learn the meaning." The words "saving trouble" sum up the dominant preoccupation, which is apparent in the illustrations as well. These are still Zaltieri's engravings, crudely reproduced. But beneath each one, an explanatory legend of several lines identifies the scene for the reader, or at least begins to make it intelligible to him. Furthermore, synoptic tables have been added at the beginning of the book: one page, divided in four compartments, presents the ensemble of the gods—gods of the heavens, the sea, the infernal regions, and the forests. Another page brings together the four seasons of the year, with their attributes and the animals sacred to them.

Lastly, Malfatti thought it best to add, as appendix, a "Catalogo . . . de 100 dei più famosi Dei, loro natura e proprietà estratto da questo e altri autori. . . ."

The intention is to make Cartari's work into a convenient sort of dictionary-album, easy of consultation when time is lacking to read text and references in their entirety.[8] Other contemporary works show the same tendency to select certain arguments from the whole body of mythology, then to classify and offer them in, as it were, predigested form "alli Poeti, Pittori, e Scultori." In addition to the abridgements of Ovid which are nothing but a sequence of pictures,[9] we must note the *Mythologia* of Tritonio, published in 1560. This aims to present the fables in a condensed and convenient form, thus making them generally accessible. "Dedi operam ut ex illius XV Metamorph. libris fabulosa breviter colligerem exempla, atque ita in communes locos redigerem, ut in scribendis carminibus ad omnia fere possint adaptari."[10] Is not such a universal passkey, generously prepared for the use of poets looking for inspiration, the counterpart of Cartari's gods who hold themselves in complete readiness and ordered array, at the disposal of artists in search of subject matter? Art, like poetry, looks to recipes and formulas for the vital sap which is beginning to fail it. Books like the *Images* and the *Mythologia* are an answer not so much to new needs as to new insufficiencies.

*

THE INSISTENCE with which theorists urge artists to read instructive texts illustrates another tendency of the period: its pedantry, or, in other words, its

[8] See in the 1683 (du Verdier) edition as well, a device aimed at making the work easy to consult: the Index is also a summary, in which the description of each god is given in full.

[9] Examples are *La Vita e Metamorfoseo d'Ovidio figurato e abbreviato in forma d'epigrammi da M. Gabriello Symeoni* (Lyons, 1584); and the album of Antonio Tempesta, *Metamorphoseon sive Transformationum Ovidii libri* XV *aeneis formis incisi, et in pictorum antiquitatisque studiosorum gratiam nunc primum editi* (Amsterdam, 1606).

[10] *Antonii Tritonii Mythologia, fabulosa exempla ad virtutum et vitiorum seriem redacta, ex Ovidiana Metamorphosi selecta* (Bologna, 1560). ("I have taken pains to collect from the fifteen books of the *Metamorphoses* fabulous examples in abridged form, and to reduce them to general arguments in such a way that in writing poetry they might be adapted to almost anything.")

taste for the niceties of mythological erudition. It is not thought sufficient, indeed, for the artist to have a general knowledge of the gods and the world of Fable; in this respect the theorists become more and more exacting and severe, always ready to underline "quam gravis, quam utilis et necessaria sit tota haec fabularis historiae cognitio."

Raffaello Borghini's dialogue, *Il Riposo,* contains a most significant controversy on this subject.[11] One of the interlocutors cites Horace:

Pictoribus atque poetis
Quidlibet audendi semper fuit aequa potestas . . .

But there is immediate agreement that artists abuse this license. A painter deserves blame for taking the slightest liberty with history or Fable, and especially for representing attributes or clothing inappropriate to the figures (p. 46). Such irrelevant details—"cose disconvenevoli" detract from a picture more than they enhance it.[12] Then follows a complaint against Titian (pp. 48–58) for not respecting Ovid's original account in his representation of Adonis trying to escape from the arms of Venus. On the other hand, Michelangelo has faithfully presented Night as the ancients depicted her, in giving her as attributes the owl and the crescent moon on her forehead. What, however, is to be said of his figures of Day, Twilight, and Dawn? These have none of the attributes assigned to them by good authors.

It is thus an inexcusable fault for an artist not to give his figures the outward signs by which they may be recognized; it is no less serious, however, to make a mistake in the choice of attributes. And Michelozzo wonders if it is his ignorance which makes the pine garlands on Ammanati's statue of Neptune appear strange to him. Vecchietta then inquires to which god the ancients gave the pine as attribute. He cites in this connection Valeriano and Cartari (with whom, for the rest, he is not always in agreement). He goes as far as to distinguish (p. 51) between the *pino* and the *arbore picea,* "a species of pine very similar to the fir." Bringing forward a mass of quotations,

[11] 1730 edition, pp. 40 ff.

[12] L. B. Alberti, who in his *Trattato della pittura* (Langlois ed., Paris, 1651), is almost exclusively concerned with mythological compositions, already asks that the artist learn from books (pp. 41–42) or from his learned friends (p. 45) all the details of the fables. He insists that each god must be represented correctly: "It is not seemly to represent Venus or Minerva in the garb of a beggar (*pitoccho*), nor to show Jove or Mars in woman's dress . . . ," etc. (pp. 30–31).

he obligingly explains that the pine belonged not only to Cybele, but to Bacchus as well, even though one rarely sees him with it as attribute. Sirigatto and Valori also enter the debate, and advance erudite hypotheses which show that they, too, are masters of the science of mythology.

The insistence with which the speakers harp upon the attributes of the gods is worthy of note, since it shows that to know them exactly is, in their eyes, a *sine qua non* of the painter's art. "If the painter wishes to give a perfect representation of Jupiter, he must first of all know who Jupiter is"; then he must give due attention to his "proportions, attitude, and coloring"; and "finally he must concern himself with the *form* of the god, by which he is made manifest and becomes recognizable: thunderbolts, eagle, scepter, costume, and all the attributes which have been given him by the poets." [13] Here we are shown the special notion of form held by theorists of this period; form was a matter of iconology, the science of "forme esteriori," and we know from Lomazzo himself "quanto il sapere la forma esteriore di ciascuna cosa sia non pur utile, ma necessario nella pittura." [14] He himself devoted some three hundred pages of his *Treatise* to a sort of universal iconography, and we have already called attention to his chapters on the pagan gods, which owe so much to Cartari's *Images.*[15]

Though this concept of form has become almost completely foreign to us, we ought nevertheless to keep it very much in mind as we seek to appreciate correctly the works of art of this time. For the art lover of today, the subject represented is very much a side issue; as long as the eye receives pleasure, the expressive detail of the subject remains a matter of indifference to him. In the sixteenth century, the *amorevolissimi della professione* looked for something quite different in a painting. What mattered to them first of all was the idea which it embodied. Hence their extreme interest in the external signs by means of which that idea was given visual form, and especially in attributes, which to them were so many symbols of the thing represented. The eagle "signifies" Jupiter, and is inseparably part of his "form."

[13] Lomazzo, *Idea del tempio della Pittura*, 2nd ed., pp. 17 ff. See also chap. XXV, p. 70: "Dell'ultima parte della pittura, e sue specie."

[14] *Trattato*, III, p. 7: ". . . how not only useful but how necessary a thing it is in painting to know the outward form of each object."

[15] See *supra*, p. 258.

In visual representation, therefore, it belongs to the god as a muscle belongs to the arm. It is even incumbent upon the artist, in order to avoid all possibility of error, to multiply the marks of identity. From this it follows that he must first of all know them. The science of mythology is neither a complement nor an appendix; it is a region within the proper domain of art.

If we add that Lomazzo, in the preamble of his *Treatise,* admonishes the painter to master the iconography "*not only of the Greeks and Romans,* but also of the Medes and Persians, and of all other peoples . . . ,"[16] we are well justified in concluding that the mythological treatises of Giraldi, Conti, and Cartari satisfied all demands of a theoretical order. They were the very aids which the time demanded: manuals both learned and easy to use, enabling everyone to reproduce correctly and without omissions the forms which were regarded as an essential element of art—their mythology extracted from the lesser-known authors,[17] enriched by the most bizarre additions, and so offering opportunity for the artist to display his learning, and the public its ingenuity.

*

THE ATTITUDE of the theologians toward mythology is even more instructive than that of the art theorists. Throughout the Middle Ages, the Church, through her scholars or pontiffs, had uttered protests and warnings—more or less severe—against those who kept alive the memory of the gods.[18] From the dawn of the Renaissance, this censure of the "pagans" who glorified the gods was revived. The outstanding episodes in the reaction which followed this attack are well known. Coluccio Salutati, Petrarch's disciple, had already been driven to defend humanism against the reproaches of the Camaldolese monk, Giovanni da San Miniato, and the Dominican, Giovanni Dominici; the latter—like Gregory of Tours before him[19]—lamented in his *Lucula noctis* that youth should be told of Jupiter and Saturn rather than of Christ and the Holy Ghost.[20] Later, as we have seen, Pope Pius II—Aeneas Sylvius

[16] *Trattato,* I, p. 17.

[17] Cf., *infra,* in connection with Bronzino, the horror felt at this period for the too familiar or "well-known."

[18] See *supra,* p. 87 and *passim;* cf. J. Adhémar, *op. cit.,* pp. 16–17.

[19] See *supra,* p. 89.

[20] *Beati Johannis Dominici Cardinalis S. Sixti Lucula Noctis,* Latin text of the fifteenth century, edited by Rémi Coulon, O.P. (Paris, 1908). This treatise is exceedingly interesting, since it contains a concise refutation of all

Piccolomini—reproached Sigismondo Malatesta for transforming San Francesco into a temple of the Gentiles "ut non tam Christianorum quam infidelium daemones adorantium templum esse videretur." [21] Finally, in the last years of the century, Savonarola let loose his formidable wrath. But all this was in vain. The Cinquecento saw the sway of mythology irresistibly established both in art and literature. At the same time, however, the indignation and the threats of the censors explain the precautions taken by contemporary mythographers, as by their predecessors, in approaching the subject, and their care to defend themselves from the charge of giving offense to the "true religion."

It might have been expected that the Counter Reformation would institute a far more systematic and profound opposition, and that after the Council of Trent a period of austerity would open for the arts, the first victims of which would be the gods. It is true that at this time we see the idols being expelled from the Vatican by Pius V, and hurled by Sixtus V from the summit of the Campidoglio. Sixtus also ordered a sculptured Moses instead of a Neptune for the Fontana dell'Acqua Felice. Preachers thundered at will against paganism, and in the same period artists like Ammanati [22] publicly repented

> *. . . d'avoir peint et sculpté, mettant l'âme en péril,*
> *O honte! Bacchus ivre ou Danaé surprise.*[23]

But in spite of symptoms like these, it is clearly apparent that the gods were not too much injured by such accesses of virtue, and that mythology

---

the arguments brought forward by the humanists in favor of ancient culture in general, and especially of mythology.

In his Introduction (p. LXI, n. 2), Coulon quotes a curious letter from Giovanni da San Miniato to Angelo Corbinelli about the reading of Virgil and Ovid: ". . . haec omnia non solum vanitas . . . sed in ore Christicolae pene blasphemiae sunt, idolorumque ignota cultura, quae velut monstruosa portenta mentem inquinant, mores dissipant," etc. (". . . all these things are not only vanity, but in the mouth of a worshipper of Christ they are almost blasphemy, and an unconscious cult of idols; they befoul the mind like horrible monsters, and overthrow morals"). The position of Coluccio Salutati concerning the gods is clearly summed up in his *Epistolario,* I, lib. IV, epist. XV, pp. 301–303.

[21] See *supra,* p. 135.

[22] He writes to his fellow members of the Florentine Academy, August 22, 1582: "Therefore to make nude statues, satyrs, fauns, or similar things is the greatest and most grievous error." See Bottari, *Raccolta di lettere* (Milan, 1822), III, 532 f.

[23] José María de Heredia, *Les Trophées:* "Le vieil orfèvre" (". . . to have painted or carved, to the peril of one's soul—ah, what shame —Bacchus in drunkenness or Danaë surprised").

continued with renewed ardor to people galleries and palaces with nude figures, acknowledged and encouraged by the Church herself in the persons of her prelates.

Their lack of instruction, and also of creative force, as we have said, made the artists dependent upon men of letters, whose meticulous instructions they received with docility, and often with gratitude. Who were these learned advisers? None other than Churchmen—the theologians and their intimates, Panvinio, Caro, Cardinal Sirleto himself.[24] Vincenzo Borghini, prior of the Innocenti in Florence, is indispensable as organizer of the *mascherate* of the gods—the helpful adviser whom Vasari cannot do without.[25] According to tradition, it was Monsignor Agucchi who furnished the Carracci with the theme for their famous Gallery.[25a] The influence of these learned ecclesiastics ought, without doubt, to have led artists away from profane subjects of this order, inspiring them with a more Christian spirit; but it had exactly the opposite effect, and at the end, as at the beginning of the century, the most important pagan decorations were executed for cardinals. Of this, the Farnese palaces at Rome and Caprarola offer convincing proof.[26] Thus the great ecclesiastics encouraged not only by their counsel, but by actual commissions, the abuses which it would rather have been their duty to check.

The situation is paradoxical only in appearance, and it would be an error to attribute this laxity solely to the epicureanism, want of conscience, and impiety of the clergy. In reality, the same conflict had existed since the first centuries of Christianity; it was part and parcel of the very culture of men of the Church. Nurtured upon ancient letters, the most scrupulous among them cannot rid themselves of their classical memories and ways of thinking; as humanists, they continue to love what they condemn, or should con-

[24] See Ch. Dejob, *op. cit.*, pp. 261 ff.

[25] See in Vasari, *Opere* (ed. Milanesi), VIII, Vasari's letters to Borghini of June 19 and 21, 1565, pp. 394–395: "I await you more eagerly than the Messiah."

[25a] D. Mahon, *Studies in Seicento Art and Theory*, Studies of the Warburg Institute, XVI (London, 1947).

[26] Among the many witnesses to the predilection for mythology among the higher clergy, see Vasari's letter to N. Vespucci (*Opere*, Milanesi ed., VIII, 234); the topic is a canvas representing Venus and the Graces, destined for Cardinal Ippolito de' Medici: "For the Cardinal and Pope Clement were so pleased with that satyr that when I have finished it, they want me to do a much larger painting showing a battle of satyrs, a bacchanalia of fauns, and other woodland deities"; also another letter, to Ottaviano de'Medici, on the Bacchanalia and the Harpocrates, *ibid.*, pp. 235–236: "For I have been made to do all this by Pope Clement, at the instance of our Cardinal."

demn, as theologians. One need but recall, in this connection, St. Augustine or St. Jerome and their inner conflicts. Their minds are haunted by the profane poetry which they ought to denounce;[27] it has penetrated their very souls. In the twelfth century, a Guibert of Nogent, a Pierre of Blois, secretly cherish the ancients whom they deny in public. Hildebert of Lavardin reminds the faithful that they are children of Christ, not of Minerva or Venus,[28] but celebrates in Latin verses the statues of the gods and their supernatural beauty.[29] Pope Pius II, who reproached Sigismondo Malatesta for having "paganized" a Christian sanctuary,[30] is the same Aeneas Sylvius, archeologist and man of letters, whose elegant prose is adorned with mythological allusions, and who upon occasion defends Ovid's *Metamorphoses.*[31] It is true that, for the most part, the pagan current prevails with these Roman prelates of the sixteenth century at the expense of morality and faith; but when they delight in composing a Ciceronian parallel between Diana and the Virgin Mary, and even when they take pleasure in watching bacchanalia,[32] they are, in the last analysis, merely being true to their education.

The indulgence shown by official—or officious—censors after the Council of Trent is to be explained in the same way; for the most part they went no further than to denounce as unseemly the use of this mythology which was, however, the most manifest symptom of the return to pagan ideas. Possibly they also thought it the most inoffensive.[33]

*

Some of them, nevertheless, were shocked by the endless repetition of mythological images—first of all, Cardinal Paleotto, who wished to recall men of learning in particular (and hence "ecclesiastical personages") to a sense of their responsibilities in this matter.

[27] See H. I. Marrou, *op. cit.*, pp. 128–131.

[28] See J. Adhémar, *op. cit.*, pp. 17–18.

[29] See *supra*, p. 212.

[30] See *supra*, p. 135.

[31] *De liberorum educatione*, in *Opera omnia* (Basel, 1551), I, p. 984: "Ovidius . . . in plerisque . . . locis nimirum lascivus: praeclarissimum tamen opus ejus cui Metamorphoseos nomen indidit; propter fabularum peritiam, quas noscere non parvi fructus est, nullo pacto postergandum est." ("Ovid in many passages is lascivious, to be sure; however, the work to which he gave the title of *Metamorphoses* is a very famous one, and for the sake of learning the fables—a knowledge of which is of considerable utility to us—we should not neglect him.") It will be seen that the Christian moralist here yields to the man of letters.

[32] See E. Rodocanachi, *Rome au temps de Jules II et de Léon X* (Paris, 1912), pp. 137 ff.

[33] See Ch. Dejob, *op. cit.*, pp. 147–149.

One chapter of the discourse [34] that he devoted to sacred and profane images is entitled: *Delle pitture di Giove, di Apolline, Mercurio, Giunone, Cerere, et altri falsi Dei.* It contains some most significant admonitions (Bk. II, chap. x), pointing out (p. 122, v.) that the abuse which consists in keeping alive the memory of the gods is all the more dangerous and blameworthy in that, under the pretext of the study of literature or antiquity, it often infects men of the greatest distinction.

He anticipates the objection that the images of the gods are the scholars' instruments, indispensable for their knowledge of antiquity or for some other laudable end, since all of them read the pagan works and the fables of the poets, which are filled with allusions to the gods. To this, Paleotto answers that his criticism is aimed above all at the custom of keeping images of the gods where they may easily be seen, and of using them as household ornaments. If a man's mind be set upon having such images in his house, solely for purposes of study, let him at least have the discretion to keep them out of sight. This precaution ought to be observed by Churchmen above all (p. 124, r., v.).

Thus, mythology is dangerous; images of the gods are "filthy and criminal," and are admissible only under the express reservation that they be kept out of sight, where they cannot exert harmful influence on the public.

This kind of severity did not act as a check upon artists, but it did not fail to trouble them—all the more, since Paleotto went further than this and condemned even *grotteschi* "in the name of reason" (Bk. II, Chaps. XXVII–XLII). He thus includes in his attack against mythology its most innocent derivatives, and would deprive artists even of motifs of pure decoration.

It is to be regretted that Paleotto published no more than a summary of his last three books. Book III was to have been entirely directed against "lascivious paintings"—in other words, especially against the world of Fable, natural habitat of nudes and of sensual images. Chapter headings, such as those for Chap. XI ("That statues and images of men and women have a peculiar power to move the senses"), Chap. XXII ("Arguments used by painters

[34] G. Paleotto, *Discorso intorno alle immagini sacre e profane . . . diviso in cinque libri, dove si scuoprono vari abusi loro . . . raccolto e posto insieme ad utile delle anime per commissione di Mons. Ill. e Rev. card. P. vescovo di Bologna* (Bologna, 1584).

to justify representation of nude and lascivious figures, or unseemly attitudes"), and Chaps. XXIII and XXIV ("Reply to painters' contrary views"; "Further replies showing that painters can on no grounds be excused for representing indecent or lascivious subjects"), are a sufficient indication that mythology itself was to have been the author's target. They show also that artists were disturbed by the attack. Feeling themselves threatened, they had constructed a system in their own defense which it would have been of interest to know and analyze.

Fortunately, in the next century, Pietro da Cortona and the Jesuit Ottonelli took the trouble to define the main points of the controversy. Taking their inspiration from the ideas of Paleotto and of the Padre Possevino,[35] they devoted an important chapter of their *Treatise on Painting and Sculpture* [36] to the images of the gods: "del giuditio che si può fare dell'immagini de'falsi dei de'gentili." The objections made by the artists are set forth and refuted one by one, and it is here that the best picture of their attitude is obtained (pp. 82–88).

It goes without saying that the artists do not allow themselves to be convinced by the solemn proclamation of some of their opponents that "Christus Dominus in mundum venit, et sanguinem profudit, ut omnem Deorum memoriam exstingueret." [37] Painting and sculpture, they reply, do not perpetuate the worship of the gods; no risk is involved in preserving their memory, now that superstition has disappeared from the world.

Besides, they hasten to add, artists have no choice: great gentlemen and princes frequently order mythological figures as decoration for their palaces, and their wishes must be followed. Furthermore, in the case of a vast decorative cycle, mythology alone gives the painter sufficient scope for the erudition and variety which are expected of him.

These are the decisive arguments; we shall soon see that they have overcome the scruples of the most devout artists. The censors can produce

[35] Antonio Possevino, *Tractatus de poesi et pictura ethnica humana et fabulosa, collecta cum vera, honesta et sacra*, dissert. introduced into the *Bibliotheca selecta* (Rome, 1593).

[36] Odomenigico Lelonotti and Britio Prenetteri (anagrams), *Trattato della pittura e scultura, uso, et abuso loro . . . in cui si resolvono molti casi di coscienza intorno al fare e tenere l'immagini sacre e profane* (Florence, 1652).

[37] "Christ the Lord came into the world, and shed His blood, in order that all memory of the gods might be extinguished."

only feeble contentions in reply: "The prince might always be urged to alter the terms of his commission," and as for erudition and variety, "these are obviously indispensable qualities, but the artist can show that he is ingenious and cultivated without resorting to the images of false gods!"

As a reply to those who persist in their strictures, the artists have in reserve a final argument—the most specious, perhaps, but for us the most interesting of all. The figures of the gods, *symbolically interpreted,* can teach and inspire love of good and hatred of evil. And this time there is no manner of use in pointing out to them that a good painter can represent the vices and virtues in some other way, or in asking how many persons are capable of understanding the moral significance of the myths. This new excuse is too convenient, and above all too well adapted to the spirit of the time, to be willingly renounced. But the artist cannot invoke it in good faith without giving his subject a more or less edifying turn; a more or less important role in his composition must be reserved for allegory. It is here that we grasp the indirect influence of the Church on the forms of "pagan" art.

*

First of all, let us see how this return to allegory, considered as a moral antidote to mythology, manifests itself in the second half of the sixteenth century.

In 1554 appeared Dolce's *Trasformationi.*[38] The dedication to the counselor of Charles V, Monsignor Perrenot, bishop of Arras (later Cardinal de Granvelle), is enveloped in precautions: "What could be less appropriate for dedication to Caesar, upon whose shoulders the infinite providence of God has placed the responsibility of upholding the Christian religion, than fables, and recitals of love? My decision to do so will be regarded by many as unwise, perhaps even as extremely unwise."

But the excuse is at hand: "Nevertheless, those who will take the trouble to look with discernment not at the surface of the fables contained in this book, but at the motives which brought about their invention and the ends

[38] Dolce, *Le Trasformationi tratte da Ovidio . . . con gli argomenti et allegorie al principio et al fine di ciascun canto* (Venice, 1554 [and 1568, 1570, etc.]).

to which they were directed by those early Masters, will see beneath the rind of fiction, all the sap of moral and sacred Philosophy."

And in order to make his position still more explicit, Dolce introduced into all the editions after 1568 an "allegoria" at the end of each canto, in which its pious meaning is unmistakably set forth.

100. Sacred and profane love

Canon Comanini follows the same line of reasoning, maintaining that no man of sense should choose as his subjects inept and hollow fables, unworthy of the name, since they serve no purpose whatever and have nothing to teach. He may, however, represent the others at will—tales which embody meaning and express some truth.[39]

This distinction, of course, leaves the artist completely free, for into what fable or figure is it not possible to read some edifying interpretation?

[39] D. Gregorio Comanini, *Il Figino, ovvero del fine della pittura* . . . (Mantua, 1591), p. 162.

The Middle Ages have offered us copious demonstration of the fact that in this domain the ingenuity of "men of virtue" knows no limits. And in this respect the Renaissance yields nothing to the earlier period.[40]

But from the day the Council of Trent uttered its warnings, allegory became more than ever a means of avoiding censure—a sort of expedient for vindicating pagan imagery and licentious tales.[41]

There are different ways of making use of this antidote. Sometimes it is administered after the fact. We may be permitted to borrow here a celebrated example from the seventeenth century, the *Daphne* of Bernini, and the words engraved on its pedestal:

> *Quisquis amans sequitur fugitivae gaudia formae*
> *Fronde manus implet, baccas seu carpit amaras . . .*[42]

These lines are by Cardinal Barberini (later Urban VIII), who improvised them in order to counteract the disturbing charms of the nymph, and to allay the scruples of Cardinal de Sourdis.[43]

What Urban VIII achieved with an epigram, the Carracci had attempted in the Farnese Gallery—perhaps more seriously—by means of small emblems discreetly placed in the corners of the hall. These four "dottissimi immagini," we learn from Malvasia (after Bellori),[44] are the basis of the whole work: they represent phases in the combat between sacred and profane love, symbolized by the two Eros figures struggling for a palm branch (*fig. 100*). These *putti*, who pass at first quite unnoticed by the spectator, should serve upon closer examination to inform him that all the mythological figures which decorate the Gallery are in reality so many allusions "to the punishments of vice and the reward of virtue."[45]

40 See *supra*, pp. 89 ff.

41 Ch. Dejob, *op. cit.*, p. 184.

42 ("Whoever, being in love, pursues the delight of a fleeing appearance, finds his hands full of foilage, or plucks only bitter berries.")

43 *Journal du Cavalier Bernin en France* (Paris, 1930), pp. 42–43. Cf. the edifying interpretations given to the Daphne myth in the Middle Ages, as for example in the *Moralia* of Robert Holkott, where Phoebus is said to aspire to the vain glory of the world, which is Daphne; or where Daphne is called a Christian soul menaced by the Devil and saved by prayer (see *supra*, p. 93).

For the Jesuits, the same fable signifies that flight is the surest means of escaping temptation. See C. F. Menestrier, *L'Art des emblèmes*, p. 71. Cf. W. Stechow, *Apollo und Daphne*, Studien d. Bibl. Warburg (1932).

44 *Felsina pittrice* (1844 ed.), pp. 314–315: "four most learned images."

45 These two *amorini* struggling for a palm branch are represented in Cartari (1571 ed.), p. 504 (see *fig. 101*). Cf. E. Panofsky, "Der gefesselte Eros," *Oud-Holland*, L (1933), pp. 193–217, esp. pp. 193–198; S. Reinach, *Repert.*

Often indeed, it is to the gods themselves that the artist, with more or less conviction, entrusts the task of incarnating ideas or moral principles. Vasari says as much, somewhat pretentiously, with regard to his frescoes in the Palazzo Vecchio in Florence: "E se in questa sala ed in altre vo dichiarando queste mie invenzioni sotto nome di favolosi dei, siami lecito in questo imitar gli antichi, i quali sotto questi nomi nascondevano allegoricamente i concetti della filosofia." [46]

101. Eros and Anteros

At one stroke, the artist's mythology becomes "philosophical" and is no longer subject to censure. Even those who, like Jacopo Zucchi, refuse to recognize the "sapientia veterum" beneath the outward shell of Fable, cannot resist invoking the traditional allegories: "Just as the eye-spangled peacock's tail and the rainbow"—attributes of Juno—"dissolve into nothing, so do ambition and wealth." [47]

Thus the admonitions of the Church did not remain wholly ineffective. Without turning painters away from pagan subjects (or even trying to do so), they gave decisive encouragement to the taste for allegory.

*

THE SPIRIT of the time, indeed, was already leading artists in the same direction; everything predisposed them to see painting as essentially a means of "rendering thought visible." It was with the artist in mind that Raffaello Borghini [48] translated, word for word, the formula of Gregory the Great—

---

des Reliefs, III, p. 73. There seems to be no doubt that the Carracci made use of Cartari; in any case, we find again in the Palazzo Magnani in Bologna, which they decorated, an "Apollo with four vases" which comes from the *Imagini* (Venice ed., 1580), p. 85.

[46] Milanesi ed., VIII, *Ragionamenti del Sig. Giorgio Vasari sopra le invenzioni da lui dipinte in Firenze*, etc., *Ragion.* I, p. 18: "And if for this and other halls I proceed to explain my compositions under the names of the gods of Fable, it should be permitted me thus to follow the example of the ancients, who beneath these names concealed philosophical concepts by means of allegory."

[47] J. Zucchi, *Discorso sopra li dei de'gentili e loro imprese* (Rome, 1602), p. 51: "Si come l'ornata e pennuta ruota dell'occhiato pavone, overo il celeste arco dissolvendosi sparisce, cosi l'ambitione, le ricchezze fanno."

[48] *Il Riposo*, p. 77.

"Quod legentibus scriptura, hoc idiotis praestat pictura" [49]—an argument which was to be used to the point of satiety, for a long time to come. "The principal reason," wrote the Abbé Pluche in 1748, "for the painters' continued use of fables and allegory is that intellectual subjects are not susceptible of direct visual presentation and, in order to be apprehended by the senses, must be given bodily form and habiliment." [50]

This is the cause, furthermore, of the extraordinary popularity of symbolic figures at the end of the sixteenth century.[51] We have already sketched the history of this movement, seeking its immediate origins in Quattrocento Neoplatonism, and in the supposed disclosure of the enigmatic meaning of the hieroglyphs.[52] The growing vogue of emblems witnesses the extent of the movement and gives us a true picture of the role played by the Church in its propagation.

In fact, this pseudo science, which teaches us to hide, or to discover, the most serious precepts beneath the most frivolous outward appearances, offered a providential means of reconciling the pagan and Christian worlds, the profane and the sacred, at the very moment when a rupture between them seemed imminent. Fables, for example, could be "sanctified" merely by the attribution of a spiritual meaning. This play of concealed meanings authorizes all sorts of combinations and transpositions. "Christian" emblems [53] utilize elements of pagan iconography to illustrate the teachings of the faith: Cupid, wearing a halo as disguise, becomes the Infant Jesus, and Ovid is

[49] *Epist.*, IX, 9: "What writing offers to those who know how to read, painting provides for the uneducated."—Giordano Bruno, furthermore, states in his *De umbris idearum* that ideas can be conceived and represented by the human mind only in the shape of images. See the comments of E. Cassirer, *Individuum und Cosmos*, p. 78.

[50] *Histoire du ciel*, II, p. 427. Pluche adds: "But the artist should realize from the failure of his allegories how little the public demands this sort of thing. Who gives himself the trouble to read in the allegorical paintings of M. LeBrun and many others what the artists have intended to make known? All these enigmatic figures make a burden of what ought to amuse or instruct me . . . Since the sole purpose of a painting is to show me what cannot be said in words, it is ridiculous that an effort should have to be made in order to understand it. . . . And ordinarily, when I have succeeded in divining what these mysterious figures mean, I find that the substance has hardly been worth so elaborate a concealment." Cf. our discussion of emblems, *supra*, pp. 100 ff.

[51] R. Van Marle (*Iconographie de l'art profane*, II: *Allégories et symboles* [The Hague, 1932]), emphasizes this "tendency toward the abstract image."

[52] See *supra*, pp. 99 ff.

[53] See in particular those of Georgette de Montenay, *Emblèmes ou devises chrétiennes* (Lyons, 1571); also those of Othon Vaenius, *Amoris divini Emblemata* (Antwerp, 1615).

made to yield devout imagery. Père Menestrier expressly sanctions this sort of thing when he says that figures from profane history, and even from Fable, may be used as sacred emblems: "Les figures de l'histoire prophane et de la fable même peuvent servir à faire des emblèmes sacrez." [54]

These strange products of Catholic humanism have been studied by Mario Praz [55] and the Abbé Bremond.[56] They offer abundant proof that it was both legitimate and easy to juggle with mythology in a symbolic sense, in order to make it reveal the truths of Scripture. The Roman Church inviting the Protestants to return to her bosom could even be represented as the nymph Salmacis calling Hermaphroditos! [57]

*

ONE CAN view these absurd analogues as the result of a harmless obsession, and smile upon them indulgently.[58] Without doubt, many sincere believers who were at the same time ardent students of literature associated their profane erudition and their faith naïvely and with no mental reservation. For them allegory was merely a flower-strewn path leading from one to the other.

But it must be admitted that, basically, allegory is often sheer imposture, used to reconcile the irreconcilable—just as we have seen it lending decency to the manifestly indecent.[59] On both grounds, it is a dangerous fraud.

The Church had seen this danger. In the Tridentine *Index,* in which the works of Ovid are not even mentioned, the moralized versions are expressly

[54] *L'art des Emblèmes où s'enseigne la morale par les figures de la fable*, etc. (Paris, 1684). Menestrier would also have it that all the ancient fables were in reality nothing more than emblems, at least if Francis Bacon is to be believed, who has given interpretations of them in a special treatise. How often, for example, has the fable of the giants been converted into emblems of the ungodly, etc. (*ibid.*, p. 21). Cf., by the same author, *La philosophie des images énigmatiques* (Paris, 1694), p. 15: parallel drawn between the attributes of the pagan gods and the sacred figures of the Church.

[55] *Op. cit.*, esp. chap. iv.

[56] *Histoire littéraire du sentiment religieux*, I: *L'Humanisme dévôt,* Pt. 2, chap. i, p. 2: "L'humanisme dévôt et les poètes païens."

[57] Filère, *Discours poétique à Messieurs de la religion prétendue réformée* (1607).

[58] This is the attitude taken by H. Bremond, *loc. cit.:* "They are children," he says, "pure in heart, and joyous in imagination; let us leave them to their singing."

[59] See *supra*, p. 271; cf. R. Schevill, *Ovid and the Renascence in Spain*, Univ. of Calif. Publications in Modern Philology, IV (1933), p. 17: "The allegorical interpretations of Ovid's myths . . . can be found . . . in the form of prefaces or appendices, which were probably never read . . . no doubt a concession to the official censors who had to grant their imprimatur."

prohibited: "In Ovidii metamorphoseos libros commentaria sive enarrationes allegoricae vel tropologicae."[60] The meaning of this proscription is clear: the ecclesiastical censors do not intend to allow erotic stories to be published under a pious disguise,[61] nor the sacraments of the Gospels to be hidden within the amours of the gods.[62]

Thus, in principle, the Church condemned the use of allegory, but she encouraged it in fact. The crisis of the Counter Reformation had clearly shown the discord between the pagan spirit and Christian morals; for that very reason the need of reconciliation and justification which had never ceased secretly to torment the *literati* and artists of the Renaissance became more urgent than ever. The same uneasiness and false modesty which gave birth to hypocritical or petty concessions, such as the vine leaves or breeches applied by Daniel da Volterra to Michelangelo's nudes, found in allegory the ideal expedient—a concealing veil and an honorable formula of compromise.

The educational program elaborated by the Jesuits[63] shows what good use can be made of so convenient and supple an instrument as allegory had become. This program, as is well known, resolutely integrated pagan letters into the scheme of Christian instruction—and this at a time when logic, prudence, and good faith would seem rather to have dictated their banishment. In circumstances not unlike those in which the Fathers of the fourth century had found themselves[64]—face to face, that is, with a culture which they knew to be contrary to their own faith, but which enjoyed immense traditional prestige and had played a part in their own development[65]—the Jesuits adopted a similar attitude and accepted what they knew they were powerless to uproot or replace. The Church once more accepted the pagan heritage, and proceeded to transmit it.

[60] H. Reusch, *Die Indices librorum prohibitorum des sechszehnten Jahrhunderts* (Tübingen, 1886), p. 275.

[61] This abuse had already annoyed Savonarola: *De divisione* (1491), I, IV.

[62] Methods of this kind had been denounced by certain Fathers and Doctors of the church: see *supra*, pp. 87, 89. Cf. also the letter of Giovanni da San Miniato to Corbinelli (*Beati Johannis Dominici . . . Lucula Noctis* [Coulon ed.], Introd., pp. LXI–LXII): "If you would attain to true knowledge of right and wrong, you will do so far more readily by studying the Scriptures—where truth is revealed directly and without lying concealment."

[63] *Monumenta paedagogica Societatis Jesu quae primam rationem studiorum anno 1586 editam praecessere* (Madrid, 1901).

[64] G. Boissier (*La Fin du paganisme*, II, pp. 498–499) underlines the similarity of the two epochs. Cf. Ch. Dejob, *op. cit.*, p. 149: Cardinal Antoniani, like Saint Basil, approves the use of pagan literature in training the young.

[65] See *supra*, p. 265.

Mythology, in consequence, occupied a place of honor in the Jesuit colleges;[66] furthermore, the two treatises on mythology which came to be regarded as authoritative in seventeenth-century France were the work of Jesuit authors, the Pères P. Gaultruche and F. A. Pomey.[67] The gods, officially consecrated as elements of rhetoric that it would be a disgrace not to know ("in quorum ignoratione versari non potest, sine summo dedecore, qui liberalium disciplinarum peritos audire vult"), again became the indispensable ornaments of formal discourse, as they had been in the time of Ausonius or Claudian.[68]

But it is not on literary grounds alone that the teaching of Fable is justified. It is exalted for its edifying value as well; it, too, aims at "the greater glory of God."[69] Mythology, in fact, say the Fathers, is not a jumble of absurd or shocking tales ("Non sunt hae fabulae anilia commenta aut insulsae narrationes somniorum"), it is a body of moral precepts, cunningly hidden under the mask of fiction "as the stone is hidden in the fruit." In this light, there is in mythology nothing to alarm the most delicate conscience: "Nec te fabulae nomen deterreat. . . ."

And to inculcate in their pupils this special form of casuistry, which excuses pleasure on the grounds of profit and concedes that sin may be purified by good intention, the Jesuits teach them the science of emblems[70] along with their mythology, the first being the method constantly to be applied to the second. Are not all the fables of the ancients emblems, and all the attributes

[66] See J. B. Herman, *La Pédagogie des Jésuites au* XVIe *siècle* (Brussels, 1914), and A. Schimberg, *L'Éducation morale dans les collèges de la Compagnie de Jésus en France sous l'ancien régime* (Paris, 1913), chap. iii.

[67] Bayle writes to his brother, January 30, 1675: "As for Fable, one must know it *ad unguem;* and if you see a little book called *L'histoire poétique* by Père Gaultruche, make it your *vade mecum.*" And, on March 15: "Do, for pity's sake, learn how each god was represented. . . . The *Pantheum mythicum* [of Père Pomey] describes nicely enough how each god is turned out ("l'équipage de chaque dieu"). Take good note as you read." In the eighteenth century, a third Jesuit, Père de Jouvancy, was to write an *Appendix de diis et heroibus poeticis,* translated almost literally from Gaultruche.

[68] They even penetrate the churches, where they serve to enhance ceremonial pomp. Menestrier (*op. cit.,* p. 383) notes that on great feast days the churches are sometimes hung with mythological tapestries (representing the Labors of Hercules, or the Metamorphoses of Jupiter), and refers to a service celebrated in Notre Dame in Paris for the Queen, for which a painting had been prepared showing the star of Venus and the eagle of Jupiter.

[69] In the preface to his *Pantheum mythicum,* Pomey declares that his aim is "propagatio Divinae gloriae." Cf. the statement of de Jouvancy (*De ratione docendi,* I, 3) that the pagan authors are to be regarded as heralds of Christ.

[70] See Herman, *op. cit.,* chap. vii, paragraphs 17 and 18; and Schimberg, *op. cit.,* pp. 571–583 (*pièces justificatives*).

of the gods hieroglyphs? [71] And does not the art of emblems consist precisely in imparting moral instruction through figures drawn from Fable? [72]

In fact, as Mario Praz has observed,[73] emblems were marvelously adapted to the pedagogical principles of the Jesuits. They seem to have been made for the express purpose of imprinting truth on the mind by way of the senses ("for there is nothing," says Richeome in his *Peinture spirituelle,* "which gives more delight and more easily permits outside things to slip into the soul than does painting; nothing which so deeply engraves them in the memory"), for reconciling the useful and pleasurable,[74] and for combining diversion with instruction. As La Fontaine was to point out:

> *Une morale nue apporte de l'ennui:*
> *Le conte fait passer le précepte avec lui. . . .*[75]

These didactic advantages were to make of painting one of the favorite instruments of Jesuit propaganda. But there is a pleasing detail to prove that while serving the Jesuit cause, emblems were also serving the cause of mythology: the Company represented itself in the guise of Mercury coming down from heaven as the messenger charged with orders from the gods! [76]

*

Let us now look back at the manuals of Giraldi, Conti, and Cartari. They offer a material ready prepared for transmutations and exegeses of this kind. Their origins and nature were such as to disarm the scruples of some and serve the pious ends of others; their gods, heirs of the Middle Ages, were once more easily adapted to the mould of allegory from which they had never fully emerged. The oddity of their forms, the multiplicity of their attributes, the Oriental elements which endowed them with mystery—to say nothing of the "Neoplatonic" significance with which they were already shrouded—allowed them to be moralized and spiritualized at will.

The mythologies designed for use in the colleges were therefore to draw

[71] See Menestrier, *op. cit.,* pp. 253–254.

[72] As is witnessed by Menestrier's title: *L'art des Emblèmes, où s'enseigne la morale par les figures de la fable.*

[73] *Op. cit.,* p. 156.

[74] "Utilitatem maximam pari delectione conditam," says Pomey in the preface to the *Pantheum mythicum.*

[75] "Unadorned moralizing is tiresome; embodiment in a tale wins acceptance alike for the precept."

[76] Menestrier, *op. cit.,* p. 69.

largely upon these earlier works;[77] but as early as the end of the Cinquecento they, too, had been absorbed into the monumental *Iconologia* of Cesare Ripa,[78] which Emile Mâle saw as "the key to the painted and sculptured allegories of the seventeenth century."[79] Ripa not only used for the most part the same sources as Giraldi, Conti, and Cartari—that is to say, the medieval mythographers, hieroglyphs, and numismatics—but he borrowed from them the very images which he converted into abstractions.[80] In his bible of symbols, the figures of the gods lose all value of their own, all independent existence; "made," in his own expression," to signify something other than meets the eye," they are no more than "veils or garments intended to conceal that part of philosophy which has to do with the generation and corruption of natural things, the disposition of the Heavens, etc. . . . and with what is within man himself: his concepts and habits. . . ."[81] In other words, mythology proclaims philosophical truths and moral concepts.

[77] The foreword to the *Pantheum mythicum* (1777 ed.) recalls Pomey's close adherence to Boccaccio, Giraldi, and Conti: "Horum vestigia legens, imo ex his . . . multa transcribens" ("following their traces, or rather transcribing many things from them").

[78] Rome, 1593. Editions of this work, repeatedly enriched with new illustrations, were issued up to the end of the eighteenth century.

[79] *L'Art religieux après le concile de Trente* (1932), chap. ix.

[80] This has been shown by E. Mandowsky, *Ricerche intorno all' Iconologia di Cesare Ripa* (Florence, 1939): *La mitologia della seconda metà del sec.* XVI *e l'Iconologia del Ripa*, pp. 32 ff.

[81] *Iconologia*, Proemio.

III

The Influence of the Manuals

WE HAVE just reviewed the circumstances which in the last half of the sixteenth century appeared favorable to the diffusion of mythology in literature and art, and hence to the success of the manuals. Even the factor which at first glance would seem most likely to have weighed in the opposite direction, the offensive of the Council of Trent against profane images, finally operated in their favor.

The manuals, in fact, attained an outstanding success; the number of editions justifies the conclusion that during more than a century, in Italy and in the rest of Europe, they had their place in the library of every artist and man of letters. Thus, editions of Conti's *Mythology* succeeded one another at very short intervals: it appeared three times in Venice, in 1551, 1568, and 1581; four times in Frankfort, in 1581, 1584, 1585, and 1596; three times in Paris, in 1583, 1588, and 1605 (issued that year by three different publishers simultaneously). Furthermore, it was published in Geneva, 1596; in Lyons, 1602; in Hanau, 1605; in Padua, 1616. The French translation, by J. de Montlyard, was printed five times: Paris, 1599; Lyons, 1604, 1607; Rouen, 1611; and again in Paris, 1627.

Cartari's *Images of the Gods* went through twelve Italian editions: Venice, 1556, 1566, 1571, 1580; Lyons, 1581; Padua, 1603, 1608, 1615; Venice, 1624; Padua, 1626; Venice, 1647, 1674. Five Latin editions appeared: Lyons, 1581; Rothenburg, 1683; Mainz, 1687; Frankfort, 1687; Mainz, 1699. Five were in French: Lyons, 1581; Tournon, 1606; Lyons, 1610, 1624, 1631. There was an English version, *The Fountain of Ancient Fiction, wherein is lively depictured the images of the gods of the ancients* (London,

1599), also a German one, entitled *Neu eröffneter Götzen Tempel* (Frankfort, 1692).

However, when we attempt to specify the precise role and influence of the manuals it is difficult to find evidence. The books that everyone consults and keeps constantly at his elbow are never, or hardly ever, mentioned; by reason of their very popularity, they soon become anonymous handbooks;[1] no one quotes a dictionary. Furthermore, a writer or artist who wishes to display his erudition is not particularly eager to reveal the source of the learning that he has acquired with so little expenditure of time or energy: those who owe the most to Giraldi, Cartari, and Conti are usually careful not to acknowledge their indebtedness.

102. Apollo, Hadad, and Atargatis

It is, however, possible to recover traces of these borrowings; we shall look for them first in Italian art, and then in European humanism.

*

WE DISCOVER such traces first of all in the festivals, processions, and "triumphs"—in other words, in that middle sphere between art and life in which Renaissance Italy produced so many ephemeral masterpieces.[2]

In spectacles of this type, mythology normally played an important, if not the essential role. But toward the end of the Cinquecento, this mythology took on a curiously hybrid character. We take as examples some of the fetes celebrated in Florence between 1565 and 1589: the "Masque of the Genealogy of the Gods," staged for the marriage of Francesco de'Medici to Johanna of Austria (1565), and the *apparati* arranged for two other weddings—those

[1] Roger de Piles, in *L'Art de peinture de C.-A. du Fresnoy* (Paris, 1673), pp. 127–129, lists the "books most useful to those of the profession." He includes the *Iconologia* and the *Imagini degli dei,* but does not give the authors' names.

[2] See J. Burckhardt, *The Civilization of the Renaissance in Italy,* v, 8: "The Festivals."

of Cesare d'Este and Virginia de'Medici (1585), and of Ferdinando de'Medici and Christine of Lorraine (1589).

For these different spectacles, extremely detailed accounts have come

103. Apollo's chariot

down to us, and many drawings.[3] It is thus easy for us to ascertain that the gods, who are the chief actors, are not the classical originals, but those very figures which we know from the manuals.

[3] For the "Masque of the Gods" we have two descriptions: that of Baccio Baldini, *Discorso sopra la Mascherata della Genealogia degl' Iddei dei gentili* (Florence, 1565); and a second, probably by Cini, which appears in Vasari (Milanesi ed.), VIII, pp. 567–614. Furthermore, we have three series of drawings, one in the Uffizi (Gabinetto delle Stampe, Disegni di figura, 2666–2945); the two others in the Biblioteca Nazionale, Florence (Giulio Parigi, *Disegni originali*, Vol. I, and mss. Follini II, I, 142). See our article, "La Mascarade des dieux à Florence en 1565," *Mélanges d'archéologie et d'histoire* (1935), p. 224.

For the two *apparati*, see Bastiano de' Rossi: (1) *Descrizione del magnificentissimo apparato e dei meravigliosi intermedi fatti per la Commedia rappresentata in Firenze nelle felicissime nozze degl' Ill. ed. Ecc. Sigg. il Sig. Don Cesare d'Este e la Signora Donna Virginia Medici* (Florence, 1585); (2) *Descrizione dell'apparato e degli intermedi fatti per la Commedia rappresentata in Firenze nelle nozze di Ferdinando Medici e Madama Cristina di Lorena gran Duchi di Toscana* (Florence, 1589).

Thus, on the first carriage in the *Mascherata*, we see an old man in his cavern—the famous Demogorgon of Boccaccio;[4] again, a woman dressed in black and white, bearing thunderbolt and *tympanon* in her hands, is the Juno of Martianus Capella. Further along in the procession appears a strange Venus, with a burning torch on her breast, and in her left hand three apples of gold. We recognize in her the Venus of the *Saxon Chronicle* and the *Mer des hystoires.*[5] Even more surprising is the Apollo mounted on the chariot of the Sun, bearded and wearing a cuirass, a basket on his head and a flower in his hand, preceded by two eagles, three women, a serpent, etc. This figure we also know: he is not in any sense the god of Olympus, but the Assyrian Apollo described by Macrobius in the *Saturnalia.*[6] We have already met all these figures, and scores of others, in Giraldi and Cartari (*figs. 102* and *103*).

The same thing is true of the *intermedi* composed in 1585 and 1589 in honor of the two princely couples. At the marriage of Cesare d'Este and Virginia de' Medici, Jupiter appears with a trident, shod in green, and seated on a cushion of peacock's feathers;[7] for the wedding of Ferdinando de' Medici and Christine of Lorraine, Saturn, Apollo, and Bacchus once more wear the costumes which they displayed at the marriage of Mercury and Philology.[8] However unusual they may seem, none of these figures succeeds in baffling us, any more than do Diana's serpents or Juno's poppies,[9] or the curious attributes of Pan, Sosipolis, Mars, Hymenaeus, or Necessity. On the contrary, such images make clear to us at a glance the source from which the organizer of these fetes, Giovanni Bardi, has drawn his material.

So numerous and striking are the parallel details, in fact, that there can be no possible doubt of the extent to which the manuals served him as guide —as they served Monsignor Vincenzo Borghini, organizer of the *Mascherata.* In most cases it is enough merely to compare the illustrations in Cartari with the drawings of the stage designers: thus, in the *apparato* of 1589 we have a Mercury and an Aesculapius "like those," de' Rossi assures us, "shown us by

[4] The title of *Mascherata della Genealogia degl' Iddei* would of itself also seem to indicate that the whole procession was nothing but a *mise en scène* of Boccaccio's *Genealogia;* actually, except for Demogorgon, little more than the names of the gods and their grouping into families is taken from Boccaccio.

[5] See *supra*, p. 240.

[6] See *supra*, p. 239.

[7] De'Rossi, 1st *Intermedio*, pp. 7 ff.

[8] *Apparato* of 1589, pp. 27, 66, 69.

[9] *Ibid.*, 6th *Intermedio*, p. 71.

the ancients." [10] That may well be, but by the "ancients" as relayed by Pietrus Apianus [11] and recopied by the illustrator of Cartari.[12]

*

If we admit, with Lasca,[13] that the chief merit of a festival procession intended for the amusement of the crowd is to be intelligible to everyone, we may well have our doubts as to whether these mythological entertainments satisfied that condition. However cultivated the Florentine public may have been, it must have found itself slightly nonplussed by the baroque pantheon thus made to file before its eyes. This is, indeed, one of the reasons why explanatory accounts were published after the fact.[14] The organizers, annoyed at finding the depth of their knowledge and the subtlety of their intentions misunderstood, attempt to justify themselves by setting forth in detail the secret beauties that the crowd has shown itself unable to appreciate. Another producer of mythological pageants, Raffaello Gualterotti,[15] complains that his figures and devices have been thought displeasing by reason of their obscurity ("spiacevoli per oscurità"). He has, however, composed them for a cultivated public; so great an expense of care and thought would not have been justified had the popular audience alone been concerned. Indeed, it often happens—so he says—that he who sets out to please the ignorant ends by making himself appear ignorant in the eyes of those whose approval ought by

[10] *Ibid.*, pp. 26 and 72.

[11] *Inscriptiones*, p. 15 (Aesculapius) and p. 422 (Mercury).

[12] *Imagini* (1571 ed.), p. 87 (Aesculapius), p. 311 (Mercury). On Cartari's borrowings from Apianus, see *supra*, pp. 245 f.

Other drawings of the same sort, designs for Florentine fetes (1581–90), are preserved in the Museum Ferdinandeum, Innsbruck (cod. 2717).

See also the drawings by Primaticcio for a masked cortege, now in the Stockholm Museum; they are described in L. Dimier (*Le Primatice* [1900], Catalogue raisonné, nos. 188–212), where they are dated between 1559 and 1570. Dimier thinks that they may have served for a fete at Chenonceaux (pp. 187–188, 380–381). Some of the figures and the notes accompanying them (in Primaticcio's own hand) appear to be borrowed from Cartari's *Imagini.* An example is Saturn, no. 198: "Saturn, as the Phoenicians painted him, with four eyes, two open and two closed, and four wings, two open and two closed, to denote that when . . ."

[13] *Tutti i Trionfi, Carri, Mascherate o Canti carnascialeschi andati per Firenze dal tempio del Magnifico Lorenzo Vecchio de' Medici fino all'anno 1559*, dedicated to Francesco de'Medici.

[14] Baldini confesses that the *Mascherata* was not understood or even liked by everyone. Cf. Enea Vico, *Sopra l'effigie e statue, motti, imprese, figure, ed animali, poste nel arco fatto al vittoriosissimo Carlo Quinto* (Venice, 1551)—a work dedicated to Philip II.

[15] *La montagna Circea, torneamento nel passagio della Sereniss. Duchessa Donna Margherita Aldobrandini, sposa del Sereniss. Ranuccio Farnese duca di Parma . . . festeggiato in Bologna* (1600).

rights to be sought first of all. Here we catch a glimpse of the pedantry of the time, and also of the dilemma in which the authors of *argomenti* found themselves, caught between the demands of the public and those of the more cultivated audience.

The artist was faced with the same dilemma. If too obvious, his subject matter risked the scorn of the connoisseur; if too complicated, the indifference of the larger public. We see a problem of this sort in a letter written by Bronzino to Vincenzo Borghini on July 25, 1578,[16] commenting on the choice of the life of Hercules as theme for a set of tapestry designs. The subject, he concedes, may be too well known; but he has noted that people sometimes take more pleasure in what is familiar to them than in something which they find it difficult to understand.

To be clear without being trivial, profound without being obscure[17]—this would have been the ideal formula. But with the new tendencies of taste, it became more and more difficult to apply. And as it was the "learned" who must first of all be satisfied, we shall soon see the painters themselves, like our "inventors" of pageants, explaining their works by means of long notices which at times have the air of being written in order to justify them in the eyes of the larger public.

For the rest, it was by taking part in the planning of festivals that artists learned to complicate a theme to the point of unintelligibility. Throughout the fifteenth and sixteenth centuries, the work of decorators and producers was entrusted not to obscure artisans, but to painters and sculptors of renown. In the fetes of 1565, for example, the collaborators included Ammanati, Bronzino, Giovanni da Bologna, Vasari, Zucchi, and Federigo Zuccaro;[18] some of the work which they produced for the occasion deserved to last longer than a single day.[19] But the artists, it should be emphasized, were here serving

[16] See V. Borghini, *Carteggio inedito*, publ. by A. Lorenzoni (Florence, 1912), Letter LXIX, pp. 126–128.

[17] "Chiari non triviali, gravi non oscuri": Gualterotti, *op. cit.* p. 17.

[18] The names are given us by Domenico Mellini in a note at the end of his description: see Vasari, *op. cit.*, VIII, pp. 617–622.

[19] See Vasari, *op. cit.*, VIII, p. 604, speaking of Bronzino: "For the wedding festivities of Queen G. [Archduchess Johanna] of Austria . . . he painted, on three large canvases . . . certain incidents from the marriage of Hymen, in such wise that they seemed not like festival furnishings, but rather worthy to be kept in some honored place, so carefully were they finished and worked out."

merely as willing tools. Nothing was left to their imagination or initiative. The *régisseur général* of the spectacle, Vincenzo Borghini, not content with merely assigning the tasks, overwhelmed his collaborators with exact instructions which he expected them to follow literally.[20] In so doing, he doubtless fed their own imagination, but he also irritated and sometimes greatly embarrassed them.

In fact, not only were they being subjected to the tyranny of a text, but the text itself was sometimes strangely stubborn and unpromising. The figures that it imposed were such as to defy all possibility of plastic expression or harmonious composition. As we have already observed,[21] all the mongrel or barbaric divinities which in these texts, as in the manuals, supplant the classical gods, are rich in mysterious attributes, but poor in grace and majesty. How could artists breathe life into these buffoons and monsters, these pedantic fictions and Oriental charades? The illustrators of the *Mascherata,* in their praiseworthy efforts at stylization, occasionally found a happy compromise.[22] But how were they to represent Thetis, with a tree on her head, and four feet (two lion paws and two bird claws), or Vitumnus, whose figure was composed of an eye, three human heads, a hawk, a fish, and a hippopotamus? [23]

Such oddities may pass muster in spectacles of this type—processions, masques, ballets, where the designer need not fear an excess of variety or overloading; a multiplicity of figures, motley brilliance in the total effect, and profusion and extravagance of detail are even desirable in this domain.[24] But taste and restraint would seem to exclude them from among veritable works of art.

*

[20] See Bottari, *Raccolta di lettere,* I, Letters LVII to LXVI. V. Borghini, it is true, denies that he wishes to impose his ideas too strictly; see *ibid.,* Letter LXII (to Bronzino): "But pay no heed to my words unless you think they will produce the right result; since I mean only to set forth my own ideas, and not to lay down the law."

[21] See *supra,* pp. 252 f.

[22] See our art. cit., pp. 237–239.

[23] Here we have a "hieroglyph," reconstructed from Plutarch (*Isis and Osiris*), where a similar figure is described as seen in the temple of Sais. Vincenzo Borghini in all probability took this figure from the *Hieroglyphica* of Pierio Valeriano (Basel, 1556), Bk. XXXI, p. 219, and fig.: *Humanae vitae conditio.* Baldini, too, refers to Valeriano, and to Horapollo.

[24] See Lasca (*op. cit.,* Dedication), which calls for "rich and gay garments, unsparingly decorated (*lavorati senza risparmio*)"; de' Rossi has much to say, in both his accounts, of the brilliance and variety of the costumes; Baldini maintains that the organizer of the affair wished to array the gods as "strangely" as possible. In other words, all three write like costume designers.

AND NEVERTHELESS these gods of carnival find their way into art as well—first of all, into the monumental frescoes which, from the middle of the sixteenth century on, people the palaces of Rome, Florence, and Venice with a world of strange and hitherto unknown creatures. Examples are the Sala Regia and the Cappella Paolina in the Vatican, the Florentine Palazzo Vecchio, the Doge's Palace in Venice, and the Farnese Palace at Caprarola.

These vast decorative ensembles are typical products of the culture of the time. Their aim is less to give pleasure (*delectare*) than to teach (*prodesse*).[25] Each one of them develops a program elaborated at length by a humanist; this program has as center and primary aim the glorification of an individual, a family, a city, or an institution—but it is supported by a scaffolding of philosophical or religious ideas. Thus the decoration of the palace at Caprarola naturally revolves around two members of the Farnese family, Cardinal Alexander Farnese and Pope Paul III; but it is entirely based on the double theme of the Active and the Contemplative Life, which determines the total disposition—the first being illustrated in the summer and the second in the winter apartment. Each room belonging to the two suites illustrates some one aspect of "action" or "contemplation." For example, in the winter apartment, the Sala del Mappamondo invites us to consider Earth and Heaven, the splendor of Creation itself; the Sala dei Angeli and the Sala dei Sonni call to mind the celestial apparitions with which man is sometimes favored in wakeful hours or in dreams; lastly, the Sala dei Giudizi and the Sala della Penitenza invite solitary meditation upon Divine Justice.[26] Seen as a whole, the halls of the palace thus form a cycle, an unbroken system of thought.

Without doubt, nothing of all this is entirely new. We have already met with examples of such figurative encyclopedias, even in profane art, in the late medieval centuries. We have also seen how the Renaissance took up these didactic programs again, either retaining their theological disposition, or concentrating their emphasis on the mortal glory of some pontiff or *condottiere*.[27]

[25] See G. Toffanin, *La fine dell'umanesimo* (Turin, 1920), pp. 21–28.

[26] See Fritz Baumgart, *La Caprarola di Ameto Orti* (Rome, 1935); this is an extract from Vol. xxv of the *Studi Romanzi*. It deals with a Latin poem written around 1585, which describes all the paintings of the Palace, with commentary. Baumgart's introduction (pp. 1–19) develops some very interesting ideas on the great decorative cycles of the Counter Reformation and the new connections between art and humanism.

[27] See *supra*, Book I, Part 1, chap. iv.

But the decorations of the Palazzo Trinci, the Tempio Malatestiano, the Borgia Apartments, or the Stanza della Segnatura differ profoundly from those which concern us at present. The first group, as we have shown, were *Summae*—more or less debased or fragmentary, but for all that syntheses still essentially scholastic in character, bringing together the traditional elements (stars, sciences, virtues, Biblical and pagan heroes), and translating into visual form man's relationship with the world and the harmonies within nature, morality, and history. Now, on the other hand, we have to do in each case with one particular system, hatched by the ingenious brain of a humanist, who has mustered all his erudition to build an artificial edifice out of disparate elements—scenes, episodes, motifs chosen from the immense reservoir of pagan or Christian antiquity for this express purpose and by reason of their very singularity.

In the earlier ensembles, established data and accepted relations appeared beneath a familiar iconography; now, unfamiliar and apparently disconnected images mask a train of ideas which we fail to grasp. Each time we are faced with a new riddle. Mythology still plays a considerable role (even more so than in the past), but it is fatally submerged in allegory.

The humanists, who are the sovereign dictators of themes, draw their material from Fable as readily as from history or Scripture—often, indeed, being led in that direction by personal predilection;[28] but there is no doubt, also, that Fable, as they understand it, lends itself admirably to their purpose. This purpose is to translate a series of concepts into a succession of images; now, as we fully understand, the images of the gods are "emblems" replete with meaning.[29] They thus have an incomparable utility.

It therefore results that the humanist, less concerned with the plastic qualities of an image than with its symbolic possibilities, turns by preference to the most complex, overcharged, and bizarre mythological figures, believing them best fitted to exhibit all the nuances of his thought and the subtlety of his intentions. Another consequence is the strictness with which he insists upon the literal execution of his program by the artists whom he is called upon to direct. He is not content merely to provide a theme, or to trace the canvas in

[28] See *supra*, p. 265.
[29] See *supra*, p. 276.

its general lines; he enters into every detail—the position of a hand, the color of a fabric. And in truth such details are not a matter of indifference, since each is a *sign*, invested with meaning. Omission or modification might not affect the beauty of the image, but would threaten something of far greater importance—its truth to the thought which it is to embody.

*

Now it is precisely here, in the singular choice of figures for representation and in their detail, that the influence of the contemporary mythographers is apparent. We shall draw our examples from three famous cycles: Vasari's mythological decorations in the Palazzo Vecchio, in Florence; those of Taddeo Zuccaro in the Palazzo Farnese at Caprarola; and those of Jacopo Zucchi in the Palazzo Ruspoli, in Rome.

For the analysis and interpretation of these three decorative ensembles, we are fortunate in possessing explanatory texts of great value. Vasari, indeed, has left us marginal comments on his own work in the *Ragionamenti;* Zucchi deals with his in his *Discorso;* for Zuccaro, we have the extremely detailed instructions which he received from Annibale Caro.[30]

The *Ragionamenti* of Vasari was composed after the completion of his frescoes in the Palazzo Vecchio, in 1558, and published only after his death. In an imaginary conversation with Francesco de' Medici, he explains to the prince all the mythological representations and allegories with which he has covered the palace walls. In reality, his aim is certainly to make known to the wider public the meaning of a work which he himself knows to be unintelligible, especially since it is still further complicated by all sorts of allusions to the Medici family.

But Vasari himself is not the author of the commentaries which, with a somewhat naïve complacency, he showers upon his fictitious interlocutor. He

[30] Giorgio Vasari, *Ragionamenti del sig. cav. G. V. sopra le inventioni da lui dipinte in Firenze nel Palazzo di loro Altezze Serenissime, con lo Ill. et Ecc. sig. Don Francesco Medici allora Principe di Firenze . . .* (Florence, 1588).

Jacopo Zucchi, *Discorso sopra li dei de'gentili, e loro imprese* (Rome, 1602).

Annibale Caro, *Delle lettere familiari del commendatore A. C. . . . colla vita dell'autore scritta da Antonfederigo Seghezzi* (Bassano, 1782), II.

utilizes (though of course without acknowledgment) the letters of 1555 and 1556 in which Cosimo Bartoli provided him with the whole program for the Sala degli Elementi, and the rooms of Lorenzo, of Cosimo, and of Leo X.[31] And has he not made use of other documents as well? It is at all events curious to compare the description of Ops by Vasari himself[32] with that found in Cartari's *Imagini.* Not only are the attributes assigned to the goddess identical in the two texts; the explanations of these attributes are also alike, as will be seen in the accompanying comparative tabulation.

VASARI	CARTARI
Ragionamenti, III, in *Opere,* VIII (Milanesi ed.) [pp. 44–46]	*Imagini degli dei degli antichi* (1571 ed.) [pp. 204–6]
The coronet of towers	
The ancients caused this goddess to wear a coronet because . . . they wished to show that the whole earth with its coronet of cities, castles and villas was under her protection.	. . . she had on her head a coronet made of towers because the circumference of the earth, like a coronet, is full of cities, castles and villages.
The robe	
The robe full of flowers and branches shows the infinite variety of woods, fruit and herbs . . . which the earth . . . produces; the scepter in her hand denotes the multitude of realms and earthly powers.	The robe is woven of green herbs and on its hem are leafy boughs, this shows the trees, plants and herbs with which the earth is covered. She has a scepter in her hand and this signifies that on earth are all the realms . . . and shows the power . . . of the earthly lords.
The lions	
According to the poets, the cart drawn by lions has various meanings, but I think myself that the intention is to show that just as the lion . . . the king of all	Lions draw it, either . . . or . . . or again to show, by putting the lion, king of the other animals, under the yoke of the goddess Ops, that in the same way the

[31] See *Carteggio di Giorgio Vasari, edito e accompagnato di commento critico dal dott. Carlo Frey* (Munich, 1923), vol. I. (Vol. II issued by H. Frey in 1930, with the title: *Der literarische Nachlass G. Vasaris mit kritischem Apparate*). Frey attributes to Bartoli rather than Borghini the letters which have to do with the decoration of the Palazzo Vecchio: Sala degli Elementi, CCXX, CCXXI, pp. 409–414; Stanza di Lorenzo il Magnifico, CCXXXII, p. 436; Stanze di Cosimo il Vecchio, Cosimo il Duca, and Giovanni delle Bande Nere, CCXXXIV, pp. 438–440; Stanza di Leone X, CCXXXVI, pp. 446–449.

[32] Bartoli in *Carteggio di G. Vasari,* CCXXI, pp. 412–414.

Vasari	Cartari
the quadrupeds . . . is tied to the yoke of this goddess, so all the human kings and princes should remember that they are placed under the yoke of law.	lords of the world themselves are subject to the laws.
The empty seats . . . are to show . . . that on earth there are still many wild places which are not cultivated.	. . . they signify . . . that on this earth there are many uninhabited places.
The Corybantes . . . mainly to show to the princes who have the charge of their peoples that they should not always remain seated nor be idle, but should leave the seats vacant and stand upright, always in readiness for the needs of the people. . . . The armed Corybantes are to show that it behooves every worthy person to take up arms for the defense of the country and its lands.	. . . they stand upright and armed to demonstrate that not only the cultivators of the soil, but also the priests and those who rule the cities and kingdoms, must not remain seated and idle, but that each of them must take up his arms . . . for the defense of the country.
The tympana . . . by the cymbals we understand the two hemispheres of the world.	By the cymbals . . . one understands the rotundity of the earth, divided into two hemispheres.

For the moment, no final conclusions as to the influence of the *Imagini* can be drawn from this parallel, since the painting of the Camera di Opi was begun before the first publication of the book; it cannot be denied, however, that even if we did not have the *Ragionamenti,* Cartari's text would apply perfectly to the Palazzo Vecchio goddess, and would account for her slightest attribute.[33]

Bartoli's choice of an Eastern divinity to personify the Earth should also be noted: under the name of Ops he describes, not the Roman goddess of the harvest, but Cybele with her Phrygian train. At Caprarola, however, we shall see figures even more frankly exotic.

33 The fresco may also be compared with Zaltieri's engraving (Cartari [1571 ed.], p. 207).

On November 11, 1562,[34] Annibale Caro addresses a long epistle to Taddeo Zuccaro, setting forth for the painter's benefit the terms in which he himself has conceived the decoration of the bedchamber "ordered" by the Farnese cardinal. The plan leaves no room for discussion, and we shall see that Taddeo Zuccaro carried it out with complete docility. Now from Caro's first lines, so close an analogy with Cartari's *Images of the Gods* is displayed that a detailed comparison of texts is again warranted (see tabulation of parallels below).

CARO in Vasari, *Opere,* VII (Milanesi ed.)	CARTARI *Imagini degli dei* (1571 ed.)
Aurora [p. 118]	[p. 99]
This I find can be done in several ways, but from all these I shall choose what seems to me can be painted gracefully.	They have described her in various ways, which are much more useful for writers than for those who want to represent her in images; consequently I shall not discuss them all, but only those few which seem to me better adapted to pictorial representation.
Let us make . . . a young woman of the kind of beauty which the poets use their ingenuity to express in words.	I will make a portrait of her, from the one which the poets have given.
Place in her hand a lamp or a lighted torch . . . Show her seated upon a chair . . . on a cart . . . drawn by a winged Pegasus or by two horses: paint her in one way or the other.	Some of them . . . place a lighted torch in her hand, and give her a cart drawn by the winged horse, Pegasus . . . Homer, however, gives her not Pegasus, but two other horses. . . . To sum up, everyone describes her as he pleases.
The Night [p. 120]	[p. 330]
She should have . . . black wings, spread out as if she were flying.	She was . . . made in the shape of a woman with two great black wings at her shoulders, spread out so that she seemed to be flying.
She should have . . . in one (hand) a sleeping white child to signify Sleep, in the other a black one that seems asleep, and signifies Death.	She had on her left arm a white infant asleep, and a black one, also asleep, on her right arm . . . the latter was Death, the former Sleep.

[34] *Delle lettere* (cf. *supra,* p. 288, n. 30), II, pp. 204–215, Letter CLXXXVIII.

Caro	Cartari
Her cart should be of bronze, with the wheels clearly spaced at four places to signify the four vigils.	The poets imagine her with a four-wheeled cart, which signifies, according to Boccaccio, the four parts of the night, as soldiers divide it.
Her complexion should be dark, her cloak black, and black her hair . . . the sky around her should be the darkest blue and dotted with many stars.	She is dark all over, but her dress is somewhat shining, and painted so as to represent the decoration of the sky.
The Moon–Isis [p. 121]	[p. 122]
. . . with long, abundant and rather curly hair . . .	Her head was adorned with long and abundant hair, lightly curled.
[p. 122] . . . with a flat disk, polished and shining like a mirror, in the middle of her forehead, on which there are snakes here and there, and above them, some ears of corn . . .	. . . and in the middle of her forehead . . . a sort of round, flat, and polished object, which shone like a mirror; on both sides were snakes, above which there were ears of corn . . .
. . . with a crown on her head, made either of dittany . . . or of various flowers, according to Martianus, or of sunflowers, as others say.	[p. 119] . . . a garland of southern wood . . . [p. 122] . . . crowned with a beautiful garland of various flowers . . .
. . . some want her dress to be long, down to her feet, some want it short, up to her knees.	[p. 109] . . . with a dress that covered it . . . (the statue of Diana) . . . down to her feet . . . The thin dress . . . descended below her knees.
Pausanias . . . describes her clothed in a deerskin.	[p. 104] We read in Pausanias that there was in Arcadia one of her (statues) clothed in a deerskin.
. . . a dress of very thin veiling in different colors, white, yellow, red.	[p. 122] . . . her dress, of different colors, was of very thin veiling; and it looked now white, now yellow . . . and now . . . red.

CARO	CARTARI
. . . and another dress all black, but bright and shining, dotted with numerous stars, with a moon in the middle and a border all around decorated with flowers and fruits which hang like tassels.	She had still another dress all black, and yet bright and shining: this one was almost covered with glittering stars, in the middle of which there was a glittering moon; all around the border were hung all sorts of flowers and fruits, most beautifully arranged.
	[p. 100]
You must represent her with bare arms.	. . . with bare arms . . .
	[p. 101]
. . . she should carry a lighted torch in her right hand, and a slackened bow in the left; this bow, according to Claudian, is made of horn; according to Ovid, it is made of gold.	This same Claudian says that her bow . . . is made of horn, thereby contradicting Ovid, who makes it golden . . .
	[p. 104]
. . . and two snakes in her left hand . . .	. . . a lighted torch in one hand, two snakes in the other . . .
	[p. 122]
. . . with a golden vase, whose handle is a snake, looking swollen with venom, and whose base is decorated with palm leaves.	. . . hanging from her left hand she had a golden vase, which had for a handle a snake which looked swollen with venom, and at the base there was some decoration made with palm-leaves . . .
	[p. 106]
She should ride a chariot drawn by two horses, a black one and a white one.	Of these two (horses) one was black, the other white, according to Boccaccio.
. . . or . . . by a mule, according to Festus Pompeius . . .	Festus Pompeius writes that the chariot of the Moon was drawn by a mule.
[pp. 122 f.]	[p. 107]
. . . or by steers, according to Claudian and Ausonius. And if you make them steers, they should have very small horns, and a white spot on the right flank.	There are those who had the chariot of the Moon drawn by steers, like Claudian . . . Ausonius Gallus does the same . . . In Egypt an ox was consecrated to the Moon . . . it was necessary for him to have a white spot on the right flank, and very small horns . . .

Caro	Cartari
Harpocrates and Angerona [p. 127]	[p. 374]
The figure of (Harpocrates) is that of a youngster, or of a boy . . . with a finger on his mouth, commanding silence.	His statue, according to Apuleius and Martianus, was that of a young man, who kept his finger on his mouth, as one does when signalling others to keep silent . . .
	[p. 376]
He should carry in his hand a branch of peach-tree and, if you like, a garland of leaves from that tree.	The peach-tree was dedicated to Harpocrates, because that tree has leaves similar to the human tongue.
	[p. 374]
Others represented that same god as a figure without a face, with a small hat on its head, clothed in a wolfskin, and all covered with eyes and ears.	To represent the god of silence they sometimes also made a figure without a face, with a very small hat on its head, clothed in a wolfskin, and almost entirely covered with eyes and ears.
	[pp. 373 f.]
(Angerona) Her figure was that of a woman placed on an altar, with the mouth gagged and sealed.	Angerona was placed on an altar . . . her statue had a piece of cloth around its neck, which gagged its mouth also.
The Lares [p. 124]	[pp. 448 ff.]
. . . one could make the Lares two young men, who were the protecting geniuses of private houses: two youngsters, clothed in dogskins, each with a sort of short coat thrown over his left shoulder in such a way that it would come under the right one, to show that they are alert and ready to guard the house.	The Lares were considered to be spirits, private protectors of houses; for this reason they were represented in the shape of two young men clothed in dogskins. They were also . . . furnished with short cloaks thrown back upon the left shoulder in such a way that they would come under the right, so that they might be quickly ready for their duty.
Mercury [p. 123]	[p. 334]
. . . Mercury should be represented in the usual way.	Poets describe him without (a beard).

Caro	Cartari
. . . beardless, or with the first down of a young man . . .	. . . Many, however, say that he is starting to grow his first down.
Some put wings above his ears, and make gold feathers come out of his hair.	[p. 322] . . . with two little wings above his ears . . . [p. 323] . . . with . . . hair . . . in which were some golden feathers . . . the points just showing (Apuleius).
The House of Sleep [p. 125] Let us represent Sleep . . . in the first place one must represent his house; Ovid sets it in Lemnos and in the country of the Cimmerians, Homer in the Aegean sea, Statius among the Ethiopians, Ariosto in Arabia. . . . a bed, which, being supposedly made of ebony, should be black, and covered with black sheets; on this bed you will place Sleep.	[p. 334] Ovid . . . has described the place where Sleep dwells; according to him it is in the country of the Cimmerians . . . according to Homer it is in Lemnos . . . according to Statius among the Ethiopians; finally, Ariosto places it in Arabia. Ovid makes him sleep on a bed of ebony, all covered with black sheets . . .
According to some others, he has two coats, a white one outside, a black one inside, with wings on his shoulders . . . He should carry a horn under his arm . . . and a stick in one hand.	[pp. 333 f.] (Philostratus) depicts Sleep . . . with two coats, a white one outside, a black one inside . . . and puts a horn in his hand . . . Besides, he carries . . . a stick in his hand.
[p. 126] Let us imagine that in this place there are two doors: one made of ivory, out of which come the false dreams, and one made of horn, out of which come the true dreams.	[p. 333] Virgil imagined that there are two doors through which the dreams come, one made of horn, the other of ivory; through the former pass the true dreams, through the latter the false ones.
. . . this elm, described by Virgil, under whose foliage he places innumerable images . . .	Virgil also held that in the middle of the entrance to hell there is a great elm . . . and that from its leaves . . . hang the false and empty dreams.

This comparison is again conclusive. From the first, one is struck by the small number of "classical" figures proposed by Caro. Though his description of the House of Sleep (not, for that matter, easily translatable into painting) is taken from Ovid and Virgil, the details which he furnishes to the artist are for the most part bizarre and overwhelmingly complex.

Zuccaro, however, seems to have accommodated himself to them well enough; at all events, he has rendered them with servile accuracy. True enough, whenever a possibility of choice is left open, he has managed to reject the more complex image in favor of the simpler one. He has preferred the Diana of Claudian to the Isis of Apuleius, freeing her forehead of the wings, horns, ears of wheat, mirror, serpents, and crown with which his over-learned author would have endowed her.[35] But in a larger sense, the painter has not ventured to modify in any way the compositions proposed for the arches and lunettes of the hall, which are as enigmatic as could be desired: Harpocrates (the infant Horus, wrongly identified by the Greeks as the god of silence) is there carrying his fishing rod, Angerona wearing her gag, and Brizos standing under the elm with enchanted foliage.

Even if Caro had not taken the trouble to give us his sources, we would have no difficulty in seeing that they are always those used by Cartari. The frequent textual identity of the descriptions proves that Caro made use of the *Imagini* in drawing up his instructions—just as Vasari was able to do in commenting on his own finished work.

In the light of these observations, the role of the scholar as adviser of artists may seem to lose some of its importance and interest. Indeed, one of two things is true: either Caro had read Cartari, and acted merely as an intermediary between the book and the artist; or (and this is improbable) Caro did not know the book, but himself took the trouble of looking in earlier authors for the elements of his descriptions. But as his authors are the same ones quoted in the *Imagini*—Pausanias, Apuleius, Macrobius, and Martianus Ca-

[35] The Hours have not been shown preceding Aurora's chariot. On the other hand, Night is burdened with her two children, Sleep and Death; this is to be regretted, especially in view of what Guercino was later able to do with this beautiful allegory. In a small room near the Sala dell'Aurora, Federigo Zuccaro painted a monstrous figure, the Hermathena, which is of course described in Cartari (1571 ed.), p. 356.

104. Harpocrates and Angerona

pella—we are led to the same conclusion. Caro's intervention was not necessary. Had Taddeo Zuccaro held the *Imagini* in his hands, and known no more than the names of the personages whom he was to represent, the result would have been exactly the same paintings we see today in the Camera dell'Aurora. For any painter whose library contains such a reference work as this, the counsels of the humanists are superfluous. We need only look, for example, at the passage in Caro's letter dealing with Harpocrates and Angerona:

"The figure of Harpocrates is that of a youth, or rather a child . . . holding his finger to his mouth. He holds a fishing rod in his hand."

"Others have represented the same god as a faceless figure, wearing a small hat on his head, wrapped in a wolfskin, and entirely covered with eyes and ears."

"The figure of Angerona is that of a woman standing upon an altar, her mouth bound with a gag."

It would have been simpler to say, "Represent Harpocrates and Angerona according to the *Imagini degli dei,*" where, indeed,[36] they appear fully described and ready for use (*fig. 104*).

The painter needed nothing else; the explanatory text is a mere accessory, as Caro himself recognizes in a letter to Luca Martini where, after having briefly sketched the figures of certain gods—in particular that of Juno according to Martianus Capella—he concludes: ". . . I have given you a

[36] The picture, it is true, dates from 1571; but since it exactly illustrates Cartari's text it none the less supports our case.

summary description of the costumes, according to the written descriptions which I have found. To tell you the meaning of each would be a lengthy undertaking; for that matter, they are ordinarily known."[37]

Thus the letters of the scholars—busy men, overburdened with commissions, preparing tasks for other busy men—come to assume the terse, practical form of a reference list, toward which Cartari's *Images* also tends. One other set of instructions (of Cosimo Bartoli to Vasari)[38] presents an especially curious feature. The author is proposing a certain number of allegories for use in the Sala di Lorenzo in the Palazzo Vecchio, and in the margin opposite the mention of each, he enters a brief descriptive note. Examples are:

"Prudentia: donna con lalie e serpi alla conciatura della testa."

"Buonevento: un povero in un mano la tazza, in l'altra spighe di grano."

"La Fama: la sapete, fatta da voi mille volte."[39]

The last words seem to betray Bartoli's impatience—his weariness at having, like a manual, continually to offer the same recipe. The letter dates from 1556, the year of the publication of the *Imagini*. Cartari's work came as an answer to this very need, making it unnecessary for artists to turn elsewhere for information, or for scholars to furnish texts and repeat themselves indefinitely. There was, none the less, a continuation of demands from artists, and advice from scholars. But from this time on, the names of individual program makers become increasingly unimportant; we know in advance the sources from which they draw, and we hold the key to the most obscure representations. Whoever may have been their immediate provider, the "arguments" are a needless repetition of those which henceforth are to be found conveniently brought together and classified in the *Imagini* and the other mythological treatises.

Further confirmation will be found in the *Discorso* of Zucchi and in his frescoes on the ceiling of the Palazzo Ruspoli. Like the *Ragionamenti* of his master Vasari, Zucchi's *Discorso* is a commentary intended to render his own

[37] Bottari, *Lettere*, III, pp. 206–208, Letter XCV.

[38] *Carteggio di G. Vasari*, ed. cit., p. 436, Letter CXXXII.

[39] "Prudence: a woman with wings and serpents as headdress."

"Good Fortune: a poor man holding a cup in one hand, in the other stalks of grain."

"Fame: you know this figure, you've painted it a thousand times."

painting intelligible: "chiarire il pensier nostro circa alla nostra pittura."[40] To revive a play upon words which his admirers abused, *penna* and *pennello* were rivals in his hands, each illuminating the other, and greatly to our ad-

105. Diana

106. Saturn

vantage. For if the analysis of the frescoes is a laborious task, at least we have no difficulty, thanks to the *Discorso,* in recognizing once more the mythographical traditions for which our manuals have served as a vehicle.

The title gives us a first hint—*Discorso sopra li dei de' gentili.* This is the title of the medieval treatises—of the *De diis gentium* of Rabanus Maurus; Zucchi makes no secret, indeed, of the dependence of his composition on the *Genealogia deorum* of Boccaccio.

The Oriental element is equally apparent. Zucchi knows the gods worshipped by the Libyans, Scythians, Persians, Egyptians, and Assyrians (p. 5); he knows both Jupiter "Heliopolites" and Jupiter Ammon (p. 18). When he describes Apollo, he does not forget to include among his attributes the hawk, the crocodile, and the scarabaeus (p. 25).

[40] Like Vasari's *Ragionamenti,* the *Discorso* did not appear till after the author's death, in 1602. The text, which is very rare, has been published, with a valuable introduction, by Saxl, *Antike Götter in der Spätrenaissance; ein Freskenzyklus und ein Discorso des Jacopo Zucchi,* Studien der Bibl. Warburg, VIII (Leipzig, 1927).—Cf. also A. Calcagno, *Jacopo Zucchi e la sua opera a Roma* (Rome, 1933).

After this, when he writes of Saturn (p. 15), "There would still be much to say of this god, but two things restrain me: one is that I fear my own ignorance; the other is the great number of scholarly books dealing with this material which have recently been published, where every detail will be found noted," we have every reason to think that he is alluding to Giraldi, Conti, or Cartari. Furthermore, there is an indubitable connection between Zucchi's frescoes and the engraved illustrations in Cartari. Each god painted by Zucchi is surrounded by an unbelievable number of attributes, many of them highly unusual. Diana, for example, holds not only her bow and arrows, but a key (recalling the functions of Lucina), while at her feet are seen three animal heads—dog, horse, and boar—recalling the Luna Triformis.[41]

But the *Discorso* has a special interest for us. Obviously, Zucchi is satisfied neither with the subject matter of his paintings nor with his commentary on it. Mythology is displeasing to him; it would not be too much to say that it inspires him with horror. He rails unceasingly against "the vain and false religion of the Gentiles," their blind ignorance, their obstinacy, and the foulness and criminality of their gods.[42]

If he is sincere, one wonders why he has chosen a theme which so repels him. He attempts to give an explanation, though not without some confusion (p. 9). Troubled by the dimensions of his task, he had to turn to mythology as the only possible source for so elaborate a program.[43] Furthermore, he felt himself constrained by tradition, for does not Armenini cite as the prime model for palace decoration the ceiling of the Palazzo del Te in Mantua, where there are "many gods, with Jove at the center"? So Zucchi resigned himself to reproducing the traditional forms, but he did so reluctantly.

There was, however, one means of reconciling the demands of art and conscience—that is, to endow these shameful images with allegorical meaning. Zucchi is not unaware of this possibility, but he shows himself much more scrupulous with regard to it than do most of his contemporaries. He agrees that Fable contains the sap of truth beneath its rind, but he has no praise for those who would muffle this truth beneath a cloak of lies or hide it behind a

[41] See *figs. 105* and *106*. Cf. the engraving in Cartari (1571 ed.), p. 117, fig. 93.

[42] This is the same expression used by Cardinal Paleotto: "sporcizie sceleratissime"; cf. *supra*, p. 267.

[43] Cf. *supra*, p. 268.

veil of obscenities: "Se ben sò, che senza dubbio mi sarà imputato . . . ad ignoranza il pensare che sotto queste scorze non ci sia del suco. . . . Dico che nol niego. Ma non loderò mai, chi con il velame degl'adulterii, i latrocinii, stupri, e mille cose oscene, e brutte, e con la veste della bugia, vorrà ornare, ò coprire l'istessa verità della potenza e sapienza divina" (p. 8).[44]

In spite of this declaration, and with manifest inconsistency, Zucchi cannot resist offering allegorical interpretations upon occasion, as of the attributes of Pan or Juno; [45] but, in the last analysis, both his discomfort and his remorse are characteristic. He is among those who were most profoundly touched by the spirit of the Counter Reformation, and we have already seen the source of attitudes such as his in the writings inspired by the Council of Trent which deal with the essential character of art, its duties, and its aim.

*

THERE ARE few occasions other than in monumental painting on walls and ceilings for this learned mythology to display its weighty paraphernalia in complete freedom. Sculpture, as Armenini observes,[46] is not fond of dealing with images of such complexity, and Michelangelo may after all be forgiven for not having adorned his statue of Night with a sheaf of poppies and a star-strewn mantle, since "these are things more appropriate to the painter than the sculptor." [47] Paintings in smaller dimensions seldom permit of such a lavish display of figures and attributes; a canvas cannot be overloaded like a carnival chariot. Certain allegories of Bronzino, however, meet this challenge successfully—among them the enigmatic *Fortuna* in the Uffizi, and the *Time and Folly with Venus and Cupid* in the National Gallery, London. And Federigo Zuccaro succeeds in massing in his *Olympus* a crowd of divinities, each weighed down by his burden of symbols in illustration of the motto "Cuique suum" (*fig. 107*).

[44] "I well know that I shall undoubtedly be charged with ignorance if I question that there is sap under rind of this sort. . . . I do not deny that it may be found. But I shall never laud him who attempts, under the veil of adultery, theft, rape, and a thousand obscene and ugly things, and with the garb of deceit, to dress up or to conceal the very truths of the divine power and wisdom."

[45] *Discorso*, p. 66 (of the god Pan): "But there would be much to say here of this figure, and *of the disguises* which it assumes"; p. 51 (of Juno), see *supra*, pp. 92 f. and p. 272, n. 47.

[46] *Il Riposo*, p. 49.

[47] The point that Vasari thought he was proving when he painted the same figure of Night (Rome, Galleria Colonna), giving her the attributes that Michelangelo had denied her.

107. *Olympus*

Rome and Florence appear to be the leading centers of this new iconography. Though it is true that the Venetians generally disliked bookish programs and overprecise schemes,[48] even they show the erudite and expository tendencies of the art of this time. In the garlands of mythological nudes with which Veronese and his disciples, the Fasolos and the Zelottis,[49] decorated the Palladian villas,[50] one is inclined at first to see nothing more than an irruption of fantasy; but they, also, form cycles, "subjects in sequence, connected by one general idea." They are variations on an edifying theme, "inventioni morali," as Ridolfi defines them;[51] sometimes true psychomachies, combats of the soul. As for the mythological paintings in the Doge's Palace, where everything sings the glories of the "Most Serene Republic" and the wisdom of the senators, political maxims are there given visual translation. Thus, when Tintoretto in 1577 paints his famous series—*Ariadne and Bacchus, Minerva and Mars, Vulcan's Forge, Mercury and the Three Graces*—he wishes to express union, the true strength of the Republic. Ariadne, receiving the homage of a god near the sea, is Venice herself; Minerva repels Mars, just as the Senate keeps the horrors of war at a distance, thereby assuring abundance and prosperity. The Graces represent the rewards in store for the good citizen. Vulcan and his Cyclopes, alternately striking the forge, symbolize the joint effort of the senators to forge arms for the city, as guarantee of her power and glory.

There is nothing exceptional in these subjects themselves, but careful observation will reveal many details which may at first escape notice. Thus, one of the Graces holds a rose, another a myrtle branch, while the third is leaning on a die, of the sort used in games of chance.[52] What is the explanation of these attributes? The myrtle and rose, both dear to Venus, are symbols of enduring love. The die marks a reciprocity of benefits, since dice come and go. Finally,

[48] E. Müntz, *Histoire de l'art pendant la Renaissance*, points this out on several occasions: II, pp. 63, 770, etc. Cf. Dolce, *Dialogo della pittura* (1745 ed.), p. 251.

[49] Zelotti is particularly known for his decorations in the Villa Cataio; we have the detailed program of this decoration, which was influenced by Caprarola, in G. Betussi, *Ragionamento sopra il Cathaio* (Padua, 1573).

[50] See G. Loukomski, *Les fresques de Paul Veronèse et de ses disciples* (Paris, 1928), esp. p. 90; and Pallucchini, *Gli affreschi di Veronese a Maser* (Bergamo, 1939).

[51] *Le meraviglie dell'arte* (Venice, 1648).

[52] Veronese and his pupils have represented them with the same attributes at the Villa Porto-Barbaran, near Vicenza. See reprod. in Loukomski, *op. cit.*, p. 241.

if the Graces have Mercury as their companion, it is because they are to bestow themselves only in due measure, and as reason decrees (*fig. 108*).

This is the explanation offered by a contemporary commentator;[53] it coincides, almost word for word, with what is said by Cartari in describing and reproducing an identical image.[54]

The four bronze statues of Sansovino's Loggetta, to which we have already alluded,[55] teach the same lesson as the canvases of Tintoretto. Pallas sets forth the wisdom and ability of the senators; Mercury, their knowledge and eloquence; Apollo, their truly unexampled harmony and accord. The figure of Peace, lastly, is "that peace so dear to the Republic," which assures her prosperity and hegemony. In short, these four divinities give expression to the principles and effects of sound government.[56]

But how does it happen that in Venice these uplifting intentions remain for the most part unsuspected? Elsewhere, our wonder and curiosity are constantly aroused; enigmas confront us wherever we turn. But here, nothing urges us to look deeper, so completely are mind and senses satisfied by the splendor of the forms. The mannerism of Florence and Rome, hollow and grudging in spite of its bombast, makes a virtue of obscurity. Its pedantry and its labored hieroglyphics are completely foreign to the splendid abundance of the Venetians, whose overflowing vitality makes them scorn the artificial fruit, lacking all aroma and taste, that ripens in libraries. Never, for their part, will the Venetians consent to sacrifice the "plastic" to the "intellectual," or to allow form to degenerate in the paralyzing embrace of the symbol. Hence the superb ease with which they free the gods from their entangling accessories. Like a certain character in Flaubert, the divinities of Vasari or Zucchi "disparaissent sous l'abondance de leurs attributs." The great robust bodies painted by Tintoretto and Veronese refuse to be stifled by such accretions. They extend their athletic limbs freely in space—richer in mean-

[53] See F. Sansovino, *Venetia descritta* (1663), p. 338. The same text, with only slight differences in wording, appears in C. Ridolfi, *Le Meraviglie dell'Arte* (Berlin ed., 1924), II, p. 43 (life of Tintoretto).

[54] *Imagini* (1571 ed.), pp. 562–563 and fig., p. 564. On another celebrated painting by Tintoretto, *The Milky Way*, see the analysis by E. Mandowsky, "*The Origin of the Milky Way* in the National Gallery," *The Burlington Magazine* LXII (1938), pp. 88–93.

[55] See *supra*, pp. 210 f.

[56] See F. Sansovino, *op. cit.*, pp. 307–308. The artist himself gives this interpretation; the figures of Venus and Jupiter in the bas-reliefs symbolize respectively Cyprus and Crete.

ing, in their opulent nudity, than all possible emblems: "Is not the human form the most expressive of symbols?" [57] In instinctively preferring the classical types to exotic or barbaric figures, the Venetians were restating a verity which was that of Greece. "When the Greek sculptors," says L. Ménard,[58]

108. Mercury and the Graces

"use symbolic references it is always in an inconspicuous way. . . . The attributes consecrated by tradition accompany the images of the gods, emphasizing by means of allegorical allusion the physical characteristics of each, and recalling his special role in the universal republic; whereas the figure itself expresses directly through its forms, its bearing and gestures, the moral aspect of the god, and his relations with mankind, his distinctive function in the city."

[57] E. Renan, *Etudes d'hist. relig.: Les relig. de l'antiquité*, p. 36.

[58] L. Ménard, *Du polythéisme hellénique*, IV, p. 159.

It was the mission of the gods of Veronese and Tintoretto to celebrate the glory and prosperity of Venice, and they are not unworthy of that mission. The superb architecture of backs and thighs, the mellow contours of satiny flesh, sing the pride of power and the delights of peace.[59]

*

IF ITALIAN ART, after 1550, is indebted to the mythological manuals, the same may be said of literature; but here we turn for our examples to France, England, Germany, and Spain. Again we shall be following the gods in their migrations.

In France, as early as the beginning of the sixteenth century, before Ronsard, Jean Le Maire de Belges becomes "the popularizer of mythology in French letters."[60] The gods, in fact, play a prominent part in his *Illustrations des Gaules et singularités de Troie.*[61] To be sure, they most often appear decked out in unaccustomed fashion, but this is because Jean Lemaire's knowledge of Fable stems not from ancient sources, but from medieval or contemporary compilations:[62] the *Mythologies* of Fulgentius, the *Etymologies* of Isidore, the *Supplementum chronicarum* of Jacopo da Bergamo; above all, the *Antiquitates* of Annius of Viterbo, and the *Genealogia deorum* of Boccaccio, with Demogorgon and his progeny[63]—a list of titles long familiar to us.

Jean Le Maire adopts not only the subject matter of these compilations but their spirit as well. Convinced that mythology is "rich in great mysteries and in poetic and philosophical meanings, containing fruitful substance beneath the artificial rind of Fable" (I, 4), he does his best to make it reveal at one moment historical allusion, at another some cosmic or moral meaning.

[59] A further comparison may be made between the pure allegories of Veronese, personifying abstractions like Respect and Scorn, Constancy and Infidelity (National Gallery), and allegories of the type used by Ripa. On the one hand we have noble forms, spontaneously living out the moral idea; on the other, the human figure treated as a mere scaffolding upon which to attach a whole panoply of attributes.

[60] See G. Doutrepont, *Jean Lemaire de Belges et la Renaissance* (Brussels, 1934), p. 386.

[61] Esp. chap. xxviii: "Les Dieux convoqués aux noces de Thétis et de Pélée"; see the edition, by Stecher, of *Oeuvres* (Louvain, 1882), I, pp. 204 ff.

[62] See Doutrepont, *op. cit.*, chap. i: "L'Erudition de seconde main dans les 'Illustrations'" (abstract of the borrowings, Annexe I): esp. paragraph 2, on the borrowings from the *Genealogia deorum.*

[63] See *Oeuvres*, I, pp. 344–346: "Les noms des acteurs alleguez en ce premier livre."

Thus, after telling of the marriage of Thetis and Peleus, he undertakes, in his Chapter xxv, "the moral as well as the philosophical and historical explanation of the nuptials described above"; and when, in Chapter xxxi, he reports "the petitions and proposals made to Paris Alexander by the two mighty goddesses, Juno and Pallas," he does not fail to add to his account "the explanation in full of their clothing and adornments, their importance and power; from which things he who looks carefully may find much allegorical and moral fruit hidden under the colors of poetry." Allegory, for him, is even something more than a method of interpretation: it justifies lascivious scenes and sensual images by virtue of the weight of truth which they conceal.[64] For the rest, his pseudo-classical divinities are intimately fused with the moral abstractions of the *Roman de la Rose*.[65]

Thus the work of Jean Le Maire is seen to be grafted to a mythological tradition with whose origins and ramifications we are well acquainted; it has, nevertheless, its own original savor and charm. The author's imagination, naïve and precious at the same time, lends new grace to these debased immortals, recreating around them a poetic atmosphere which, if not that of Olympus, at least belongs to another enchanted kingdom, the realm of faërie.

*

NEXT we must ask whether the poets of the Pléiade looked, in their turn, to anthologies and manuals for elements of their vast erudition. Did they, at need, consult the new and invaluable repertories of information assembled by such men as Giraldi, Conti, and Cartari, who were almost their contemporaries?

As to Ronsard, the question is a complicated one; it has, indeed, given pause to two critics, Pierre de Nolhac and Paul Laumonier. Both express the opinion that the poet often gets his mythological information at second hand.[66] But who is his intermediary? Ronsard began to write before the publi-

[64] Doutrepont, *op. cit.*, p. 317.

[65] P. Laumonier, *Ronsard, poète lyrique* (Paris, 1910), pp. 409 ff.

[66] See P. Laumonier, *op. cit.*, pp. 379–380 and n. 1; and the article on "La bibliothèque de Ronsard," *Revue du* XVIe *siècle*, XIV (1927), pp. 4, 5, 6, 14. Laumonier notes among books owned by the poet the *Dictionary* of Hesychius, several collections of *sententiae* and *exempla;* and especially the *Florilegium* of Stobaeus, by which he was extensively inspired from 1553 to 1555. P. de Nolhac (*Ron-*

cation of the great Italian manuals; but he was a pupil of Dorat, who still made use of Boccaccio's *Genealogia deorum,* and of the 1535 collection already referred to [67] which included the treatises on fables by Hyginus and Fulgentius and was augmented in later editions by the *Libellus* of Albricus and extracts from Giraldi. From these various treatises, and from his impassioned and feverish reading of classical texts, Ronsard appears to have composed his own mythological reference file.[68]

On the other hand, when the *Mythologia* of Natale Conti appeared, Ronsard in all probability knew the work, for its second edition was dedicated to Charles IX, and Ronsard was Charles' official poet. This dedication resulted in "naturalizing" the *Mythologia* in France, where, as we already know,[69] it was to have an outstanding vogue. We cannot, however, prove any specific borrowing by Ronsard from Conti, though K. Borinski claims to have detected a direct influence of the *Mythologia* in the *Hymnes.*[70] But on the other hand, the work is cited in the famous commentary on the *Amours* by Marc-Antoine Muret, and this is worthy of note. Muret's commentary, indeed, constitutes a sort of catalogue of what was known to the poets of the Pléiade; almost all the authors whom they read are mentioned in it.[71] After the death of Muret, from 1587 on, successive editors several times added to the glosses of the learned humanist, as if to sum them up: "Voyez la *Mythologie française* de Noël Le Comte. . . . Noël Le Comte décrit et expose excellement cette histoire. . . ." [72] It would seem, in other words, that they considered Conti's dictionary a wholly fitting—perhaps even sufficient—source of clarification for obscurities found in Ronsard.

And, in fact, Ronsard's mythology and that of Conti have more than one

---

sard et l'humanisme [Paris, 1921], p. 99) thinks that Ronsard must have used the *Dictionarium nominum propriorum* of Robert Estienne.

[67] See *supra,* p. 226, n. 22.

[68] See Laumonier, *op. cit.,* p. 379.

[69] See É. Picot, "Les Italiens en France au XVIe siècle," *Bulletin Italien,* III (1903), p. 128. From 1583 on, Conti's work was printed with the treatise on the Muses (*Mythologiae musarum Libellus*) written by Geoffroi Linocier, a relative of the publisher and a friend of Ronsard. One proof of Conti's popularity in France in the seventeenth century occurs in the *Dictionnaire* of Furetière (1690); in the article *Mythologie,* the definition of the term is followed by the following reference: "Noël Le Comte, also called Natalis Comes, has written of mythology."

[70] K. Borinski, *Renaissance und Reformation,* p. 30.

[71] P. de Nolhac, *op. cit.,* p. 101.

[72] See *Les Amours de Pierre de Ronsard commentées par Marc-Antoine de Muret,* ed. Vaganay (Paris, 1910): p. 21, the Gorgons; p. 33, Bellerophon; p. 37, the Sirens.

point in common. Ronsard, too, draws indiscriminately and simultaneously from all possible sources: [73] he welcomes all divinities—whether from Asia, Greece, Rome, or Egypt, whether primitive, classical, or decadent.[74] He even turns by preference to the least known and most bizarre texts, as a display of erudition, showing himself in this more pedantic than du Bellay, who did not think that "Lycophron feust plus excellent qu'Homère, pour estre plus obscur." [75] Lastly, faithful here to the teachings of Dorat, who had transmitted to him "this troublesome medieval heritage," [76] Ronsard conceives of Fable as a "philosophia moralis." On his own account, he enjoys deifying abstractions and likes to "disguise the truth of things beneath a mantle of Fable." In this, again, he resembles the Italian mythographer.

But with Ronsard, as needs hardly be said, through the intensity and fire of study this bookish learning comes to life and is transfigured.[77] In the true sense of the word, the poet lives in a state of *enthusiasm:* he is haunted by these divinities, who from his earliest youth have accompanied his footsteps "au profond des vallées" and under the "ombrage incertain" of the forest. The confused, ill-digested mythology with which he has gorged himself does not stifle his imagination, but rather intoxicates and exalts it, for within that mythology there vibrates for him the deep pulse of nature.

*

THE PIOUS du Bartas, Protestant though he was, and author of a poem on Biblical subjects, did not feel that he could deprive his *Sepmaine* [78] of the charms of mythology. He explains himself in his "Avertissement au lecteur" not without a certain embarrassment: "Others [i.e., other critics] would have me banish the words Flora, Amphitrite, Mars, Venus, Vulcan, Jupiter, Pluto, etc., from my book. They are indeed to some extent right, but I would have

[73] Laumonier, *op. cit.*, p. 379; de Nolhac, *op. cit.*, pp. 85–86.

[74] Laumonier, *ibid.*, and p. 380.

[75] (". . . that Lycophron was more excellent than Homer, through being more obscure.") *Deffence et illustration* (ed. Chamard [1904]), p. 158.

[76] G. Cohen, *Ronsard, sa vie et son oeuvre* (1932 ed.), p. 53; cf. *supra*, pp. 97 f. and nn. 63, 64.

[77] On the "living" character of mythology in Ronsard, see E. Bourciez, *Les Moeurs polies et la littérature de cour sous Henri* II, pp. 231–238.

[78] The first *Sepmaine* appeared in 1578; the second in 1584. We quote from the Rouen edition, with commentary (1602).

them note that I have used the names sparingly. And when one does appear, it is by metonymy, or through some allusion to their fables: something which has always been practiced by authors of Christian poems! Poetry has for so long been in possession of these terms of fable that she can only rid herself of them little by little. . . ."

As a matter of fact, the mythological allusions in the *Sepmaine* are so many and so learned that Simon Goulart, in his painstaking commentary on the poem (which, in this respect, recalls the commentary of Muret on Ronsard's *Amours*),[79] seems to find it necessary to pause long over them in explanation. Now to what authors does Goulart turn?

For Aeolus (p. 7) and Latona (p. 31) he consults "Noël des Contes, Vénitien," and recommends the same source to the reader: "Whoever wishes an explanation of this poetic invention, together with most others, should read the *Mythologie* of Noël des Contes, the Venetian."

Again, we find him invoking for Jupiter Ammon (p. 83) an authority who is equally familiar to us: "See fuller treatment in Gyraldus, in the second commentary of his *Histoire des dieux*." Shortly afterward (on Phoebus, p. 99) he cites Conti and Giraldi together.

Only Cartari is still lacking, but not for long. In explaining an allusion to Mars (p. 117), Goulart writes: "See Gyraldus, in the tenth book of his *Histoire des dieux*, Noël des Contes in his *Mythologie*, and Vincent Cartari in his *Images des dieux*."

Here, then, are our three Italian mythographers reunited, as we find them in several other passages of the same text.[80] Goulart, it is evident, had the works constantly at his elbow; they provided him with the key to all his difficulties.

*

IN FRANCE, as in Italy, the gods figured at this time in court entertainments, solemn *entrées*, and princely wedding celebrations. On occasions of this sort,

[79] See *supra*, p. 308. Goulart's commentary on the first *Sepmaine* dates from 1583; that on the first and second, from 1588–1589.

[80] As on p. 183, where Goulart cites "une figure" of Cartari's, in connection with the Furies, and gives exact references to the chapters of Conti and Cartari which deal with the matter. Similarly, in the *Seconde Sepmaine*, p. 87: "All this fully explained by N. des Contes, L. Gyrald, and Cartari in their mythologies" (in speaking of Rhea).

as one would expect, the influence of the Italian manuals also made itself felt. Thus, in the published text of the *Ballet comique de la Royne,* organized in 1582, the name of Natale Conti recurs.[81] The fact is of particular interest since the poets of the Pléiade—Dorat, Baïf, Ronsard himself—collaborated in these fetes. Thus, for the triumphal entrance of Charles IX into Paris and the crowning of Elizabeth of Austria, on March 6 and 25, 1572, Ronsard composed sonnets which were inscribed on the bases of statues set up along the processional way, statues of Juno, the Dioscuri, and Hymenaeus.[82]

*

RABELAIS and Montaigne saw in mythology, as in history, little more than a collection of curiosities; but the examples and anecdotes which they drew from it were again taken for the most part either from the compilations of late antiquity or from the manuals of their own time. Thus Rabelais [83] finds details about Juno Moneta or Apollo Loxias in the *Saturnalia* of Macrobius; [84] but he makes use also of the *Officina* of Textor,[85] and the *Dies geniales* of Alexander of Naples.[86] And though, as we have seen,[87] he derides the abuses of allegorical mythology, Horapollo engages his interest in the hidden significance of sacred sculpture, "which should be understandable to any initiated person able to read the worth, the properties, and the nature of things by means of such images." [88] As for Montaigne, we know that, for all his apparent unconcern, he relied extensively upon catalogues and reference lists of all sorts.[89] He had in his own library the same collection of works on my-

[81] *Ballet comique de la Royne faict aux nopces de M. le Duc de Joyeuse et Mademoiselle de Vaudemont* "par B. de Beaujoyeulx" (Paris, 1582); as Appendix, "Allégorie de la Circé," "taken by Natalis Comes from commentaries on the Greek poets." See F. Yates, *The French Academies of the Sixteenth Century* (London, 1947), esp. chap. xi.

[82] *Bref et sommaire recueil de ce qui a esté faict et de l'ordre tenu à la joyeuse et triumphale entrée de . . . Charles IX . . .* etc. (Paris, 1572); see pp. 26, 27–29. On the part taken by the poets in these *entrées,* see P. de Nolhac, *op. cit.,* p. 59. Dorat, in his *Chant nuptial* on the marriage of Anne de Joyeuse to Marie of Lorraine (1581), speaks of the contribution of Desportes, Baïf, and Ronsard; he also describes the mythological scenes painted on the triumphal arches in honor of Henri III. On Primaticcio and the court *mascarades,* see *supra,* p. 283, n. 12.

[83] See J. Plattard, *L'Oeuvre de Rabelais* (Paris, 1910), chap. vi: "Catalogue des sources anciennes et modernes de l'érudition antique de Rabelais."

[84] *Tiers Livre,* 16, 18, etc.

[85] *Quart Livre,* 38: Erichthonius; *Pantagruel,* 1: "les Géants anciens."

[86] *Quart Livre,* 62: "sur la statue de Mercure."

[87] See *supra,* p. 95.

[88] *Gargantua,* 9; a copy of the *Hieroglyphica* is known which contains Rabelais' *ex-libris* (see Plattard, *op. cit.,* p. 202).

[89] See P. Villey, *Sources et évolution des Essais de Montaigne,* I.

thology which had been used by the pupils of Dorat;[90] also the *Officina* of Textor, du Choul's *Religion des anciens Romains* (which he used in writing the *Apologie de Raimond Sebond*), and, finally, the *De deis gentium* of Giraldi, an author for whom, as we already know,[91] he professed the greatest esteem.

From this cursory review, it becomes clear that the French humanists, even the greatest among them, utilized upon occasion books of very mixed erudition—thereby avoiding the trouble of consulting the ancient sources. Nevertheless, in a more general sense, these works do not appear to have decisively influenced their intellectual development or their view of the ancient world; it is also clear that the most recent writings of the type we are considering, the manuals of Giraldi, Conti, and Cartari, were not well known or commonly used in France till the last years of the sixteenth century or even later—and then thanks to translations or adaptations made by du Verdier,[92] Jacques de Montlyard,[93] and Baudouin.[94]

*

THE INVASION of England by the gods was no less widespread. The Elizabethan poets were not outdone by the Pléiade in their taste for mythological lore. But they, too, derived their learning from indirect sources—sources for the most part Italian.[95]

In the first place, they knew the *Genealogia deorum* of Boccaccio, whose Demogorgon is found in Spenser, Marlowe, and Dryden, just as he appears later in Milton, and even in Shelley;[96] also, the *De deis gentium* of

90 See *supra*, p. 308; Montaigne owned the 1549 edition, which included the *Libellus* of Albricus.

91 See *Essais*, I, 35; cf. *supra*, p. 231, n. 41.

92 Translator of Cartari (Lyons, 1581) into Latin and French.

93 Translator of Conti (Paris, 1599).

94 Author of a compilation which appeared in Paris in 1627: *Mythologie ou Explication des Fables* (i.e., of Conti), *ci-devant traduite par J. de Montlyard, exactement revue, . . . et augmentée d'un Traité des Muses* (Giraldi), *de diverses moralitez . . . et d'un abrégé des Images des dieux* (the *Libellus*). The illustrations in this work are derived from those of Cartari.

95 See D. Bush, *Mythology and the Renaissance Tradition in English Poetry* (London, 1932); F. Schoell, *Etude sur l'humanisme continental en Angleterre à la fin de la Ren.*, chap. ii; "Les Mythographes italiens de la Ren. et la poesie Elizabethaine," *Bibl. rev. litt. comp.*, XXIX (Paris, 1926), pp. 21–42. See also our article, "Les manuels mythologiques italiens et leur diffusion en Angleterre à la fin de la Renaissance," *Mélanges d'hist. et d'arch.* (1933), pp. 276–292; and Frances A. Yates, "Italian Teachers in Elizabethan England," *Journal of the Warburg Institute*, I (1937–38), esp. p. 114.

96 See M. Castelain, "Démogorgon ou le barbarisme déifié," *Bull. Assoc. G. Budé*, No. 36 (July, 1932), pp. 22–39.

Giraldi, from whom George Chapman borrows a gloss for his "Hymn to Cynthia,"[97] and who alone gives the complete key to his allegories.[98] Giraldi, again, early in the seventeenth century was to furnish many details to Burton, author of the strange *Anatomy of Melancholy*.[99] But Giraldi was not the only compendium that Burton had at hand, as he himself tells us: "Their carved idols [speaking of the Gentiles] were most absurd. . . . Jupiter with a ram's head, Mercury a dog's, Pan like a goat, Hecate with three heads. . . . See more in Carterius and Verdurius of their monstrous forms and ugly pictures."[100] These references are to Cartari and his translator, du Verdier, and it was evidently one of the illustrated editions of Cartari that Burton had seen.[101] He appears to have been so impressed with the ugliness of these illustrations that he came to regard mythology as one of the manifestations of melancholy—a product, that is, of diseased imagination.

As for Natale Conti, Schoell has shown us that he, even more than Giraldi, was Chapman's constant companion. The poet, probably intrigued by Conti's systematic inquiry into the moral meaning of the myths,[102] pillaged his work (without admitting it) not only in the *Shadow of Night* and the *Andromeda Liberata*, in *Ovid's Banquet of Sence* and the tragedies, but even for the pedantic notes that he appends to the hymns. Bacon, in turn, is greatly indebted to the *Mythologia* of Conti, from which, as the analyses and comparisons of Lemmi have proved,[103] the *De sapientia veterum* borrows not only subject matter, but method as well.

Finally, we have a piece of evidence of the highest interest concerning the popularity of Cartari and Conti in the late sixteenth century. In his *Satire* II, written in 1598, John Marston takes issue with one of those poets who cram so many scholarly allusions into their work that it becomes unintelli-

[97] *Poems* (1904 ed.), p. 17, no. 8: "This is expounded as followeth by Geraldus Lilius."

[98] For example, *Bussy d'Ambois*, I, 1, 113–117 (Fortune); cf. Giraldi, *Syntagma* XVI.

[99] *The Anatomy of Melancholy* (1621; London ed., 1931), p. 370 (of Tityus): "for so doth Lilius Gyraldus interpret it"; p. 712: "When Jupiter wooed Juno first (Lilius Gyraldus relates it,") etc.

[100] *Ibid.*, p. 905.

[101] For example, the French edition of du Verdier (Lyons, 1581) presents on p. 199 the Jupiter with ram's head; p. 401, the cynocephalic Mercury (Anubis); p. 125, Hecate Trigemina.

[102] F. Schoell, *op. cit.*, p. 31; see, in Appendix I (pp. 179–197), his detailed list of Chapman's borrowings from Conti.

[103] *Op. cit.*, see *supra*, p. 249, n. 109.

gible. Oedipus himself, he says, could not find his way through these Cimmerian shades. And he exclaims:

> *O darknes palpable! Egipts black night!*
> *My wit is stricken blind, hath lost his sight;*
> *My shins are broke with groping for some sence,*
> *To know to what his words have reference . . .*
> *Reach me some poet's index that will show.*
> *Imagines deorum, Booke of Epithetes,*
> *Natales Comes, thou I know recites . . .*
> *. . . ayde me to unrip*
> *These intricate deepe oracles of wit*
> *These dark enigmaes, and strange ridling sence,*
> *Which pass my dullard braines intelligence.*[104]

Thus the *Imagines deorum* (Cartari) and the *Mythologia* of Natales Comes (Conti) are the works which Marston calls upon spontaneously to help him resolve the enigmas posed by contemporary poets. As for the *Booke of Epithetes,* it may be Ravisius Textor's which is meant.[105] It would seem that Marston had all these works conveniently at hand ("reach me") on his library shelves—proof that they were currently consulted at the time, and that they served as indices not only for poets, but for their readers as well.

We have left till the last a problem of great difficulty, that of the mythological sources in Shakespeare.[106] This problem, which has frequently been raised, invariably arouses controversy. Some critics share the belief that Shakespeare, also, got his knowledge of Fable indirectly, perhaps by way of contemporary compilations or manuals.[107] It has been conjectured that he

[104] *Works of Mr. John Marston* (Halliwell ed. [London, 1856]), III, p. 218.

[105] *Epithetorum opus absolutissimum . . . lexicon vere poeticum* (Basel, 1558); an "epitome" of this work appeared in London in 1595. There existed, besides, many other manuals of the same type, as for example those of Montefalco, *De cognominibus deorum* (Perugia, 1525), and Conrad Dinner, *Epithetorum Graecorum farrago locupletissima* (Frankfort, 1589).

[106] See W. Ebisch, *A Shakespeare Bibliography* (Oxford, 1931): pp. 64–69, "Shakespeare and Classical Literature" (pp. 68–69, "Classical Mythology"). The *Supplement* (1937) contains the literature for 1930–1935.

[107] N. Delius, "Klassische Reminiscenzen in Sh.'s Dramen," *Jahrbuch der deutschen Shakes. Gesellschaft* (Berlin, 1883), pp. 81–103 (pp. 89–93, the gods in Sh.; pp. 93–99, the demigods and heroes); R. Anders, "Shakespeare's Books, a Dissertation on Shakespeare's Readings and the Immediate Sources of his Works," *Schriften d. deutsch. Sh. Gesell.* (Berlin, 1904); Robert K. Root, *Classical Mythology in Shakespeare,* Yale Studies in English, XIX (New York, 1903); and more recently, E. I. Fripp, *Shakespeare Studies*

made use of Textor's *Officina.* With more precision, his indebtedness to the emblematists Alciati, Symeoni, Sambuc, and Whitney has been postulated, not only for "devices" and allegories, but also for a large number of mythological allusions scattered throughout his work.[108] Finally, there are certain indications pointing to Shakespeare's having known the *Imagini* of Cartari. At all events, it is to the *Imagini* that one must turn for help in solving the enigma posed by a Shakespearean heraldic emblem devised by Bacon.[109]

*

Mythological pageants and other entertainments were much in vogue in England, as they were in France and Italy; masquerades and ballets, in particular, flourished under the name of "masques" in the second half of the sixteenth century and the first half of the seventeenth.[110] Their brilliance may be inferred from the fact that many of them were composed collaboratively by one of the leading poets of the time and one of the finest artists—Ben Jonson[111] and Inigo Jones. Jonson's verses have come down to us, and Jones' drawings for settings and costumes. In these Festivals of Thetys and Triumphs of Neptune, the gods are for the most part caparisoned with accessories so mysterious that it is very difficult to identify them. It is obvious that Ben Jonson, as a humanist, searched his memory for curious details not

(London, 1930) pp. 98–128 ("Shakespeare's Use of Ovid's Metamorphoses"), have maintained that Shakespeare drew his knowledge of mythology, in all essentials, directly from Ovid and Virgil.

108 See H. Green, *Shakespeare and the Emblem Writers* (London, 1870), esp. chap. vi, 3: "Emblems for Mythological Characters." See also A. von Mauntz, *Heraldik in Diensten der Shakespeare-Forschung* (Berlin, 1903); and F. Brie, "Shakespeare und die Impresa-Kunst seiner Zeit," *Jahrb. d. deutsch. Sh. Gesellsch.* (1914), pp. 9–30. Brie studies the use of emblems in several other Elizabethan poets. There was in fact a widespread taste for emblems in English Renaissance literature, as witness *The Arte of English Poesie* of George Puttenham (London, 1589), which treats at length of devices or emblems.

109 See William Goldsworthy Lansdown, *Shakespeare's Heraldic Emblems, their Origin and Meaning* (London, 1928). The author shows (pp. 75–77) that the figures of Castor and Pollux in the emblem reproduce an engraving from Cartari (1581 ed.) p. 224; and their meaning is made clear by the text of the *Imagini, ibid.*, p. 222.

110 See P. Reyher, *Les Masques anglais, étude sur les ballets et la vie de cour en Angleterre* (Paris, 1909); Enid Welsford, "Italian Influence on the English Court Masque," *Modern Language Review* (Oct., 1923), pp. 394–409, and Allardyce Nicoll, *Stuart Masques and the Renaissance Stage* (London, 1937), esp. chap. vi: "Court Hieroglyphics."

111 See A. H. Gilbert, *The Symbolic Persons in the Masques of Ben Jonson* (Durham, 1948); also D. J. Gordon, "The Imagery of Ben Jonson's *The Masque of Blacknesse* and *The Masque of Beautie,*" in *Journal of the Warburg and Courtauld Institutes,* vi (1943), pp. 101–121, and "*Hymenaei:* Ben Jonson's Masque of Union," *ibid.*, viii (1945), pp. 107–145.

known to the vulgar; but it was not only in his memory that he searched. He consulted, in addition to several emblem books, that *Iconologia* by Ripa into which, as we have seen,[112] all the elements of late fifteenth-century learning were drawn together, there to be converted into a set of moral charades.

*

NOT ONLY France and England, but Germany and Spain offer evidence of the diffusion of the manuals, and especially of the Italian group.

We have already spoken of Georg Pictor,[113] and have shown that his *Magazine of the Gods* represents a link in the tradition connecting Boccaccio and Giraldi. We also know that the *Heydenwelt* of Johann Herold,[114] coming after Giraldi's *Historia,* is directly derived from it. The author—who, incidentally, makes use of other contemporary works of learning as well—explains in his "Address to the Reader" that he has felt it necessary to set forth in the vulgar tongue, for the benefit of those unfamiliar with any other, the subject-matter treated by his Italian predecessor. He has tried, he says, within the limits of his own ability, to take the earlier work as his model.

The *Roman Antiquities* of Johann Rosen,[115] published in 1583, continues the same tradition. Book II, dealing with the gods and their temples, is a compilation of Albricus (that is to say, the author of the *Libellus*), Boccaccio, Pictor, and above all Giraldi. Following Giraldi's example, Rosen's iconography contains borrowings from sculptured reliefs, from medals (for the allegories), and from emblems (for the figures of Cupid, Hercules, etc.); but it is a curious fact that in describing the major gods he limits himself, for the most part, to copying the exact words of the *Libellus.*[116]

Rosen gives little space to interpretations. He mentions the euhemeristic explanations, including the extravagant genealogies of Goropius Becanus (in connection with Saturn); and parallel to these gives, without discussing them,

112 See *supra,* p. 278.

113 See *supra,* p. 228.

114 *Heydenwelt und irer Götter anfangcklicher Ursprung* (followed by a translation of Diodorus Siculus; Basel, 1554). See *supra,* p. 229, n. 36.

115 *Romanarum antiquitatum libri* x . . . (Basel, 1583).

116 Examples are chap. iv, Saturn; chap. vi, Juno (in part); chap. vii, Apollo (in part) and Diana (Rosen adds: ". . . sicut adhuc in nummis antiquis cernitur"—". . . as she is still to be seen on old coins"); chap. ix, Jupiter.

the physical explanations of the Stoics (apropos of Juno, for instance). He seems to know, but disregards, the moral interpretations.

Finally, in the seventeenth century, the monumental *Iconologia deorum* of Sandrart [117] reveals its remoter origins from the first page on; Boccaccio's Demogorgon is given the place of honor. The work, it is true, boasts of its use of antique monuments: "Greek and Roman statues, objects in marble, ivory, agate, and onyx"; but it is still in large part founded on the Italian mythographers and emblematists of the preceding century—Alexander of Naples, Alciati, Valeriano, Conti, Cartari. The very illustrations derive to some extent from the *Imagini degli dei*: the plates executed for the Cartari work by the engraver Ferroverde under the direction of Pignoria represented, as we have seen,[118] a certain progress toward archeological correctness. Sandrart continues this effort, but it is not difficult to recognize his prototypes.

In Spain, in 1585, there appeared in Madrid an imposing work entitled *Philosophia secreta donde debaxo de historias fabulosas, se contiene mucha doctrina provechosa a todos estudios, con el origgen de los idolos, o dioses de la gentilidad.* The author, Juan Pérez de Moya, known especially as a mathematician, was also a learned humanist; but though he seems to be familiar with the classics, his scholarship has a distinctly medieval cast. The names of the Fathers and the encyclopedists (that of Isidore in particular) come constantly to his pen; he quotes Albricus several times, and follows Boccaccio in establishing the genealogy of the gods. He even utilizes more recent sources, like Alexander of Naples and Natale Conti. In its general conception, furthermore, his work has more than one point of resemblance with Conti's *Mythologia.* Like his Italian predecessor, Pérez de Moya distinguishes clearly between the different types of interpretation which can be given to a single fable (Chap. II: "De los sentidos que se puede dar a una fabula"), and applies them all in succession. The description of each divinity and of his adventures are in most instances followed by a triple *declaración,* historical, physical, moral. The third type of interpretation is of greatest concern to him, for, as the title of the work indicates, he sees in mythology above

[117] J. von Sandrart, *Iconologia deorum, oder Abbildung der Götter, welche von den Alten verehrt worden . . .* (Nuremberg, 1680).

[118] See *supra,* p. 252, n. 117.

all its "hidden philosophy." One whole book, the fifth, is devoted to the study of fables "which exhort men to flee vice and to follow virtue"; and in the seventh and last he treats of those which were invented in order to "inspire the fear of God."

The *Philosophia secreta* went through many editions;[119] but the collection which was to attain the greatest popularity in Spain was the *Teatro de los dioses de la gentilidad* by Fray Baltasar de Victoria, prior of the convent of San Francisco in Salamanca. This book appeared in 1620, with an "approbation" by Lope de Vega himself—a curious document which makes clear once again that allegorical interpretation formed the ideal safe-conduct for the gods. Lope declares that nothing in mythological history contravenes faith or morality; on the contrary, it is a science of great importance for literary understanding. The ancients shrouded philosophy in Fable, beneath the surface beauties of poetry, painting, and astrology. All the pagan theologians, from Hermes Trismegistus to the divine Plato, hid their explanations of nature in symbols and hieroglyphs—as the *Timaeus* and the *poimandres* tell us of the Egyptians—so that the sacred truths might be hidden from vulgar minds.

Lope de Vega goes on to say that a book of this sort in the Spanish language, showing great erudition on the part of the author, has been much needed. Italy and France have already produced several such works.

Now the *Teatro de los dioses* is a compilation based on these very French and Italian manuals: the *Officina* of Textor, the *Discours de la religion des anciens Romains* of du Choul; the emblem books of Alciati and Valeriano, with the glosses added by their commentators; lastly, the *Mythologia* of "Natal Comite" (Natale Conti), and the *Imagini* of Cartari.[120] It is by way of these intermediaries that Fray Baltasar de Victoria harvests the classical tradition, encumbered with all its medieval accretions.

*

FROM WHAT has gone before, we have a right to conclude that the manuals of mythology had their place in the library of every cultivated gentleman of the

119 Saragossa, 1599; Alcala, 1611; Madrid, 1628 and 1673. The work was reissued in Madrid in 1928 in the series *Los clásicos olvidados*, VI (2 vols.), with introduction by Gómez de Baquero.

120 All these works are cited in marginal notes, with precise references.

sixteenth and seventeenth centuries, and that several of them, in fact, knew the touch of illustrious hands.

It is too soon to arrive at conclusions as to the real influence which they exerted on the various literatures; only long and detailed research can determine the exact nature and extent of that influence—which, for that matter, did not reach its height till the seventeenth century. But one fact is clear, which seems to us of far-reaching importance—the Renaissance humanists did not in every case nor at all times drink directly from the pure and life-giving waters of antiquity. Their mythological science is derived, at least in part, from contemporary compilations.

The greater number of these compilations, and the most important of them, come from Italy; in this domain, as in so many others, it is thus frequently by way of Italy that sixteenth-century Europe gains its knowledge of antiquity. But of what antiquity? The heritage which Italy in this case distributes among the other nations is not the treasure of classical mythology, suddenly brought to light, recovered intact; it is a deposit that she herself has received, in part, from alien sources—a deposit made up of a variety of contributions, where some gold pieces shine among the time-worn copper coins. Many of the gods whom Italy sends out for the conquest of other peoples have come to her—or come back to her—from great distances; they are adventurers who have been roaming the world for hundreds of years.

*

At the conclusion of this study, let us attempt to formulate what we have been able to learn from it of the Renaissance, its nature, and the causes of its decline.

The long history of the gods, as we have outlined it here, brings forward a supporting argument for those who refuse to see the Renaissance as a break with the past, an initiation of something completely new.[121] One can no longer speak—at least or not literally—of a "rebirth" of the gods, when one has followed their fortunes, as we have done, from late antiquity on; when one has watched them being absorbed into medieval culture, which saves them from

[121] See, for instance, G. Doutrepont, *Jean Lemaire de Belges et la Renaissance*, Introduction.

oblivion and protects them from hostility; when one has seen elaborations and new glosses constantly added to that tenacious, uninterrupted tradition which gathers up all that has survived of the fabulous world of the ancients and transmits it as common currency down through the ages; when one has gazed at the great mass of naïve or barbaric images, scattered offshoots of the Olympian line—obscure in their descent, no doubt, but still endowed with the divine right of immortality.

For these last, the survivors, the Renaissance was no more than a Fountain of Youth within which to bathe their deformed and impotent limbs. But then, for a time, other divinities did eclipse them by their triumphant beauty, rising from their ancestral soil after a sleep of a thousand years, having known neither decadence nor exile.

It is indeed worthy of note that during the most radiant period of the Renaissance, the iconographical types that had been "handed down," and therefore altered, were almost everywhere abandoned in favor of types "rediscovered" in their primal purity. It is also significant that during the same period there seems to be an interruption in the mythographical tradition, at least in Italy (no Italian history of the gods appeared between Boccaccio and Giraldi). It is as if nothing more was now needed, in order to know and understand the gods, than to look out at the surrounding world and listen to the voice of instinct; as if man had at last penetrated to the inner meaning of mythology, now that he was engaged in rehabilitating, along with physical beauty, the realm of nature and the flesh.

But beneath this gaiety and enthusiasm lurks a stubborn disquiet; just because a "pagan" cult of life is now being professed, with the gods as its incarnation, the need is felt of bringing that cult into line with the spiritual values of Christianity—of reconciling the two worlds. Humanism and art appear, for a brief moment, to have succeeded in accomplishing this result; the Renaissance, in its moment of flowering, is this synthesis—or rather, this fragile harmony. But the equilibrium is disturbed after only a few decades. The sixteenth century, as it advances, is forced to avow the disaccord which it thought had been successfully hidden. An era of crisis and reaction then dawns. The gods no longer arouse the same sentiments. Zeal is succeeded by admiration grown reticent and overscrupulous; intoxication with beauty, by a cold archeological interest, by scholarly curiosity. From being objects of love, the gods are transformed into a subject of study. Thus the medieval tradition of the *libri de imaginibus deorum* is born again, and by a strange cycle of return, the gods of Martianus Capella once more appear. Once more, as in the twilight of the ancient world, the Olympians give way before the idols of Egypt and Syria. But at the same time, since the gods cannot be excluded from art, poetry, or education, a compromise is more than ever necessary to satisfy the demands and conventions of morality, and the traditional compromise consists in presenting each of the gods as an edifying symbol. Thus the allegorical method dear to the Middle Ages flourishes again with new vigor. All mythology is nothing more—or pretends to be nothing more—than a system of ideas in disguise, a "secret philosophy."

Increasingly erudite and diminishingly alive, less and less felt but more and more intellectualized [122]—such, from now on, it seems, is to be the inescapable evolution of mythology. Indeed, the discussions which take place in seventeenth-century France, for example, on the topic of the "merveilleux païen"—the arguments advanced by the defenders of the gods, as well as by their adversaries [123]—give proof of the drying up of poetic sentiment in the realm of Fable, which is now regarded as no more than "un amas de nobles fictions" and "ornements reçus" [124] or as an adjunct in teaching, intended for the edification of the young, and especially for the instruction of princes.[125]

Nevertheless, in this same century, the very gods who have been reduced

[122] See E. Bourciez, *op. cit.*, chap. iv: "Caractères de l'art et de la mythologie au XVIe siècle: la mythologie moralisée," pp. 257–262; "The gods were condemned to re-enter a more abstract system," etc.

[123] See V. Delaporte, *Du merveilleux dans la littérature française sous le règne de Louis* XIV (Paris, 1891). In the following century, the controversy was to be resumed between Pluche, *Histoire du Ciel* (1748 ed.), pp. 412 ff., who violently attacked mythology, and Voltaire, who defended it, *Dict. philos.*, article *Fable*: "On certain fanatics who have attempted to proscribe the ancient fables."

[124] Boileau, *Art poétique*, III, 173 and 194; see the entire passage, 163–232.

[125] At the direction of Richelieu, mythology was taught to Louis XIV in his childhood by means of a card game representing the gods, invented by Desmarets de Saint-Sorlin (who was later to become the chief opponent of the gods and goddesses). Bossuet, as he himself told Innocent XI, taught the Dauphin "the fables of pagan Theology." Fénelon, in turn, taught them to the Duke of Burgundy, "who loved fables and mythology." Cf. Abbé de Villiers, *Poésies*, p. 207: "De l'éducation des rois."

to the functions of chamberlains or tutors experience astonishing revivals of power and acquire new prestige. At precisely the moment when, in Italian art, mythology is being relegated to the stage machinery of opera, Flanders, with Rubens, recalls it to primitive realities, to brute and elemental force. Sated with wine, gorged with meats and fruits, the gods are nourished to a point where their majesty, it is true, may be lost, but their animal vigor reappears. The naturalism of the North once more lends them its own flesh and blood, while the intoxicating effects of pantheism free them from all restraint.

With Poussin, meditating in Rome in the silence of the ruins, the gods are surrounded by a different atmosphere, strangely dreamlike and grave. We feel that for this artist the world of Fable represents the Golden Age, gone never to return; everything breathes regret for that lost world and for its serene delights.

The fact is that the ancient world has become irrevocably detached from our own; it is an enchanted isle, lost beyond a luminous horizon, forever invisible. The sentiment of nostalgia which pervades the work of Poussin is the fruit, at once bitter and delicious, of the Renaissance; it means that the perspectives of the mind have changed. The notion of antiquity as a distinct historical milieu, as a period that had run its course, did not exist in the Middle Ages; and this is the cause of the relative facility, so surprising to us, with which, in spite of the immense revolution created by Christianity, medieval thought found points of agreement and formulas for reconciliation with the pagan spirit. The Renaissance, on the other hand, perceived this historical distance, and had to make a conscious effort to establish harmony between two worlds separated by a lapse of centuries. When this effort failed, "the antique world . . . which had proved incompatible with Christian culture, appeared all the more as a perfect harmony in itself. . . ." In that world, "physical beauty and carnal desires, heroic pathos and playful amorousness, had never entered into conflict with moral or theological conceptions."[126]

[126] Panofsky and Saxl, "Classical Mythology in Mediaeval Art," *Metropolitan Museum Studies,* IV (1932–1933), conclusion; and Panofsky, "Et in Arcadia ego," in *Philosophy and History, Essays Presented to E. Cassirer* (Oxford, 1936), pp. 223 ff., esp. pp. 229–232.

Thus the classical past becomes, in Baudelaire's words,

. . . le souvenir de ces époques nues

—the memory of those ages when beings stronger and more beautiful than ourselves

jouissaient sans mensonge et sans anxiété . . .

tasted without deceit or disquiet the joys of that imaginary kingdom, that serene Arcadia, toward which the anguished mind of modern man turns for refuge among the gods.

BIBLIOGRAPHY

AND

INDEX

Bibliography

Abbreviations used throughout this volume:

LCL	Loeb Classical Library
MGH	*Monumenta Germaniae historica*, Berlin-Hannover, 1874–1894
PG	*Patrologia Graeca* } *see* Migne (*II*)
PL	*Patrologia Latina* } *see* Migne (*II*)

The Roman numerals *I* and *II* (italic) refer respectively to the sections of this bibliography.

I. SOURCES

AGRIPPA VON NETTESHEIM, HEINRICH CORNELIUS. *De occulta philosophia libri* III. Cologne, 1533.

ALBERTI, LEONE BATTISTA. *De pictura . . . libri* III. Basel, 1540.

ALBRICUS. *Allegoriae poeticae seu de veritate ac expositione poeticarum fabularum libri* IV. . . . Paris, 1520. *See also* Raschke (*II*).

ALCIATI, ANDREA. *Emblematum liber.* [*s.l.*] 1531.

ALDROVANDI, ULISSE. *Tutte le statue antiche che in Roma si veggono* (app. to Mauro, Lucio, *Antichità*). Venice, 1556. *See also* Reinach (*II*).

ALEXANDER OF NAPLES. *Dies geniales.* [*s.l.*] 1522.

ALIACO, PETRUS DE (AILLY, PIERRE D'). *Ymago mundi.* Louvain, 1480–1483. Latin text . . . publ., with French transl., by Buron, E., Paris, 1930.

ANNIUS OF VITERBO. *Commentaria fratris Joannis Annii . . . super opera diversorum auctorum de antiquitatibus loquentium confecta. . . .* Rome, 1498.

APIANUS, PETRUS. *Inscriptiones sacrosanctae vetustatis. . . .* Ingolstadt, 1534.

APOLLODORUS OF ATHENS. *Bibliotheca sive de deorum origine. . . .* Rome, 1555.

APOLLONIUS OF RHODES. *See* La Ville de Mirmont (*II*).

ARATUS. *Phaenomena.* Venice, 1499.

ARMENINI, GIOVANNI BATTISTA. *Precetti della pittura.* Ravenna, 1586–1587.

ARNALDO D'ORLÉANS. *See* Ghisalberti (*II*).

Auctores mythographi Latini. Ed. by Staveren, Augustinus van. Leyden and Amsterdam, 1742.

BACON, FRANCIS. *De sapientia veterum liber.* London, 1609. *See also* Lemmi (*II*).

BALDINI, BACCIO. *Discorso sopra la Mascherata della genealogia degl'iddei de'gentili.* Florence, 1565.

BARTOLI, BARTOLOMEO DI. *See* Dorez (*II*).

BAUDOUIN, JEAN. *Mythologie ou explication des fables . . . ci-devant traduite par J. de Montlyard. . . .* Paris, 1627.

BAUDRY DE BOURGUEIL. *See* Abrahams (*II*).

BERSUIRE, PIERRE. *Ovide moralisé*, in *idem, Reductorium morale*, bk. XV: *De fabulis poetarum*. Bruges, 1484.

BOCCACCIO, GIOVANNI DI. *See* Baldini (*I*); Castelain (*II*), Coulter (*II*), Hauvette (*II*), Hortis (*II*), Landi (*II*), Wilkins (*II*).

BOETHIUS. *See* Jourdain (*II*), Patch (*II*).

BORGHINI, RAFFAELLO. *Il riposo*. Florence, 1584.

BORGHINI, VINCENZO. *Relazione al Duca sul l'apparato da farsi . . .* (nuptials of Francesco de'Medici and Johanna of Austria), in Bottari, G., and Ticozzi, S., *Raccolta di lettere. . . .* Milan, 1702.

———. *Carteggio artistico inedito*. Coll. by Lorenzoni, A., *q.v.* (*II*).

BOTHO, CONRAD. *Cronecken der Sassen*. Mainz, 1492.

BURTON, ROBERT. *The Anatomy of Melancholy*. London, 1621.

CARO, ANNIBALE. *See* Seghezzi (*II*).

CARTARI, VINCENZO. *Le imagini colla sposizione degli dei degli antichi*. Venice, 1556.

CHRESTIEN DE TROYES. *See* Lewis (*II*).

COLONNA, FRANCESCO. *Hypnerotomachia Poliphili*. Venice, 1499. *See also* Fierz-David (*II*).

COMANINI, GREGORIO. *Il Figino, ovvero del fine della pittura. . . .* Mantua, 1591.

CONTI, NATALE. *Mythologiae sive explicationis fabularum libri* X. Venice, 1551. *See also* Bassi (*II*).

DOLCE, L. *Le trasformationi tratte da Ovidio . . . con gli argomenti et allegorie al principio et al fine di ciascun canto*. Venice, 1553.

———. *Dialogo della pittura*. Venice, 1557.

DOMINICI, GIOVANNI. *Lucula noctis*. Latin text, 15th cent., ed. by Coulon, R., *q.v.* (*II*).

DU CHOUL, GUILLAUME. *Discours de la religion des anciens Romains*. Lyons, 1556.

DU VERDIER, ANTOINE. *Prosopographie. . . .* Lyons, 1589.

ESTIENNE, ROBERT. *Dictionarium nominum virorum, mulierum, populorum, idolorum, urbium et quae passim in libris prophanis leguntur*. Paris, 1512.

FABRICIUS, JOHANN ALBERT. *Bibliographia antiquaria*. 3d ed. Hamburg, 1760. (Cf. esp. chap. viii: "Scriptores de diis.")

FULGENTIUS, FABIUS PLANCIADES. *Fulgentii Episcopi Carthaginensis Mythologiarum ad Catum Presbyterum Carthaginensem . . .*, in Hyginus, C. J., . . . *Fabularum liber*, Basel, 1535.

Fulgentius metaforalis. *See* Ridewall (*I*); Liebeschütz (*II*).

GAULTRUCHE, PIERRE. *L'Histoire poétique pour l'intelligence des poètes et des auteurs anciens*. 6th ed. Caen, 1671.

Ghâya. See Dozy and Goeje, de (*II*).

GIRALDI, LILIO GREGORIO. *De deis gentium varia et multiplex historia in qua simul de eorum imaginibus et cognominibus agitur. . . .* Basel, 1548.

GRAZZINI, ANTONIO FRANCESCO (IL LASCA). *Tutti i trionfi, carri, mascherate o canti carnascialeschi andati per Firenze dal tempo del magnifico Lorenzo de'Medici fino all'anno 1559.* Lucca, 1750.

GUALTEROTTI, ROBERTO. *Feste nelle nozze del Serenissimo Francesco Medici G. Duca di Toscana e della Sereniss. sua consorte la Sig. Bianca Cappello.* Florence, 1579.

GUILLAUME DE CONCHES. *See* Jourdain (*II*).

HERACLITUS. *De allegoriis apud Homerum.* Venice, 1505.

HERMES TRISMEGISTUS. *See* Festugière (*II*).

HEROLD, J. *Heydenwelt und irer Götter anfangcklicher Ursprung.* Basel, 1554.

HORUS APOLLO (HORAPOLLO). *Hieroglyphica.* Venice, 1505. *See also* Boas (*II*).

HYGINUS. *Fabularum liber.* Basel, 1535.

JACOPO DA BERGAMO. *Supplemento alle croniche. . . .* Venice, 1520. (1st ed., Bergamo, 1483.)

JONSON, BEN. *See* Sartorius (*II*), Wheeler (*II*).

LAFRERI, ANTONIO. *Speculum Romanae magnificentiae. . . .* [*s.l.*] 1564.

LEGOUAIS, CHRESTIEN. *See* Paris (*II*).

LE MAIRE DE BELGES. *See* Doutrepont (*II*).

LEONARDI, CAMILLO. *Speculum lapidum.* Venice, 1502.

Libellus (*De deorum imaginibus*). Publ. (in *Fulgentius metaforalis . . .*) by Liebeschütz, H., *q.v.* (*II*).

LOMAZZO, GIOVANNI PAOLO. *Trattato dell'arte della pittura.* Milan, 1584.

———. *Idea del tempio della pittura.* Milan, 1590.

LUBINUS, EILHARDUS. *Fax poetica sive genealogia et res gestae deorum gentilium, virorum, regum et Caesarum Romanorum.* Rostock, 1598.

MACROBIUS. *In somnium Scipionis; Saturnalia.* Florence, 1515.

MARLOWE. *See* Frey (*II*).

MARTIANUS CAPELLA. *De nuptiis Philologiae et Mercurii libri* II. Basel, 1532.

MASUDI. *See* Mehrens (*II*).

MENESTRIER, CLAUDE FRANÇOIS. *La Philosophie des images énigmatiques où il est traité des énigmes, hiéroglyphes. . . .* Paris, 1682.

———. *L'Art des emblèmes, où s'enseigne la morale par les figures de la fable, de l'histoire et de la nature.* Paris, 1684.

Mer des hystoires (*La*). Paris, 1488.

MILTON. *See* Osgood (*II*).

MONTAIGNE. *See* Villey (*II*).

MONTEFALCO. *De cognominibus deorum.* Perugia, 1525.

MONTENAY, GEORGETTE DE. *Emblèmes ou devises chrétiennes.* Lyons, 1571.

Opicinus de Canistris. In Cod. Palat. Lat. 1993. Publ. by Salomon, R. G., *q.v.* (*II*).

Opuscula mythologica physica et ethica, Graece et Latine (Palaephatus, Heraclitus, Phornutus, Sallustius, etc.). Cambridge, 1671.

Ortelius, Abraham. *Deorum dearumque capita ex vetustis numismatibus.* Antwerp, 1572.

Ottonelli, Giovanni Domenico, and Cortona, Pietro da. *Trattato della pittura e scultura, uso et abuso loro, composto da un theologo e da un pittore. . . .* Florence, 1652.

Ovid. *See* Bersuire (*I*), Dolce (*I*); Boer, de (*II*), Born (*II*), Ghisalberti (*II*), Hauréau (*II*), Henkel (*II*), Pansa (*II*), Paris (*II*), Rand (*II*), Sant, van't (*II*), Schevill (*II*).

Ovide moralisé. Publ. by Boer, C. de, *q.v.* (*II*).

Palaephatus. *De non credendis historiis.* Venice, 1505.

Paleotto, Gabriele. *Discorso intorno alle imagini sacre e profane.* Bologna, 1581.

Pansa, Mutio. *De osculo ethnicae et christianae philosophiae.* [*s.l.*] 1601.

Pausanias. *Commentarii Graeciam describentes.* Venice, 1516. (Greek text.)

———. *De tota Graecia libri* x. . . . Basel, 1550. (Latin text.)

Pérez de Moya, J. *Philosophia secreta donde debaxo de historias fabulosas, se contiene mucha doctrina provechosa a todos estudios, con el origgen de los idolos, o dioses de la gentilidad.* Madrid, 1585. Reprinted with Intro. by Gómez de Baquero, E. (Los clásicos olvidados, vi), Madrid, 1928.

Petrarch. *See* Essling, d', and Müntz (*II*), Nolhac, de (*II*), Weisbach (*II*).

Phornutus. *De natura deorum.* Venice, 1505.

Picatrix. Arabic text publ. by Warburg Library, Hamburg, 1927. *See also* Ritter (*II*).

Pictor, G. *Theologia mythologica ex doctiss. virorum promptuario . . . videlicet de nominum deorum gentilium ratione, de imaginibus aut formis. . . .* Freiburg im Breisgau, 1532.

———. *De apotheosi tam exterarum gentium quam Romanorum deorum libri* iii. . . . Basel, 1558.

———. *Physicarum quaestionum centuriae* iii . . . *quis verus Deus, unde gentiles dii.* Basel, 1568.

Pignoria, Lorenzo. *Vetustissimae tabulae . . . sacris Aegyptiorum simulachris coelatae . . . explicatio.* Venice, 1605.

———. *Discorso intorno le deità dell'Indie orientali et occidentali con le loro figure.* . . . Padua, 1615.

Pomey, François Antoine. *Pantheum mythicum, seu fabulosa deorum historia. . . .* 3d ed. Lyons, 1675.

Possevino, Antonio. *Tractatus de poesi et pictura ethnica humana et fabulosa. . . .* Diss. inserted in *idem, Bibliotheca selecta . . . ,* Rome, 1593.

Proclus. *De sphaera.* Basel, 1523.

Prudentius. *See* Lavarenne (*II*).

RABANUS MAURUS. *See* Amelli (*II*).
RABELAIS. *See* Plattard (*II*).
RAVISIUS TEXTOR. *See* Texier (*I*).
RHODIGINUS, CAELIUS. *Lectionum antiquarum libri* XXX. Venice, 1516.
RICHARD DE FOURNIVAL. *See* Delisle (*II*).
RIDEWALL, JOHN. *Fulgentius metaforalis.* Publ. by Liebeschütz, H., *q.v.* (*II*).
RIPA, CESARE. *Iconologia. . . .* Rome, 1593.
RONSARD. *See* Cohen (*II*), Laumonier (*II*), Nolhac, de (*II*), Vaganay (*II*).
ROSEN, J. *Romanarum antiquitatum libri* X. Basel, 1583.

SALUTATI. *See* Martin, von (*II*).
SERVIUS. *Commentarii in Bucolica, Georgica et Aeneidem Virgilii.* Venice, 1471.
SHAKESPEARE. *See* Green (*II*), Root (*II*).
SPENSER. *See* Lotspeich (*II*).
STAVEREN, AUGUSTINUS VAN. *See Auctores mythographi latini* (*I*).
STRUVE, BURCKHARD GOTTHELF. *Antiquitatum Romanarum syntagma sive de ritibus sacris systema absolutius:* "Mythographi Latini"; "Recentiores scriptores de diis." Jena, 1701.
———. *Bibliotheca antiqua.* Frankfort, 1701.
SÛFÎ. *See* Hauber (*II*).

TEXIER DE RAVISI (RAVISIUS TEXTOR). *Officina partim historicis partim poeticis referta disciplinis.* Paris, 1520.
TORY, GEOFFROY. *Champfleury.* Paris, 1529. Facsimile ed., with Intro. and notes, by Cohen, G., *q.v.* (*II*).
TRITONIUS, ANTONIUS. *Mythologia. . . .* Bologna, 1560.
TRIVETH. *See* Jourdain (*II*).

VALERIANO, PIERIO. *Hieroglyphica.* Basel, 1556.
VASARI, GIORGIO. *Ragionamenti . . . sopra le invenzioni da lui dipinte. . . .* Florence, 1588.
———. *Le vite de'più eccellenti pittori, scultori ed architettori . . .* (*Le opere di Giorgio Vasari*). Annotated and commentated by Milanesi, G., Florence, 1878–1885. 9 vols.
———. In *Carteggio di Giorgio Vasari,* ed. with critical commentary by Frey, Carlo. Vol. I, Munich, 1923. Vol. II publ. in Frey, H., *Der literarische Nachlass Vasaris mit kritischem Apparate,* 1930.
VICTORIA, B. DE. *Teatro de los dioses de la gentilidad.* Salamanca, 1620.
VIRGIL. *See* Servius (*I*); Comparetti (*II*), Drew (*II*), La Ville de Mirmont (*II*).
VIRGIL POLYDORE. *De gli inventori delle cose, libri* VIII. Transl. by Baldelli, Francesco. Florence, 1592.
VOSSIUS, GERARDUS JOANNES. *De theologia gentili sive de origine ac progressu idololatriae.* Amsterdam, 1641.

ZUCCHI, J. *Discorso sopra li dei de'gentili e loro imprese.* Rome, 1602. *See also* Calcagno (*II*), Saxl (*II*).

II. STUDIES

ABRAHAMS, PHYLLIS. *Les Oeuvres poétiques de Baudri de Bourgueil.* Paris, 1926.

ADHÉMAR, JEAN. *Influences antiques dans l'art du moyen âge français.* Studies of the Warburg Institute, VII. London, 1939.

AFFÒ, IRENEO. *Ragionamento . . . sopra una stanza dipinta dal celeberrimo Antonio Allegri da Correggio nel monastero di San Paolo in Parma.* Parma, 1794.

ALPHANDÉRY, PAUL. *L'Evhémérisme et les débuts de l'histoire des religions au moyen âge.* Paris, 1934. (Reprinted from *Revue de l'histoire des religions,* vol. CIX, Jan.–Feb., 1934.)

———. "La Science des religions dans le moyen âge occidental." Résumé of course, publ. in *L'Annuaire de l'Ecole des Hautes Etudes* (Paris), 1920–1921, pp. 55–56; 1922–1923, pp. 65–66.

AMELLI, A. M. *Miniature sacre e profane dell'anno 1023 illustranti l'enciclopedia medioevale di Rabano Mauro.* Monte Cassino, 1896.

ANCONA, PAOLO D'. "Le rappresentazioni allegoriche delle arti liberali nel medio evo e nel Rinascimento," *L'Arte,* V (1902), 137–55, 211–27, 269–89, 370–85.

BALTRUŠAITIS, JURGIS. "L'Image du monde céleste du 9me au 12me siècle," *Gazette des beaux-arts,* XX (1938), pt. 2, pp. 134–48.

BARZON, A. *I cieli e la loro influenza negli affreschi del Salone in Padova.* Padua, 1924.

BASSI, DOMENICO. "La mitologia nelle prime imitazioni della Divina Commedia," *Aevum,* XI (1937), 203–35.

———. "Un'opera mitologica del secolo XVI," Reale Istituto Lombardo di Scienze e Lettere (Milan), *Rendiconti,* LXX (1937), 9–20.

BAUMGART, FRITZ. *La Caprarola di Ameto Orti.* Rome, 1935.

BAYOT, ALPHONSE. *La Légende de Troie à la cour de Bourgogne.* Mélanges de la Société d'Emulation de Bruges, I. 1908.

BEVAN, E. R. In Hastings, J., *Encyclopaedia of Religion and Ethics* (Edinburgh, 1908–1915), vol. IV, *s.v.* "Deification."

BEZOLD, CARL. *See* Boll and Bezold (*II*).

BEZOLD, FRIEDRICH VON. *Das Fortleben der antiken Götter im mittelalterlichen Humanismus.* Bonn-Leipzig, 1922.

BLOCHET, EDGAR. *Les Peintures des manuscrits orientaux de la Bibliothèque Nationale.* Portfolio. Société Française de Reproduction des Manuscrits à Peinture. Paris, 1914–1920.

BLOCK, RAYMOND DE. *Evhémère, son livre et sa doctrine.* Mons, 1876.

BOAS, GEORGE. *The Hieroglyphics of Horapollo.* Transl., with Intro. and notes. Bollingen Series XXIII. New York, 1950.

BODE, GEORG HEINRICH. *Scriptores rerum mythicarum Latini libri* III. Celle, 1834. 2 vols. (Cf. esp. vol. I.)

Boer, C. de. *Ovide moralisé: poème du commencement du quatorzième siècle, publié d'après tous les manuscrits connus. . . .* Koninklijke Akademie van Wetenschapen te Amsterdam, *Verhandelingen, Afd. Letterkunde,* new ser., vol. xv (1915), vol. xxi (1920), vol. xxx, no. 3 (1931), vol. xxxvii (1936), vol. xliii (1938).

Boissier, Gaston. *La Religion romaine d'Auguste aux Antonins: étude sur les dernières luttes religieuses en Occident au 4me siècle.* Paris, 1874. 2 vols.

———. *La Fin du paganisme.* Paris, 1891. 2 vols.

Boll, Franz. *Sphaera: neue griechische Texte und Untersuchungen zur Geschichte der Sternbilder.* Leipzig, 1903.

——— and Bezold, Carl. *Sternglaube und Sterndeutung: die Geschichte und das Wesen der Astrologie.* Ed. by Gundel, W. 4th ed. Berlin, 1931.

Borinski, Karl. *Die Antike in Poetik und Kunsttheorie vom Ausgang des klassischen Altertums bis auf Goethe und Wilhelm von Humboldt.* Leipzig, 1914–1924. 2 vols.

Born, Lester K. "Ovid and Allegory," *Speculum,* ix (1934), 362–79.

Bouché-Leclercq, Auguste. *L'Astrologie grecque.* Paris, 1899.

Bourciez, Edouard. *Les Moeurs polies et la littérature de cour sous Henri II.* Paris, 1886.

Bréhier, Louis. *L'Art byzantin.* Paris, 1924.

Bremond, Henri. *Histoire littéraire du sentiment religieux en France.* Paris, 1916–1933. 11 vols. (Cf. esp. vol. i: *L'Humanisme dévot,* pt. 2.)

Brockhaus, Heinrich. "Ein edles Geduldspiel: die Leitung der Welt oder die Himmelsleiter, die sogenannten Taroks Mantegnas vom Jahre 1459–60," in *Miscellanea di storia dell'arte in onore di I. B. Supino,* Florence, 1933, pp. 397–416.

Burckhardt, Jakob. *The Civilization of the Renaissance in Italy* (*Die Cultur der Renaissance in Italien*). Authorized transl. (of 15th ed., Basel, 1860) by S. G. C. Middlemore. London and New York, 1929.

Burdach, Konrad. "Nachleben des griechisch-römischen Altertums in der mittelalterlichen Dichtung und Kunst," in *idem, Vorspiel: gesammelte Schriften zur Geschichte des deutschen Geistes,* Halle, 1925–1926, i, 49–100.

Burges, W. "La Ragione de Padoue," *Annales archéologiques,* xviii (1858), 331–43; xix (1859), 241–51; xxvi (1869), 250–71.

Burmeister, Ernst. *Der bildnerische Schmuck des Tempio Malatestiano zu Rimini.* (Diss.) Breslau, 1891.

Burroughs, Bryson. "Ceiling Panels by Pinturicchio," *Bulletin of the Metropolitan Museum of Art,* vol. xvi, no. 1 (Jan., 1921), pt. 2.

Buschner, Hans. *Die Bedeutung der antiken Mythologie für die französische Ode bei deren Entstehung.* Weida, 1909.

Bush, Douglas. *Mythology and the Renaissance Tradition in English Poetry.* Minneapolis, 1932.

Calcagno, A. *Jacopo Zucchi e la sua opera a Roma.* Rome, 1933.

Carcopino, Jérôme. *La Basilique Pythagoricienne de la Porte Majeure.* 3d ed. Paris, 1926. (Cf. esp. pt. 2, chap. i: "Mythologie et mystères.")

CASSIRER, ERNST. *Individuum und Cosmos in der Philosophie der Renaissance.* Studien der Bibliothek Warburg, X. Leipzig-Berlin, 1927.

CASTELAIN, MAURICE. "Démogorgon, ou le barbarisme déifié," *Bulletin de l'Association Guillaume Budé,* no. 36 (July, 1932), pp. 22–39.

CHASTEL, A. "Art et religion dans la Renaissance italienne," *Bibliothèque d'humanisme et Renaissance,* VII (1945), 7–61.

COHEN, GUSTAVE. *Geoffroy Tory: Champfleury.* Paris, 1931. (Cf. Intro. and notes.)

———. *Ronsard, sa vie et son oeuvre.* 2d ed. Paris, 1932.

COLVIN, SIDNEY. *A Florentine Picture Chronicle: being a series of ninety-nine drawings representing scenes and personages of ancient history sacred and profane, reproduced from the originals with a critical and descriptive text.* London, 1898.

COMPARETTI, DOMENICO. *Virgilio nel medio evo.* New ed. Florence, 1937–1946. 2 vols.

COOKE, JOHN DANIEL. "Euhemerism: a Mediaeval Interpretation of Classical Paganism," *Speculum,* II (1927), 396–410.

COULON, RÉMI. *Beati Joannis Dominici Cardinalis S. Sixti Lucula noctis.* Paris, 1908. (Cf. Intro.)

COULTER, CORNELIA C. "The Genealogy of the Gods," in *Vassar Mediaeval Studies,* New Haven, 1923, pp. 317–41.

COURAJOD, LOUIS. *Les Origines de la Renaissance,* in *idem, Leçons professées à l'Ecole du Louvre,* vol. II. Paris, 1901.

CUMONT, FRANZ. *Les Religions orientales dans le paganisme romain.* 4th ed. Paris, 1929.

———. "Les Noms des planètes et l'astrolâtrie chez les grecs," *L'Antiquité classique,* IV (1935), 5–43.

———. In SAGLIO, DAREMBERG, and POTTIER, *Dictionnaire des antiquités grecques et romaines, s.v.* "Zodiacus."

DAREMBERG. *See* Saglio (*II*).

DECHARME, PAUL. *La Critique des traditions religieuses chez les Grecs, des origines au temps de Plutarque.* Paris, 1904.

DEJOB, CHARLES. *De l'influence du Concile de Trente sur la littérature et les beaux-arts chez les peuples catholiques.* Paris, 1884.

DELAPORTE, VICTOR. *Du merveilleux dans la littérature française sous le règne de Louis XIV.* Paris, 1891.

DELISLE, LÉOPOLD. "La *Biblionomia* de Richard de Fournival," in *idem, Le Cabinet des Manuscrits de la Bibliothèque Imperiale et Nationale,* Paris, 1868–1881, II, 518 ff.

DENECKE, LUDWIG. *Ritterdichter und Heidengötter (1150–1220).* Leipzig, 1930.

DEONNA, WALDEMAR. "Le Groupe des trois Grâces nues et sa descendance," *Revue archéologique,* ser. V, vol. XXXI (1930), 274–332.

DOLLMAYER, HERMANN. "Giulio Romano und das klassische Altertum," *Jahrbuch der kunsthistorischen Sammlungen des Allerhöchsten Kaiserhauses* (Vienna), XII (1901), 178–220.

DOREN, A. "Fortuna im Mittelalter und in der Renaissance," *Vorträge der Bibliothek Warburg*, II (1922–1923), 71–144.

DOREZ, LEONE. *La canzone delle virtù e delle scienze di Bartolomeo di Bartoli. . . .* Bergamo, 1904.

DOUTREPONT, GEORGES. *La Littérature française à la cour des ducs de Bourgogne.* Paris, 1909.

———. *Jean Lemaire de Belges et la Renaissance.* Brussels, 1934.

DOZY, REINHARD, and GOEJE, MICHAEL JAN DE. "Le 'Ghâya,' " in *Actes du VIe Congrès International des Orientalistes* (Leyden, 1885), II, 285 ff.

DRACHMANN, ANDERS BJÖRN. *Atheism in Pagan Antiquity,* London-Gyldendal, 1922. Transl. from University of Copenhagen, *Festskrift,* 1919.

DREW, DOUGLAS L. M. *The Allegory of the Aeneid.* Oxford, 1927.

EBERSOLT, JEAN. *Mélanges d'histoire et d'archéologie byzantines.* Paris, 1917.

EGIDI, FRANCESCO. "Le miniature dei codici barberiniani dei *Documenti d'amore,*" *L'Arte,* V (1902), 1–20, 78–95.

EISLER, ROBERT. *Weltenmantel und Himmelszelt: religionsgeschichtliche Untersuchungen zur Urgeschichte des antiken Weltbildes.* Munich, 1910. 2 vols.

ESSLING, VICTOR D', and MÜNTZ, EUGÈNE. *Pètrarque: ses études d'art, son influence sur les artistes, ses portraits et ceux de Laure, l'illustration de ses écrits.* Paris, 1902.

EVANS, JOAN. *Magical Jewels of the Middle Ages and the Renaissance, Particularly in England.* Oxford, 1922.

FARAL, EDMOND. *Recherches sur les sources latines des contes et romans courtois du moyen âge.* Paris, 1913.

———. *Les Arts poétiques du 12me et du 13me siècle; recherches et documents sur la technique littéraire du moyen âge.* Paris, 1924.

FARNELL, LEWIS RICHMOND. "The Value and the Methods of Mythologic Study," *Proceedings of the British Academy,* IX (1919), 37–51.

FESTUGIÈRE, ANDRÉ JEAN. *L'Astrologie et les sciences occultes.* Paris, 1944–1949. 2 vols. (Cf. esp. vol. I: *La Révélation d'Hermès Trismégiste.*)

FEULNER, ADOLF. *Peter Vischers Sebaldusgrab in Nürnberg.* Munich, 1924.

FIERZ-DAVID, LINDA. *Der Liebestraum des Poliphilo.* Zurich, 1947. (English transl. by Hottinger, Mary: *The Dream of Poliphilo,* Bollingen Series XXV, New York, 1950.)

FISCHER, KUNO. *Francis Bacon und seine Schule: Entwicklungsgeschichte der Erfahrungsphilosophie.* 3d ed. Heidelberg, 1904.

FLUTRE, LOUIS FERNAND. *Li Fait des Romains dans les littératures française et italienne du 13me au 16me siècle.* Paris, 1933.

FOERSTER, RICHARD. *Farnesina-Studien.* Rostock, 1880.

———. "Die Verleumdung des Apelles in der Renaissance," *Jahrbuch der preussischen Kunstsammlungen* (Berlin), VIII (1887), 29–56, 89–113; XV (1894), 27–40.

———. "Die Hochzeit des Alexander und der Roxane in der Renaissance," *ibid.,* XV (1894), 182–207.

FOERSTER, R. "Philostrats Gemälde in der Renaissance," *ibid.*, XXV (1904), 15–48.

———. "Wiederherstellung antiker Gemälde durch Künstler der Renaissance," *ibid.*, XLIII (1922), 126–36.

FOWLER, WILLIAM WARDE. *Roman Ideas of Deity in the Last Century before the Christian Era.* London, 1914.

FRAZER, JAMES GEORGE. *The Golden Bough: a Study in Comparative Religion.* 3d ed., rev. and enl. London, 1911–1915. 12 vols.

FREY, KARL. *Die klassischen Götter- und Heldensagen in den Dramen von Marlowe, Lyly, Kyd, Greene und Peele.* (Diss.) Strassburg, 1909.

———. *Carteggio di Giorgio Vasari. See* Vasari (*I*).

FREY-SALLMANN, ALMA. *Aus dem Nachleben antiker Göttergestalten: die antiken Gottheiten in der Bildbeschreibung des Mittelalters und der italienischen Frührenaissance.* Leipzig, 1931.

GABRICI. *See* Levi and Gabrici (*II*).

GARIN, E. "Magia e astrologia nella coltura del Rinascimento," *Belfagor*, vol. V (1950).

GEFFCKEN, J. In Hastings, J., *Encyclopaedia of Religion and Ethics* (Edinburgh, 1908–1915), vol. V, *s.v.* "Euhemerism."

GHELLINCK, JOSEPH DE. *L'Essor de la littérature latine au 12me siècle.* Brussels, 1946. 2 vols. (Cf. esp. vol. I.)

GHISALBERTI, FAUSTO. *Integumenta Ovidii, poemetto inedito del secolo* XIII. Milan, 1933.

———. "Arnaldo d'Orléans, un cultore di Ovidio nel secolo XII," Reale Istituto Lombardo di Scienze e Lettere (Milan), *Memorie*, XX (1932), 157–234.

GIEHLOW, KARL. "Die Hieroglyphenkunde des Humanismus in der Allegorie der Renaissance," *Jahrbuch der kunsthistorischen Sammlungen des Allerhöchsten Kaiserhauses* (Vienna), XXXII (1915), 1–24.

GÖBEL, HEINRICH. *Wandteppiche.* Leipzig, 1923–1934. 3 vols. in 6. (Cf. esp. vol. II: *Die romanischen Länder.*)

GOEJE, DE. *See* Dozy and Goeje, de (*II*).

GOLDSCHMIDT, ADOLPH. "Das Nachleben der antiken Formen im Mittelalter," *Vorträge der Bibliothek Warburg*, 1921–1922, pp. 40–50.

———. "Frühmittelalterliche illustrierte Enzyklopädien," *ibid.*, 1923–1924, pp. 215–26.

——— and WEITZMANN, KURT. *Die byzantinischen Elfenbeinskulpturen des* X.–XIII. *Jahrhunderts.* Berlin, 1930–1934. 2 vols.

GÓMEZ DE BAQUERO, EDUARDO. *See* Pérez de Moya (*I*).

GRAF, ARTURO. *Roma nella memoria e nelle immaginazioni del medio evo.* Turin, 1882.

GREEN, HENRY. *Shakespeare and the Emblem Writers: an Exposition of Their Similarities of Thought and Expression.* London, 1870.

GREIF, WILHELM. *Die mittelalterlichen Bearbeitungen der Trojanersage: ein neuer Beitrag zur Dares- und Dictysfrage.* Marburg, 1886.

GRENIER, ALBERT. *Le Génie romain dans la religion, la pensée et l'art.* L'Evolution de l'humanité, no. 17. Paris, 1925.

Gruppe, Otto. *Griechische Mythologie und Religionsgeschichte.* Handbuch der klassischen Altertums-Wissenschaft, vol. v, pt. 2. Munich, 1906. 2 vols.

———. *Geschichte der klassischen Mythologie und Religionsgeschichte während des Mittelalters im Abendland. . . .* Leipzig, 1921. Suppl. to Roscher, W. H., *Ausführliches Lexikon . . . , q.v. (II).*

Gundel, Wilhelm. *Dekane und Dekansternbilder: ein Beitrag zur Geschichte der Sternbilder der Kulturvölker.* Studien der Bibliothek Warburg, xix. Hamburg-Glückstadt, 1936.

——— (ed.). *See* Boll and Bezold (*II*).

Haskins, Charles H. *The Renaissance of the Twelfth Century.* Cambridge, Mass., 1927.

———. "Arabic Science in Western Europe," *Isis,* vii (1925), 478–85.

Hauber, Anton. *Planetenkinderbilder und Sternbilder: zur Geschichte des menschlichen Glaubens und Irrens.* Strassburg, 1916.

———. "Zur Verbreitung des Astronomen Sûfî," *Islam,* viii (1918), 48–54.

Hauréau, Barthélemy. "Mémoire sur un commentaire des Métamorphoses d'Ovide," *Mémoires de l'Académie des Inscriptions et Belles-Lettres* (Paris), xxx (1883), pt. 2, pp. 45–55.

Hauvette, Henri. *Boccace, étude biographique et littéraire.* Paris, 1914.

Heckscher, W. S. "Relics of Pagan Antiquity in Mediaeval Settings," *Journal of the Warburg Institute,* i (1937–1938), 204–20.

Heiss, Alois. *Les Médailleurs de la Renaissance florentine.* Paris, 1891.

Henkel, M. D. *De Houtsneden van Mansion's Ovide moralisé, Bruges, 1484.* Amsterdam, 1922.

———. "Illustrierte Ausgaben von Ovids Metamorphosen im xv., xvi. und xvii. Jahrhundert," *Vorträge der Bibliothek Warburg,* 1926–1927, pp. 58–144.

Herman, J. B. *La Pédagogie des Jésuites au 16me siècle.* Louvain-Brussels, 1914.

Highet, Gilbert. *The Classical Tradition: Greek and Roman Influences on Western Literature.* Oxford, 1949.

Hind, Arthur M. *Early Italian Engraving: a Critical Catalogue, with Reproduction of All Prints Described,* vol. iv. London, 1938.

Hinks, Roger P. *Myth and Allegory in Ancient Art.* Studies of the Warburg Institute, vi. London, 1939.

Hortis, Attilio. *Studij sulle opere latine del Boccaccio.* Trieste, 1879.

Huebner, Paul Gustav. *Le statue di Roma: Grundlagen für eine Geschichte der antiken Monumente in der Renaissance.* Leipzig, 1912.

Huet, Pierre Daniel. *Dissertation de l'origine de la langue hébraïque.* Ed. by Tillardet. The Hague, 1720.

Jahn, Otto. "Cyriacus von Ancona und Albrecht Dürer," in *idem, Aus der Altertumswissenschaft,* Bonn, 1868, pp. 333–52.

JOURDAIN, CHARLES. "Des commentaires inédits de Guillaume de Conches et de Nicolas Triveth sur la Consolation de la philosophie de Boèce," *Notes et extraits des manuscrits* (Paris), XX (1865), 40–82.

KATZENELLENBOGEN, ADOLF. *Allegories of the Virtues and Vices in Mediaeval Art.* Studies of the Warburg Institute, X. London, 1939.

KLACZKO, JULIAN. "Jules II," in *idem, Rome et la Renaissance,* Paris, 1898.

KRISTELLER, PAUL. *Die Tarocchi: zwei italienische Kupferstichfolgen aus dem* XV. *Jahrhundert.* Graphische Gesellschaft. Berlin, 1910. (Cf. Intro.)

KUHN, A. "Die Illustration des Rosenromans," *Jahrbuch der kunsthistorischen Sammlungen des Allerhöchsten Kaiserhauses* (Vienna), XXXI (1912), 1–66.

LABORDE, ALEXANDRE DE. *Les Manuscrits à figures de la Cité de Dieu de Saint Augustin.* Paris, 1909. 3 vols.

LA BOULLAYE. *See* Pinard de la Boullaye (*II*).

LALANNE, JEAN PHILIPPE AUGUSTE. *L'Influence des Pères de l'Eglise sur l'éducation publique pendant les cinq premiers siècles de l'ére chrétienne.* Paris, 1850.

LANCI, MICHEL ANGELO. *Trattato delle simboliche rappresentanze arabiche.* Paris, 1845–1846.

LANDI, C. *Demogorgone, con saggio di nuova edizione delle Genealogie deorum gentilium del Boccaccio e silloge dei frammenti di Teodonzio.* Palermo, 1930.

LANGLOIS, CHARLES VICTOR. *La Connaissance de la nature et du monde au moyen âge, d'après quelques écrits français à l'usage des laïcs,* in *idem, La Vie en France au moyen âge,* III. Paris, 1927.

LANGLOIS, ERNEST. *Origines et sources du Roman de la Rose.* Paris, 1891.

LAUMONIER, PAUL. *Ronsard, poète lyrique.* Paris, 1910.

———. "La Bibliothèque de Ronsard," *Revue du seizième siècle,* XIV (1927), 315–35.

LAVALLÉE, PIERRE. *Le Dessin français du 13me au 16me siècle.* Paris, 1930.

LAVARENNE, M. *La Psychomachie de Prudence.* Text, with Intro. and commentary. Paris, 1933.

LA VILLE DE MIRMONT, HENRI DE. *Apollonius de Rhodes et Virgile: la mythologie et les dieux dans les Argonautiques et dans l'Enéide.* Paris, 1894.

LEHMANN, PAUL. *Pseudo-antike Literatur des Mittelalters.* Studien der Bibliothek Warburg, XIII. Leipzig-Berlin, 1927.

LEMMI, CHARLES W. *The Classical Deities in Bacon: a Study in Mythological Symbolism.* Baltimore, 1933.

LESSING, GOTTHOLD EPHRAIM. *Wie die Alten den Tod gebildet.* Berlin, 1769.

LEVI, EZIO, and GABRICI, ETTORE. *Lo Steri di Palermo e le sue pitture.* Regia Accademia di Scienze, Lettere ed Arti di Palermo. Suppl. to *Atti,* no. 1. Palermo [1932].

LÉVY-BRUHL, LUCIEN. *La Mythologie primitive.* Paris, 1935.

LEWIS, CHARLES B. *Clasical Mythology and Arthurian Romance: a Study of the Sources of Chrestien de Troyes' "Yvain" and other Arthurian Romances.* St. Andrews University Publications, 32. London, 1932.

LIEBESCHÜTZ, HANS. *Fulgentius metaforalis: ein Beitrag zur Geschichte der antiken Mythologie im Mittelalter.* Studien der Bibliothek Warburg, IV. Leipzig-Berlin, 1926. (Cf., for *Libellus . . .* , pp. 117–28.)

LIPPMANN, FRIEDRICH. *The Seven Planets.* Engl. version by Simmonds, Florence, printed (as also German original) by Reichsdruckerei, Berlin, for International Calcographic Society. London and New York, 1895.

LOGA, VALERIAN VON. "Beiträge zum Holzschnittwerk Michel Wolgemuts," *Jahrbuch der preussischen Kunstsammlungen,* XVI (1895), 224–40.

LORENZONI, A. *Carteggio artistico inedito di d. Vinc. Borghini,* in *idem, Scritti inediti . . .* (1515–1580), vol. I. Florence, 1912.

LOTSPEICH, HENRY G. *Classical Mythology in the Poetry of Edmund Spenser.* Princeton, 1932.

LOUKOMSKI, G. K. *Les Fresques de Paul Véronèse et de ses disciples.* Paris, 1928.

MAHON, DENIS. *Studies in Seicento Art and Theory.* Studies of the Warburg Institute, XVI. London, 1947.

MAI, ANGELO. *Classicorum auctorum e Vaticanibus codicibus editorum tomus* I–X (Rome, 1828–1838), vol. III (1831).

MÂLE, EMILE. *L'Art religieux de la fin du moyen âge en France.* Paris, 1908.

———. *L'Art religieux du 13me siècle en France.* 6th ed. Paris, 1925.

———. *L'Art religieux après le Concile de Trente.* Paris, 1932.

MANDOWSKY, ERNA. "*The Origin of the Milky Way* in the National Gallery," *Burlington Magazine,* LXXII (1938), 88–93.

———. "Ricerche intorno all'Iconologia di Cesare Ripa," *Bibliofilia,* XLI (1939), 7–27, 111–24, 204–35, 279–327.

MARLE, RAIMOND VAN. *Iconographie de l'art profane au moyen âge et à la Renaissance.* The Hague, 1931–1932. 2 vols. (Cf. esp. vol. II: *Allégories et symboles.*)

MARROU, HENRI IRÉNÉE. *Saint Augustin et la fin de la culture antique.* Bibliothèque des Ecoles Françaises d'Athènes et de Rome, fasc. 145. Paris, 1938.

MARTIN, ALFRED VON. *Coluccio Salutati und das humanistische Lebensideal: ein Kapitel aus der Genesis der Renaissance.* Leipzig-Berlin, 1916.

MEHRENS, A. F. *Mas'ûdî, manuel de cosmographie.* Transl. Copenhagen, 1874.

MÉLY, FERNAND DE. "Du rôle des pierres gravées au moyen âge," *Revue de l'art chrétien,* new ser., XXXVI, vol. IV (1893), 14–24, 98–105, 191–203.

———. "Les Très Riches Heures du duc de Berry et les trois Grâces de Sienne," *Gazette des beaux-arts,* VIII (1912) pt. 2, pp. 195–201.

MÉNARD, LOUIS. *Du polythéisme hellénique.* Paris, 1863. (Cf. pp. 81 ff.)

MENNER, ROBERT J. "Two Notes on Mediaeval Euhemerism," *Speculum,* III (1928), 246–48.

MEYER, PAUL. "Les Premières compilations françaises d'histoire ancienne," *Romania,* XIV (1885), 38–81.

MEYER-WEINSCHEL, ADY. *Renaissance und Antike.* Reutlingen, 1933.

MIGNE, J.-P. (ed.). *Patrologiae cursus completus accurante J.-P. Migne.* Ser. I, II

(*Latina*), Paris, 1844–1864; 221 vols. Ser. III (*Graeca*), Paris, 1857–1886; 165 vols.

MILANESI. *See* Vasari, *Le vite . . .* (*I*).

Monumenta paedagogica Societatis Jesu quae primam rationem studiorum anno 1586 editam praecessere. Madrid, 1901.

MÜNTZ, EUGÈNE. *Les Précurseurs de la Renaissance.* Paris, 1882. *See also* Essling, d', and Müntz (*II*).

MURRAY, GILBERT. *Five Stages of Greek Religion.* Oxford, 1925.

NICOLL, ALLARDYCE. *Stuart Masques and the Renaissance Stage.* London, 1937.

NILSSON, MARTIN PERSSON. *A History of Greek Religion.* Oxford, 1925.

NOLHAC, PIERRE DE. *Pétrarque et l'humanisme.* 2d ed. Paris, 1907. 2 vols.

———. *Ronsard et l'humanisme.* Paris, 1921.

NOURRY. *See* Saintyves (*II*).

OLSCHKI, LEONARDO. "La cattedrale di Modena e il suo rilievo arturiano," *Archivum Romanicum*, XIX (1935), 145–86.

OSGOOD, CHARLES G. *The Classical Mythology of Milton's English Poems.* New York, 1900.

OULMONT, CHARLES. "La Fresque de la Tour de la Ligue au château de Tanlay," *Revue de l'art*, II (1933), 183–84.

PANOFSKY, ERWIN. *Dürers Stellung zur Antike.* Vienna, 1922. (First issued in *Wiener Jahrbuch für Kunstgeschichte*, I [1921–1922], 43–92.)

———. *Herkules am Scheidewege und andere antike Bildstoffe in der neueren Kunst.* Studien der Bibliothek Warburg, XVIII. Leipzig-Berlin, 1930.

———. "Et in Arcadia ego," in *Philosophy and History: Essays Presented to E. Cassirer*, Oxford, 1936, pp. 223–54.

———. "Der gefesselte Eros," *Oud-Holland*, L (1933), 193–217.

——— and SAXL, FRITZ. *Dürers Melencolia I: eine quellen- und typengeschichtliche Untersuchung.* Studien der Bibliothek Warburg, II. Leipzig, 1923.

———, ———. "A Late Antique Religious Symbol in Works by Holbein and Titian," *Burlington Magazine*, XLIX (1926), 177–81.

———, ———. "Classical Mythology in Mediaeval Art," *Metropolitan Museum Studies*, IV (1932–1933), 228–80.

PANSA, GIOVANNI. *Ovidio nel medioevo e nella tradizione popolare.* Sulmona, 1924.

PARIS, GASTON. "Chrestien Legouais et les autres traducteurs ou imitateurs d'Ovide," *Histoire littéraire de la France*, XXIV (1885), 455–525.

PASCALE, C. *Dei e diavoli: saggi sul paganesimo morente.* Florence, 1904.

PATCH, HOWARD R. *The Goddess Fortuna in Mediaeval Literature.* Cambridge, Mass., 1927.

———. *The Tradition of Boethius.* New York, 1935.

PELLIZZARI, ACHILLE. *I trattati attorno le arti figurative in Italia dall'antichità classica al Rinascimento*, vol. I. Naples, 1915.

Pfister, Friedrich. *Die Religion der Griechen und Römer: mit einer Einführung in die vergleichende Religionswissenschaft, Darstellung und Literaturbericht (1918–1929/30)*. Leipzig, 1930.

Piano, G. del. *L'enigma filosofico del Tempio Malatestiano.* Bologna, 1928.

Picard, Charles. *Les Origines du polythéisme hellénique.* Paris, 1930. 2 vols. (Cf. esp. Intro.)

Picot, Emile. "Les Italiens en France au 16me siècle," Faculté des Lettres de Bordeaux et des Universités du Midi, *Bulletin italien,* iii (1903), 118–42.

Pinard de la Boullaye, Henri. *L'Etude comparée des religions.* 3d ed. Paris, 1929. 2 vols.

Piper, Ferdinand. *Mythologie und Symbolik der christlichen Kunst von der ältesten Zeit bis ins* xvi. *Jahrhundert,* i: *Mythologie.* Weimar, 1847–1851.

Planiscig, Leo. *Venezianische Bildhauer der Renaissance.* Vienna, 1921.

Plattard, Jean. *L'Oeuvre de Rabelais.* Paris, 1910. (Cf. chap. vi: "Catalogue des sources anciennes et modernes de l'érudition antique de Rabelais.")

Pottier. *See* Saglio.

Praz, Mario. *Studies in Seventeenth-Century Imagery.* Studies of the Warburg Institute, iii. 2 vols. London, 1939.

Prunières, Henry. *Le Ballet de cour en France avant Benserade et Lully.* Paris, 1914.

Rand, Edward Kennard. *Ovid and His Influence.* London, 1926.

Raschke, Robert. *De Alberico mythologo.* (Diss.) Breslau, 1913.

Reinach, Salomon. *L'Album de Pierre Jacques, sculpteur de Reims, dessiné à Rome de 1572 à 1577.* Complete reprod., with Intro. and French transl., of Aldrovandi, *Tutte le statue. . . .* Paris, 1902.

———. "Essai sur la mythologie figurée et l'histoire profane dans la peinture italienne de la Renaissance," *Revue archéologique,* ser. v, vol. i (1915), 94–171.

Renan, Ernest. *Etudes d'histoire religieuse.* 2d ed. Paris, 1857. (Cf. esp. chap. i: "Les Religions de l'antiquité.")

Répertoire des ouvrages pédagogiques du 16me siècle, in *Mémoires et documents scolaires publiés par le Musée Pédagogique* (Bibliothèques de Paris et des Départements), iii. Paris, 1886.

Reusch, Heinrich. *Die Indices librorum prohibitorum des* xvi. *Jahrhunderts.* Tübingen, 1886.

Reyher, Paul. *Les Masques anglais, études sur les ballets et la vie de cour en Angleterre (1512–1640)*. Paris, 1909.

Ricci, Corrado. *Il Tempio Malatestiano.* Milan-Rome, 1925.

Ridolfi, Carlo. *Le Maraviglie dell'arte, overo le vite degl'illustri pittori veneti, e dello stato.* Ed. by Hadeln, D. von. Berlin, 1914–1924. 2 vols.

Ritter, Helmut. "*Picatrix,* ein arabisches Handbuch hellenistischer Magie," *Vorträge der Bibliothek Warburg,* 1921-1922, pp. 94–124.

Roger, Maurice. *L'Enseignement des lettres classiques d'Ausone à Alcuin.* Paris, 1905.

Root, Robert Kilburne. *Classical Mythology in Shakespeare.* Yale Studies in English, xix. New York, 1903.

ROSCHER, W. H. *Ausführliches Lexikon der griechischen und römischen Mythologie.* Leipzig, Leipzig-Berlin, 1884–1937. 6 vols. in 9.

ROSE, HERBERT JENNINGS. *Modern Methods in Classical Mythology.* Three lectures delivered at University College, London. St. Andrews, 1930.

SAGLIO, E., DAREMBERG, C., and POTTIER, E. *Dictionnaire des antiquités grecques et romaines.* Paris, 1877–1919. 5 vols. in 10.

SAINTYVES, P. (*pseud.* of NOURRY, EMILE). *Essais de mythologie chrétienne: les saints successeurs des dieux.* Paris, 1907.

SALMI, MARIO. "Gli affreschi del Palazzo Trinci a Foligno," *Bolletino d'arte,* XIII (1919), 139–80.

SALOMON, RICHARD G. *Opicinus de Canistris: Weltbild und Bekenntnisse eines Avignonesischen Klerikers des* XIV. *Jahrhunderts.* Studies of the Warburg Institute, I. London, 1936.

SANDYS, JOHN E. *A History of Classical Scholarship.* Cambridge, 1903–1908. 3 vols.

SANT, JEANNETTE VAN'T. *Le Commentaire de Copenhague de l'Ovide moralisé.* Amsterdam, 1929.

SAPORI, F. *Jacopo Tatti, detto il Sansovino.* Rome, 1928.

SARTORIUS, H. *Die klassische Götter- und Heldensage in den Dramen Beaumonts und Fletchers, Chapmans, Ben Jonsons und Massingers.* (Diss.) Strassburg, 1912.

SAXL, FRITZ. *Antike Götter in der Spätrenaissance: ein Freskenzyklus und ein Discorso des Jacopo Zucchi.* Studien der Bibliothek Warburg, VIII. Leipzig-Berlin, 1927.

———. *La Fede astrologica di Agostino Chigi.* Rome, 1934.

———. *Verzeichnis astrologischer und mythologischer illustrierter Handschriften des lateinischen Mittelalters:* vol. I, *Handschriften in römischen Bibliotheken,* in *Sitzungsberichte der Heidelberger Akademie der Wissenschaften, Phil.-hist. Kl.,* Abhandl. 6, 7 (1915); vol. II, *Die Handschriften der Nationalbibliothek in Wien, ibid.,* Abhandl. 2 (1925–1926 [publ. 1927]); vol. III, *Catalogue of Astrological and Mythological Illuminated Manuscripts of the Middle Ages: Manuscripts Preserved in the Libraries of London, Oxford, and Cambridge* (to be published by Warburg Institute, London).

———. "Beiträge zu einer Geschichte der Planetendarstellungen im Orient und Okzident," *Islam,* III (1912), 151–77.

———. "Probleme der Planetenkinderbilder," *Kunstchronik und Kunstmarkt,* new ser. XXX, vol. LIV (1918–1919), 1013 ff.

———. "Rinascimento dell'antichità: Studien zu den Arbeiten A. Warburgs," *Repertorium für Kunstwissenschaft,* XLIII (1921–1922), 220–72.

See also Panofsky and Saxl (*II*).

SCHEVILL, RUDOLPH. *Ovid and the Renascence in Spain.* Berkeley, 1913.

SCHIMBERG, ANDRÉ. *L'Education morale dans les collèges de la Compagnie de Jésus en France sous l'ancien régime* (*16me, 17me, 18me siècles*). Paris, 1913.

SCHLOSSER, JULIUS VON. *Beiträge zur Kunstgeschichte aus den Schriftquellen des frühen Mittelalters.* Vienna, 1891.

———. "Giustos Fresken in Padua und die Vorläufer der Stanza della Segnatura," *Jahrbuch der kunsthistorischen Sammlungen des Allerhöchsten Kaiserhauses* (Vienna), XVII (1896), 11–100.

———. "Die ältesten Medaillen und die Antike," *ibid.*, XVIII (1897), 64–108.

SCHNEEGANS, FRIEDRICH. "A propos d'une fresque mythologique du 16me siècle," *Humanisme et Renaissance*, II (1935), 441–44.

SCHOELL, FRANCK LOUIS. *Etudes sur l'humanisme continental en Angleterre à la fin de la Renaissance.* Bibliothèque de la Revue de littérature comparée, XXIX. Paris, 1926. (Cf. esp. pp. 21–42.)

SCHUBRING, PAUL. *Cassoni: Truhen und Truhenbilder der italienischen Frührenaissance.* Leipzig, 1915.

SEGHEZZI, A. *Delle lettere familiari del comm. Annibale Caro.* Bassano, 1782.

SEZNEC, JEAN. "Un Essai de mythologie comparée au début du 17me siècle," Ecole Française de Rome, *Mélanges d'histoire et d'archéologie,* XLVIII (1931), 268–81.

———. "Les Manuels mythologiques italiens et leur diffusion en Angleterre à la fin de la Renaissance," *ibid.*, L (1933), 276–92.

———. "La Mascarade des dieux à Florence en 1565," *ibid.*, XLII (1935), 224–43.

———. "Apollo and the Swans on the Tomb of St. Sebald," *Journal of the Warburg Institute,* II (1938–1939), 75.

SOLDATI, BENEDETTO. *La Poesia astrologica nel quattrocento.* Florence, 1906.

SPRINGER, ANTON. *Das Nachleben der Antike im Mittelalter.* Paris, 1927.

STRZYGOWSKI, JOSEPH. *Die Calenderbilder des Chronographen vom Jahre 354. Jahrbuch des Königlichen Deutschen Archaeologischen Instituts* (Berlin), suppl., 1888.

SUDHOFF, KARL. *Beiträge zur Geschichte der Chirurgie im Mittelalter.* Studien zur Geschichte der Medizin, X–XII. Leipzig, 1914–1918. 2 vols.

TAYLOR, HENRY OSBORN. *The Mediaeval Mind: a History of the Development of Thought and Emotion in the Middle Ages.* London, 1911.

THIELE, GEORG FRIEDRICH. *Antike Himmelsbilder, mit Forschungen zu Hipparchos, Aratos und seinen Fortsetzern, und Beiträge zur Kunstgeschichte des Sternhimmels.* Berlin, 1898.

THORNDIKE, LYNN. *A History of Magic and Experimental Science during the First Centuries of Our Era.* New York, 1923–1941. 6 vols.

TIETZE, HANS. *Der junge Dürer.* Augsburg, 1928.

TIRABOSCHI, GIROLAMO. *Storia della letteratura italiana.* Modena, 1772–1781. (Cf. vol. VII, pp. 190–95, for Giraldi; pp. 195–96, for Conti.)

TOFFANIN, GIUSEPPE. *La fine dell'umanesimo.* Turin, 1920.

TOUTAIN, JULES. *Etudes de mythologie et d'histoire des religions antiques.* Paris, 1909.

———. *Nouvelles études de mythologie et d'histoire.* Paris, 1935.

VAGANAY, HUGUES. *Les Amours de Pierre de Ronsard, commentés par M.-A. de Muret.* Paris, 1910.

VENTURI, ADOLFO. "Il libro di Giusto per la cappella degli Eremitani in Padova," *Le Gallerie nazionali italiane,* IV (1899), 345–76.

VENTURI, ADOLFO. "Il libro di disegni di Giusto . . . ," *ibid.*, v (1902), 391–92. (Cf. also plates.)

VENTURI, LIONELLO. "Una risorta casa del Rinascimento italiano," *L'Arte*, XVII (1914), 72 ff.

VILLEY, PIERRE. *Sources et évolution des Essais de Montaigne*, vol. I. Paris, 1908.

VOLKMANN, LUDWIG. *Bilderschriften der Renaissance, Hieroglyphik und Emblematik in ihren Beziehungen und Fortwirkungen.* Leipzig, 1923.

WARBURG, ABY. "Sandro Botticellis 'Geburt der Venus' und 'Frühling': eine Untersuchung über die Vorstellung von der Antike in der italienischen Frührenaissance," in *idem, Gesammelte Schriften* (Leipzig, 1932, 2 vols), I, 1–61. (Cf. also App., pp. 307–29.)

———. "Eine astronomische Himmelsdarstellung in der alten Sakristei von San Lorenzo in Florenz," *ibid.*, I, 169–72.

———. "I Costumi teatrali per gli intermezzi del 1589," *ibid.*, I, 259–300. (Cf. esp. pp. 271 ff. and App., pp. 412–15.)

———. "Italienische Kunst und internationale Astrologie im Palazzo Schifanoja zu Ferrara," *ibid.*, II, 459–81.

———. "Über Planetengötterbilder im Niederdeutschen Kalender von 1519," *ibid.*, II, 483–86.

———. "Heidnisch-antike Weissagung in Wort und Bild zu Luthers Zeiten," *ibid.*, II, 487–558.

WEDEL, THEODORE O. *The Mediaeval Attitude toward Astrology, Particularly in England.* Yale Studies in English, LX. New Haven, 1920.

WEISBACH, WERNER. *Trionfi.* Berlin, 1919.

———. "Petrarca und die bildende Kunst," *Repertorium für Kunstwissenschaft*, XXVI (1903–1904), 265–87.

WEITZMANN. *See* Goldschmidt and Weitzmann (*II*).

WELSFORD, ENID. "Italian Influence on the English Court Masque," *Modern Language Review*, XVIII (1923), 394–409.

WELTER, J. T. *L'Exemplum dans la littérature religieuse et didactique du moyen âge.* Paris, 1927.

WHEELER, CHARLES FRANCIS. *Classical Mythology in the Plays, Masques, and Poems of Ben Jonson.* Princeton, 1938.

WICKERSHEIMER, ERNEST. "Figures médico-astrologiques des 9me, 10me et 11me siècles," *Janus*, XIX (1914), 157–77.

WICKHOFF, FRANZ. "Die Bibliothek Julius' II," *Jahrbuch der königlich preussischen Kunstsammlungen* (Berlin), XIV (1893), 49–64.

WILKINS, E. H. "The Genealogy of the Editions of the *Genealogia deorum*," *Modern Philology*, XVII (1919), 423–38.

WIND, EDGAR. "Platonic Justice, Designed by Raphael," *Journal of the Warburg Institute*, I (1937–1938), 69–70.

WINKLER, FRIEDRICH. *Die flämische Buchmalerei des* XV. *und* XVI. *Jahrhunderts.* Leipzig, 1925.

———. *Die Zeichnungen A. Dürers.* Berlin, 1936–1939. 4 vols.

WITT, ROBERT C. "Notes complémentaires sur la mythologie figurée," *Revue archéologique,* ser. V, vol. IX (1919), 173–78. (Cf. Reinach, "Essai sur la mythologie figurée . . ." [*II*].)

YATES, FRANCES A. "Italian Teachers in Elizabethan England," *Journal of the Warburg Institute,* I (1937–1938), 103–16.

———. *The French Academies of the Sixteenth Century.* Studies of the Warburg Institute, XV. London, 1947.

YRIARTE, CHARLES. *Un condottiere au 15me siècle, Rimini.* Paris, 1882.

Index

Dates of rulers, including popes, are regnal. A single date indicates a *floruit* or the appearance of a book or work of art mentioned in the text. Place names are indicated by small capitals. Page references to the illustrations are included. As these are not differentiated in type, the index should be used in conjunction with the list of illustrations, pp. xi–xvi.

A

Abano, Pietro d', Italian astrologer and physician (1250–1316), 74 n
Abel, 23
Abélard, Pierre, French philosopher (1079–1142), 48 n
Abraham, 14, 28, 30 n, 51
Abrahams, Phyllis, 127
Abricus, *see* Albricus
Abundance, 118
Achilles, 163 n f
Actaeon, 93, 101, 163 n f
Acron Helenus, grammarian (late 4th c.), 227 n
Active Life, 286
Adam, 23, 27 f, 30 n, 50, 55
Adhémar, Jean, 3 n, 56 n, 206 n, 211 n, 263 n, 266 n
Admetus, 249
Ado of Vienne, St., French martyrologist (799–874), 15
Adolescence, 132
Adonis, 117, 130, 261
Adriani, A., 105 n
Aeneas, 19, 21
Aeneas Sylvius, *see* Pius II
Aeolus, 310
Aeschylus (525–456 B.C.), 86
Aesculapius, 22, 282
Aeson, 222
Affò, Ireneo, Italian monk and historian (1741–1802), 118
Agave, 105
Ages of Life, 47, 120, 123 ff, 127, 131
Agostini (Agustín), Antonio, Spanish prelate and numismatist (1517–86), 256 n
Agostini, Niccolò, Venetian poet (1515–61), 96 n
Agostino di Duccio, Florentine sculptor and architect (1418–after 1481), 132, 192, 194, 253, 254 n; *Apollo*, 133; *Jupiter*, 133; *Mars*, 192
Agrippa von Nettesheim, Heinrich Cornelius, German physician and occultist (1486?–1535), 62, 72 n
Agucchi, Giovanni Battista, Italian art critic (1570–1632), 265
Ailly, Pierre d', French theologian (1350–1420), 122
Air, 47, 141
Albani, Francesco, Italian painter (1578–1660), 258 n
Albericus, *see* Albricus
Alberti, Leone Battista, Italian architect and writer on art (1404–72), 134; and Botticelli, 115, 116 n; and Horapollo Niliacus, 100; and 16th-c. writers, 234; and temples to the gods, 136 n; *De re aedificatoria*, 100, 119 n, 136 n; *Trattato della pittura*, 261 n
Albricus/Albericus Londoniensis, mythographer (12th c., but not positively identified), 90 n, 170 ff, 181, 190, 193, 208, 211, 228 n; and allegory, 172; and Boccaccio, 179, 221; editions of his work, 225 f; and 15th-c. painters, 204, 213; illustrations of works of, 193 ff,

K

L

W

OTHER TITLES IN ART AND ARCHAEOLOGY AVAILABLE IN PRINCETON AND PRINCETON/BOLLINGEN PAPERBACKS